Socially Relevant Policy Analysis

Socially Relevant Policy Analysis

Structuralist Computable General Equilibrium Models for the Developing World

edited by Lance Taylor

The MIT Press
Cambridge, Massachusetts
London, England

This book was set in Palatino by Asco Trade Typesetting Ltd., Hong Kong and printed and bound in the United States of America.

Library of Congress Cataloging-in-Publication Data

Socially relevant policy analysis: structuralist computable general equilibrium models for the developing world / edited by Lance Taylor.

p. cm.
Includes bibliographical references.
ISBN 0-262-20075-9
1. Developing countries—Economic conditions—Econometric models. 2. Equilibrium (Economics)—Mathematical models. I. Taylor, Lance.
HC59.7.S8738 1990
330′.01′5195—dc20 89-13624
CIP

Contents

List of Contributors

Nazli Choucri
Massachusetts Institute of Technology, Cambridge, MA

William Easterly
The World Bank, Washington, DC

Bill Gibson
University of Vermont, Burlington, VT

Motaz Khorshid
Kuwait Institute of Scientific Research, Kuwait, and Cairo University, Cairo, Egypt

Supriya Lahiri
University of Lowell, Lowell, MA

Juan Luis Londoño
FEDESARROLLO, Bogotá, Colombia, and Harvard University, Cambridge, MA

Nora Lustig
El Colegio de Mexico, Mexico City, Mexico, and the Brookings Institution, Washington, DC

Anne Maasland
The World Bank, Washington, DC

Manoj Panda
National Council of Applied Economic Research, New Delhi, India

Jørn Rattsø
University of Trondheim, Trondheim, Norway

Jeffrey Rosensweig
Emory University Business School, Atlanta, GA

Hiren Sarkar
National Council of Applied Economic Research, New Delhi, India

Lance Taylor
Massachusetts Institute of Technology
Cambridge, MA

Preface

This book presents a sample of work from the structuralist tradition in formulating and applying computable general equilibrium models in economies in the developing world. The endeavor dates back several decades, inspired originally by the late Leif Johansen's multisectoral growth model for Norway (published in 1960) and demonstration models put together by Hollis Chenery and associates in the late 1950s. (Chenery's models, incidentally, were solved using virtually the same algorithms as the authors in this book apply today; fixed-point approaches of the sort proposed in the neoclassical tradition by Herbert Scarf in the late 1960s have fallen by the practical wayside.)

A further step in the direction of structuralist models was a prototype for Brazil put together by Frank Lysy and me in the mid-1970s. It emphasized forced saving and some output adjustment in an economy with several sectors and social classes. Slightly earlier, Irma Adelman and Sherman Robinson constructed a model for South Korea, emphasizing shifts in the internal terms of trade. The Adelman-Robinson model led to a large number of country exercises sponsored by the World Bank. As structuralists learned to rely more explicitly on their analytical heritage from Keynes, Kalecki, and Kaldor, they began to put together applied models of the type presented here. An emphasis on class relationships and income distribution changes underlying macroeconomic adjustment naturally emerged.

The models in this book were mostly put together in the 1980s. Some, like the set for India and the one for Egypt, have been used actively to inform policy practitioners about the problems they confront; others, like the one for Thailand, were designed to advance methodology (to incorporate financial markets in the Thai case). The rest have all had an impact on the policy discussions of the countries in which they were made.

All in all, the work herein suggests that structuralist CGE models have a promising future. By not emphasizing abstraction and trying to include institutional content, they come closer to economic reality than other work. Its focus on practical, socially relevant issues has to be a decisive advantage for the structuralist tradition in the long run.

Socially Relevant Policy Analysis

1 Structuralist CGE Models

Lance Taylor

Computable general equilibrium (CGE) models were first applied to developing economies in the early 1970s. Work has expanded rapidly since then, with two recent compendia (Devarajan, Lewis, and Robinson 1986; Decaluwe and Martens 1987) each listing fifty-odd models for two dozen countries around the world. It is clearly time to take stock of this effort, to see what has been learned and ask whether the CGE trail merits further pursuit. Robinson's (1989) survey paper is one such assessment. This book is another.

The emphasis here is on "structuralist" models, which account for only some of the CGEs. Their perspective is broader than that of other, more "neoclassical" constructs. Lustig (1988) nicely summarizes the ideas around which they are built: "Structuralist thought considers that structural characteristics (the repetition is appropriate) of the economy are fundamental to its behavior. Among the structural factors are the distribution of income and wealth, tenancy relationships on the land, the type and degree of specialization in foreign trade, the density of chains of production, the degree of concentration in markets, control of the means of production by distinct types of actors (the private sector, the state, or transnational capital), the functioning of financial intermediaries, and penetration of technical advance, as well as sociopolitical factors associated with the extent of organization of the working class and other influential sectors and classes, the geographical and sectoral distribution of the population, and its level of skills."[1] These factors are at the foundations of the models in this book. Indeed, basing economic analysis on institutions and political economy is the hallmark of the structuralist approach. Neoclassical authors start from hypotheses of optimizing agents and full employment; their moves toward incorporating social classes and market power come as afterthoughts at best.

This chapter aims at showing how structuralist models work. It opens in section 1.1 with a discussion of how model builders strive to incorporate political economy into their machines. The organization of data for economywide models into social accounting matrixes is described in sections 1.2 and 1.3, first with a numerical example and then in terms of symbols. Possible directions of macroeconomic causality (or model "closures") are outlined in a one-sector model without foreign trade in section 1.4. Additional causal links and the implications of opening the model to trade are taken up in sections 1.5 and 1.6, followed by a review of multisectoral data and closure issues in sections 1.7 and 1.8. Sections 1.9 and 1.10 show how the models can be extended to deal with flows of funds and finance, first in terms of data organization and then specification. Section 1.11 is about the treatment of nonproportionalities and substitution, and section 1.12 takes up dynamics. Section 1.13 reviews computational procedures for model solution. Finally, section 1.14 is a preview of the models presented in this book.

1.1 Political Economy

Structuralism is more a program of research and policy formation than a well-defined set of rules for putting a model in place. Any economy is a maze of structural detail—more than one could ever build into equations or use in policy design. However, general hypotheses about how the system functions are shared by structuralist authors. They include the following:

1. Economically powerful actors—"institutions" such as the state or corporations, "groups" such as landlords or rentiers, and "classes" such as organized labor—are not price-takers. They can influence price and/or quantity changes in certain markets. The seats of power differ from economy to economy, and change with local institutional arrangements and history. Identifying powerful actors and specifying the inflexibilities they can create is an indispensable first step in model design.

2. Macroeconomic causality is influenced by microeconomic detail, but on the whole it flows from investment, exports, and fiscal demand as predetermined variables (or demand "injections") to income distribution, import, and output flows which generate savings supplies (or "leakages"). Changes in income and wealth distributions play an essential role in macro adjustment to historical processes such as capital accumulation and to exogenous shocks. There is no particular reason to assume that macro-

economic equilibrium will involve full employment of either labor or installed capacity economywide.

3. The money supply is often endogenous or "passive," adjusting to the level of activity and rate of inflation. In many sectors production responds to demand as just indicated, while the roots of inflation lie in unresolved distributional conflicts and propagation mechanisms such as the indexation of contracts.

4. Forms of financial intermediation that have developed over time strongly influence the macro system. Feedbacks between the real and financial sides of the economy can be mediated by large portfolio shifts (e.g., capital flight) as well as changes in asset rates of return. In developing economies the onset of "financial fragility" is an ever-present risk.

5. In part due to the process of import-substituting industrialization, imported intermediate and capital goods are required to support local production; foreign exchange to buy these imports can be a binding constraint.

6. Development is not a balanced or harmonious process. Technical change tied to new investment on the part of independently acting firms is an important contributor to growth. Private capital formation is as likely to be "crowded in" by public investment through complementarities as "crowded out" by rising interest rates charged by banks.

How are these views about the economy built into a model? Structuralists's practice has five key features. First, they begin their analysis by singling out economically relevant sets of people and institutions and specifying how they fit into available data on income and wealth distributions. In Adelman and Robinson's (1989) phrase, they create an "extended functional distribution" based on the institutional structure of the economy at hand. Each set of economic actors typically is related to a functional category of the income distribution (wages, corporate profits, receipts of unincorporated enterprise) or a production sector; it has different behavior patterns and partial controls over the system. In practice, a group, class, or institution may be labeled by specific income flows rather than membership in an identifiable cluster of firms or individuals, but that is a shortcut. The justification for taking it is the belief that actions both of legal persons such as the state or corporate sector and of real households reflect their positions in the economic system as revealed by their principal income source. They interact according to behavioral rules the modeler specifies, with consequent repercussions on macroeconomic equilibrium.

In this book all the models incorporate extended functional distributions, across which savings propensities, consumption and investment behavior, portfolio choices, and power over price formation are assumed to differ. Typical entries in the distributional matrix include nonagricultural firms which gather profit income from markup pricing and undertake investment projects costing more than their own savings flows; rentiers who receive distributed profits, interest, and other financial incomes, suffer capital losses and gains on their (often considerable) assets, and save more than they invest; workers who get income from wages nominally fixed in the short tun, don't save very much, and battle with firms about how wage increases will respond to unemployment and price inflation; agriculturalists whose saving rates are often high but whose income fluctuates sharply, following flexible price movements; and urban and rural "marginals" who pick up residual income flows, suffer from deprivation of basic needs, and save at low, often negative rates. The state in its fiscal, public investment, and central banking roles, the commercial banks, and foreigners also enter as partially independent and powerful actors. The degrees of freedom available to any actor depend on the institutions and history of the economy at hand; incorporating them in convincing fashion is part of the model-building art.

Starting from such notions of economic structure and institutions or class runs counter to neoclassical practice. Economists presently in the "mainstream" devote their time to "deriving" macro behavioral functions from stylized optimization exercises that individual persons, firms, and even the government are supposed to undertake. If clever, the analyst can fold the separate optimizations into a Pareto first-, second-, or *n*th-best equilibrium that can be represented as the extreme value of a social welfare function. A harmonious, welfare-maximizing economy (perhaps with a few "distortions" to be removed) represents the mainstream vision. Neoclassical modelers such as Scarf and Shoven (1983) or Shoven and Whalley (1984) reflect it in their computations by measuring welfare costs of distortions, or looking at effects of extra saving on growth. More adventurous neoclassicals may build in rent-seeking bureaucrats and other obstructions, but few go far in trying to bring class and economic power into their models through the rational agent back door.[2]

A second distinctive feature of structuralist models is that they are *not* set up in "real" terms (i.e., with only relative prices). Rather, they explicitly include prices and income flows in nominal or money terms, of the sort that actual firms, poeple, and ministers of finance face. Examples abound: Workers may be concerned about their "real" purchasing power (e.g., a wage index divided by a price index), but in practice they struggle or negotiate with management over a money wage. Rapidly rising money wage rates in turn can trigger price inflations that affect everybody's economic decisions. Governments may be concerned with a "real" exchange rate (e.g., the ratio of indexes of prices of traded and nontraded goods), but they manipulate the nominal peso to yen conversion factor—real or relative prices of traded goods may or may not respond. The finance minister worries about meeting payment obligations from a nominally fixed budget—if she underestimates inflation, money will have to be printed or the government's real spending will have to fall.

Third, these examples suggest that different prices are under varying degrees of control by distinct groups in the economy—a focus on nominal magnitudes permits realistic treatments of financial markets and economic power. The models herein postulate that power plays a role in price formation. For example, econometric studies almost always show that firms (especially in manufacturing) mark up variable production costs by a fixed margin to fix prices. The markup rate is usually interpreted as the outcome of an oligopoly position on the output side and perhaps efficiency wage considerations for inputs. Other markets may have more flexibly varying prices, reflecting competitive behavior on the part of actors on both sides. The state may be able to intervene directly to control markups or public enterprise prices (e.g., the sale prices of gasoline and diesel fuel from refineries it controls) but finds controlling flex-prices costly in terms of holding stocks, importing, and "making" markets. Nominal price accounting provides the flexibility to include these and similar considerations in applied models.

Working with money income accounts also makes it easy to link the goods-producing and financial sectors of the economy through flows of funds. Each economic class or actor (e.g., wage earners, the government, or the rest of the world) has a "financial surplus" defined as the excess of its saving over its investment. The sum of nominal surpluses across the economy must be zero, though each one separately may be positive or negative. For example, rentiers and (perhaps) farmers usually save more than they invest, and industrial firms do the opposite. Among households, wage earners typically save far less than farmers or rentiers. The overall public sector may save substantially or dissave, but after it pays for public investment, its financial surplus is usually negative.

Shifts in surpluses depend on nominal price movements. Further price and quantity financial adjustments (at times involving asset and liability stocks that are the cumulations of flows) in response to changed positions can be built into CGE models. The feedbacks to commodity prices and quantities are often important. Effects of interest rate movements on investment demand are a classic example. Others involve portfolio movements and changes in wealth. For example, if rentiers hold assets abroad in the wake of capital flight, nominal currency devaluation will make them richer in local currency terms. A consequent reduction in their saving rate could have important macroeconomic implications, either for output changes or inflation.

Fourth, there is the question of how much economic rationality and price-mediated substitution to include in the specification. As a matter of convenience and common sense, the models here all incorporate some degree of consumer response to relative price shifts. If the staple food becomes more expensive, people will consume more or less of it, depending on income and substitution effects in complete systems of demand equations which are easy to build in. More important, dearer food may lead purchases of other goods to fall if its own demand is income inelastic. When there is a large agricultural sector, we will see in section 1.8 that the macroeconomic implications can be profound.

Elsewhere in the system, asset holders usually try to shift their portfolios to keep up with changing rates of return. Price-induced substitution among production inputs may be considered, if it seems practically relevant—econometric evidence rarely supports strong firm-level changes in labor demand as real wages vary, but there may be price-induced shifts among inputs such as copper and aluminum, citizens and guest-workers, or gas and oil. On the output side, the total volume of agricultural production is not very price responsive, but acreages devoted to specific crops are. Export volumes and investment are at times sensitive to prices and asset returns, depending on the economy at hand.

The moral from these examples is that price responsiveness may or may not be empirically important, or central, to the questions the model is supposed to address. If not, it can usefully be suppressed to focus attention on issues that are more relevant. A secondary observation is that one may or may not wish to characterize sensitivity to relative prices in an optimizing framework. Such machines are often convenient and neat but are not the end of the model builder's art. Consumers in an economy with several staple crops are likely to switch consumption to, say, rice from wheat flour if the price of wheat goes down, regardless of whether one believes they are doing careful optimizations or not. A model should include the demand switch in parsimonious fashion, not its utility-based textbook rationalization.

The fifth point about models is that their behavior depends crucially upon their description of causal linkages in the macroeconomic system. As discussed below, there are many ways in which the economy can adjust when it is perturbed—output levels or the income distribution across classes may change, interest rates may vary, positions of wealth may expand or erode. A model builder has to select *which* of these adjustment mechanisms to build into his or her equations—the qualitative nature of the solutions will depend upon the choice. In the jargon, a model's "closure" has to be chosen and justified on the basis of empirical and institutional analysis of the economy at hand. Setting closure is impossible unless class structures and economic power relationships have already been defined. Searching for sites of power and macro causal links is the key to the structuralist approach.

In summary, an emphasis on interactions between groups of households and institutions such as the state, banks, and firms characterizes the models in this book. Distributional shifts are the hinge for macro adjustment, mediated by output changes and movements of nominal prices against one another. How prices and production equilibrate is determined primarily by a model's causal structure, and only secondarily by substitution response. Estimating elasticities and elaborating substitution patterns in production or demand play second fiddle in model design to specifying its structures of causality and class.

1.2 The Data Base

CGE modelers make a fetish of accounting consistency. The numbers they feed into models must be consistent with the national income and input–output accounting their equations contain. The models are then used for comparative static exercises around the base data set or to make conditional projections for the future, all the while maintaining the accounting rules. It has become customary to impose tight bookkeeping from the start by arraying the data in the form of a social accounting matrix (SAM), of the sort proposed by Stone (1966) and elaborated by Pyatt and Round (1985) and many others. In this section we discuss SAM's for the nonfinancial part of the economy, postponing analysis of asset flows and stocks to sections 1.9 and 1.10.

Table 1.1 is a representative SAM for a one-sector economy—the numbers are fabricated, but for many developing economies their composition would be roughly right. They are put together subject to two main accounting considerations:

First, totals for corresponding rows and columns are always the same, a defining characteristic of a SAM. For example, total uses of output in row 1 (= 100) are the same as the first column's total production costs. Wage

Table 1.1
Illustrative numerical SAM for a one-sector economy

		Production costs	Uses of incomes					Export subsidy	Capital formation	Competitive imports	Total
			Firm	Wage	Rentier	Government	Foreign				
		1	2	3	4	5	6	7	8	9	10
1	Sales	30		25	4	12	23	2	7	−3	100
2	Wages	20				4					24
3	Profits	23									23
4	Indirect taxes	7									7
5	Import tariffs	2			1						3
6	Value added	52			1	4					57
7	Firm income	13									13
8	Wage income	20				4					24
9	Rentier income	10									10
10	Government income	9	3		2		5				19
11	Foreign income	18	5		1				5	3	32
12	Direct taxes		3		1						4
13	Subsidies			−2		4		−2			0
14	Saving		5	1	3	−1	4				12
15	Totals	100	13	24	10	19	32	0	12	0	

income of 24 in row 8 is exhausted by the entries in column 3—workers's consumption of 23 (producers's price purchases of 25 in row 1 less a consumer subsidy of 2 in row 13) plus saving of 1 in row 14. The latter example shows that row and column numbers for corresponding income sources and uses do not coincide in table 1.1, for reasons of presentation to be explained below.

The second principle is that the matrix is set out in nominal or current-value terms. All entries in a row are valued in the same unit of account (typically an index based on producers's prices). Experience shows that the mapping from SAM to CGE is easier to grasp if the price used for "most" transactions along a row is the same. For example, row 1 gives the different uses of output, valued at producers's prices. It is assumed that the domestic price value of exports is 25, whereas foreign buyers benefit from an export subsidy of 2. The subsidy is in column 7, and the world price value of 23 is in column 6. They sum to exports in producers's prices.

Exceptions to the uniform price rule come up when there are well-entrenched price differentials across columns. For example, in the wage payment rows 2 and 8, production workers in column 1 and government employees in column 5 may receive different average remunerations. A purist would put the two sorts of wage payments in different rows to maintain single prices, but for such a simple case the extra space seems wasteful—one doesn't want to paper a wall with a SAM. It is easy enough to write down two separate wage rates in a model based on the social accounts.

The rows in table 1.1 are arranged in the following fashion: Sales by destination are in row 1. Components of value added at market prices are in rows 2 through 5, with totals in row 6. The payments entries are regrouped from production inputs (including indirect taxes) into income flows in rows 7 through 11. Besides receipts from productive activity, items such as transfers and direct taxes appear in these rows as well. Rows 7 through 11 correspond to the income recipient categories split out in the SAM—firms, wage recipients, rentiers who receive distributed profits from the firms, the government, and foreigners. Rows 12 and 13 summarize direct tax and subsidy flows, and row 14 gives savings from the different income categories.

In the columns, number 1 summarizes production costs, and the entries down numbers 2 through 6 show how the recipient groups dispose of their incomes. For example, column 6 gives foreigners' spending in border prices (foreign exchange prices converted to national terms by the exchange rate), for "our" exports in row 1, a transfer to the government of 5 in row 10, and the current-account deficit (or "foreign saving") of 4 in row 14. Foreigners' inflows in row 11 are also in border prices. They include our imports of intermediates (column 1), rentiers' consumer goods (column 4), capital goods (column 8), and "competitive" items (column 9) as well as firms's transfers to abroad (profit remittances, etc.) of 5 in column 2.

The remaining columns include the export subsidy of 2 in number 7—note that it adds to export value in row 1 and is "reflected" through the negative entry to column 7, row 13, into the subsidy total of 4 in the government spending column 5 (the other subsidy items is 2 for workers' consumption in column 2). Column 8 gives investment spending (inventory changes are suppressed for simplicity), and column 9 shows that there are competitive imports of 3. Such commodities are assumed to substitute easily for domestic products. For simplicity, world and domestic prices for competitive imports are assumed to be the same, although it would be easy enough to include a price differential column like number 7. Of course, one would also have to specify to which income flow(s) the differential between world and domestic prices should be charged or accrue.

Other observations about table 1.1 include the following:

1. Errors and omissions are usually ironed away when a SAM is constructed. This procedure is at times inappropriate as, for example, when errors and omissions in the balance of payments are a proxy for rentier's capital flight, offset domestically by borrowing and dissaving by the government or private firms.

2. Spending differentials across classes appear in the numbers. The share of wage income saved is lower than the shares from incomes of firms and rentiers. Rentiers consume imported goods (row 11, column 4) and also pay tariffs upon them (row 5, column 4). Workers' spending in column 3 goes only for consumption of national goods in row 1, with their costs reduced in row 13 by a well-targeted subsidy.

3. Government wage payments, indirect taxes, and tariffs are included in GDP, following standard practice. The wage bill appears in the government-spending column 5, adding to the labor cost of production in column 1 to give total wage income of 24 in row 2.

4. Investment in column 8 is split 7 to 5 into nationally produced and imported components, a plausible breakdown for a developing economy. The intermediate import share of gross output is 18 percent, also a reasonable number.

5. Saving flows from all sources in row 14 sum to total investment as a check on the overall accounting consistency of the SAM. In section 1.9 we

show how savings from the different income groups feed into flows of funds.

Lore about the fabrication of SAM's is presented in later chapters. Broadly speaking, the matrixes are based on national income and product accounts, interindustry data, and consumer budget information for the base year. Typically these sources are inconsistent, and judgment must be applied in modifying estimates that don't agree with one another to set up the consistent accounting of the SAM. The payoff comes from the fact that production and income numbers which tally with each other (even if they are "wrong") provide a powerful base for economic analysis. CGE models are designed to exploit the fruits of consistency to the greatest possible extent.

1.3 The SAM in Symbols

Table 1.2 restates the numbers of table 1.1 in algebraic notation, to pave the way for later economic analysis and also to show how many parameters in CGE models can be estimated (or "calibrated") as ratios of entries in the basic data source.

It is simplest to go through the table rowwise. Row 1 gives different uses of output with price P and volume X. Intermediate uses of domestically produced goods (or competitive imports) are proportional to production via the input–output coefficient a_1. Workers's and rentiers's consumption volumes are, respectively, C_1^w and C_1^r. Government real consumption of domestic goods is G_1, exports are E and competitive imports are M^c. Total real investment is I, and fractions β_1 and β_0 (summing to 1) are devoted to purchases of national and imported goods, respectively. The subscript 0 refers to an import.

A world price (and occasionally a foreign exchange stock or flow) is denoted by an asterisk. The world price of exports P_e^* comes from the relationship $P_e^* = P(1 - z_e)/e$, where z_e is the rate of subsidy. Rearrangement of this equation gives $P = eP_e^* + z_e P$, which explains the decomposition of the value of exports PE into world price and subsidy components in columns 6 and 7, respectively.

Going back to table 1.1, one would estimate the input–output coefficient a_1 by the ratios of entries in rows 1 and 15 of column 1: $a_1 = 30/100 = 0.3$. The export subsidy rate is figured relative to the producers's value of exports: $z_e = 2/25 = 0.08$. Finally, the share of national goods in the investment basket is $\beta_1 = 7/12 = 0.5833333$. Evidently $\beta_0 = 1 - \beta_1 =$

Table 1.2
Illustrative symbolic SAM for a one-sector economy

		Production costs 1	Firm's income use 2	Current spending by income type: Wage 3	Rentier 4	Government 5	Foreign income use 6	Export subsidy 7	Capital formation 8	Competitive imports 9	Total 10
1	Sales	Pa_1X		PC_1^w	PC_1^r	PG_1	eP_e^*E	z_ePE	$P\beta_1 I$	$-PM^c$	PX
2	Wages	wbX				w_gL_g					Y_w
3	Profits	rP_iK									rP_iK
4	Indirect taxes	t_1BX									Ind
5	Import tariffs	$t_0eP_0^*a_0X$			$t_ceP_0^*C_0^r$						Tar
6	Value added	V			$t_ceP_0^*C_0^r$	w_gL_g					GDP
7	Firm income	$(1-d)rP_iK$									Y_f
8	Wage income	wbX				w_gL_g					Y_w
9	Rentier income	drP_iK									Y_r
10	Government income	T_x	T_f		T_r		U_{fg}				Y_g
11	Foreign income	$eP_0^*a_0X$	U_{ff}		$eP_c^*C_0^r$				$eP_0^*\beta_0 I$	PM^c	Y_{for}
12	Direct taxes		$t_f^dY_f$		$t_r^dY_r$						Dir
13	Subsidies			$-z_cPC_1^w$		Z		$-z_ePE$			0
14	Saving		S_f	S_w	S_r	S_g	S_f				P_iI
15	Total	PX	Y_f	Y_w	Y_r	Y_g	Y_{for}	0	P_iI	0	

Definitions

$$B = Pa_1 + wb + (1 + t_0)eP_0^* a_0, \qquad r = [P - (1 + t_1)B]X/(1 + t_1)P_i K$$

$$P_i = \beta_1 P + \beta_0 e P_i^*, \qquad V = [wb + t_1 B + t_0 e P_0^* a_0]X + (1 + t_1) r P_i K$$

$$T_x = [t_1 B + t_0 e P_0^* a_0]X, \qquad T_f = t_f^d Y_f, \qquad T_r = t_r^d Y_r + t_c e P_c^* C_0^r$$

0.4166667. These fractions are carried out to seven places because such precision would be wise in computational practice. In the numerical illustrations hereafter there is more rounding off for presentational ease.

Row 2 shows that wages are paid to production workers and government employees. It is usually convenient to normalize base year prices to unity: $P = w = e = 1$. The implication is that volume numbers are measured in units such as "rupees worth of output in prices of 1990." Input coefficients such as the labor–output ratio can be computed as $b =$ base-year employment/X. The government wage w_g could be given a value different from 1, to account for intersectoral wage differentials.

Skipping down to row 11, note in column 1 that intermediate imports are made proportional to output through a coefficient a_0 and (in row 5) pay a tariff rate t_0. Such imports are usually assumed not to compete with domestic goods: They are "complementary" or "noncompetitive." They have a world price P_0^*, which could be set equal to one in the base year. From table 1.1 the input coefficient is $a_0 = 18/100 = 0.18$, and the tariff rate is $t_0 = 2/18 = 0.1111$.

In the definitions at the bottom of table 1.2, B stands for variable cost per unit output—this concept is used to calculate a markup rate in section 1.4. The numbers in rows 1, 2, 5, and 11 of table 1.1 show that $B = (30 + 20 + 2 + 18)/100 = 0.7$. Indirect taxes in row 4 are figured on the basis of variable cost plus profits, so that the rate is $t_1 = 7/(70 + 23) = 0.0753$. By raising B, a higher tariff rate t_0 "cascades" into increased indirect taxes. Such effects occur often in developing country tax systems.

Row 3 of table 1.1 shows that total profits are 23. They give rise to a profit rate r in table 1.2, measured relative to the value of capital stock (at replacement prices) P_iK. The price index P_i is based on the investment proportions β_0 and β_1. They sum to one, implying that $P_i = 1$ in the base year. If the capital stock is, say, 250, then $r = 23/250 = 0.092$.

We have now discussed the breakdown of value added in production, namely, V in row 6. To it must be added consumer tariffs and government wages to get GDP at market prices in the last column. The next step is to investigate income flows.

Foreigners' income in row 11 is made up of intermediate imports (column 1), firms' external remittances or transfers U_{ff} (column 2), rentiers' consumption imports C_0^r (column 4), investment imports with world price P_i^* (column 8), and competitive imports M^c (column 9). Competitive imports enter the accounting with a negative sign in row 1 since they offset demand or add to supply, and with a positive sign to contribute to foreign exchange outflows in row 11. The consumer imports carry a tariff in row 5. Its rate is $t_c = 1/1 = 100$ percent.

Various taxes enter government income in row 10—they are defined at the bottom of the table. The government also gets a transfer from abroad, U_{fg} in row 10, column 6. Rentiers in row 9 receive a fraction d ("dividends") of total profits. The rest goes to firms in row 7. From table 1.1, $d = 10/23 = 0.4348$.

Direct taxes are accounted for in row 12. The rates for firms and rentiers are $t_f^d = 3/13 = 0.2308$ and $t_r^d = 1/10 = 0.1$, respectively. Subsidies are cumulated in row 13, entering as a government expenditure item in column 5. The subsidy rate z_c on wage earners's consumption is $z_c = 2/25 = 0.08$.

1.4 Macro Causality in the One-Sector Economy

With data and accounting rules exemplified, we are ready to discuss causal relationships in a one-sector CGE. As noted in section 1.1, structuralists often assume that macroeconomic causality runs broadly from demand injections to leakages under conditions of passive money supply.[3] They treat the extended functional distribution and at least some sectors's outputs as endogenous in their macro models, subject to rules such as markups and fix-price/flex-price distinctions (see section 1.8) regarding price adjustment. Neoclassicals, by contrast, typically presuppose full labor employment and capacity utilization under an "active" money supply that fixes the overall price level. They root their firms upon cost and input demand functions derived from clever optimization games.

Maintained hypotheses as diverse as these have notable effects upon the different models's qualitative results. For example, greater investment demand in a structuralist model will make output rise and/or the income distribution shift to generate the complementary saving supply. With available saving determined from full employment output, distribution, and prices (or the forces of "productivity and thrift") in a neoclassical world, an upward jump in investment is an impossible event. Such distinct outcomes arise throughout nonstructuralist and structuralist policy analysis, as we will see in discussing the contrasting effects under different causal schemes of exogenous changes in the income distribution as well as higher government spending, currency devaluation, and other policy moves.

The notation defined in table 1.2 serves as a basis to describe causal relationships in a one-sector CGE model or to define its "closure" (a term proposed by Sen 1963 and reinvented for the CGE field by Taylor and Lysy 1979). In formal algebra, prescribing closure boils down to stating

Table 1.3
Basic macro relationships for a one-sector model

Markup pricing	Neoclassical cost function	
$P = (1+\tau)wb$	$P = f(w, rP)$	(1)
$L/X = b$	$L/X = f_w(w/P, r)$	(2)
$u = X/K$	$u = X/K$	(3)
$r = [\tau/(1+\tau)]u = \pi u$	$K/X = f_r(w/P, r)$	(4)
Investment–saving balance		
$g^s = sr$		(5)
$g^i = g^i(r, u)$		(6)
$\gamma + g^i - g^s = 0$		(7)
Definitions		
$\pi = rPK/PX = \tau/(1+\tau)$, $w/P = (1-\pi)/b$, $\gamma = PG/PK$		

which variables are endogenous or exogenous in an equation system largely based upon macroeconomic accounting identities, and figuring out how they influence one another. When one is setting up a model for any economy, the closure question becomes more interesting, transforming itself to one of empirically plausible signs of "effects" and, more important, a perception of what are the driving macroeconomic forces in the system. A sense of institutions and history necessarily enters into any serious discussion of macro causality. We can easily run through the algebra here; the models in this book give good examples of applied institutional perspective.

Table 1.3, based on table 1.2 but without its accounting complications, sets the stage. It contains two similar but not identical macro models—the neoclassical version to the right is itself more internally constrained or closed than the one with markup pricing. Properties of different closures can be illustrated by adding restrictions to the seven that appear, but first the table itself should be explained.

Consumption, investment, and government spending are the only components of demand, meaning that the material balance condition (comparable to row 1 in table 1.2) is

$$PC + PI + PG - PX = 0.$$

As written, this equation signifies that excess commodity demand vanishes. In what follows, we interpret it both as ex post accounting relationship that will be observed in a SAM and as a defining condition for macroeconomic balance. Note for later reference that macro balance does not presuppose either full capacity use or full employment of labor (the two are not the same thing). Output X can in principle be determined by either effective demand or input supply.

For simplicity, we consolidate incomes of firms and rentiers. Then (ignoring intermediate inputs and indirect taxes) the income statement is

$$PX = wbX + rPK.$$

The saving rate from profit incomes rPK is s. We set workers's saving to zero, without much loss of generality in analyzing current output-expenditure interactions so long as the saving rate from wages is well less than that from profits.[4] Total consumption becomes

$$PC = wbX + (1 - s)rPK.$$

Combining the material balance, income, and consumption equations gives

$$PG + PI - srPK = 0.$$

This equality of private saving to investment plus government spending (or, more generally, the fiscal deficit[5]) is a familiar condition for macro balance. It is clearly not independent of the material balance condition—one is derived by accounting manipulation from the other.

Closure rules in a one-sector system are easier to illustrate if the foregoing equations are restated in a normalized or "intensive" form, with all nominal income and expenditure flows divided by the value of the capital stock PK.[6] We will follow this practice until multisectoral models appear in section 1.7. We let $g^s = srPK/PK = sr$ and $g^i = PI/PK$ stand, respectively, for the capital stock growth rate permitted by national saving and created by investment demand. Also let $\gamma = PG/PK$, that is, government outlay relative to the capital stock. Then the condition for macro equilibrium (or the investment-saving balance) is $\gamma + g^i - g^s = 0$, equation (7) of table 1.3. The growth rates possible from saving and investment appear in lines (5) and (6).

The arguments in the investment function are quite standard. Capacity use u represents the accelerator term that enters worldwide into econometric investment demand functions. Without going into fancy formulas for dynamic expectations (which don't make a lot of sense in applied models), the profit rate r in (6) can be interpreted as an index of expected future returns. Alternatively, it is a proxy for firms's available cash flow when investment is largely self-financed under credit rationing.

As the table headings indicate, we work with two pricing theories. Contrasting assumptions about pricing rules and the presence or absence of full employment or capacity use will provide the gist for the discussion that follows. On the left, the markup rule in row (1) simply states that output prices are based on variable costs (here, wages) with producers taking a margin at rate τ. In the more complete accounts of tables 1.1 and 1.2, the markup is defined by profit flows relative to variable costs: $\tau = rP_iK/BX = 23/70 = 0.3286$.

Markup pricing equations have the advantage of fitting the data, at least in nonprimary goods producing sectors where producers's margins are often stable. There is no dearth of theoretical explanations for both the level and stability of τ. They may follow from considerations of market power (Kalecki 1971; Sylos-Labini 1984), efficiency wages (Bowles and Boyer 1989) setting prices high enough to generate corporate savings sufficient to finance the bulk of planned capital formation (Duesenberry 1958; Eichner 1980), or ease in internal coordination in multiproduct, multiplant firms (Semmler 1984). The presence of a markup can thus be supported by optimizing models or—more plausibly—by empirical observation of enterprises and common sense. Its rate may change with the current macro situation, institutional evolution, and redistributive policy, as the models in the following chapters emphasize.

Following down the left-hand column, in line (2) the labor–output ratio is b, and the output–capital ratio u (which we treat as a measure of capacity utilization) is defined in row (3). With regard to (4), it is easy to see from (1) that the share of profits in output is $\pi = rPK/PX = \tau/(1 + \tau)$. Since the profit rate is the product of the profit share and the output/capital ratio u, (4) follows directly. This definition also implies that investment can be treated as a function of π (instead of r) and u.

The markup model (1) through (7) is a full macro system. It is of interest because markup pricing imposes few restrictions on supply. The markup rate τ and profit share π follow from institutions and policy, whereas the labor use coefficient b comes from technology and market custom. There is no mechanism via which τ (or other distributional parameters) and b interact. Such independence of distribution and resource allocation does not occur in the neoclassical model of the right-hand columns of table 1.3.

Equation (1) in the neoclassical model is a cost function. When production takes place under constant returns to scale (the standard hypothesis), the function f will be homogeneous; that is, it can be written in the form

$$1 = f\left[\frac{w}{P}, r\right].$$

This version is often called a "factor-price frontier" since it sets up an inverse relationship between the real wage w/P and the profit rate r. In the markup model such a conflict between real returns to labor and capital need not occur for macroeconomic reasons. The story goes as follows: The real wage is $w/P = 1/b(1 + \tau) = (1 - \pi)/b$, while from (4) r depends on τ and capacity utilization u. A distributional shift toward labor would be represented by a lower τ (or π), directly increasing w/P. The overall saving rate would decline but (under expectations that the distributional shift is "permanent") investment could fall as well if it responds more to a lower profit share than higher consumer demand. The net effect on output could go either way. With investment more sensitive to u than π, the outcomes could include higher output, faster growth, and higher values of both r and w/P, something the factor-price frontier does not allow. These possibilities underline the fact that the seemingly innocuous optimization exercises underlying neoclassical production theory strongly constrain its results.

When some degree of input substitution is assumed, neoclassical equations (2) and (4) are based on a relationship known as Shepard's lemma (cf. Varian 1984, 54–57), which states that factor input ratios are equal to the partial derivatives of the cost function, f_w and f_r. Equation (2) ties the labor–output ratio to the real wage—if w/P rises, L/X goes down. Labor use is linked to distribution. Greater employment is necessarily associated with a lower real wage—another strong neoclassical result.

From neoclassical equations (3) and (4), the output–capital ratio is positively related to the profit rate, as in the markup formula (4). The cost function (1) and the marginal productivity conditions (2) and (4) imply (and are jointly implied by) the existence of a constant returns production function, $X = g(L, K)$. When marginal productivity rules for input demands are postulated, a neoclassical model can be set up around either a production or cost function. For comparison with markup pricing, the latter is more convenient.

The causal structure of both versions rests on determination of price and input–output relationships from (1) through (4), and the level of demand from (4) through (7). How the two sets of equations interact is determined by additional restrictions, or closure. We discuss three standard cases—models characterized by output adjustment, forced saving, and determination of investment by saving supply—and in the following section consider additional adjustment mechanisms through which rigidities of the last version can be relaxed.

Output Adjustment

In the markup model assume that the nominal wage w is fixed by historical wage bargains and custom, the capital stock K by previous investment, and government spending G and (for the given K) the spending ratio γ by policy. Then with a fixed markup rate τ, the price level P and income distribution follow from (1). The demand equations (5) through (7) and the distributional identity (4) jointly determine r and u. Output X follows from (3) and employment L from (2). We have a macro system in which causality runs toward employment and output from the side of demand; output is implicitly assumed to lie below the full capacity level κK determined by the available capital stock. A classic formulation of the markup causal scheme is by Kalecki (1971).

The neoclassical story is similar, but more tightly constrained. Only γ, w, and K can be predetermined—distributional variables such as τ, the profit share, and the real wage are endogenous to the system. This complication is reflected in the fact that (1) must be combined with (4) through (7) to solve jointly for u, r, and w/P. Output and employment follow from (3) and (2) as before, whereas (1) gives the price level. Keynes's (1936) *General Theory* model of the real side of the economy is fundamentally the neoclassical equations (1) through (7) closed from the side of demand.

Comparative statics of the two versions can be illustrated with three experiments: changing government spending γ, the money wage w, and the real wage w/P.

In both versions a higher value of γ raises u and X through a multiplier process that converges so long as saving supply increases more strongly than investment demand as a function of u. In the neoclassical model, (1) can be inserted into (4) to eliminate w/P. The upshot is a positive relationship between r and u. But then from (1) interpreted as a factor-price frontier, w/P must fall as u goes up. An increased demand injection is associated with greater output and a lower real wage, with decreasing returns setting in as more labor is combined with the available capital stock. Since the nominal wage is fixed, P must rise to reduce w/P—the demand injection drives up the price level as well as with output.

Neither the real wage decrease nor the price increase occurs in the markup model since τ is set from the outside and diminishing returns do not set in so long as capacity exceeds output. A demand injection could cause real wage *in*creases and price *de*flation if the markup rate or the labor–output ratio is an inverse function of u, as some evidence suggests (Schor 1985). However, we do not pursue these possibilities here since they are not often included in CGE models.

A change in the money wage w has no real effects in the markup system. From (1), P just adjusts in proportion, and the real side is unchanged. The neoclassical equations can easily be seen to depend only on w/P; therefore the same conclusion applies. For a given level of effective demand (i.e., γ), the real wage is an outcome of the neoclassical model. Hence money wage changes will affect only the price level and not employment—this is basically Keynes's argument about the uselessness of money wage reduction in chapter 19 of *The General Theory*.

Since the real wage is endogenous in the neoclassical system, it cannot be shifted exogenously in a thought experiment. In the markup model, if the rate τ is changed by macroeconomic shocks or policy (price controls, revised public enterprise charges, trade policy, etc.), the real wage will also move. As noted above, a real wage increase may make capacity utilization go either up or down. It will fall if there is a small differential between rentiers's and workers's saving shares and/or the responsiveness of investment demand to the profit share is strong. However, real wage increases will stimulate output if investment rises with the consumption surge that redistribution toward labor is likely to trigger. Through the same linkage, the growth rate may also go up.[7]

Dutt (1984) drew attention to this possibility for expansion, which can occur for additional reasons in an open economy model (section 1.6). It seems to apply in the developing world (Taylor 1988a).

Forced Saving

Forced saving occurs when u and X cannot vary, for instance, because the economy is at full capacity (u is at its "technical" maximum κ) or employment L is predetermined at a "full" level or otherwise. We work in the following discussion with a fixed L, but the analysis extends to a supply-side restriction on output by available capital or by a labor supply function such as $L = L(w/P, X, K)$. A surplus labor specification, for example, would make L highly elastic to the real wage, effectively setting w/P.

In the markup model, setting employment adds a restriction to (1) through (7). In algebraic terms the system becomes overdetermined, and some variable must become endogenous to meet the new constraint. If incipient excess demand with fixed output leads to upward pressure on prices, the obvious candidate for endogeneity is the markup rate τ, and thereby the price level P from (1). The causal structure is that (2) determines X, and (3) u. The demand equations (5) through (7) give the profit rate r. The markup rate comes from (4) and P from (1). Through price movements relative to the fixed money wage (presupposing a greater saving propensity from profits than wages), the income distribution adjusts endogenously to force the creation of enough saving to meet the new injection of demand.

In the neoclassical version, (1) and (4) through (7) determine u, r, and w/P as in the output adjustment closure. But then the model falls apart. Equations (2) and (3) give inconsistent values for X—the only recourse is that one equation be dropped. Two excisions generally appear in the literature. The first is to leave out the investment demand function, with implications to be taken up below. The other is to omit (2) and replace (4) by the identity $r = \pi u$. These moves are tantamount to abandoning marginal productivity input demand functions and returning to the markup system since $\pi = \tau/(1 + \tau)$.

This forced retreat underscores Kaldor's (1955) doubts about the usefulness of distribution theory based on marginal productivity. Alternatively, forced saving can be viewed as a macro adjustment scenario in which the neoclassical combination of output and price increases in response to higher demand degenerates into a pure price (and distribution) change when output is determined from the side of supply.

This last observation leads into comparative statics in the markup model. With u fixed, if the demand injection γ increases, then in (5) through (7) the profit rate is the free variable that goes up to provide the corresponding saving supply. From (4) and (1) the markup and price level rise and the real wage goes down. Reduced real spending (or "automatic lacking" in Dennis Robertson's 1933 phrase) on the part of wage earners caused by higher prices is the adjustment vehicle.

Since τ follows from effective demand, a money wage increase would just drive up the price level proportionally under forced saving. A worse outcome could befall an attempt at redistribution. Suppose in a simple case that investment is stable at the level $\bar{g}$ and that a tax $trPK$ is levied on profit income and transferred to wage earners. Saving-investment balance becomes $r = \bar{g}/s(1 - t)$. The profit rate rises along with the tax rate increase, and the real wage correspondingly falls.

Straightforward manipulation shows that the derivative of real post-transfer income per worker [which is $(w + trPK/L)/P$] with respect to t is $-t/(1 - t)$. If there is an existing tax-cum-transfer in place, increasing its rate *worsens* the position of wage earners. This is an example of the so-called paradox of thrift that accompanies forced saving. It bedevils any transfer attempt when the economy approaches full use of labor and/or available capital stock.

In closing, two observations should be added. First, although forced saving has been described here in terms of wages and profits, similar redistributional effects can occur among any number of saving flows. Applied models will include saving from one or more income classes, the rest of the world, and the government. Movements in financial surpluses (saving less investment) as prices shift will differ across these classes and institutions, allowing forced saving to occur. The presence of flows fixed in nominal terms—transfers and state spending are common examples—makes redistribution induced by changing prices even more important.

Second, it bears note that the inverse effect of price changes on consumption demand resulting from forced saving was the adjustment mechanism used by the economists who Amadeo (1986) calls the "post-Wicksellian" generation, such as Schumpeter, Robertson, and the Stockholm school. It was the basis of Keynes's (1930) *Treatise on Money*. After the publication of *The General Theory*, output adjustment came to the fore. When employment recovered in the industrial economies after World War II, macro theorists again wanted an inverse relationship between the price level and effective demand at hand. Instead of forced saving, a wealth effect was used to rationalize a negatively sloped schedule for aggregate consumer demand. Whether empirical relevance or ideological acceptability was the main reason for this choice would be an interesting inquiry, especially since we will see in section 1.5 that wealth effects provide a channel via which money wage cuts unambiguously make output rise.

Determination of Investment by Saving

Forced saving provides one means for accommodating a labor supply function into the macro system. As we have already noted, dropping the independent investment demand function (6) is another. This artifice is widely used. For example, it is the heart of the neoclassical growth model of Solow (1956).

Causal links are straightforward. In the markup model, K, L, w, and τ are predetermined. In table 1.3, P comes from (1), X from (2), u from (3), r from (4), and g^s from (5). In a savings-driven economy there is no room for (6), so capital stock growth g^i comes from (7). The solution of the neoclassical version is similar, except that as usual there is no room for a predetermined distributional index such as τ. With w fixed, equations (1) through (4) solve jointly for P, X, r, and u, and the story thereafter goes as in the markup model.

Output, income distribution, and saving all come from the supply side in the neoclassical version of this closure, which emphasizes productivity and thrift. A higher value of γ reduces g^i from (7)—government spending "crowds out" investment demand. The real wage can't be altered, and a money wage increase reflects itself solely in higher prices.

The markup model also demonstrates a pure price increase from a higher money wage and investment crowding-out by γ. A real wage increase is represented by a lower τ. From (4) and (5) the profit rate and saving supply fall. Hence (7) shows that the growth rate must decline. Such outcomes are opposite those possible in the output adjustment closure discussed above. To reiterate, with potential results so different, empirical awareness and institutional understanding of the economy are required to judge how an apposite macro model should be closed.

1.5 Additional Adjustment Mechanisms

Since the publication of *The General Theory*, mainstream macroeconomics has devoted great efforts toward putting independent investment demand and labor supply functions into the same model—its theoretical pursuit of equilibrium full employment (ideally to be induced by real wage cuts) does not cease. In terms of table 1.3 this quest takes the form of adding endogenous variables or by postulating new adjustment mechanisms. The examples discussed in this section have all influenced neoclassical CGE work. They appear only rarely in models designed by structuralists, who are not wedded to the idea that full employment of resources is a part of macroeconomic equilibrium.

Adding Endogenous Variables to the System

In table 1.3 suppose that the investment demand function (6) is reinstated along with predetermined employment but that γ is endogenous. Then all equations can be retained, with γ coming from (7). The interpretation would be that the government regulates its spending to ensure full employment. Another possibility would be for the government to adjust some tax variable (e.g., the rate t in the tax-cum-transfer program discussed above) to the same end. The spending scenario is spelled out in Meade (1961), whereas Johansen (1960) implicitly used an endogenous income tax to permit both an independent investment function and full employment in the first practical CGE. Rattsø (1982) provides illuminating simulations around Johansen's and other closures.

Postulating such government interventions perhaps make sense in models designed to explore distributionally "neutral" medium-run plans. In a shorter run, stock changes and/or trade flows such as competitive imports or exports might vary to equilibrate demand with a predetermined domestic supply. Such balancing seems improbable at the aggregate level. Under a foreign exchange shock, for example, imports can only be reduced to zero, and export volume may be limited by world market conditions. However, trade and/or inventory adjustments are more plausible for specific sectors and are built into several of the models discussed in this book.

Loanable Funds

Changes in "the" interest rate (say, i) mediate an adjustment mechanism that has been suggested at least since Thornton's and Ricardo's day. If the saving rate s rises as a function of i while investment demand g^i declines, then all seven equations of table 1.3 comprise a well-behaved system. An exogenous increase in γ will make the left-hand side of (7) positive, and i will rise to restore equilibrium by cutting investment and inducing extra saving.

This story sounds sensible, but it is subject to at least two objections (both emphasized by Keynes). The first is structural. Rates of return to assets in principle are determined in markets for stocks, not by savings and investment flows. As we will see in sections 1.9 and 1.10, this problem can be addressed in practical models by cumulating flows of funds, so we leave it for the moment. Extending a CGE model to include financial linkages does not change the *directions* of effects of interest rate changes from those that happen with loanable funds.

The more serious question is about the *strength* of interest rate effects. There is not much evidence in the Third World that overall saving responds to interest rate movements (although portfolio compositions certainly do). With much investment controlled by the state and large enterprises with good access to finance, interest rate influences on aggregate demand will be limited to only part of gross capital formation (housing construction?) and perhaps consumer purchases of durable goods. Empirical questions obviously arise, but low elasticities can cripple adjustment based on interest rate movements. For that reason this mechanism does not usually figure in applied CGE work.

The Real Balance Effect

If output is predetermined and there is an independent investment function, consumption is the main demand component that must vary to permit macro equilibrium. If consumer demand is an inverse function of the price level, the linkage is straightforward: Increased investment crowds out consumption by driving prices up. As noted in the last section, forced saving provides such a linkage but lost theoretical favor (apart from Kaldor and colleagues) fifty years ago. In contemporary macroeconomics its place is taken by the real balance effect.

The story is familiar, although, as we will see, it leads toward an overdetermined model in a neoclassical specification. It rests upon an exogenous money supply, say, H. A price increase will reduce national wealth by eroding "real balances," H/P. Wealth holders might be expected to try to restore their position by saving more; hence the saving rate becomes $s = s(H/P)$. A higher P cuts consumption by increasing the saving rate. Crowding-out becomes feasible again.

In the markup model with variable output and employment, money wage cuts now have some bite. A lower w will reduce P via (1), increasing wealth and making consumption rise. Indeed, real balances were first given prominence by Pigou (1943) as a counterargument to Keynes's insistence that money wage reduction is of no use. If their impact on saving is strong enough, price-induced changes in real wealth make the "principle of effective demand" as enunciated by Keynes and Kalecki beside the point.

If L is predetermined while the markup varies, then the real balance effect complements forced saving since both mechanisms lower consumption demand. With an endogenously determined markup rate, more investment or state spending will crowd out real consumption by reducing both the real wage *and* real wealth.

In a neoclassical specification the argument when L is free to vary runs along the same lines as with markup pricing—money wage changes affect real balances by shifting the level of P through costs. However, with L and K set exogenously or by supply functions, the model leaves no room for a predetermined money wage. Equations (1) through (4) in table 1.3 solve for r, u, X, *and* w/P. Since the saving rate depends on H/P, the demand equations (5) through (7) set a value for P with the real balance effect in force. But then the money wage w has to be endogenous to permit supply-side determination of w/P. There is no room left for historical or institutional elements in the wage bargain!

These observations suggest that a short-run neoclassical specification incorporating predetermined employment along with the real balance effect makes no sense. In the long run the appropriate level of w can be made the equilibrium point of a wage adjustment process, for example, as in Friedman (1968), Fischer (1977), and Taylor (1980), but even these authors allow determination of employment by aggregate demand until a vertical Phillips curve is reached. Their scenario is remote from the world of applied CGEs.

The problem with the real balance effect is that it picks out an absolute level of P as a function of the money supply H—it basically operates in the same way as the equation of exchange. In a full employment neoclassical economy all other nominal prices such as w must follow. Markup pricing allows two nominal magnitudes—w and H—to be fixed. Producers's margins and the overall price level take up the adjustment burden if full employment is imposed. If L can vary, it adjusts in place of τ. Ultimately a model builder must decide which of these mechanisms applies in the economy at hand. Using markup pricing instead of a marginal productivity black box forces one to think through one's prejudices about causality and class.

Similar considerations carry over to other liabilities and assets—valuations of stocks of wealth besides money are bound to change as prices adjust. As sensible financial analysts from Keynes (1931) and Fisher (1933) to Tobin (1980) have emphasized, *all* classes and *all* financial claims are affected by price movements in complex fashion. These changes and their consequent effects on economic behavior are only beginning to be addressed by CGEs. For what has been done, see sections 1.9 and 1.10.

The *inflation tax* is a dynamic version of the real balance effect. Inflation can only be described in models with more than one period, since it means growth of the price level over time. Its rate can be defined as $\hat{P} = [P(t) - P(t-1)]/P(t-1)$, where the arguments in t denote explicit time periods. An inflation tax makes saving a positive function of $\hat{P}$.

The rationale rests on real balances. When prices are rising, the reduction of one's real wealth over a period is given by $[P(t) - P(t-1)] \times [H/P(t-1)] = \hat{P}H$. It may be sensible to offset at least part of this loss by saving, so that the saving function becomes $g^s = sr + \alpha\hat{P}H$ with $\alpha \leq 1$. Faster inflation makes aggregate demand decline by acting as a tax on real balances.

This story is central to monetarist inflation theory. The full plot is set out elsewhere (e.g., Taylor 1988b), so we do not bother with it here. The effect at times is practically relevant, for example, in the consumption surges that have followed attempts to stabilize inflations by banning indexed contracts and imposing price controls (Taylor 1988a). For that reason it makes sense to incorporate an inflation tax into dynamic CGE models, where in structuralist variants inflation will stem from distributional conflict and propagation mechanisms, as discussed in sections 1.1 and 1.12.

Positive Effects of Inflation on Demand

Finally, inflation may activate demand. Suppose that i, the nominal loan rate of interest, is pegged or comes from the financial side of the model (section 1.10). Then faster inflation reduces the real rate $i - \hat{P}$, perhaps stimulating capital formation. If this possibility is deemed relevant, it is easy enough to build into an investment function. The same observation obviously applies to effects of inflation on competitive imports, demand for consumer durables, the efficiency of tax collection, or other variables.

1.6 Open Economy Extensions

The stylized data in tables 1.1 and 1.2 suggest that for short-run analyses the model just discussed should be extended to include exports and intermediate uses of imports and national goods. The demand-supply and cost equations become

$$PX = a_1 PX + PC + PI + PG + PE$$

and

$$PX = a_1 PX + wbX + rPK + eP_0^* a_0 X,$$

respectively. If we include saving from both rentiers (at rate s_r) and workers (rate s_w), the consumption function is

$$PC = (1 - s_r)rPK + (1 - s_w)wbX.$$

Putting these equations together gives an investment-saving balance of the form

$$PI = s_r rPK + s_w wbX + (eP_0^* a_0 X - PE) + (-PG).$$

National intermediates don't enter this accounting because they cancel out between the cost and demand decompositions. The saving counterpart of investment comes from several sources: rentiers ($s_r rPK$), wage earners ($s_w wbX$), the trade deficit ($eP_0^* a_0 X - PE$), and government dissaving ($-PG$). The last term would include taxes and other revenues as positive items if they were carried in the accounting.

These equations could easily be extended to incorporate consumer and capital goods imports, as well as emigrant workers's remittances and interest on foreign debt, which would have to enter into some domestic actors's income flows as positive and negative items, respectively. In numerical

Table 1.4
Macro relationships for a one-sector open economy model

Markup pricing	Neoclassical cost function	
$P = [1/(1-\pi)](wb + eP_0^* a_0)$	$P = f(w, eP_0^*, rP)$	(1)
$L/X = b$	$L/X = f_w(w/P, eP_0^*/P, r)$	(2)
$M_0/X = a_0$	$M_0/X = f_e(w/P, eP_0^*/P, r)$	(3)
$u = X/K$	$u = X/K$	(4)
$r = \pi u$	$K/X = f_r(w/P, eP_0^*/P, r)$	(5)
Investment–saving and trade balances		
$\epsilon = \epsilon(eP_e^* P)$		(6)
$g^s = [\pi s_r + (1-\pi)(\phi + (1-\phi)s_w)]u - \epsilon - \gamma$		(7)
$g^i = g^i(\pi, u)$		(8)
$g^i - g^s = 0$		(9)
$\epsilon - (1-\pi)\phi u = et$		(10)

Definitions

$\pi = rPK/PX$, $\phi = eP_0^* a_0/(wb + eP_0^* a_0)$, $w/P = (1-\pi)(1-\phi)/b$

$\epsilon = PE/PK$, $\gamma = PG/PK$, $\tau = T/PK$

$s = \pi s_r + (1-\pi)[\phi + (1-\phi)s_w]$, $\Gamma = \eta\epsilon - (1-s_w)(1-\pi)\phi u$

models these extra foreign transactions would influence the role of the trade (or current-account) surplus in model responses as derived below—the formal modifications are left to the reader. Depending on the economy at hand, remittances, interest, and imports of capital goods would be the practically important foreign exchange flows.

In what follows, we will concentrate upon the comparative statics of changing two nominal magnitudes—the money wage w and exchange rate e. Even leaving out monetary considerations of the type discussed last section, these variables act through several channels and are subject to different institutional forces. For these reasons it is again helpful to work with a model set up in nominal terms. The equations appear in table 1.4, normalized by the value of the capital stock, PK. With minor loss of generality (rectified below), the markup and neoclassical price equations (1) net out intermediate uses of national goods as a component of cost.

The concept of output in table 1.4 is larger than value added. With national intermediates netted out, the cost equation in nonintensive form can be written as

$$PX = rPK + wbX + eP_0^* a_0 X,$$

which includes imported intermediates with their input coefficient a_0 and world price P_0^* (for simplicity, tariffs are ignored). The import share of variable cost,

$$\phi = \frac{eP_0^*a_0}{wb + eP_0^*a_0},$$

turns out to be useful in analyzing the model. From this definition it readily follows that the import–capital ratio is $eP_0^*a_0X/PK = (1 - \pi)\phi u$, where π is the share of profits in output PX. The share of wages in the value of output is $(1 - \pi)(1 - \phi)$. Finally, the real exchange rate, e/P, is equal to $\phi(1 - \pi)/a$ so that responses of the model can be discussed equivalently in terms of ϕ or e/P (we stick with the former in the analysis that follows).

Since π enters the import–capital ratio directly, it is convenient to set up the markup function (1) using it as well. The version in table 1.4 follows from one based on a markup rate τ because $1 + \tau = 1/(1 - \pi)$.[8] In the neoclassical version the cost function and its partial derivatives have the import cost eP_0^* as an argument.

An export function appears in equation (6), where $\varepsilon = E/K$. Exports are assumed to be sold in an imperfectly competitive world market. The world price of national goods (ignoring export taxes and subsidies) is P/e, while the price of foreign "similars" is P_e^*. Equation (6) shows that volume increases with devaluation (a higher e), and when local prices fall or foreign ones go up. This demand-based specification is broadly appropriate for industrial goods. It will not work well for primary commodities. A brief digression on how primary exports can be treated in CGE models follows.

Primary exports typcially have a predetermined world price (call it P_e^* also), so that the f.o.b. local currency price is eP_e^*. This "border price" may or may not determine the internal market price P. Whether trade arbitrage and the "law of one price" are effective is an institutional question—in many primary exporting economies, institutions such as marketing boards rule arbitrage strictly out. If the two prices equalize, then the restriction $P = eP_e^*$ is added to the model. The markup rate (or, more generally, some national component of production cost) will have to be an endogenous variable from (1). If P and eP_e^* move independently, then their differential (multiplied by export volume) will represent a profit or loss for someone in the economy. It can be accounted for in the same way as the export subsidy in tables 1.1 and 1.2. Finally, depending on one's views about the market, primary export volumes may be fixed exogenously, or else determined endogenously as the excess of domestic supply over demand. The first option is a special case of (6) in table 1.4, whereas the other has already been noted as a convenient means to close a supply-determined model.

How currency devaluation works under these variant specifications is taken up below.

Returning to the discussion of table 1.4, equation (7) gives saving normalized by the value of capital. For later use, let s stand for the bracketed expression multiplying u, or saving per unit of capacity use:

$$s = \pi s_r + (1 - \pi)[\phi + (1 - \phi)s_w].$$

Equation (8) is the investment function, and (9) defines macroeconomic balance. If T is the trade surplus in foreign currency, and $t = T/PK$, then the trade balance is (10). Depending on closure, T may or may not be endogenous. Indeed, to avoid tedious taxonomy, we consider only two closures here. The first has u determined by demand and T endogenous. The second fixes T exogenously (a binding trade constraint) and asks how the rest of the system adjusts.[9]

Output Adjustment

Either higher government spending γ or an upward shift in the export demand function ε will increase capacity utilization in the markup model—in this regard the open economy version differs little from table 1.3. More interesting are the effects of movements in the key nominal prices, the exchange rate and the wage. Since their effects through π and u on investment demand are straightforward, in the following discussion g^i is held constant.

Nominal devaluation influences the system in several ways. From (1), it pushes up the price level with elasticity ϕ, shifting income shares from workers toward higher saving rentiers and the rest of the world. Since ϕ itself is an increasing function of e (the elasticity is $1 - \phi$), (7) shows that devaluation raises saving due to intermediate imports while cutting back on wage earners's saving by a lesser amount (since $s_w < 1$). Aggregate demand falls—an example of forced saving at work. Finally, exports respond to a higher e (and a lower P) with elasticity η.

Putting these effects together in equations (6) through (9) shows that devaluation increases u when $\Gamma = \eta\varepsilon - (1 - s_w)(1 - \pi)\phi u$ is positive. A bit of manipulation shows that this condition is equivalent to

$$\eta > \frac{(1 - s_w)eP_0^*a_0X}{PE}.$$

Output expansion is likely with high values of the export elasticity η, the workers's saving share s_w, and the ratio of exports to imports. If the world demand elasticity and workers's saving are low or the trade deficit is large, output contraction after devaluation is likely to result. Such a response shows up econometrically in many developing countries, as well as in structuralist CGEs.

The money wage enters the present model as a mirror image of the exchange rate, affecting all variables in (6) through (9) with the same magnitude but opposite sign. A higher w makes output increase when devaluation is contractionary, when $\Gamma < 0$ or the inequality above is violated. This result suggests that in the Third World, last section's arguments in support of money wage cuts to raise employment should be taken with a grain of salt. Output expansion in response to higher wages shows up in applied CGE work for the reasons just discussed (not to mention the investment responses mentioned in section 1.4), although we will see shortly that strict opposite sign symmetry of e and w is broken in more complicated specifications.

If prices are formed according to a neoclassical cost function, the analysis becomes more complicated. It can be illustrated with an example. Suppose that national and imported intermediates trade off for one another with a constant elasticity of substitution σ. As explained in section 1.11, this basically means that the intermediate input demand functions can be written in the form $a_1 = \bar{a}_1(P/Q)^{-\sigma}$ and $a_0 = \bar{a}_0(eP_0^*/Q)^{-\sigma}$, where the "bars" indicate constant terms and Q is a CES agggregate cost function for intermediates: $Q = Q(P, eP_0^*)$. An increase in e will raise Q with an elasticity equal to the cost share of imports (say, ξ) in total intermediates. Elasticities of a_1 and a_0 with respect to e are $\sigma\xi$ and $-\sigma(1 - \xi)$, respectively.

Now consider a devaluation. It increases the cost ratio ϕ directly but also makes it decline by reducing a_0 as national goods become cheaper relative to imports. The increase in potential saving from a higher ϕ is less than in the case with no substitution, so output contraction becomes less likely. Formally, the condition for expansion becomes

$$\eta > [1 - \sigma(1 - \xi)](1 - s_w)eP_0^*a_0X/PE,$$

which is more easily satisfied the higher is σ. If σ takes an empirically plausible value (well less than 0.5), the inequality may still not hold.

The story in this neoclassical model about wage increases goes the same direction as in the markup specification; however, the opposite sign but equal magnitude effects of w and e don't occur for substitution only between intermediate inputs. Substitution between labor and imported intermediates would make symmetry come back. It is a matter of judgment which version is more realistic. Regardless of which applies, dedicated econometricians have a hard time coming up with high values for the relevant elasticities of substitution in most economies of the Third World.

A Binding Trade Constraint

Frequently in developing countries, it seems as if trade deficits beyond a certain level cannot be financed. At the same time, political forces make aggregate demand (and therefore intermediate imports) impossible to cut back. In such a case of a binding trade constraint, capacity utilization will be determined from equation (10) of table 1.4, with a fixed value (negative or positive, depending on the external debt situation) of the dollar trade surplus T. Formally, we have $u = (\varepsilon - et)/(1 - \pi)\phi$, where $t = T/PK$.

Another restriction has been added to the model. As usual we have to come up with a corresponding endogenous variable. One possibility is the nominal exchange rate itself, although if there is a nonconvertible currency (the usual case in the Third World), it is more naturally treated as being a policy tool. The obvious alternative is the profit share π, especially when we observe that adverse external shocks in developing countries are usually followed by output stagnation and inflation. Forced saving (perhaps supplemented by real balance effects or inflation taxes) is the adjustment vehicle. Any foreign transfer or capital inflow will reduce t, permitting u to increase and cutting back on prices. The relevance of this scenario is corroborated by the anti-inflationary effects of foreign resource transfers that have been observed in externally strangled developing countries in recent years as well as the inflations the spring up when inflows are cut off (Taylor 1988a).

What will be the effects of devaluation in these circumstances? It is simplest to tell the story in terms of the trade constraint, which can be rewritten as

$$X = \frac{(P/e)E(eP_e^*/P) - T}{a_0 P_0^*}.$$

The only terms that depend on the exchange rate here are the price level P, export volume E, and the input coefficient a_0. Devaluation will permit X to increase if

$$\frac{PE}{ea_0 P_0 X}(\eta - 1)(1 - \phi) + \sigma(1 - \xi) > 0.$$

Broadly speaking, if σ is near zero (intermediate input substitution is weak), then the demand elasticity η will have to be not far below one to permit output to expand. The reason is simple. Devaluation reduces P/e, the foreign price of exports. It must generate an elastic volume response to offset this terms of trade loss. Such reasoning underlies trade theory's familiar Marshall-Lerner condition (which can be derived from the inequality above).

The effect of e on the profit share π is more complex. It goes through equation (7), in which devaluation affects exports ϵ, capacity utilization u, and the import cost share ϕ all at once. Leaving aside intermediate input substitution, one can show analytically from (7) through (10) as a simultaneous system that π will rise with devaluation if

$$\Gamma(1 - \pi)\phi - s(\eta - 1)\epsilon > 0.$$

This expression is not terribly illuminating. However, if we focus on the export elasticity η as a key parameter, it can be restated as

$$\eta < \frac{s - (1 - \pi)\phi[(1 - s_w)(eP_0^* a_0 X/PE)]}{s - (1 - \pi)\phi}.$$

The bracketed term multiplying $(1 - \pi)\phi$ in the numerator will exceed one if s_w is small and there is a substantial trade deficit. Therefore the upper bound on η is less than one. A value below the bound means that devaluation cuts back on u, increasing excess demand and exacerbating forced saving. A larger elasticity means that devaluation generates enough foreign exchange to allow forced saving to abate. Only detailed computation would reveal which way the influences run.

Finally, two words should be added about the effects of exchange rate changes when primary product exports are included in the model as discussed above. First, if the relevant sectors use imported intermediates, a change in e will affect their cost structures, with implications similar to those just discussed.

Second, the domestic price level may be related to the foreign one via the law of one price $P = eP_e^*$ or some more complex formulation. (For example, P might be made more or less elastic to eP_e^* depending on the cash position of an export marketing board.) If, further, supply in the export sector responds to the price/cost ratio as discussed in section 1.11 *and* export volume is the variable that adjusts to bring sectoral demand-supply balance, then devaluation will stimulate exports by raising output, while perhaps having a negative effect by driving up costs. The outcome will depend on details of the specification, subject to as many uncertainties as in the "industrial" export version. CGE models are of use not because they give the "right" quantitative assessments about policy responses but because they help one trace the directions in which they are likely to run.

1.7 Models with Many Sectors

The last exercises suggest that algebra is reaching its limits in deriving comparative static results. In this and the following section, we shift focus to discuss in more qualitative fashion the data and closure questions that arise when a CGE model contains more than one sector. Sections 1.9 and 1.10 take up financial accounts and models based upon them.

Table 1.5 gives two sectors's worth of SAM, suppressing government transactions to save space. The first sector is called "agriculture" and the other "industry" for reasons that will become clear in section 1.8. All agricultural value added is lumped into that sector's income Y_a, and industrial incomes are split into wages and profits as before. The underlying assumption is that income classes by sector have disparate saving and consumption patterns, as discussed in section 1.1. Columns 3 through 5 are dedicated to these differences.

Two sets of parameters in the intersectoral accounts stand out in the table, and two more are implicit. The most visible are the input–output coefficients a_{ij}, where i runs from 0 to 2 (or N, in an N-sector model), and j from 1 to 2 (or N). As before, the 0 subscript denotes a foreign input, of intermediate goods in this case. These coefficients can be estimated as ratios from the base year flow accounts of a SAM, as discussed in section 1.3. Indeed, SAM's are usually put together for years in which an input–output table has been constructed (or seriously updated from the past), so the a_{ij} represent an essential part of a model's data base.

The other explicit parameters are the capital coefficients β_{ij}. The investment flows I_1 and I_2 in table 1.5 stand for real gross capital formation "by destination," namely, in the sectors in which the investment takes place. However, sectoral demand-supply accounting is done "by origin" or "source," namely, in terms of the sectors producing the relevant goods. The β_{ij} coefficients transform investment by destination into investment by source.

Information about capital coefficients is usually far more scanty than about their input-output cousins. They typically are pieced together on an ad hoc basis from industrial and agricultural cost surveys and similar sources. Lacking such data, a common artifice is to make all columns of the β-matrix the same. Each column must sum to one for accounting consistency, and proportions between the entries could come from the values of

Table 1.5
Illustrative symbolic SAM for a two-sector economy

	Production costs		Uses of incomes					
	Agriculture 1	Industry 2	Agriculture 3	Wage 4	Rentier 5	Foreign 6	Gross capital formation 7	Totals 8
Sales								
1. Agriculture	$P_1 a_{11} X_1$	$P_1 a_{12} X_2$	$P_1 C_1^a$	$P_1 C_1^w$	$P_1 C_1^r$	$P_1 E_1$	$P_1(\beta_{11} I_1 + \beta_{12} I_2)$	$P_1 X_1$
2. Industry	$P_2 a_{21} X_1$	$P_2 a_{22} X_2$	$P_2 C_2^a$	$P_2 C_2^w$	$P_2 C_2^r$	$P_2 E_2$	$P_2(\beta_{21} I_1 + \beta_{22} I_2)$	$P_2 X_2$
Incomes								
3. Agriculture	V_1							Y_a
4. Wage		$w_2 b_2 X_2$						Y_w
5. Rentier		$r_2 P_2^i K_2$						Y_r
6. Foreign	$eP_0^* a_{01} X_1$	$eP_0^* a_{02} X_2$					$eP_i^*(\beta_{01} I_1 + \beta_{02} I_2)$	Y_{for}
Saving								
7. Saving			S_a	S_w	S_r	S_{for}		I_{tot}
Totals								
8. Total	$P_1 X_1$	$P_2 X_2$	Y_a	Y_w	Y_r	Y_{for}	I_{tot}	

Definitions

$P_j^i = P_1 \beta_{1j} + P_2 \beta_{2j} + eP_i^* \beta_{0j}, \qquad j = 1, 2$

$I_{tot} = P_1^i I_1 + P_2^i I_2$

investment flows by origin (e.g., $P_i J_i, i = 0, 1, \ldots, N$) from the input–output table. This asumption of identical columns could be relaxed to capture broad sectoral differences; for example, if one has independent information on the makeup of the capital stock in agriculture, then the nonagricultural capital goods composition can be derived from economywide totals as a residual. In any case, only a few industries produce capital goods (e.g., machinery, construction, producers's services, and imports), so most rows of the β-matrix in a model with more than a few sectors will be zero.

Capital coefficients (ideally set up with a time dimension to reflect investment gestation lags) are essential parameters if one wants to cumulate investments by destination into capital stocks over time in a dynamic model as described in section 1.12. On the other hand, they can be dispensed with in comparative statics, if one sticks with investments by origin as the relevant components of final demand. The other main use of the β_{ij} in the models of this book is to set up capital goods price indexes P_j^i (the superscript stands for "investment" and the subscript for sectors) which are used to figure costs of investments by destination and value capital stocks for use in calculating rates of profit. Absent a full matrix, using the same set of coefficients for all sectors can suffice for these purposes.

The first set of implicit parameters in table 1.5 enters into consumer demand functions. To see what is involved, note that column 3 can be written in the form $P_1 C_1^a + P_1 C_2^a = Y_a - S_a = D_a$, where D_a stands for total consumption spending from agricultural sector incomes. As the models in previous sections illustrate, variables such as D_a are functions of income flows (e.g., Y_a) and saving and tax parameters. Somehow in the model specification, a value sum of consumer purchases like $P_1 C_1^a + P_2 C_2^a$ must be forced into equality with the corresponding spending flow.

The simplest means to enforce consumption adding-up (or "Engel aggregation") is complete system of demand equations based upon the neoclassical pretense that consumers maximize utility subject to a budget constraint—the constraint is what forces outlays by sector to sum to total spending. A clever choice of utility function gives convenient equations. Since it is easy to use and interpret, the models in this book mostly adopt a specific formulation called the "linear expenditure system" (LES). How the LES is parameterized is discussed in section 1.11.

Finally, similar adding-up restrictions are implicit in columns 1 and 2 of table 1.5. Total costs must sum to $P_i X_i$, and the components of value added to the correct total. The first requirement is satisfied if the numerical model is based upon ratio estimates of input–output coefficients, tax and tariff rates, and so on, from the base-year SAM. With markup pricing, computation of the markup rate from the SAM takes care of adding-up for value added. The assumption of constant returns to scale does the same for a neoclassical cost function. The function's scaling parameters will be determined by base-year data, as described in section 1.11.

1.8 Closure Issues with Many Sectors

Multisectoral models repeat in many dimensions the questions about how economic classes are defined and interact that we have already addressed. They can be phrased in terms of the circular flow of income from production to demand and back to the level of output. From this perspective *each* sector in a CGE model requires a four-part specification:

1. Its value added (plus imported intermediates) must be broken down into income flows that fit the issues the model is trying to address. Also needed are functional relationships via which these flows are determined from the output level and input prices, subject to the column identity in the social accounts stating that the sector's value of output must just be exhausted by costs.

2. Rules for mapping input costs into price formation must be specified. Possible formulations include a markup specification or some sort of neoclassical cost function, both of which determine the sector's price level as a function of costs. Alternatively, there may be a freely varying sectoral output price that equilibrates supply and demand and also acts as a vehicle for forced saving at the macro level. In the latter case some component of cost (e.g., the markup rate) will have to be endogenous to allow the SAM column identity to remain in force when the model is perturbed.

3. To describe circular flow, the model also needs rules for mapping each sector's value flows into real demands for output from itself and other sectors. Examples include input–output coefficients, and equations saying how saving is determined from each income flow (generated from one or more sectors, e.g., total wages) and how each nonsaved portion is distributed across demand by sector. Such a sectoral spending breakdown will have to satisfy adding-up restrictions as discussed in the preceding section.

4. Finally, there has to be a rule for each sector's quantity adjustment, obeying the SAM row identity stating that its value of output must equal the sum of values of components of demand. For example, output may be determined by demand only. Alternatively, there may be a sector supply restriction, in which case some other quantity variable will have to adjust to bring sectoral demand into equality with supply. Price-sensitive compo-

nents of demand provide one such vehicle—as we will see shortly a combination of forced saving and consumer expenditure responses may be involved. If prices are determined from the supply side, trade flows or state purchases are obvious candidates to be adjusting variables in some sectors, as discussed in sections 1.5 and 1.6.

Besides these within-sector specifications, cross-sectoral relationships also apply. The most important stems from the savings leakages that are built into all applied CGE models. With saving present in the system, there must be a demand injection in at least one sector to permit a sensible solution to exist. The simplest Keynesian model (with P normalized to unity) illustrates. The four sets of rules just discussed take the following form:

1. Income equals the value of output, or $Y = PX$.
2. Prices are normalized, or $P = 1$.
3. Consumption is a fraction of real income, or $C = (1 - s)Y/P$.
4. Output adjusts to satisfy demand-supply balance, that is, $X = C + A$.

It is clear that a nontrivial solution cannot exist without a nonzero demand injection A. A variable like A may be a *function* of other variables in the system, for example, a contemporaneous investment accelerator $I = I(X)$ or an export demand $E = E(P)$, but it cannot be determined identically from income flows. This general argument carries over to other adjustment mechanisms and many sectors.

Besides demand injections one may also choose to impose cross-sectoral supply constraints. Obvious examples are supply functions for total labor or specific skill classes, or a binding trade balance. Each additional restriction will require a corresponding endogenous variable. We have seen in section 1.5 how a labor supply constraint can be met by forced saving or an endogenous nominal wage (in which case institutional factors in wage formation have to be omitted). Similarly section 1.6 shows how a binding trade constraint again requires forced saving, or perhaps an endogenous nominal exchange rate.

Any number of examples could be concocted to illustrate these general observations. To wind up this section, we content ourselves with just one. It underlies several models in this book as well as an influential investigation of the agricultural/nonagricultural terms of trade (deJanvry and Sadoulet 1987). The two-sector specification blends forced saving, Engel demand effects, and output adjustment in an illuminating fashion. The equation set is simplified from table 1.5 and appears in table 1.6.

We maintain the identification of sector 1 with "agriculture" and sector 2 with the rest of the economy, or "industry." Agricultural supply X_1 responds to the price P_1 in the first equation, presumably with a low elasticity. Equation (2) shows that P_2 is determined by a markup over labor costs. Equations (3) through (5) determine income flows, and (6) deducts each class's saving from income to determine total consumption demand D.

Although they have different saving rates, we save symbols and space by assuming that consumer behavior of the groups is the same (ignoring the aggregation error that results from not using separate demand functions for each). On this hypothesis, (7) and (8) describe consumer demand. The equations are simplified from the linear expenditure system described in section 1.11. They show first that adding-up is assured, that is, $P_1 C_1 + P_2 C_2 = D$. Second, it is easy to verify that the elasticity of C_1 with respect to D is $\alpha D/(\alpha D + \theta P_1)$ which is less than one for $\theta > 0$. Equations (7) and (8) provide an easy way to assure that Engel's law for consumption of agricultural commodities is satisfied.

Equation (9) is an excess demand function for agriculture. With the supply function (1) imposed, P_1 must vary to bring demand in line with supply. Demand components are exports E_1 and consumption C_1. Since industry's price is determined by a markup from (2), its output X_2 adjusts to satisfy the excess demand equation (10). If industry is the only sector supplying capital goods, its demand is made up of investment by destination $I_1 + I_2$, plus consumption C_1. The investment-saving balance (11) can be derived from (1) through (10). It is always a good check on the data and accounting consistency of an applied model, but is not an independent equation.

We have a simple fix-price/flex-price specification, combining price-sensitive supply and demand, forced saving, and output adjustment. To see how the three mechanisms mix, we can boil the model down to excess demand functions for agriculture,

$$\frac{\alpha\gamma_2 P_2 X_2}{P_1} - (1 - \alpha\gamma_1)X_1(P_1) + \theta + E_1 = 0,$$

and industry,

$$I_1 + I_2 - [1 - (1 - \alpha)\gamma_2]X_2 + \frac{[(1 - \alpha)\gamma_1 X_1(P_1) - \theta]P_1}{P_2} = 0,$$

in which the γ_i stand for consumer spending from sectoral output flows $P_i X_i$, and are defined in table 1.6.

Table 1.6
Macro relationships for a simplified two-sector model

Structural relationships	
$X_1 = X_1(P_1)$	(1)
$P_2 = (1 + \tau_2)w_2 b_2$	(2)
$Y_a = P_1 X_1$	(3)
$Y_w = w_2 b_2 X_2$	(4)
$Y_r = \tau_2 w_2 b_2 X_2$	(5)
$D = (1 - s_a)Y_a + (1 - s_w)Y_w + (1 - s_r)Y_r$	(6)
$C_1 = [\alpha D + \theta P_1]/P_1$	(7)
$C_2 = [(1 - \alpha)D - \theta P_1]/P_2$	(8)
$E_1 + C_1 - X_1 = 0$	(9)
$(I_1 + I_2) + C_2 - X_2 = 0$	(10)
Investment–saving balance	
$P_1 E_1 + P_2(I_1 + I_2) - (s_a Y_a + s_w Y_w + s_r Y_r) = 0$	(11)
Definitions	
$\gamma_1 = 1 - s_a,$ $\quad \gamma_2 = [(1 - s_w) + (1 - s_r)\tau]/(1 + \tau)$	

The second equation determines X_2 as a function of P_1 and other variables. Greater investment demand or an upward shift in the agricultural supply function makes X_2 rise. On the other hand, a higher P_1 will make X_2 decline if the supply response to a higher price is weak and θ is large. The latter condition is tantamount to a low income elasticity of demand for agriculture. The story is that a higher P_1 reduces real wage income, leading to forced saving. With income-inelastic sector 1 demand, "automatic lacking" largely cuts demand for industrial goods, and X_2 falls. Alternatively, X_2 could rise if agricultural supply is elastic, farmers account for a big proportion of demand, or Engel effects are weak.

The first equation is simpler. It simply shows that higher exports or sector output will raise demand for sector one products, causing the price P_1 to rise. The two equations together determine a macroeconomic equilibrium based upon the agricultural price and industrial output.

The obvious comparative static experiments are to raise agricultural exports (or assume an adverse agricultural supply shock) and investment demand. The former drives up P_1. The subsequent effect on demand may make industrial output either rise or fall. Higher investment increases industrial output; the induced demand response causes agricultural price inflation. Outcomes of these combinations of forced saving, output changes, and shifts in demand composition are important for policy formation in developing countries, as illustrated in several models in this book.

Finally, note that the fix-price/flex-price specification carries over to a number of other areas of interest, such as traded goods with prices fixed from abroad as opposed to nontraded goods with market-clearing prices. This so-called dependent economy model can be given a structuralist interpretation (Taylor 1983) and also underlies a number of more neoclassical CGE models of trade policy surveyed by deMelo (1988).

1.9 Financial Flows and Stocks

So far, the models (passing remarks about real balances included) have addressed only the part of the economy that produces goods and services. Most CGE work has been devoted to this IS side of the system, but computable models can deal with LM issues as well.[10] A sample data base for real–financial models is set out in this section. The one following takes up modeling questions per se.

Table 1.7 is a SAM with a compressed but illustrative set of financial stocks and flows. It builds upon the matrixes already presented (especially in being set out in nominal terms) and extends them in three ways. First, the new SAM shows how saving by each class or institution feeds into changes in asset and liability positions in current prices. Second, financial flows are cumulated into stocks that fit into a portfolio balance model. Finally, the matrix helps one visualize channels for interaction between the real and financial sides of the economy.

The real side is described by rows 6 through 10 and columns 1 through 6. Value added is broken down into income flows to firms (V_f), households (V_h), and the government (V_g) in rows 7 through 9 of column 1. In row 10 foreigners receive income from imports of intermediates and capital goods. Row 6 shows components of demand. Columns 2 through 5 give uses of incomes, and column 6 shows national (row 6) and imported (row 10) provision of investment goods by origin. Government revenue in row 9 comes from value added (indirect taxes and public enterprise profits) and direct taxes on firms (T_f) and households (T_h).

The first big difference between table 1.7 and the SAM's presented heretofore is that savings flows from the different income categories are shown in separate rows—11 for firms, 12 for households, and so on. Across a row, saving goes into net accumulation of assets by the corresponding income class. The sign convention in these flows of funds is that

Table 1.7
Illustrative symbolic SAM combining the real and financial parts of the economy

		Uses of incomes					Firm portfolio			Household portfolio	Government portfolio		Foreign portfolio		Bank portfolio			
	Production cost 1	Firm 2	Household 3	Government 4	Foreign 5	Capital formation 6	Physical capital 7	Bank borrowing 8	Foreign borrowing 9	deposits 10	Bank loans 11	Foreign loans 12	Loans 13	Reserves 14	Loans 15	Reserves 16	Deposits 17	Totals 18
Initial portfolio																		
1. Capital							$-P_i\bar{K}$											$-P_i\bar{K}$
2. Bank loan								$\bar{L}_f$			$\bar{L}_g$				$-\bar{L}$			0
3. Foreign loan									$e\bar{L}_f^*$			$e\bar{L}_g^*$	$-e\bar{L}^*$					0
4. Reserves														$e\bar{R}^*$		$-e\bar{R}_b^*$		0
5. Deposits										$-\bar{H}_h$							$\bar{H}$	0
Sales																		
6. Product	Pa_1X		PC	PG	PE	$P\beta_1I$												PX
Incomes																		
7. Firm	V_f																	Y_f
8. Household	V_h																	Y_h
9. Government	V_g	T_f	T_h															Y_g
10. Foreign	$eP_0^*a_0X$					$eP_i^*\beta_0I$												Y_{for}
Flows of funds																		
11. Firm		S_f					$-P_iI$	ΔL_f	$e\Delta L_f^*$									0
12. Household			S_h							$-\Delta H_h$								0
13. Government				S_g							ΔL_g	$e\Delta L_g^*$						0
14. Foreign					S_{for}								$-e\Delta L^*$	$e\Delta R^*$				0
15. Bank															$-\Delta L$	$-e\Delta R_b^*$	ΔH	0

Table 1.7 (continued)

		Uses of incomes					Firm portfolio				Government portfoilo		Foreign portfolio		Bank portfolio			
	Production cost 1	Firm 2	Household 3	Government 4	Foreign 5	Capital formation 6	Physical capital 7	Bank borrowing 8	Foreign borrowing 9	Household portfolio deposits 10	Bank loans 11	Foreign loans 12	Loans 13	Reserves 14	Loans 15	Reserves 16	Deposits 17	Totals 18
Asset balance																		
16. Bank loan								$-L_f$			$-L_g$				L			0
17. Foreign loan									$-eL_f^*$			$-eL_g^*$	eL^*					0
18. Reserves														$-eR^*$		eR_b^*		0
19. Deposits										H_h							$-H$	0
Totals																		
20. Total	PX	Y_f	Y_h	Y_g	Y_{for}	P_iI	$-P_iK$	0	0	0	0	0	0	0	0	0	0	

Definition $P_i = P\beta_1 + eP_0^*\beta_0$

increases in assets are negative and increases in liabilities positive. Thus row 11 can be stated as

$$S_f + \Delta L_f + e\Delta L_f^* - P_i I = 0.$$

Investment by firms ($P_i I$) is financed by their own saving (S_f), increased loans from the banking system (ΔL_f), and increased foreign currency loans converted to domestic price terms by the exchange rate ($e\Delta L_f^*$). The difference operator Δ refers to changes between the end of last period (e.g., a year) and the end of this one: $\Delta L_f = L_f(t) - L_f(t-1)$.

A simple, though not atypical, financial structure is assumed.[11] In row 11 household saving goes entirely toward building up net assets (ΔH_h) with the banks. In practice, households in any given period run up both bank loans and balances, but as a shortcut here their net asset increase is called new "deposits."

Banks in turn engage in new lending (ΔL) and build up foreign reserves ($e\Delta R_b^*$) to offset their higher deposits (ΔH) in row 15. The banking system's net saving is set to zero (or accumulated in firms's accounts), so there is no saving entry toward the left end of its flow of funds row.

We have already seen in row 11 that firms take loans from both the domestic banking system and foreign sources. In row 13 the government does the same. Since the row sum must be zero, one of its entries has to be negative. Either the government is paying off loans or—no great surprise—its current outlays (PG) exceed revenues (Y_g) in column 4 so that $S_g < 0$.

The final flow of funds is the balance of payments in row 14, stating that

$$e\Delta R^* = e\Delta L^* - S_{\text{for}}.$$

The net increase in reserves equals capital inflows less the current account deficit.

The next step to add these flows to existing asset and liability stocks to get current positions. The time convention is that the asset and liability balances in rows 16 through 19 refer to the end of the current period and are evaluated in end-of-period prices where relevant. Stocks coming into the period are identified by overbars and appear in rows 1 through 5. They are also valued at end-of-period prices. Thus capital gains between periods have already been taken into account. Difficult valuation problems are swept under the rug by these conventions, but they substantially ease applied modeling. For a recital of the difficulties, see Foley (1975).

Reading down columns 7 through 17 shows how assets accumulate. For firms's capital stocks, for example, column 7 shows that

$$P_iK = P_iI + P_i\bar{K},$$

or end-of-period capital equals investment plus capital at the beginning of the period (for simplicity, depreciation is ignored). Using explicit time arguments, this equation can be restated as

$$P_i(t)K(t) = P_i(t)I(t) + P_i(t-1)K(t-1) + [P_i(t) - P_i(t-1)]K(t-1),$$

where $K(t)$ and $P_i(t)$ are the capital stock and its asset price at the end of the period, $I(t)$ is investment during the period, and $K(t-1)$ and $P_i(t-1)$ are the stock and asset price at the end of last period or the beginning of this one. The capital gain term $[P_i(t) - P_i(t-1)]K(t-1)$ accrues over the current period.

The capital stock is carried down to row 20 ("totals") since it is difficult to model the market for old buildings and machines. Otherwise, end-of-period stocks appear in the asset balance rows 16 through 19. In row 16 outstanding bank loans (L) go to firms (L_f) and the government (L_g). Foreign loans (eL^*) are taken by the same two borrowers in row 17. By the signs in table 1.7, both these balances can be interpreted as excess loan supply equations. Similarly, the supply of foreign reserves (eR^*) is held by banks (eR_b^*) in row 18. Bank deposits (H) are equal to the amount supplied by households (H_h) in the last asset account.

These ending balances are stated for beginning-of-period stocks in rows 2 through 5 (with signs reversed). It is illuminating to sum the flows of funds rows 11 through 15, and then insert the initial asset balances. The outcomes are the *equalities*

$$\begin{aligned} P_iI - (S_f + S_h + S_g + S_{\text{for}}) &= 0 \\ &= (L_f + L_g - L) + e(L_f^* + L_g^* - L^*) \\ &\quad + (H - H_h) + e(R^* - R_b^*). \end{aligned}$$

In the first line we already know that investment will equal saving from the real side of the model. The second line states that macro balance implies that the sum of excess asset demands must be zero. In equilibrium therefore only three out of four (or $N-1$ out of N) of the asset balances represent independent restrictions on the system. How they interact with the real side of the model is the topic we take up next.

1.10 Real–Financial Models

A description of all the models that can be built around the accounts in table 1.7 is out of the question—that is what textbooks in macroeconomics are about. Rather, we will take up formulations appropriate to the developing country context, starting with complete systems and then going on to models tailored to fit available financial data (chiefly of the monetary sort).

Table 1.7 is best read top to bottom, or north to south. We start the discussion from a consistent real side solution (with only one sector, for simplicity) and the saving flows it generates toward the west of the matrix. Available savings put restrictions on the changes in assets and liabilities that appear in rows 11 through 15. These changes together with initial stocks in the northeast feed into the closing asset balances in the southeast. The first task is to describe how asset markets clear. The effects of financial market outcomes on price and quantity adjustment is the next topic, reading the matrix from southeast back to west and northwest.

A rather Keynesian story can be told along the lines suggested by Tobin (1982). Suppose that output is the variable that adjusts on the real side, with either markup or neoclassical pricing. At a price-quantity equilibrium, there will be a government saving flow (possibly negative) S_g. If the government is subject to an external credit limit, it will be able to find "new money" in a fixed amount ΔL_g^* from abroad. Its new domestic borrowing ΔL_g follows from row 13 of table 1.7, and its total loan obligations L_g and L_g^* from columns 11 and 12.

Next, in row 12 household saving supply S_h generates an increment in desired deposits ΔH_h and thereby total deposits H_h from column 10. These are accepted by banks in row 19, determining the money supply H. We suppose that banks choose to lend out some fraction $\lambda(i, e)$ of their deposit base, where i is a market-clearing loan rate of interest and e is included to reflect the attractiveness of holding reserves. Loan supply to firms comes from row 16,

$$L_f^s = \lambda(i, e)H - L_g.$$

Firms's loan requirements depend on their initial stocks together with their flows of funds in row 11,

$$L_f + eL_f^* = \bar{L}_f + e\bar{L}_f^* + P_i I - S_f = Q_f.$$

It is reasonable to postulate that firms borrow more domestically when the interest rate is low or the exchange rate high:

$$L_f^d = \delta(i, e)Q_f.$$

The excess demand equation, $L_f^d - L_f^s = 0$, solves for the interest rate i and level of bank loans L_f. Foreign loans L_f^* are determined by the firms's initial asset position and their flows of funds. The asset balances in rows 16 and 17 sum outstanding loan stocks to get the bank and foreign totals L and L^*.

Now we are virtually done. Initial assets and the foreign flow of funds in row 14 determine reserves held abroad R^*. The quantity R_b^* that banks wish to hold comes from initial positions, the household and banking system flows of funds in rows 12 and 15 and the deposit balance in row 19. These two variables will take the same value, in accord with our observation last section that there is no need to impose the reserve balance in row 18 as an independent restriction on the system.

These manipulations basically produce portfolio allocations and a rate of interest i, which can feed back to the real side. The interest rate will be affected by both incoming asset and liability stocks and current financial flows, in line with the market's conventional wisdom. The influence of commonly used instruments of monetary policy—rediscount, reserve requirements, credit controls—could be modeled by separating the accounts of the central and commercial banks which are consolidated in table 1.7. If there were a market in government securities used as an arena for open market operations, it would be easy to include. Finally, the exchange rate will affect loan market equilibrium via both demand and supply.

In the model just sketched, the interest rate is the main variable mediating effects of finance on output and prices. Three channels are often specified. First, net interest payments should be included in income statements. Such flows are often ignored as being small, but this is not always the case.

Second, investment demand is presumably a negative function of the nominal (i) or real ($i - \hat{P}$) interest rate—this is the traditional LM channel. It may be supplemented by positive effects of the interest rate on savings rates (or on the flow incomes of high-saving households), if there is reason to believe that strong responses exist.

Third, there is evidence in some economies that interest rates affect prices directly by raising the cost of financing working capital. If a fraction ξ of variable costs BX must be financed by bank loans, then the markup equation may take the form

$$P = (1 + \tau)(1 + i\xi)B,$$

so that interest rate increases drive up the price level. Loans demanded by firms may also be tied directly to their working capital requirements as opposed to their overall financial deficit. Both specifications have been used in applied models.

Comparative statics in the Tobin-style model go along conventional lines. Expansionary fiscal policy is associated with greater government credit needs and commercial bank borrowing. Deposits also rise, increasing loan supply. Disequilibrium in the loan market is eliminated by interest rate adjustments (presumably increases) that then influence investment demand and the price level. The less flexible is the interest rate, the greater is the part of the expansionary impetus that will spill aborad in the form of reduced bank reserves and higher foreign borrowing by firms.[12]

More monetarist-sounding outcomes could also be arranged. With labor supply predetermined, the real side would have to be closed by forced saving and/or real balance effects as discussed in sections 1.4 and 1.5. Fiscal expansion would cause inflation as well as increased borrowing from the banks. Nominal savings flows from rentier incomes would also rise, increasing the end-of-period deposit base. With appropriate parameters, rough proportionality between the money supply and price increases would be observed, "ratifying" the equation of exchange. Results would go in the same direction even with variable employment, via a neoclassical cost function or an assumed positive elasticity of the markup rate with respect to the level of capacity use.

Several other effects can be built into applied models, and bear mention in passing. First, fixing the sum of changes in reserves and total foreign borrowing would amount to a foreign exchange constraint. It effects could be modeled by endogenizing the exchange rate or assuming forced saving adjustment on the real side, as discussed in section 1.6. Expansionary policy would lead to price and interest rate increases.

Second, the interest rate might be controlled. There would have to be some sort of quantity adjustment in financial markets. Government foreign borrowing and/or the banking system's foreign exchange reserves could be made endogenous.

Finally, asset valuation issues have to be considered. Devaluation would increase the borrowing requirement of firms Q_f (defined above) by appreciating initial foreign liabilities $e\bar{L}_f^*$ in local currency terms. The outcomes could involve drops in investment for reasons of reduced cash flow, interest rate increases, and stagflation. Contrariwise, foreign asset positions would be enhanced by devaluation. If rentier or firm-owning households have substantial holdings abroad (the fruits, perhaps, of previous capital flight), devaluation would make them wealthier in local currency terms. Their saving rates might decline, with expansionary consequences.

In closing, a word should be added on incomplete asset market specifications. One important version uses only the flow of funds 13 through 15 in table 1.7—private sector net savings surpluses are left out. Such a model hinges around determination of the money supply by government borrowing and the balance of payments, and its effects on prices and quantities. Depending on the assumptions one makes, either monetarist or structuralist outcomes can appear.

The implication is that even when full information on financial stocks and flows is not available, it is still feasible to incorporate monetary considerations into CGE models. Whether they are of sufficient importance to justify the labor involved is of course a matter for the model builder to judge. The fact that the International Monetary Fund often bases its stabilization programs on a rudimentary version of table 1.7 closed with the equation of exchange and forced saving or Meade/Johansen rules (Taylor 1988a) suggests that alternative specifications might usefully be thrown into the policy debate.

1.11 Nonproportionalities and Substitution

In this section functional specifications for applied models are quickly reviewed—the use of intercept terms, constant elasticity functions, input substitution as captured by CES functions, and consumer demand behavior in the LES specification. All these tricks are used extensively in the models of this book. The section closes with observations about the use of time series information to specify parameters.

Intercept Terms

All the ratio estimates of parameters discussed in section 1.3 can easily be extended to include intercepts. For example, suppose that wage income and saving from it take respective values of Y_w and S_w in the base year SAM. One can easily estimate an average (= marginal) saving rate s_w as the ratio $s_w = S_w/Y_w$. Alternatively, one might believe that the marginal saving rate differs from the average so that the saving function is $S_w = s_w Y_w + \bar{s}_w$. The intercept term $\bar{s}_w$ can be computed from the SAM data base if one assumes a value for the marginal rate s_w (e.g., obtained from consumer budget surveys or a time series regression). S_w will be an elastic (inelastic) function of Y_w when $\bar{s}_w$ is negative (positive). This intercept trick can be extended to more general systems in which one wants to avoid purely proportional (or unit elastic) relationships. It is the secret of the linear expenditure system of consumer demand equations discussed below, for example.

Intercepts often prove useful in saving, investment, and export functions. They have the advantage that the intercept terms can be manipulated to take into account intuitive or exogenous information (supply shocks, likely changes in behavior, political events) about how the economy is behaving. If I take the intercepts and you take the slopes, I'll be better able to tune a model solution to fit my views about the current economic situation than you.

Constant Elasticities

This same observation applies to constant elasticity functions, for example, $E = \bar{E}[eP_e^*/(1 - z_e)P]^\eta$ for exports in the notation of table 1.2. The constant term $\bar{E}$ can be calcuated from the base-year SAM once one knows the export level E, subsidy rate z_e, the price terms, and postulates the elasticity η. Like the linear functions just discussed, constant elasticity formulations are convenient to use when an isolated quantity variable responds to a price and vice versa. Export functions, markup rates (which may depend on the level of activity or monetary variables), money demand functions, import coefficients, and sectoral supply functions making output a function of the price–cost ratio (or $1 + \tau$) are all examples. Economists often have stylized elasticities for such relationships in their heads, and they are easy to plug into a model.

CES Functions

One often wants to specify substitution possibilities between production inputs—capital and labor, imported and domestically produced intermediate inputs, oil and gas as energy sources. A load of distributional baggage is carried along with any such neoclassical specification, as we have seen in section 1.4. Nonetheless, where substitution is deemed to be potentially important, it should be included in a CGE model. Constant elasticity of substitution (or CES) functions are often convenient, for reasons to be indicated shortly.

A CES cost function (e.g., for labor L and capital K) takes the form

$$P = [\alpha_L w^{1-\sigma} + \alpha_K (rP)^{1-\sigma}]^{1/(1-\sigma)},$$

in a one-sector model in which w is the wage rate, P the output price level, and r the rate of profit. The constant elasticity of substitution is σ.

Applying Shepard's lemma (see section 1.4) shows that input demand functions take the form

$$\frac{L}{X} = \alpha_L \left(\frac{w}{P}\right)^{-\sigma},$$

and

$$\frac{K}{X} = \alpha_K (r)^{-\sigma},$$

where X is the level of output. These equations have the advantage of making input–output ratios depend *only* on the cost variable relevant to the input at hand—the real wage for labor and the profit rate for capital. Cross-cost terms do not appear, as they do in the general neoclassical input demand functions in table 1.3.

This feature of CES functions makes them easy to interpret and manipulate. "Distribution" or scale parameters like α_L can be calculated readily from a SAM once one specifies the elasticity of substitution σ, since the labor share of output is equal to $\alpha_L(w/P)^{1-\sigma}$. The functions also "nest" nicely. For example, aggregate labor cost w could be constructed as a CES index of wages w_i of different skill classes L_i. Employment of each skill group (L_i/X) would depend only on the cost ratios w_i/w and w/P.

Besides input substitution harmonic means of the CES type can also be used to indicate trade-offs such as the one between domestic and imported goods in satisfying intermediate requirements (see section 1.6), or between domestic and export destinations of the same sector's products in a constant elasticity of transformation (CET) setup. These formulations are often adopted in World Bank sponsored CGE models (Robinson 1989) and add a degree of price responsiveness to the competitive versus noncompetitive trade categories used in most models in this book.

LES Demand Specifications

It would seem natural to carry the CES framework over to price substitution in consumer demand. However, a glance at the labor and capital input demand functions shown above reveals a major drawback—the functions are "homothetic," displaying unitary elasticities of inputs such as L with respect to output X. Since income elasticities of demand for most goods differ from unity (recall Engel's law), one needs a more general formulation. Applied CGE models often incorporate the linear expenditure system or LES.

The LES is derived in the usual way by maximization of a specific utility function,

$$U = \sum_{i=0}^{N} \mu_i \log(C_i - \theta_i),$$

subject to the budget constraint,

$$\sum_{i=0}^{N} P_i C_i = D.$$

A bit of manipulation shows that the demand functions coming from this exercise take the convenient linear form

$$C_i = \theta_i + \left(\frac{\mu_i}{P_i}\right)(D - F),$$

where

$$F = \sum_{i=0}^{N} P_i \theta_i.$$

The interpretation of these equations goes as follows: The μ_i parameters are "marginal budget shares," which can be estimated as

$$\mu_i = \eta_i \left(\frac{P_i C_i}{D}\right) = \eta_i \psi_i,$$

where η_i stands for the income elasticity of demand for commodity i and ψ_i is its budget share in the spending of the relevant consumer class from the base year SAM.

The θ_i parameters are fixed levels of consumption of each commodity, independent of income or price. The quantity F is the value of a "floor" consumption basket defined by the θ_i and the current set of prices P_i. Any excess of total spending D over the floor is directed to commodities in line with their marginal budget shares μ_i. If all the θ_i were zero, then all commodities would have constant budget shares, implying unitary income elasticities of demand. These intercept terms permit the LES to produce income elasticities differing from one.

Further algebra shows that the θ_i must satisfy the condition

$$\theta_i = \left(\frac{D}{P_i}\right)(\psi_i - \xi \mu_i),$$

where

$$\xi = \frac{D - F}{D}.$$

The new parameter ξ is usually called the "supernumerary income ratio" because it measures the amount of available spending power that consumers have above the floor level F. A larger value for ξ indicates that consumer behavior will show more sensitivity to changes in income and prices.

The foregoing discussion shows that the equations of an LES for $N + 1$ commodities (domestic goods plus imports) can be fully parameterized from $N + 1$ budget shares ψ_i (which come from the base-year SAM), $N + 1$ income elasticities η_i, and the parameter ξ. The income elasticities and ξ can often be inferred from household budget data and/or time series information. Absent any other knowledge, the stylized fact is that ξ often takes a value near 0.5 (Lluch, Powell, and Williams 1977).

These same data also serve to parameterize any other consumer demand system derived from an additive utility function of the form

$$U = \sum_{i=0}^{N} f_i(C_i).$$

If the f_i are exponential functions (same exponent but different constant terms for each good), one gets a "direct addilog" set of demand equations that come close to having constant income and own-price elasticities. For the details, see Taylor (1979, app. E).

Using Time Series Information

All the manipulations we have discussed boil down to making functions with specified slope or curvature parameters (elasticities, marginal rates or shares, etc.) consistent with the base-year SAM by adjusting their scaling parameters or constant terms.

The reason one wants to do this sort of "calibration" is to ensure that solutions for a CGE model take off from an initial position that incorporates all the consistency conditions that its accounting and behavioral equations contain. Consistency and clear causal links are the main strengths of the CGE approach.

Time series information can be used to specify slope and curvature parameters for CGEs—all one has to do is rescale the regression intercept terms so that the regression line passes through the SAM data points instead of the statistical sample's mean. Whether this is advisable in wholesale fashion depends on three considerations.

First, data over time are usually not available for the interindustry flows, origin-to-destination investment flows, consumer budget breakdowns, and so on, that figure in applied CGEs. Model builders are necessarily driven toward more ad hoc calibration procedures based on partial information.

Second, economies (especially developing economies) change. It is never clear what numbers from even ten years ago have to do with the current economic situation, especially when model closures or directions of macroeconomic causality may be very different. Relying on regression equations which amount to averages of past years's data with equal weights may not be an illuminating procedure. However, for key relationships such as investment demand functions and wage indexation rules, incorporating time series information often makes sense. Fully wedded CGE and econometric models are probably impossible, but both parties may be happier if they flirt a little bit.

Third, one may try to use theory to express SAM calibrations in terms of "deeper" parameters to be estimated cross-sectionally or over time. Neoclassical economists are fond of setting up optimization models to this end. When cleverly done, such formulations have intuitive content, as the CES and LES equations illustrate. They also have their drawbacks. There is no clear evidence that "agents" such as households, firms, or the state truly optimize. Memory is a good test, and anyone who has ever balanced a home's or enterprise's books or participated in IMF negotiations in full tilt has vivid recollection of groping, satisficing, irrationality in the common usage of the word, and worse. Moreover, although setting up and solving simple optimizations is an interesting game, it can easily divert attention from fundamental questions of political economy, macroeconomic causality and class. Making sensible judgments about slopes, intercepts, and closure is far more crucial than incorporating "deep" (and ultimately unobservable) parameters to an applied model's success.

1.12 Dynamic Relationships

It is straightforward to simulate CGE models over a number of periods, to get projections of possible future behavior of the economy. These solutions are conditioned by the assumptions one makes about comparative static properties of the model, as well as exogenous time trends. If these dynamic exercises are carefully thought through and executed, they can provide useful information.

Obviously, any parameter in a model can be given a time index and a trend. In addition many variables have to be updated from period to period in simple ways. The main examples of both types go as follows:

1. Asset and liability stocks should be cumulated from within-period flows along the lines indicated in table 1.7. If δ_i is the physical depreciation rate for the capital stock K_i in sector i, the accumulation rule will be

$$K_i = I_i + (1 - \delta_i)K_i,$$

where I_i is the sector's gross captial formation by destination. Parameters like δ_i can be estimated as ratios from depreciation flows in a SAM and initial capital stock estimates (or adivinations).

2. Productivity increases are typically observed in time series output data. They are usually not well understood in terms of explanatory factors, but at least can be modeled by attaching trends to the relevant production input parameters. Growing labor productivity, for example, would be reflected by a steady geometric decrease in the labor input coefficient b in a markup formulation or the parameter α_L in the CES labor demand function discussed last section. Time trends in consumption can be captured by attaching growth rates to the floor parameters θ_i in an LES specification, subject to the adding-up requirement that

$$\sum_{i=0}^{N} [\theta_i(t) - \theta_i(t-1)] = 0.$$

3. Predetermined nominal prices may have to be updated from one period to the next in line with inflation and other economic variables, for example, by a rule such as

$$w(t+1) = w(t)\left\{1 + \varepsilon\hat{P}(t) + \alpha\left[\frac{L(t) - \bar{L}(t)}{\bar{L}(t)}\right] + \beta\left[\frac{\bar{\omega}(t) - \omega(t)}{\bar{\omega}(t)}\right]\right\}.$$

Here, wages next period are indexed to the current period's price inflation (with a "pass-through coefficient" ε which usually takes a value between zero and one). The between-period wage increase also depends on employment L relative to a "full" level $\bar{L}$ in a Phillips curve specification as well as distributional tension as measured by the shortfall of the real wage ω $(= w/P)$ from a target level $\bar{\omega}$. Such relationships underlie cost-based structural inflation and are used in several models in this book.

4. Similar considerations apply to other price variables such as the exchange rate e. It may be indexed to ongoing inflation in a "crawling peg" and also adjusted between periods in light of the balance of payments results from the model.

5. These trending price variables can also have feedbacks to the rest of the system. The inflation tax and other effects of price inflation $\hat{P}$ as discussed

in section 1.5 are prominent examples. Also unless savings rates and stocks of assets held by different classes are broadly consistent, dynamic simulations can give unstable wealth distributions unless there are improbably large relative shifts in asset prices.

6. Various exogenous items have to be specified—government spending (in real or nominal terms), external and internal credit limits, investment levels by destination and export and import flows (if not determined by closure or behavioral relationships), and inventory changes are the obvious examples. It is often convenient to set up their changes over time in growth rate form.

1.13 Solution Techniques

CGE models aren't terribly useful unless they can be solved numerically in a reasonable amount of time. Computer speeds go up by about a factor of ten every decade, so that by the late 1980s solving a model with up to a few dozen sectors is no major task (though the same cannot be said about putting its data together). Despite computer speed one does have to think a bit about setting up solution algorithms. Basically, four approaches appear in the literature (Robinson 1989).

First, in each period the model boils down to a set of nonlinear equations with a certain structure, around which solution techniques can be devised. Details for models like the ones in this book are set out below. Such model-specific procedures are often convenient (and help one think about how the model works) but they are not essential. Nonlinear algorithms on mainframes (or even spreadsheeet packages on microcomputers) now deal easily with more than 100 equations. That is enough for a model with quite a few sectors.

Second, models in the Arrow-Debreu tradition without forced saving and other nonhomogeneous consequences of nominal flows can be solved by finding fixed points of their excess demand functions in nonnegative prices. The Scarf fixed-point algorithm provided the original impetus for neoclassical models for industrialized countries (see, e.g., Scarf and Shoven 1983; Shoven and Whalley 1984). This approach is not of much use for structuralist models. In practice, even neoclassical modelers have given up fixed-point algorithms of late in favor of standard nonlinear equation-solving computer routines.

Third, more or less neoclassical models can be set up as nonlinear programs instead of fixed-point problems. Ginsburgh and Waelbroeck (1981) provide examples and a survey of techniques.

Finally, all the equations can be linearized around the base-year SAM so that an approximate solution can be found by matrix inversion. Johansen (1960) adopted this technique for his pioneering CGE model, and it has been used widely since, such as in the large models for Australia designed by Dixon, et al. (1982).

Models of the type in this book can usually be solved by simple iterative procedures based on the circular flow of incomes discussed in section 1.8. Consider a model in which output or some other quantity variable (a trade flow or real government spending) adjusts to ensure demand-supply balance by sector. Each sector's price can be formed by a markup rule, neoclassical cost function, or the inverse of a supply function depending on the price-cost ratio.

One starts with initial (or "old") guesses at sector quantity variables. Through the equations corresponding to columns of the SAM, they permit computation of sectoral prices and income flows. These in turn feed through saving functions and complete demand systems to give real consumption levels. Together with sectoral demand injections (exports, investment, and/or government spending) the consumption flows provide "new" estimates of quantities through the input–output balance equations. One proceeds in this fashion comparing new with old quantity levels until they agree within a pre-set tolerance level. This procedure usually converges after a couple of dozen iterations with the sorts of savings leakages that appear in applied models.

One or more sectors may be characterized by flexible prices, for example, the overall price level when there is macroeconomic forced saving, the agricultural price in the model of section 1.8, or the interest rate for the loan market in section 1.10. Each such price is determined implicitly at equilibrium by the condition that its corresponding excess demand should equal zero. The question is how to fit price adjustment into an iterative procedure like the one just discussed.

Depending on the model specification, one may be able to get an explicit expression for a flex-price by inverting its excess demand function—this could be used in conjunction with output levels computed as described above. Alternatively, prices could be iteratively modified parallel to outputs in proportion to excess demands—experimentation with factors of proportionality usually gives convergent solutions. Finally, outputs could be computed as above for given prices, while in an outer iteration loop the prices are adjusted by some nonlinear equation algorithm to drive the corresponding excess demands to zero. All these procedures have been used successfully in practice.

The last complication is that the model may be subject to cross-sectoral restrictions such as labor supply functions or a balance of payments constraint. It can always be solved as above for given values of the variables that are supposed to adjust to meet the constraints. In an outer solution loop these variables can then be changed to drive their corresponding constraints toward being satisfied. For a reasonable number of restrictions (e.g., up to ten), this procedure is perfectly feasible with standard nonlinear equation packages on mainframes. If one is willing to wait a bit for solutions, the same technique can be applied on microcomputers.

In closing, it is worth noting that solution procedures for applied models always seem to give unique results, perhaps because most model variants that one considers are perturbations around the initial solution represented by the base-year SAM. One uses the model first to replicate the SAM and then do comparative statics or conditional projections. Fortunately, neither exercise is plagued in practice by different solutions for the same set of exogenous variables and parameters.

1.14 Preview of the Models

The chapters that follow describe a dozen applied structuralist CGE models. They begin with three fix-price/flex-price models of the type discussed here in section 1.8, designed to deal with food subsidy, fiscal, and macroeconomic stablilization issues in Mexico, Colombia, and Nicaragua. Chapters 5 through 7 extend this general line of analysis to effects of public enterprise pricing policy in India, energy pricing in Egypt, and subsidies and general macro policy in Sri Lanka.

Chapter 8 applies serveral "partial" CGE's to India, to ask how its growth prospects might be limited by constraints of several kinds; chapter 9 looks more in detail at different sorts of inflationary processes in that country. The next two chapters set out models with full financial sectors (monetarist linkages are already considered in other models) to explore impacts of wealth redistribution in Mexico and monetary policy in Thailand. Chapters 12 and 13, respectively, take up medium term dynamics of productivity growth and lagging oil revenue per capita in Kuwait, and inflation stablilization in Argentina.

In more detail, the models deal with the following issues:

The chapter 2 model by Nora Lustig and Lance Taylor was set up to address problems of food subsidy design in Mexico in the late 1970s. It illustrates the general nature of fix/flex models by comparing the effects on income distribution and the fiscal and external deficits of three types of policies aimed at eliminating the food intake shortfall below a norm (as a proxy for a nutritional deficit) of the low-income population. The policies are a targeted food price subsidy, an income transfer, and a general price subsidy. The latter two are unacceptably costly in fiscal and foreign exchange terms, suggesting that effective targeting of subsidies would have to be a priority in any serious program aimed at alleviating malnutrition in Mexico.

Like the ones that follow, the Mexican model is multisectoral, with some sectors reaching market balance via price changes and others via output adjustment. Several income classes are considered, with rules specified for income generation and saving and consumption behavior of each class. Nominal wages and the exchange rate are fixed and macro causality runs from investment to saving, with both output shifts and forced saving processes contributing to the attainment of macro balance.

The model for Colombia in chapter 3 was put together by Juan Luis Londoño to deal with issues of fiscal and macro stabilization policy. Because they have differing spillover effects across sectors, the model distinguishes "general" and "specific" expenditure policies and distributional shifts. An example of a demand injection specific to a sector would be its exports, while spending from increased coffee growers's income due to an export price bonanza would be a general distributional shift.

Londoño demonstrates the importance of terms-of-trade changes in macro adjustment and then goes on to consider the role of stabilization policy during three different episodes in recent Colombian history. The simulations provide useful insights, for example, how contractionary effects of devaluation in 1984–85 may have been partially offset by nonprice rationing of imports and a partial pass-through of the local currency price increase of coffee to the growers. The simulations also show that fiscal contraction is not a very effective means for reducing the external deficit in Colombia, while direct taxes (a "general" leakage) may be the best tool for cutting fiscal deficits.

Chapter 4, by Bill Gibson, takes up recent policy questions in Nicaragua. The model is foreign exchange constrained, with both internal output changes and forced saving serving as macro adjustment mechanisms. Gibson argues that recent macro policy in Nicaragua—aimed at reallocating labor toward productive activities by reducing the forced saving which shifts the income distribution toward the informal sector which controls scarce imports—makes sense. Three more controversial conclusions that follow from the logic of the model are (1) price controls may *not* be distributionally progressive, depending on their general equilibrium impacts; (2) devaluation may prove progressive and expansionary, given the binding forex constraint; (3) a smaller trade deficit is contractionary and regressive, but attempts to shield the popular classes from these effects through nominal wage increases and higher government spending can make the situation worse.

Chapter 5 describes one of several CGE models for India that have been put together over the past decade by Hiren Sarkar and Manoj Panda (with inputs by Jørn Rattsø and Lance Taylor). In the present paper Panda and Sarkar take up effects of price increases by public sector enterprises, which account for about a quarter of the nation's GDP. The overall price structure in the model is made sensitive to both cost pressure (e.g., for intermediates produced by public sector firms) and the level of aggregate demand. A detailed government accounting block of equations captures the effects of price changes on government revenue and spending, which activate a chain of macro effects.

The administered price sectors considered are petroleum, coal, electricity, and the railroads. The results first show that raising administered prices is stagflationary. However, when the resulting revenues are used to finance public investment, the outcomes are faster growth and inflation. On both counts, petroleum and coal price increases are more effective instruments for financing investment than are higher electricity or railroad rates. Finally, in a policy-relevant result, existing indirect taxes are shown to be better fund-raisers than administered prices.

The related issue of energy pricing by state-run oil refining and natural gas producing companies in Egypt is taken up by Nazli Choucri and Supriya Lahiri in chapter 6. They show, first, that if there is no substitution between oil and gas in the industrial sector and a completely elastic supply of gas, then a 10 percent oil product price increase will drive up various price indexes between 5 and 10 percent and lead to economic contraction unless state spending is raised by 8 percent.

The authors then extend the model in the neoclassical direction by permitting substitution between refined oil products and gas as intermediate industrial inputs (with an elasticity of substitution of 1.5) and considering various supply elasticities for natural gas (infinity, two, and zero). In all of these cases when GDP is held constant by fiscal intervention, the elasticities of refinery output with respect to the oil product price range between about −0.03 and −0.13 while elasticities of gas output range between zero and 0.27. The implication is that even when price-elastic substitution responses are built into the CGE model, its solutions suggest that the practical possibilities for shifting between energy sources by altering their relative prices in the short run are relatively weak.

In chapter 7 Anne Maasland sets up a model to simulate the effects of an economic liberalization strategy pursued in Sri Lanka beginning in 1977. In 1980–81 the economy experienced rapid inflation due to cost-push from import price and wage increases, removal of price subsidies, and domestic money creation to finance ambitious agricultural investment projects. To capture these inflationary pressures, the model incorporates cost-push via markup pricing equations and also allows the markup rate to rise in response to increases in the money supply and capacity utilization, in keeping with the way the Sri Lankans view the inflationary process in their own economy.

The key policy issues center around income distribution, in a country where saving and consumption patterns differ between the poor and rich. An illustrative simulation maintains a food price subsidy to the poor and lowers public investment—it is counterfactual in both regards. The outcomes include lower prices, higher exports, and increased national consumption (especially of food by the poor). Increased tariffs on nonfood consumer goods imports can be used to pay for the subsidy and improve the current account which otherwise is adversely affected by consumer imports.

Chapter 8, by Lance Taylor, uses simple macro models that could be extended into full-fledged CGEs of the type presented in this book to try to isolate the binding constraints on the rate of growth of capacity (or potential output) in India. In a medium-term context the limits to growth from saving, productivity increases, foreign exchange, food supply, inflation from both monetarist and structuralist causes, and potential internal and external debt traps are considered.

Since they are parameterized over the same period in one economy, all the potential constraints are located near current Indian levels of the fiscal and trade deficits, and inflation and growth rates. In comparative dynamic analysis, they show that 6 instead of 5 percent capacity growth would involve widening the current account deficit or increasing the export share by 0.5 percent of the value of gross output (GDP plus intermediate imports), a 1 percent annual trend in the terms of trade toward agriculture, 2 or 3 percent faster inflation, and additional buildups of both external and internal debt.

These costs seem mild, suggesting that Indian policy has been conservative in the sense of keeping the economy demand constrained. The paper concludes by discussing the political economy of various means to change this situation.

Chapter 9, by Jørn Rattsø, goes into more detail in Indian inflation. Recent experience suggests that agricultural droughts and external terms of trade shocks are important sources of increasing prices. Conflicting claims among income groups act as propagation mechanisms to sustain inflations based upon these and other disturbances. The distribution of income among agriculturalists, wage earners, profit recipients, foreigners, and the state reflects the social structure. Five inflationary processes involving these groups—based on food prices, money wages, markups, import prices, and demand pressure from higher public investment—are investigated in a dynamic CGE.

The agricultural market emerges as the main ground on which macroeconomic disturbances play. Government regulation of agricultural prices becomes a key anti-inflationary policy in the short run, while investment in the sector will be essential for price stability over time. Nominal wage growth and manufacturing profitability both turn out to be sensitive to food price inflation.

Chapter 10, by William Easterly, introduces a CGE model for Mexico which includes portfolio balances. These permit the analysis of important financial channels usually ignored in applied CGE work. Topics treated include (1) capital flight, which has been a major contributor to the Latin American debt crisis; (2) "dollarization" (or denomination of loans and deposits in dollars) of the local banking system; and (3) capital gains and losses on existing stocks of assets and liabilities due to price movements. With regard to the last topic, the inclusion of dollarized assets and liabilities broadens the usual analysis of real balances (see section 1.5) to cover revaluations induced by exchange rate changes. For example, with a local devaluation, the capital loss on dollar debt of firms has a negative effect on corporate investment in the model, while the capital gains on dollar assets of rentiers encourage their consumption. Redistributive effects of devaluation are complex, depending on the relative shares of different classes in dollar-denominated assets and liabilities, dollar expenditures, and dollar incomes.

Another novel feature of the model is incorporation of indexation of state-controlled prices and wages to endogenous price movements, introducing trade-offs for the government between its fiscal performance, the level of output, and distributional equity. Finally, the explicit inclusion of the banking system and the public sector accounts in the model permits assessment of the relationships between financial fragility and fiscal performance. For example, the government could block a financial crisis which could be caused by revaluation of dollar-denominated domestic debts by specifying a lower exchange rate for such liabilities. But this would require heavy fiscal outlays to cover the losses suffered thereby by the banks. The model helps quantify, although not ameliorate, such serious policy problems.

Jeffrey Rosensweig and Lance Taylor take up other financial issues in a model for Thailand in chapter 11. Put together in 1984, it is one of the first CGEs to incorporate financial variables, and was in part designed to illustrate the sorts of policy analysis such formulations permit. The authors concentrate on short-run portfolio balances for households, firms, the government, and the commercial and central banks, asking how monetary policy affects macroeconomic equilibrium in a relatively open economy.

One policy query that arises is the extent to which different sorts of interventions are offset by reserve changes. If the government borrows 100 billion baht from the Bank of Thailand to increase public consumption, for example, that institution's reserve losses in the new macro equilibrium amount to 93—additional state spending is essentially financed from abroad. On the real side, the counterpart of the reserve loss is a large increase in imports since the Thai economy's marginal propensity to import (with respect to real GDP) is a relatively high 0.375. Central bank policy moves—changing the volume of rediscount or reserve requirements—are also at least partly offset by foreign reserve changes, reducing their impact on the interest rate and investment demand. Finally, devaluation has expansionary effects on the real side of the economy by stimulating exports. But when capital losses on external liabilities are taken into account, the expansion may well be canceled by increased interest rates and reduced investment demand.

Chapter 12 shifts focus to long-term development issues in Kuwait, a small and prosperous country which nonetheless faces vexing policy problems in the medium run. Motaz Khorshid develops a dynamic CGE model to quantify (1) the fiscal constraint that government is likely to face as its oil revenues per Kuwaiti (with 3.5 percent population growth) inevitably decline, (2) the social problem of trying to reduce the ratio of resident non-Kuwaitis to citizens from about 1.4 down to unity over a period of 10 to 15 years, and (3) diversifying the economy away from its extreme dependence on oil.

Two main strategies are considered. The first is reduction of aggregate demand to slow output growth and thereby employment of non-Kuwaitis, and the second is directed public investment to enhance productivity of employed Kuwaitis. Productivity growth, if attained, would enhance the GDP growth rate and household income and expenditure, while reducing activity improves the Kuwaiti population ratio and reduces the rate of loss (per Kuwaiti) of public reserve funds held abroad. The author suggests a strategy combining aspects of both these approaches, with emphasis on micro-level diversification of the non-oil productive base.

Chapter 13, by Lance Taylor, uses a simple one-sector CGE elaborated with detail on financial and inflation accounting to explore options for price stabilization in Argentina. Among other complications it is assumed that (1) consumption demand responds negatively to the inflation tax (and thus rises when inflation is reduced); (2) markup inflation responds strongly to foreign exchange shortages, while wages are fully indexed; (3) there is cost-push on working capital finance due to higher interest rates; (4) exports tend to be crowded out by increases in domestic demand.

The model simulations suggest there is no need for extremely tight monetary and fiscal policy after a "heterodox shock" price freeze aimed at braking inflation; however, a surge in consumer demand from reducing the inflation tax requires attention. More fundamentally, markup inflation is likely to continue unless the country's need to make a large external transfer to service debt is somehow reduced.

Notes

Research support from the Ford Foundation and comments on previous drafts by Jaime deMelo, Bill Easterly, Nora Lustig, Sherman Robinson, and T. N. Srinivasan are gratefully acknowledged.

1. Free translation by the author.

2. In model exercises that blend neoclassical and structuralist formulations, the trade policy simulations by deMelo and Robinson (1982) represent a partial exception.

3. The word "causality" is used here to describe the selection of variables that are exogenous (or "predetermined") and endogenous in a set of equations or a model, combined with analysis of how the endogenous ones are influenced by the exogenous ones and themselves. Statistical notions of causality, according to which one variable "causes" another if it leads it in time, are ignored as irrelevant or misleading. Local earthquakes below the slopes do not "cause" a subsequent volcanic eruption, and money can either lead or lag output depending on the stance of the central bank, as Davidson and Weintraub (1973) point out. Pyatt (1988) discusses causality and closure issues from a perspective like the one adopted here in the context of a SAM.

4. Note 7 signals a case in which the relative magnitudes of the two savings rates matter. If wage earners (improbably) save at nearly the same rate as rentiers, then real wage cuts can be expansionary in a closure in which output is determined by aggregate demand; with a big differential in savings rates, overall demand can fall. Also nonzero saving from wages affects dynamic income flows. If they save, then presumably worker households have accumulated assets in the past, the returns from which should enter their income statements. We ignore this complication as being empirically unimportant, although it can in principle influence dynamic behavior of the macro system. In models with diverse asset/liability specifications, Pasinetti (1962) and Taylor (1988c) show that assets held by wage earners do not substantially alter the nature of long-run macroeconomic equilibrium, so long as "significant" differences in saving propensities and/or portfolio compositions persist.

5. We omit taxation terms in the present discussion to keep the algebra as simple as possible.

6. Note that in the short run the capital stock K is fixed so that it serves only as a scaling factor. Dividing nominal flows by the value of potential output or full capacity (e.g., $P\kappa K$, where κ is a technical parameter giving the maximum output that can be produced by a given capital stock) would be an alternative normalization. We don't adopt it simply to avoid carrying along the extra term κ.

7. Note that this is a case where the relative magnitudes of saving rates from nonwage and wage income have a significant influence on the characteristics of macroeconomic equilibrium.

8. The markup is figured on costs exclusive of national intermediates. If $\tilde{\tau}$ is the rate on costs including such purchases, then

$$\tau = \frac{\tilde{\tau} + (1 + \tilde{\tau})a_1}{1 - (1 + \tilde{\tau})a_1}.$$

9. If service payments such as remittances and interest are carried in the accounting, the current account as opposed to the trade surplus is more naturally considered to be fixed by available capital inflows.

10. Chapters 10 and 11 in this book contain applications. See also Bourguignon, Branson, and deMelo (1988).

11. One obvious omission is disaggregation of the central and commerical banks in place of the "banking system" to permit analysis of monetary policy. Also households might usefully be disaggregated to reflect their different income flows and asset holdings, for example, workers, rentiers, and (with some practical interest) enterprise-owning households who can borrow from their own firms to engage in capital flight.

12. By increasing the government's demand for loans, public capital formation formation may crowd out private investment by bidding up interest rates in this specification. Recent evidence (Taylor 1988a) suggests that public investment in

fact crowds in private investment via complementarity effects. Tracing the financial implications in a CGE would be a useful exercise.

References

Adelman, Irma, and Sherman Robinson. 1989. "Income Distribution and Development." In Hollis Chenery and Sherman Robinson (eds.), *Handbook of Development Economics*. Vol. 2. Amsterdam: North-Holland.

Amadeo, Edward. 1986 *Keynes's Principle of Effective Demand and Its Relationship to Alternative Theories of Distribution and Accumulation*. Ph.D. dissertation. Harvard University.

Bourguignon, François, William H. Branson, and Jaime deMelo. 1988. "Macroeconomic Adjustment and Income Distribution: A Macro-Micro Simulation Model." Washington: The World Bank.

Bowles, Samuel, and Robert Boyer. 1989. "A Wage-Led Employment Regime: Income Distribution, Labor Discipline, and Aggregate Demand in Welfare Capitalism." In Stephen Marglin (ed.), *The End of the Golden Age: Lessons for the 1990's*. Oxford: Clarendon Press.

Davidson, Paul, and Sidney Weintraub. 1973. "Money as Cause and Effect." *Economic Journal* 83: 1117–32.

Decaluwe, Bernard, and Andre Martens. 1987. "Developing Countries and General Equilibrium Models: A Review of the Empirical Literature." IDRC Manuscript Report No. IDRC-MR155e. Ottowa: International Development Research Center.

deJanvry, Alain, and Elisabeth Sadoulet. 1987. "Agricultural Price Policy in General Equilibrium Models: Results and Comparisons." *American Journal of Agricultural Economics* 69: 230–46.

deMelo, Jaime. 1988. "Computable General Equilibrium Models for Trade Policy Analysis in Developing Countries: A Survey." *Journal of Policy Modeling* 10: 469–504.

deMelo, Jaime, and Sherman Robinson. 1982. "Trade Adjustment Policies and Income Distribution in Three Archetype Developing Economies." *Journal of Development Economics* 10: 67–92.

Devarajan, Shantayanan, Jeffrey D. Lewis, and Sherman Robinson. 1986. "A Bibliography of Computable General Equilibrium (CGE) Models Applied to Developing Countries." Department of Agricultural and Resource Economics, University of California at Berkeley.

Dixon, Peter B., Brian R. Parmenter, John Sutton, and D. P. Vincent. 1982. *Orani: A Multisectoral Model of the Australian Economy*. Amsterdam: North-Holland.

Duesenberry, James. 1958. *Business Cycles and Economic Growth*. New York: McGraw-Hill.

Dutt, Amitava K. 1984. "Stagnation, Income Distribution, and Monopoly Power." *Cambridge Journal of Economics* 8: 25–40.

Eichner, Alfred S. 1980. "A General Model of Investment and Pricing." In Edward Nell (ed.), *Growth, Profits, and Property*. Cambridge: Cambridge University Press.

Fischer, Stanley. 1977. "Long-Term Contracts, Rational Expectations, and the Optimal Money Supply Rule." *Journal of Political Economy* 85: 191–206.

Fisher, Irving. 1933. "The Debt Deflation Theory of Great Depressions." *Econometrica* 1: 337–57.

Foley, Duncan K. 1975. "On Two Specifications of Asset Equilibrium in Macroeconomic Models." *Journal of Political Economy* 83: 303–24.

Friedman, Milton. 1968. "The Role of Monetary Policy." *American Economic Review* 58: 1–17.

Ginsburgh, Victor, and Jean Waelbroeck. 1981. *Activity Analysis and General Equilibrium Modeling*. Amsterdam: North-Holland.

Johansen, Leif. 1960. *A Multi-sectoral Study of Economic Growth*. Amsterdam: North-Holland.

Kaldor, Nicholas. 1955. "Alternative Theories of Distribution." *Review of Economic Studies* 23: 83–100.

Kalecki, Michal. 1971. *Selected Essays on the Development of the Capitalist Economy*. Cambridge: Cambridge University Press.

Keynes, John Maynard. 1930. *A Treatise on Money*. London: Macmillan

Keynes, John Maynard. 1931. "The Consequences to Society of Changes in the Value of Money." In *Essays in Persuasion*. London: Macmillan.

Keynes, John Maynard. 1936. *The General Theory of Employment, Interest, and Money*. London: Macmillan.

Lluch, Constantino, Alan A. Powell, and Ross A. Williams. 1977. *Patterns in Household Demand and Saving*. New York: Oxford University Press.

Lustig, Nora. 1988. "Del Estructuralismo al Neoestructuralismo: La Busqueda de un paradigma Heterodoxo." *Coleccion Estudios CIEPLAN*. 23: 35–50.

Meade, James. 1961. *A Neo-classical Theory of Economic Growth*. London: Allen and Unwin.

Pasinetti, Luigi L. 1962. "Rate of Profit and Income Distribution in Relation to the Rate of Economic Growth." *Review of Economic Studies* 29: 267–79.

Pigou, Arthur C. 1943. "The Classical Stationary State." *Economic Journal* 53: 343–51.

Pyatt, Graham. 1988. "A SAM Approach to Modeling." *Journal of Policy Modeling* 10: 327–52.

Pyatt, Graham, and Jeffrey I. Round (eds.). 1985. *Social Accounting Matrices: A Basis for Planning*. Washington: The World Bank.

Rattsø, Jørn. 1982. "Different Macroclosures of the Original Johansen Model and Their Impact on Policy Evaluations." *Journal of Policy Modeling* 4: 85–97.

Robertson, D. H. 1933. "Saving and Hoarding." *Economic Journal* 43: 399–413.

Robinson, Sherman. 1989. "Multisectoral Models." In Hollis Chenery and T. N. Srinivasan (eds.), *Handbook of Development Economics*. Vol. 2. Amsterdam: North-Holland.

Scarf, Herbert, and John B. Shoven (eds.). 1983. *Applied General Equilibrium Analysis*. Cambridge: Cambridge University Press.

Schor, Juliet B. 1985. "Changes in the Cyclical Pattern of Real Wages: Evidence from Nine Countries, 1955–80." *Economic Journal* 95: 452–68.

Semmler, Willi. 1984. *Competition, Monopoly, and Differential Profit Rates*. New York: Columbia University Press.

Sen, Amartya K. 1963. "Neo-classical and Neo-Keynesian Theories of Distribution." *Economic Record* 39: 54–64.

Shoven, John B., and John Whalley. 1984. "Applied General Equilibrium Models of Taxation and International Trade." *Journal of Economic Literature* 22: 1007–51.

Solow, Robert M. 1956. "A Contribution to the Theory of Economic Growth." *Quarterly Journal of Economics* 70: 65–94.

Stone, J. R. N. 1966. "The Social Accounts from a Consumer Point of View." *Review of Income and Wealth*, series 12, no. 1: 1–33.

Sylos-Labini, Paolo. 1984. *The Forces of Economic Growth and Decline*. Cambridge, MA: MIT Press.

Taylor, John B. 1980. "Aggregate Dynamics and Staggered Contracts." *Journal of Political Economy* 88: 1–24.

Taylor, Lance. 1979. *Macro Models for Developing Countries*. New York: McGraw-Hill

Taylor, Lance. 1983. *Structuralist Macroeconomics*. New York: Basic Books.

Taylor, Lance. 1988a. *Varieties of Stabilization Experience*. Oxford: Clarendon Press.

Taylor, Lance. 1988b. "Real and Money Wages, Output, and Inflation in the Semi-industrialized World." *Economica*, to appear.

Taylor, Lance. 1988c. "Regressive Redistribution, Speculation, and Financial Collapse." Department of Economics, Massachusetts Institute of Technology.

Taylor, Lance. and Frank J. Lysy. 1979. "Vanishing Income Redistributions: Keynesian Clues about Model Surprises in the Short Run." *Journal of Development Economics* 6: 11–29.

Tobin, James. 1980. *Asset Accumulation and Economic Activity*. Chicago: University of Chicago Press.

Tobin, James. 1982. "Money and Finance in the Macroeconomic Process," *Journal of Money, Credit, and Banking*. 14: 171–204.

Varian, Hal R. 1984. *Microeconomic Analysis*. 2d ed. New York: Norton.

2 Mexican Food Consumption Policies in a Structuralist CGE Model

Nora Lustig and
Lance Taylor

Studies and surveys have shown that the problem of malnutrition in Mexico is acute and affects a significant proportion of families (see, e.g., Instituto Nacional de la Nutricion 1979; COPLAMAR 1982; Lustig 1980, 1982a, 1985). The 1977 Income and Expenditure Survey by the Secretaria de Programmacion and Presupuesto, for instance, showed that food expenditure by households with an income below the minimum wage (about 45 percent of all households) was on average insufficient to cover the recommendations by the National Institute of Nutrition and the (now disappeared) Mexican Food System. This deficiency in food intake occurred despite the fact that food expenditures represented between 50 and 60 percent of these families's budgets.

Under these circumstances the Mexican government has long been concerned with how to combat undernutrition without seriously upsetting the frail public finances.[1] During the past thirty years general price subsidies have been the main policy instruments used to protect the living standard of low-income families. The outcomes include a heavy outlay burden on the fiscal budget and the fact that food subsidies—if not explicitly regressive—have benefited better-off segments of the population as well as the poor.[2]

In this chapter we use a general equilibrium model to compare the effects of three different sorts of policies aimed at increasing the food intake of low-income families: a general price subsidy of the type traditionally employed, an income transfer, and a targeted price subsidy. For a given desired increment in food consumption, we are interested in seeing how these policies affect the level and distribution of income by household classes, and the fiscal and external accounts. As one would expect, the results show that the discriminatory policy is least costly in terms of the fiscal deficit and balance of payments pressure. The income transfer produces a higher overall increase in employment and income for all classes than does a directed food price subsidy, but with a higher fiscal cost and larger trade deficit. A general price subsidy large enough to raise most poor households above the recommended food spending level proves impossible from both the fiscal and balance of payments points of view. The implication is that a serious attempt to combat malnutrition would require effective targeting of the directed policies. If a general price subsidy is made large enough to have more than marginal effects on food intake of the poor, it would have to be accompanied by other measures to reduce the government's spending or increase its income.

The presentation is organized as follows: In the next section we present a summary of the CGE model and its corresponding social accounting matrix. Section 2.2 describes the simulations and discusses their implications for policy choice. The mathematical specification of the model appears in the appendix and, in more detail, in Lustig (1982b).

2.1 The Model

Along with other structuralist CGE models, the one used here emphasizes absolute price and quantity adjustments—a detailed neoclassical description of input substitution in response to relative price changes in the short run is not relevant to the policy questions we have in mind and is deliberately suppressed. Consumer choice is thoroughly modeled via linear expenditure systems, since it is central to the issues at hand. Productive activity is separated into eight sectors: corn and bean production, other agriculture, petroleum, fertilizers, food processing, other industry, services, and commerce. This disaggregation was chosen in light of the policy simulations presented here. For example, it allows us to isolate policies directed toward basic foodstuffs that are "peasant intensive" (e.g., guarantee prices for corn and beans) and also gives a general description of how total spending is allocated among food and nonfood manufacturing and the tertiary sectors.

Private income is distributed across seven categories: income flows accruing to *campesinos* (or peasants), *jornaleros* (or agricultural workers), agricultural capitalists, urban workers, urban capitalists, merchants, and urban marginals. This grouping of income shares is based upon several criteria. On the one hand, we are interested in differentiating the effects of policies on rural incomes vis-à-vis the rest; on the other, we want to distinguish what happens with property income flows as opposed to those accruing to labor. Finally, we want to examine how policies influence the breakdown of property incomes, such as that of peasants as opposed to large landowners, and of industrialists as opposed to merchants. Within the last two classes we also split out property owners who are not able to produce an income surplus beyond their subsistence and group them with below-subsistence workers to create a class we call the urban marginals.[3]

The model's focus is on the short run, implying that the two agricultural sectors can be assumed to have fixed domestic supplies. The idea behind this specification is that while the size of the current crop may be influenced by prices in the past, the length of the growing cycle prevents it from responding immediately to market signals.[4] Equilibrium in these two markets is brought about through changes in their "flex-prices" that affect demand (if we assume that trade restrictions are in effect) or net exports. The six nonagricultural sectors are assumed to have excess capacity and their outputs adjust to effective demand. Prices in these sectors are formed by a markup over prime cost à la Kalecki.[5]

The levels of output in the nonagricultural sectors determine overall economic activity and (given our assumption of fixed labor input coefficients in the short run) employment. Labor supplies are freely variable at the negotiated money wages, meaning that there is no supply-side relationship between employment and the real wage. There are, however, effective demand linkages via which real income changes influence employment levels. Real wages are determined ex post by deflation of nominal, predetermined wages by the relevant endogenous price indexes which incorporate fluctuations from the flex-price agricultural sectors.

The foreign sector is treated in a very simple manner. The exchange rate is nominally fixed (by the central bank), exports are predetermined in real terms, and imports depend on input–output requirements except for competitive imports into the agricultural sectors. These latter trade flows in fact respond to relative price changes, although we control them exogenously in the simulations in order to underline some of the policy results (the mechanics will become clear below when we describe policy experiments). The difference between total imports and exports yields foreign saving or an endogenous resource gap.

The macroeconomic interpretation of the model's behavior is straightforward. Total investment is set exogenously, and the general equilibrium adjustment mechanism that guarantees no excess demand in any of the eight commodity markets yields at the same time the level of saving required to finance the given investment (i.e., macro balance). Shifts in the micro equilibrium in response to policy or parameter changes involve changes in net exports (and foreign savings), outputs, and nominal prices

Table 2.1
Social accounting matrix for Mexico (billion 1975 pesos)

	Corn and beans	Other agriculture	Petroleum	Fertilizers	Food processing	Industry	Services	Commerce	Total
1. Corn and beans	667.0	1,760.6	0.0	0.0	5,554.9	0.0	0.0	0.0	7,982.5
2. Other agriculture	0.0	11,159.3	2.2	5.6	70,434.0	7,658.8	532.8	0.0	89,792.7
3. Petroleum	71.0	2,656.1	21,403.8	817.2	3,128.2	13,494.0	10,073.2	3,144.3	54,787.7
4. Fertilizers	949.7	3,138.2	0.0	23.6	0.0	108.9	7.4	0.0	4,227.8
5. Food processing	0.0	11,363.1	7.3	6.2	32,434.5	2,733.7	888.9	0.0	47,433.7
6. Industry	166.0	6,667.4	3,436.7	1,070.6	13,131.1	171,012.4	28,214.1	5,462.0	229,160.2
7. Services	542.0	1,595.3	4,628.4	257.3	9,120.1	33,939.4	56,294.5	21,880.0	128,257.0
8. Commerce	461.9	5,701.4	1,031.6	339.3	10,377.6	42,472.5	11,264.5	1,973.1	73,622.0
9. Total	2,857.6	44,041.4	30,510.0	2,519.8	144,180.4	271,419.6	107,275.3	32,459.3	635,263.3
10. Campesinos	14,056.3	27,147.0							41,203.3
11. Agricultural workers	4,280.5	27,057.8							31,338.3
12. Agricultural capitalists	1,561.3	48,425.8							49,987.1
13. Urban workers			13,678.5	645.4	20,157.1	118,254.9	141,475.1	46,577.7	340,788.6
14. Urban capitalists					39,788.4	105,736.6	167,546.5	0.0	313,071.4
15. Merchants								144,383.4	144,383.4
16. Urban marginals					4,832.3	14,161.9	21,503.5	16,993.2	57,490.8
17. Total private value added	19,898.1	102,630.6	13,678.5	645.4	64,777.8	238,153.3	330,525.1	207,954.2	978,262.8
18. Net taxes	101.9	522.5	25,590.8	840.2	9,973.5	10,378.2	5,497.8	28,453.2	81,358.1
19. Imports	237.4	1,095.2	3,774.5	860.3	7,347.8	31,583.4	4,324.4	0.0	49,223.0
20. Savings									
21. Total	23,095.0	148,289.6	73,553.8	4,865.7	226,279.5	551,534.5	447,622.6	268,866.7	1,744,107.0

Note: This SAM was constructed by Bill Gibson and the authors. For data sources, assumptions, etc., see Lustig (1982b).

Table 2.1 (continued)

		Campesinos	Agricultural workers	Agricultural capitalists	Urban workers	Urban capitalists	Merchants	Urban marginals	Total private consumption	Government expenditure	Exports	Investment	Total
1.	Corn and beans	3,769.9	1,700.6	267.7	2,089.0	1,292.5	641.2	2,222.2	11,983.2	0.0	6.2	3,123.1	23,095.0
2.	Other agriculture	3,791.3	2,243.2	2,084.2	17,843.2	10,748.5	5,418.4	5,040.0	47,168.9	136.9	3,192.4	7,998.8	148,289.6
3.	Petroleum	405.7	254.7	1,070.7	3,809.7	3,437.1	1,374.8	340.8	10,693.4	1,718.0	5,784.6	570.0	73,553.8
4.	Fertilizers	0.0	0.0	0.0	0.0	0.0	0.0	0.0	0.0	13.6	398.5	225.8	4,865.7
5.	Food processing	11,466.9	8,421.8	6,788.7	65,627.7	38,544.4	20,089.2	17,526.1	168,464.8	176.3	7,378.9	2,825.8	226,279.4
6.	Industry	6,652.4	4,143.7	4,775.8	50,440.5	29,997.1	13,163.6	7,816.5	116,989.5	5,126.7	17,358.6	182,899.4	551,534.3
7.	Services	7,355.2	7,894.1	10,568.9	101,374.3	74,767.5	32,654.0	13,257.0	247,871.0	64,376.1	2,605.8	5,012.6	447,622.4
8.	Commerce	8,096.1	6,307.9	6,705.5	65,062.1	43,267.9	19,843.2	11,755.2	161,037.9	977.8	2,554.5	30,674.6	268,866.8
9.	Total	41,537.6	30,966.1	32,261.5	306,246.4	202,055.0	93,184.3	57,957.9	764,208.5	72,525.4	38,779.5	233,330.0	1,744,106.5
10.	Campesinos												41,203.3
11.	Agricultural workers												31,338.3
12.	Agricultural capitalists												49,987.1
13.	Urban workers									40,264.4			381,053.0
14.	Urban capitalists												313,071.4
15.	Merchants												144,383.4
16.	Urban marginals marginals												57,498.8
17.	Total private value value added									40,264.4			1,818,527.1
18.	Net taxes	0.0	626.8	2,783.9	19,052.6	17,435.3	8,040.9	0.0	47,939.4				229,297.5
19.	Imports	−335.1	−254.9	−406.6	−3,099.4	−2,546.4	−1,174.4	−467.6	−8,284.4	535.5	16,259.5	27,287.1	85,020.7
20.	Savings	0.0	0.0	15,348.3	58,853.6	96,128.1	44,332.7	0.0	214,662.8	15,972.2	29,981.7		260,616.7
21.	Total	41,202.4	31,337.9	49,987.1	381,053.3	313,071.9	144,383.5	57,490.3	1,018,526.3	129,297.5	85,020.7	260,617.1	3,135,551.5

that generate new levels of public and private incomes and savings flows in turn. Macro balance (or investment-savings equilibrium) is brought about by changes in activity levels, the trade gap, and income distribution that generate an amount of saving equal to nominal investment demand.[6]

The data base used in the model has been organized in the SAM presented as table 2.1. It summarizes in snapshot form the sectoral, distributional, and macroeconomic characteristics of the Mexican economy and at the same time is the base solution of the model. The model parameters detailed in the appendix were calibrated to the base year SAM.[7]

2.2 Policy Experiments and Results

In table 2.2 we present estimates of the daily per capita deficits in expenditure on processed food for the two classes whose intake fell below norms.[8] Urban marginals also have below-standard food consumption, but the shortfall is for products originating in sector 2 (other agricultual products). We concentrate here on analyzing the effects of removing the deficits for processed foods (sector 5) alone.

The three policy experiments that were simulated are the following:

1. A straight income transfer to peasants and agricultural workers to generate the required increase in expenditure on processed food.[9]

2. A targeted price subsidy (assumed to reach only the desired households without leakages) on processed food for peasants and agricultural workers.[10]

3. A general price subsidy on processed food.[11]

In the three experiments import levels for the two agricultural sectors were changed exogenously to hold the sectoral price levels equal to those of the base solution. Otherwise, there would be inflationary pressure resulting from food supply constraints. This procedure implies that greater demand caused by the transfers or subsidies spills exclusively onto the balance of payments and not on prices. Other treatments are of course possible, but this one makes evaluation of fiscal and foreign trade implications of the policy changes quite direct.

The results are shown in tables 2.3 through 2.7. In table 2.3 we can observe that the impact on the fiscal and external balances of a general food subsidy would not be practically feasible—the trade deficit would almost double and the fiscal surplus would turn into a considerable deficit. These disequilibria result from the tremendous expansionary effect that a

Table 2.2
Daily per capita deficit in food expenditure (in 1975 pesos)

	Consumption		Deficit	
	Actual	Recommended	With margin	Without margin
Food processing (section 5)				
Peasants	3.0057	3.7349	0.7292	0.5833
Agricultural workers	3.1094	3.7349	0.6255	0.5004

Source: Encuesta Nacional de Ingresos y Gastos de los Hogares: 1977 (Secretaria de Programación y Presupuesto).

Table 2.3
Percentage change in savings

	Source		
Policy measure	Private savings	Foreign savings	Government savings
Income transfer	2.12	16.60	−59.70
Targeted price subsidy	0.95	9.52	−30.62
General price subsidy	8.56	82.33	−269.58

Table 2.4
Structure of savings

	Source			
Policy measure	Private savings	Foreign savings	Government savings	Total
Base solution	82.37	11.50	6.13	100
Income transfer	84.12	13.41	2.47	100
Targeted price subsidy	83.15	12.60	4.25	100
General price subsidies	89.42	20.97	10.39	100

Table 2.5
Percentage changes in production and employment of the nonagricultural sectors

	Sector						
Policy	Petroleum	Fertilizers	Food processing	Other industries	Services	Commerce	Total
Production							
Income transfer	1.82	0.04	3.19	1.77	2.42	2.65	1.99
Targeted price subsidy	0.76	0.02	2.54	0.68	0.90	1.24	0.89
General price subsidy	6.75	0.15	22.87	6.06	8.06	11.11	8.02
Employment							
Income transfer	1.82	0.04	3.18	1.77	2.42	2.65	
Targeted price subsidy	0.76	0.02	2.53	0.68	0.90	1.24	
General price subsidy	6.75	0.15	22.86	6.06	8.06	11.11	

Table 2.6
Percentage change in real incomes

	Class						
Policy	Peasants	Agricultural workers	Agricultural capitalists	Urban workers	Nonagricultural capitalists	Merchants	Urban marginals
Income transfer	17.10	17.34	0.0	2.01	2.30	2.65	2.40
Targeted price subsidy	7.68	7.93	0.0	0.87	1.04	1.25	1.10
General price subsidy	7.51	7.61	5.73	14.04	14.84	17.72	19.07

Table 2.7
Distribution of income by class

	Class							
Policy	Peasants	Agricultural workers	Agricultural capitalists	Urban workers	Nonagricultural capitalists	Merchants	Urban marginals	Total
Original	4.05	3.08	4.91	37.41	30.74	14.17	5.64	100
Income transfer	4.59	3.50	4.75	36.98	30.47	14.10	5.60	100
Targeted price subsidy	4.30	3.27	4.83	37.20	30.62	14.15	5.63	100
General price subsidy	3.81	2.90	4.54	37.34	30.93	14.60	5.88	100

general price subsidy would have (table 2.5). Although this policy measure generates the highest increases in the real incomes of the three poorest classes (peasants, agricultural workers, and urban marginals), it also creates large increments in the incomes of the wealthier classes (table 2.6). One could interpret these simulation results as a caricature of the well-known inefficiency and cost-ineffectiveness of using a general price subsidy to improve the living standards of the poor.

At the other end of the spectrum, we have the targeted price subsidy. Its impact on public and foreign savings is about one-ninth that of the general price subsidy. At the same time the increases in real incomes of the poor are about the same under the targeted and general subsidy programs (tables 2.3 and 2.6).

To underline the cost-ineffectiveness of a general subsidy, we can show how little it would decrease the food expenditure deficits for "reasonable" losses in government and foreign saving. Specifically, we ran another simulation in which the rate of the general subsidy was adjusted to make the decrease in government and foreign saving the same as for the targeted subsidy that eliminated the food expenditure deficits of peasants and agricultural workers. The reduced general subsidy made the deficits fall by only about 11 percent.

The advantage of income transfer over a targeted subsidy is that the positive impact on real income of the rural is more than double. However, the negative effect on government and foreign savings is also doubled. The savings loss results from the greater expansionary effect of the income transfer and the larger fiscal outlay required to generate the needed increment in food expenditure via higher income as opposed to a lower price.[12]

In addition to providing quantitative information to use in ranking policies, what these simulations also show is that any attempt to eliminate food consumption deficits by fiscal measures (even in the case of targeted policies that are assumed to be well aimed) will imply a considerable effort on the government's part. For example, in the case of the two targeted policy measures, government saving decreases by over 3.5 percent for each 1 percent increase in the real incomes of peasants and agricultural workers. The savings loss points to the need to accompany state food subsidy programs with policies to sustain government net revenue. In other words, the state cannot commit itself to substantially reduce poverty or problems associated with it (such as undernutrition) without running into macroeconomic disequilibria unless it is willing and able to transform itself into an effective redistributional machine.

Appendix: Detailed Description of the Model

Variables

p	producer price	Y	income
x	production	c	consumption
τ	markup rate	SG	governments savings
p'	consumer price	SF	foreign savings
E	total expenditure	SP	private savings

Parameters

g	government current expenditure	a	input–output coefficients
z	exports	w	nominal wage
m	competitive imports	l	employment coefficients
θ	subsistence consumption	I	investment
M	marginal propensity to consume	ds	change in stocks
p^*	guarantee price	pi	international price
s	propensity to save	q	direct tax rates
u	proportion of value added that goes to peasants	b	commerce margins
v	proportion of income that goes to urban marginals	e	exchange rate
t	net indirect tax rate	wg	government wages
mi	investment imports	TR	income transfer
mg	government imports	SUB	direct subsidy on final prices

Equations of the Model

Prices

$$p_j = (1 + t_j)(1 + \tau_j) \sum_{i=1}^{9} (p_i a_{ij} + w l_j)$$

$j = 3, \ldots, 8$, $i = 1, \ldots, 9$ (subscripts refer to sectors)

Sectoral Balances

$$x_i = \sum_{j=1}^{8} a_{ij} x_j + \sum_{k=1}^{7} c_{ik} + I_i + ds_i + g_i + z_i - m_i$$

$i, j = 1, 2, \ldots, 8$ (sectors), $k = 1, 2, \ldots, 7$ (income classes)

Consumer Demand Equations

$$c_{ik} = \theta_{ik} + (M_{ik}/p'_{ik})[E_k - \textstyle\sum_{i=1}^{7} p'_{ik}\theta_{ik}]$$

$i = 1, 2, \ldots, 7$ (sectors), $k = 1, 2, \ldots, 7$ (income classes)

Total Expenditure by Class

$$E_k = (1 - s_k)(1 - q_k)Y_k, \quad k = 1, 2, \ldots, 7 \text{ (income classes)}$$

Total Income by Classes

Peasants: $Y_1 = \sum_{i=1}^{2} (p_i - \sum_{j=1}^{9} p_j a_{ji})x_i u_i + TR_1$
Agricultural workers: $Y_2 = \sum_{i=1}^{2} wl_i x_i + TR_2$
Agricultural capitalists: $Y_3 = \sum_{i=1}^{2} [(1 - u_i)(p_i - \sum_{j=1}^{9} p_j a_{ji}) - wl_i]x_i$
Urban workers: $Y_4 = \sum_{i=3}^{8} wl_i x_i(1 - v_4)$ (for $i = 3$ and 4, $w = w_g$)
Urban capitalists: $Y_5 = \sum_{i=5}^{7} \tau_i(\sum_{j=1}^{9} p_j a_{ji} + wl_i)x_i(1 - v_5)$
Merchants: $Y_6 = \tau_8(\sum_{j=1}^{9} p_j a_{j8} + wl_8)x_8(1 - v_6)$
Urban marginals: $Y_7 = \sum_{j=4}^{6} [v_j/(1 - v_j)]Y_j + TR_7$

Final Prices

$$p'_{ik} = p_i + p_8 b_{i8} + SUB_{ik}$$

$i = 1, 2, \ldots, 7$ (sectors), $k = 1, 2, \ldots, 7$ (income classes)

Consumption of Commerce (Sector 8)

$$c_{8k} = \textstyle\sum_{i=1}^{7} c_{ik} b_{ik}, \quad k = 1, 2, \ldots, 7 \text{ (income classes)}$$

Government Savings

$$\begin{aligned} SG = {} & \textstyle\sum_{j=3}^{8} t_j(1 + \tau_j)(\sum_{i=1}^{9} p_i a_{ij} w l_j)x_j + \sum_{j=3}^{4} \tau_j(\sum_{i=1}^{9} p_i a_{ij} + wl_j)x_j \\ & + \textstyle\sum_{j=1}^{7} q_j Y_j - \{\sum_{j=1}^{8} [p_j - e(pi_j)]z_j + \sum_{j=1}^{2} (p_j^* - p_j)x_j + \sum_{j=1}^{8} p_j g_j \\ & + e(mg) + TR_1 + TR_2 + TR_7 + \textstyle\sum_{i=1}^{7} \sum_{k=1}^{7} SUB_{ik} c_{ik}\} \end{aligned}$$

Foreign Savings

$$SF = e[\textstyle\sum_{i=1}^{8} (pi_i)a_{9i}x_i + \sum_{i=1}^{8} (pi_i)m_i + mi + mg - \sum_{i=1}^{8} (pi_i z_i)]$$

Private Savings

$$SP = \sum_{k=1}^{7} Y_k(1 - q_k)s_k$$

Investment-Savings Balance

$$\sum_{i=1}^{8} p_i(ds_i + I_i) + e(mi) - (SG + SF + SP) = 0$$

Notes

Research originally supported by the Sistema Alimentario Mexicano. Bill Gibson collaborated in formulating and programming the model.

1. Since 1982, the year marking the end of the oil boom and the beginning of a long-standing economic crisis in Mexico, there is indirect and scattered evidence that the malnutrition problem has worsened, while the degrees of freedom for the government to pursue subsidy policies have been considerably reduced by restrictions on the public deficit established under stabilization programs agreed to with the IMF.

2. Lustig (1986) gives a detailed discussion of food subsidy programs in Mexico and their welfare impacts.

3. The criteria used to classify private income flows into these seven categories are set out in Lustig (1982b).

4. We ignore the realistic complication that marketable surpluses are likely to respond to price changes in the short run.

5. Jimenez and Roces (1981) and Ros (1980) provide econometric evidence in support of markup pricing in nonagricultural sectors in Mexico. A ceiling for the markup is defined by the international price measured in domestic currency plus the tariff. We effectively assume that internal markups are at their ceilings, although at any time there are likely to be sectors for which this hypothesis may not be true.

6. The key assumptions underlying the macroeconomics of the model have empirical support. As noted in note 5, econometric studies of Mexico strongly suggest that markup pricing and the presence of excess capacity characterize the industrial sectors. Wages are institutionally set in money terms periodically, and the real wage is an ex post outcome that depends on the current rate of inflation. Given the rate at which the Mexican labor force is growing compared to the increase in jobs, it is safe to assume that person-hours required to support a given level of economic activity will be forthcoming at the current wage.

7. The SAM was built using 1975 data because until very recently this was the last year for which an original input–output matrix for Mexico was available. For a

description of the data sources and methodology used to construct the SAM, see Lustig (1982b).

8. These deficits correspond to the food-processing sector of the model (sector 5). They were estimated from the 1977 Income and Expenditure Survey, which gave actual daily per capita expenditures by class on the model's three food categories (sectors 1, 2, and 5). These levels were compared to the Basic Recommended Basket of the National Institute of Nutrition, and the difference between the two was taken to be a physical deficit. To make them compatible with the model, the deficits were evaluated in 1975 prices with commerce margins taken away.

9. The implied transfers are 7,063 and 5,427 billion pesos for peasants and agricultural workers, respectively.

10. Required decreases in prices of processed foods were 26 percent for peasants and 27 percent for agricultural workers.

11. The general subsidy rate was set to give a 26 percent decrease in the prices for processed foods paid by all seven income classes.

12. This outcome is a consequence of the relative magnitudes of the marginal spending propensity and the demand price elasticity for processed food.

References

COPLAMAR. 1982. *Necesidades Esenciales en Mexico*. Mexico City: Siglo XXI.

Instituto Nacional de la Nutricion. 1979. *Segunda Encuesta Nacional de Alimentacion*. Mexico.

Jimenez, E., and Roces, C. 1981. "Precios y margenes de ganancia en la industria manufacturera mexicana." *Economia Mexicana*, no. 3: 183–251.

Lustig, N. 1980. "Distribucion del ingreso y consumo de alimentos en Mexico." *Demografia y Economia* 14, 42: 107–45.

Lustig, N. 1982a. "Distribucion del ingreso y consumo de alimentos: estructura, tendencias, y requerimientos distributivos al nivel nacional." *Demografia y Economia* 16, 50.

Lustig, N. 1982b. "Politicas de precios y subsidios del Sistema Alimentario Mexicano y distribucion del ingreso." SINE/SAM, Segundo Reporte. August.

Lustig, N. 1985. "Distribution of Income, Food Consumption, and the Fiscal Cost of Alternative Policy Measures." In P. Aspe and P. Sigmund (eds.), *The Political Economy of Income Distribution in Mexico*. New York: Holmes and Meier.

Lustig, N. 1986. "Food Subsidy Programs in Mexico." *Working Papers on Food Subsidies No. 3*. Washington: IFPRI.

Ros, J. 1980. "Pricing in the Mexican Manufacturing Sector." *Cambridge Journal of Economics* 4: 211–31

3 IS-FM Macroeconomics: General Equilibrium Linkages of the Food Market in Colombia

Juan Luis Londoño de la Cuesta

The original Latin American structuralists emphasized the historical constraints that agriculture imposes on long-run urban-industrial growth. Besides providing labor and savings to be transferred to urban activities, the primary sector also is a source of foreign exchange for machinery imports. In a well-known slogan, agriculture takes the place of a capital goods sector in many dependent economies.

Neostructuralists such as Taylor (1983) extend the idea that agriculture is a bottleneck for industrial development to the short run. They postulate that sectors differ in their adjustment mechanisms to disequilibria and that sectoral and macroeconomic imbalances are interrelated. Current transactions in one market enter into other sectors's excess demand functions, so that notional and effective demands are distinct along the lines suggested by Clower (1965). For example, agricultural supply bottlenecks can disturb savings-investment equilibrium, and the urban income distribution adjusts via forced saving to food price shifts.

In this paper we apply neostructuralist ideas to industry–agriculture interactions in Colombia. The analytical approach is developed in the first section, followed in section 3.2 by a description of relevant aspects of the economy set out in a social accounting matrix. Section 3.3 presents the main features of a CGE model for Colombia, and its results are summarized in section 3.4

3.1 An Analytical Outline

We begin by describing a small consistency model to examine the implications of distinct dynamic adjustment patterns across sectors. This illustrative model in practice will be expanded to deal with the policy issues addressed in section 3.4.[1]

The point of departure is to postulate, for an economy like Colombia's, the coexistence of sectors with different short-run reactions to excess demand. Due to the atomized nature of its producers, supply inelasticity, and auction market characteristics, the food sector has a typical flex-price market. Disequilibria are resolved mainly by movements in prices and not supplies. The urban-industrial sector, on the other hand, might be described as having a typical fix-price market featuring non-arms'-length relationships between customers and firms, an oligopolistic structure and persistent capacity underutilization. Its demand shifts lead to changes in capacity use, with weak effects on prices. Demand for both sectors comes from autonomous sources such as investment, exports, and public expenditure, as well as household consumption which depends on activity levels and the distribution of income.

On the basis of these hypotheses, the economy can be viewed through demand-supply balances in three markets: food, urban-industrial, and investment-savings (as a residual to define global equilibrium). Formally, we have two unknowns—the price of food P_a and industrial (or nonfood) output X_n—linked through three equations. An FM schedule describes the agricultural market, with a positive slope in the $X_n - P_a$ plane since higher industrial income leads to excess demand for food and therefore a greater equilibrium food price. The NN schedule for the industrial market can have a slope of either sign, depending on income effects as discussed in chapter 1. The IS schedule defining macroeconomic balance has a negative slope since increases in both P_a and X_n raise potential saving. For given investment demand, if one variable goes up, the other must fall.

Any two of these three schedules jointly determine macro equilibrium. For analogy with the IS-LM diagram that emphasizes the role of a financial flex-price market, we work with FM and IS, postponing a diagrammatic treatment to figure 3.1 in favor of presenting an algebraic resolution of the model here. Let the (absolute) slopes of the FM and IS curves, respectively, be equal to a and s. Also let G_g stand for autonomous expenditure associated with agricultural exports and public employees, G_e for autonomous expenditure from investment and industrial exports, and m for the propensity to consume out of urban income. A reduced form for the two-sector model is then

$$P_a = \frac{1}{1 - \mathrm{m}} \frac{1}{a - s}\left[G_e + \frac{G_g}{m} \right]$$

and

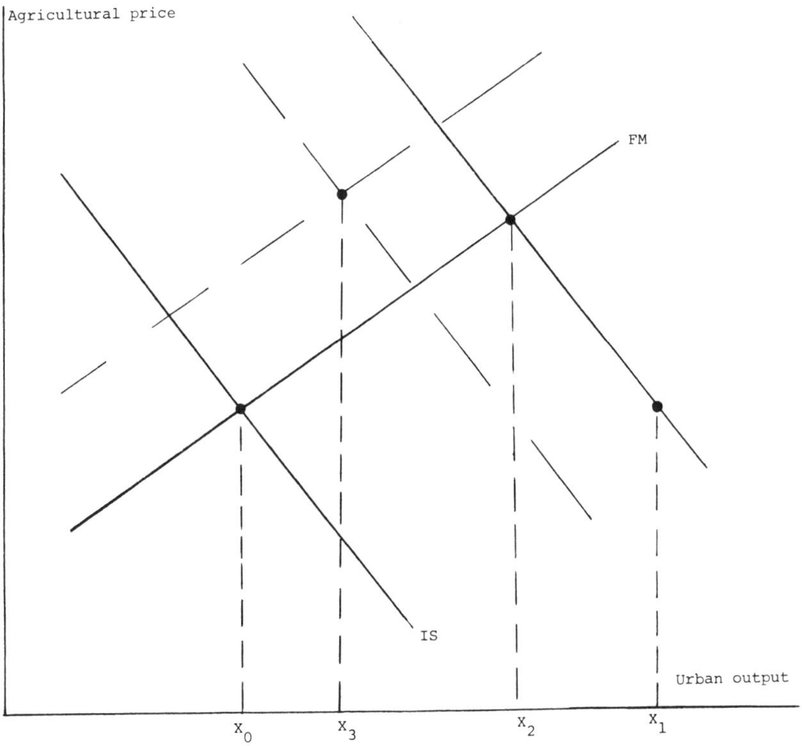

Figure 3.1
Diagrammatic presentation of the model

$$X_n = \frac{1}{1-m}\frac{a}{a-s}[G_e + G_g] + \frac{s}{a-s}\frac{G_g}{m}.$$

The lead term in both expressions is analagous to the usual multiplier, depending on savings leakages $1 - m$. In this model the multiplier also depends on the difference of slopes of the FM and IS schedules, $a - s$. The less elastic is food supply or the bigger is the macro spillover of food market disequilibrium, the more food prices will rise in response to an increase in autonomous spending.

A second observation is that there are significantly different effects of autonomous expenditure on goods from the two sectors. Investment (a component of G_e) is "specifically directed" to the industrial market, while food exports as a component of G_g are more "generally directed," affecting both the food price and overall savings. For the same nominal increments higher general expenditures are financed more through inflation and less through output expansion than specific expenditures. Different degrees of leakage toward the food market and savings explain these compositional effects.

Finally, the model's reduced form helps make precise a neostructuralist message: Macro adjustment in response to exogenous expenditure depends strongly on changes in the agricultural terms of trade. Food price changes appear as a basic transmission channel to amplify or diffuse autonomous demand impulses.

3.2 A Social Accounting Matrix for Colombia

Table 3.1 presents a social accounting matrix (SAM) for Colombia in 1980, expressed in millions of Colombian pesos (at an exchange rate of 48.03 pesos per dollar) of that year. The sectoral aggregation is designed to emphasize the connections between agriculture and the rest of the economy. We distinguish four productive sectors (coffee, agricultural raw materials, food production, and urban activity) and five social classes (rural laborers, peasants, landowners, urban wage earners, and capitalists) and use a simplified version of the external and public accounts.

There are three main points related to the production accounts in the SAM. First, if valued at purchasers's prices, agriculture accounts for 36 percent of GDP. Final food consumption is 26.4 percent of GDP. Both numbers signal the importance of the food sector in Colombia.

Second, urban and nonurban cost structures differ considerably. The import content is four times bigger in the urban sector than in agriculture. On the other hand, although intersectoral transactions between agriculture and the rest of the economy are almost equal (agriculture uses 57.375 millions of urban goods, while urban activity uses 57.337 of agricultural raw materials), the relative importance of this intermediate flow is twice as large for agriculture as the urban sector.

Third, the sectors have different demand structures. Agriculture, especially coffee, is externally oriented. Demand for urban products comes more from capital formation and the urban sector's own intermediate inputs. The import content of urban output is largely financed by agricultural exports, as the old structuralists pointed out.

Four aspects of the income distribution also are worth noting. First, nonlabor income is more important in agricultural than urban activity, due to landlords's rents (and also profits of urban capitalists in food processing and distribution), despite the higher employment intensity of agriculture. Second, at least one-quarter of food value added accrues to urban classes.

Table 3.1
Social accounting matrix for Colombia, 1980 (millions of pesos)

	Coffee	Raw materials	Food	Urban	Household consumption: Rural workers	Peas-ants	Land-lords	Salaried workers	Capital owners	Firms	Importers	Consump-tion imports	Exports	Govern-ment con-sumption	Govern-ment in-vestment	Indirect taxes	Direct taxes	Tariffs	Stocks change	Private in-vestment	Gross accu-mulation	Total
1. Coffee												116,793		422								117,215
2. Raw materials				57,337									29,268		855					5,914	6,769	93,374
3. Food					43,954	27,781	40,582	227,974	28,576			(5,527)	5,750	10,767					12,377		12,377	392,234
4. Urban	16,074	10,073	31,228	468,531	30,777	17,407	114,006	277,023	310,880			(42,676)	104,292	26,718	49,107				17,121	136,667	202,895	1,567,217
5. Rural workers	23,483	11,133	44,987																			79,603
6. Peasants	8,671	4,194	33,519																			46,384
7. Landlords	13,373	28,061	185,496																			226,930
8. Salaried workers	3,974	5,182	10,806	383,551										120,494								524,007
9a. Capitalists	3,123	26,307	70,093	177,657						91,074	39,619										407,873	
9b. Firms				240,597																		240,597
9c. Importers	204	796	1,502	20,236								10,975		579					59	5,268	5,327	39,619
10. Imports	1,626	6,341	11,963	133,826					1,692			29,879			2,541	9,257			5,796	45,077	60,130	247,998
11. Tariffs	149	581	1,096	20,527								7,351		448	218				666	12,749	13,633	43,785
12. Indirect taxes	46,538	663	1,544	64,955										967								114,667
13. Direct taxes							993	11,691	7,765	31,712												52,111
14. Revenues									1,802							114,667	52,111	43,785				212,365
15. Gross savings					4,873	1,196	71,349	7,319	57,245	117,811			(8,105)	49,429								301,117
16. Total	117,215	93,331	392,234	1,567,217	79,604	46,384	226,929	524,007	407,960	240,597	39,619		247,998	212,365	59,437	114,667	52,111	43,785	36,019	205,675	301,131	

Third, peasant participation in food producers's income is low. Peasants receive only 10 percent, and agricultural rentiers 54 percent of the total. Fourth, government employment accounts for almost a quarter of the total wage bill.

Savings and taxes stand out as important macro flows in the SAM. In 1980 the private savings surplus financed Colombia's fiscal deficit and external surplus. The private sector generated 80 percent of gross savings in that year, with the bulk coming from urban capitalists and rentiers since the saving rate from wage income is approximately 2 percent. Urban capitalists and rentiers have a similar saving rate, around 30 percent, but among the former savings originate largely from firms. Among households, rural groups have a saving propensity (21.9 percent) which exceeds the urban rate (16.9 percent).[2] Finally, direct taxes affect the different social groups unequally. Their effective rates are higher for urban than nonurban groups, due to taxation of firms. Among householders the highest tax rate is for urban wage earners.

3.3 A CGE Model for Colombia

The equations for the model are not presented in detail here.[3] However, they fall naturally into seven blocks, related to the arrangement of the accounts in the SAM.

The first block is made up of sectoral demand-supply balances, with final consumption goods provided only by the food and urban sectors, and capital goods by the raw materials and urban-industrial sectors.

The second block describes price formation. The urban sector is assumed to follow a markup pricing rule, based upon input costs (of labor, imported inputs, and agricultural raw materials). Flex-prices characterize the agricultural sectors. Freely varying agricultural prices (with respect to international prices for coffee and raw materials, and to national excess demand for food) imply that the total of agricultural profits (or "surplus") is a residual, determined by subtracting costs of national and imported inputs and wages from the agricultural sectors's gross incomes. All these hypotheses about price formation are consistent with empirical evidence in Colombia over the period 1945–80.

The third set of equations is made up of income distribution rules for the social groups. Employment of rural laborers is proportional to real agricultural production; their income follows from an institutionally determined nominal wage. The same procedure is followed for urban workers, whose income is calculated as the sum of their shares in each sector (including government). Incomes of peasants and rentiers come from their respective, fixed shares in the agricultural surplus. Overall profit income comes from production and margins on international trade. Firms retain a fixed proportion of the urban surplus. Capitalist households receive nonretained profits (after taxes) plus import margins.

Block four sets out expenditure allocations for the distinct social classes, based upon their savings rates and consumer behavior as modeled in linear expenditure systems. Consistent with Colombian institutions, consumer imports are assumed to be regulated by quotas.

The fifth block is devoted to effects of sectoral real exchange rates (the nominal rate deflated by appropriate price indexes) on foreign trade flows. Urban intermediate and private investment imports are assumed to respond to exchange rate changes, as are noncoffee exports.

The sixth block prescribes sectoral adjustment rules. As described in section 3.1, the key endogenous variables are urban-industrial capacity utilization and the market-clearing price for food products. Inventory and import changes respectively take care of short-run adjustment in the coffee and agricultural raw materials sectors.

Finally, the seventh block sums up savings flows to check on macro equilibrium. Saving of firms is made up of their retained earnings. Public income comes from direct taxes on households and firms, indirect taxes, and tariffs. Subtracting government expenditure gives public saving. External saving is the current account deficit, valued in national currency via the exchange rate. Exogenous adjustment terms are included in both the public and external balances, to account for flows the model omits.

The full model requires 98 parameters. Many are implicit in the SAM presentation of table 3.1, for example direct and indirect tax rates, tariffs and margins on imports, input–output coefficients, and distributive shares. Other parameters required information from outside the SAM, as follows:

Multiple information sources were used to estimate per capita remunerations and labor input coefficients. In Colombian pesos yearly wages were estimated as 59,119 for rural laborers, 107,545 for private urban wage earners, and 186,700 for public employees. These numbers are compatible with employment–output ratios (employment per million pesos production) of 4.0 in the agricultural sectors (7.7 for coffee, 3.4 for food, and 2.8 for raw materials), 3.5 for urban activity, and 3.7 for the public sector.

In the linear expenditure system "subsistence requirements" (or the constant terms) were based on minimal nutritional standards taken from poverty studies, international consumption patterns, and our own econometrics. Marginal budget shares were computed consistent with these data,

Table 3.2
Consumption and saving parameters

		Marginal propensities			Income elasticities		
	Committed expenditure	Food consumption	Urban consumption	Saving	Food	Urban	Cross price elasticity, *En*
Rural laborers	6252	0.383	0.532	0.084	0.69	1.38	−0.38
Peasants	3125	0.538	0.432	0.030	0.90	1.15	−0.15
Rentiers	51590	0.081	0.565	0.354	0.45	1.12	−0.12
Wage earners	11821	0.201	0.788	0.021	0.45	1.44	−0.44
Capitalists	97872	0.023	0.825	0.152	0.32	1.05	−0.05
Average	11821	0.136	0.727	0.138	0.46	1.22	−0.22

Note: Parameters are estimated econometrically for consistency.

and are presented in table 3.2. The average income elasticity of demand for food of 0.46 is low enough to generate, via price movements, strong income effects in the rest of the economy. The propensity to consume food declines with income, consistent with Engel's law, but there is a social class bias: The propensity is bigger for rural-based than urban groups. There are also important differences in saving patterns of the different social classes. Rural groups in general have higher saving rates, with agricultural rentiers having the highest rate and urban workers the lowest.

External trade parameters are consistent with various estimates for Colombia and our own work. The export price elasticities are 0.6 for noncoffee agricultural products and 0.3 for urban goods. The import demand for capital goods has an elasticity of -0.8. For intermediate consumption we estimated a function allowing some substitution between imports and national goods.[4] The short-run external parameters are consistent with the Marshall-Lerner conditions.

3.4 Simulation Results

The model was used to simulate the effects of changes in the most important exogenous variables and distributional parameters. We first analyze the effects of autonomous expenditures on economic activity, following section 3.1 in distinguishing sectoral impacts of "specific" and "general" outlays. Second, we take up food market disturbances from supply shocks and external trade. Third, the impacts of changes in distributional parameters (wages and the exchange rate) are discussed. Fourth, effects of distinct fiscal packages on economic activity and the income distribution are explored. Finally, the model is used to analyze the probable effects of economic policies followed during the first part of the 1980s in Colombia.

Changes in Autonomous Expenditures

Traditional Keynesian macroeconomics distinguishes autonomous and endogenous components of demand. The former are characterized by relative independence from income (and financial constraints) in the short run––investment, public spending, and exports are usually handled in this fashion. Endogenous demands—often treated in the form of leakages such as savings flows, imports, and taxes—are assumed to depend strongly on income.

If the entire economy has markup pricing and flexible supply, and savings is a mere by-product of output changes, such distinctions among final demand components are adequate. However, if there are flex-prices, fixed supplies, and other mechanisms for saving generation, the analysis of autonomous expenditure becomes more complex. Its impacts depend on spillovers among markets, and therefore on its sectoral breakdown.

Two types of autonomous spending should be distinguished. The first has demand which is circumscribed, in the first instance, to a given market; we call it *specific expenditure*. Industrial exports and demand for urban goods for capital accumulation are specific urban expenditures; food exports and inventory changes are specific rural expenditures. *General expenditures* directly generate demand for all sectors. Coffee income, rural exports other than food, and current public outlays are the most important examples for Colombia. We can analyze the likely effects of changes in the two types of autonomous spending, following the discussion in section 3.1.

Specific urban expenditure generates an increase in nominal aggregate demand, shifting the IS locus in figure 3.1 to the right. For a given agricultural price, this demand change would expand urban activity from X_0 to X_1. However, with higher urban output, the food market is in disequilibrium. Its excess demand will be rationed by price increases. Through spillovers in consumer demand, urban activity is cut back to X_2. The slope of the FM schedule determines the sectoral breakdown of the demand increase between the two markets and, accordingly, its impacts on price increases and urban capacity utilization. The more inelastic the food supply, the steeper is FM.

Higher general expenditure affects the food market through two channels. Some proportion of the income it generates may be saved (coffee growers's saving is a good example in the Colombian case), implying reduced aggregate demand or a smaller displacement of the IS schedule toward the right (the dashed line in figure 3.1). Another proportion is directed toward food consumption, shifting the FM curve up (the other dashed line). This displacement generates income effects from the food market that constrain urban demand. The general equilibrium urban expansion is only from X_0 to X_3. The saving and food expenditure components of incomes associated with autonomous expenditures weaken their effect on urban activity.

Our main empirical results for both types of autonomous spending appear in tables 3.3 through 3.6. The most important observation they suggest is that there is an appreciable quantitative difference between impacts of specific and general spending on output, price increases, and the distribution of consumption by class.

Table 3.3
Autonomous expenditure multipliers

	Multipliers		
	Of nominal income	Of real income	Of urban income
Urban autonomous expenditures			
Urban exports	2.30	1.92	1.92
Private investment	1.77	1.49	1.49
Public investment	1.94	1.64	1.64
General autonomous expenditures			
Coffee exports			
Prices	3.04	1.21	1.21
Quantum	3.22	2.40	1.40
Public consumption	3.41	1.58	1.58

Specific urban expenditures stimulate more expansion of real activity, with income generation biased toward urban groups. Rural expenditures are associated with inflationary pressure and forced saving, biasing the income distribution and real consumption toward recipients of the agricultural surplus. General expenditures give results intermediate between these two extremes, depending on their demand composition.

General expenditures have higher *nominal* income multipliers than specific urban expenditures (table 3.3, column 1) because they increase food and (through the markup) urban prices. Real multipliers are lower than the nominal ones, taking values not far from two. The multiplier effect of an autonomous expenditure increase depends inversely on the extent of leakages it creates. Autonomous spending on urban goods has the biggest real multiplier, despite leakages through indirect taxes and imports. Public and private investment multipliers are relatively low, because of Colombian capital formation's high import content. Agricultural exports also do not generate much urban demand because of the sector's high savings rates from surplus income, its system of taxation (especially for coffee), and rural laborers's demand for food.

With regard to prices, general expenditures are more inflationary than higher autonomous outlays for urban goods. However, even specific urban expenditure drives up prices by inducing excess demand for food.

Table 3.4 shows how the financial repercussions of the types of expenditure differ. Higher nominal spending directed toward the food sector is financed basically through forced saving by households, with real spending

Table 3.4
Marginal savings generation (percentage shares)

	Specific urban expenditures				General expenditures			Specific rural expenditures		
	En	*In*	*Ip*	*Io*	*Ec*(*q*)	*Ec*(*p*)	*G*	*Ea*	*Ma*	*Za*
1. Firms	21.9	21.9	16.8	18.4	9.7	8.2	18.0	8.9	(7.9)	8.9)
2. External sector	34.4	34.4	44.1	44.8	16.5	12.9	29.9	13.9	(24.6)	14.0
3. Public sector	25.5	25.5	24.7	21.5	51.8	50.0	23.5	12.9	(4.0)	12.9
4. Households	18.2	18.2	14.3	15.3	22.1	28.9	28.6	64.3	(63.5)	64.2
Peasants	0.1	0.1	0.1	0.1	0.4	0.8	0.3	0.8	(0.9)	0.8
Laborers	(0.2)	(0.2)	(0.1)	(0.1)	1.5	(0.2)	(0.04)	(1.2)	1.2	(1.2)
Rentiers	8.3	8.3	6.4	7.0	15.0	23.7	18.5	58.0	(58.7)	58.0
Urban workers	1.1	1.1	0.9	0.9	0.3	—	2.0	(1.6)	1.7	(1.6)
Capitalists	8.8	8.8	7.1	7.4	4.9	4.4	8.3	8.2	(6.9)	8.2
5. Total capital	30.7	30.7	23.9	25.8	14.6	12.6	26.3	17.1	14.8	17.1
Total	100	100	100	100	100	100	100	100	100	100

Note: *En* = industrial exports, *In* = urban investment, *Ip* = private investment, *Io* = public investment, *Ec*(*q*) = coffee exports (quantum increase), *Ec*(*p*) = coffee exports (price increase), *G* = public consumption, *Ea* = food exports, *Ma* = food imports, and *Za* = food inventories change.

Table 3.5
Distribution of marginal nominal income changes (percentage shares)

		Specific urban expenditures				General expenditures			Specific rural expenditures		
	Initial *Dbn*	*En*	*In*	*Ip*	*Io*	*G*	*Ec(p)*	*Ec(q)*	*Ma*	*Ea*	*Za*
Peasants	3.6	2.9	2.9	2.9	2.8	4.0	18.4	8.9	10.9	10.5	10.7
Laborers	6.2	0.0	0.0	0.0	0.0	0.0	0.0	13.1	0.0	0.0	0.0
Rentiers	17.7	15.9	15.9	15.9	15.9	22.1	44.5	32.0	60.4	58.4	59.1
Wage workers	40.9	43.8	43.8	43.8	43.8	51.0	16.9	22.8	4.7	9.1	8.5
Capitalists	31.6	37.4	37.4	37.4	37.4	22.9	20.3	23.2	20.0	22.0	21.7
Total	100	100	100	100	100	100	100	100	100	100	100

Note: For an explanation of symbols, see table 3.4.

power transferred from rural and urban workers toward recipients of the agricultural surplus. Increased general expenditures are financed both by higher real output and forced saving. They are more inflationary and less expansionary than urban expenditures, with a bigger increment in household saving (especially from rentiers) and less of a trade deficit. Policy changes can affect these outcomes in various ways. If coffee exports were strongly taxed, a high level of public saving would be the dominant result. Higher public consumption is financed mainly through saving from capitalists and rentiers.

Changes in the income distribution and consumption levels are consistent with these financial shifts. Toward the left of table 3.5, one can see that urban expenditures raise the income shares of urban workers and capitalists, especially the latter. Toward the right, higher rural expenditures bias the income distribution toward surplus recipients, especially rentiers. Public consumption preferentially benefits urban wage earners and, with less impact, rentiers. If higher international coffee prices are transmitted to internal prices, rentiers and peasants gain. With higher coffee income from new production (labeled a "quantum effect" in the tables), rural and urban workers benefit, the latter through a multiplier increase in demand.

As a rough measure of welfare, real consumption changes of the various groups are shown in table 3.6. Rural laborers, the only class with a fixed nominal income, are negatively affected by urban expansion (table 3.6, second row). Specific urban expenditures benefit all other classes, although the capitalists's relative consumption share declines. Rural groups benefit from spending packages that induce higher food prices. Agricultural exports shift real consumption from wage earners toward rentiers. The latter receive double benefits—greater nominal income from exports and the rents stemming from higher food prices. When increased coffee income comes from higher prices, urban workers's consumption may decline absolutely to permit higher rural demand. Finally, autonomous expenditures on food, by reducing the available marketed surplus, play an essentially redistributive role. They transfer real spending power from urban consumers to rural producers.

Analysis of Food Supply

The results just discussed suggest that forced saving via changes in food prices plays a substantial role in mediating exogenous shocks to the macroeconomic system—food availability strongly influences macro equilibrium. For this reason we simulated changes in distinct exogenous variables that

Table 3.6
Changes and distribution of marginal real consumption

		Specific expenditures								General expenditures					
	Initial	*En*		*In*		*Ip*		*Ig*		*G*		*Ec*(*p*)		Ec(*q*)	
	1	1	2	1	2	1	2	1	2	1	2	1	2	1	2
Peasants	4.0	4.2	1.0	1.8	0.8	1.9	0.6	2.1	0.2	2.8	1.5	31.5	6.3	12.5	2.5
Laborers	6.7	(3.7)	(0.5)	(0.1)	0	(7.7)	(1.4)	(4.3)	(0.3)	(5.9)	(1.9)	(6.9)	(0.8)	17.0	2.1
Rentiers	13.8	12.5	0.9	12.3	1.6	13.4	1.2	11.2	0.3	20.3	3.1	52.6	3.1	32.4	1.9
Wage	45.1	42.8	0.9	42.4	1.7	45.7	1.3	50.2	0.4	53.3	2.5	(6.0)	(0.1)	5.3	0.1
Capital	30.4	44.2	1.4	43.5	2.6	46.7	1.9	40.9	0.5	29.5	2.1	28.8	0.8	32.8	0.9
Total	100.0	100.0		100.0		100.0		100.0		100.0		100.0		100.0	

Note: For an explanation of symbols, see table 3.4. Under column 1 appears the distribution of marginal real consumption among social classes, and under column 2 appears the percentage change in real consumption affect the food market in a positive or negative way. Table 3.7 synthesizes that main outcomes of food supply increases (production and imports) and decreases (crop crisis, exports, and inventory accumulation).

The principal result is that a strong positive link between output in the urban-industrial and food sectors goes together with distributive conflict between urban and rural groups. Demand inelasticity of food consumption is the key to the issue. Given Colombia's income level—and its associated significant share of food in household consumption—food price increases create an income effect strong enough to shrink effective demand for urban goods. From this point of view increasing the food supply is an essential condition for sustained urban output growth.

Food demand inelasticity has two further important implications. First, for given effective demand, a greater food supply will reduce rural incomes. Second, large relative price fluctuations and induced distributional shifts are required for adjustment of macro equilibrium to shocks. Strong dependence of growth, inflation, and distribution on flex-prices in the food market appears to be the Colombian rule.

To follow through these linkages in detail, the first step is to verify empirically the complementarity between urban and food production. The bottom rows of table 3.7 show that a 10 percent fall in food production causes a 2.4 percent decline in urban output and a 25.5 percent increase in the food price. Higher food output thus stimulates urban activity, with a multiplier comparable to that of private investment.

Compositional effects enter via differences in the source of food supply. Rather than increasing effective demand as does higher food production, food imports hold it down. An import increase amounting to 10 percent of household consumption would cut prices as much as 26 percent but lead urban output to fall by 2 percent. From a macroeconomic perspective extra food imports represent an excess of foreign saving that leads to a fall in global demand. Other sources of saving must decline—rural savings flows fall along with agricultural prices (and surpluses), while urban savings is cut back by reduced output.

Finally, changes in food supply have big distributional impacts. A 10 percent crop loss leads to a more than proportional decrease in consumption of groups not linked to the agricultural surplus (fourth column of table 3.7): Urban and rural workers's consumption levels fall respectively by 12.1 and 14.7 percent. Higher food imports in the model have effects that recall nineteenth-century discussions in Britain about repeal of the Corn Laws. Extra foreign purchases amounting to 10 percent of initial household demand lead rentiers's real consumption to decline by 19.4 percent. Real

Table 3.7
The impact of changes in food supplies

		Increased supply		Decreased supply		
	Basic run	Production	Imports	Crop crisis	Exports	Inventory accumulation
Income share (%)						
Peasants	3.6	3.3	3.0	4.1	4.3	3.7
Laborers	6.2	6.6	8.2	5.7	6.1	6.1
Rentiers	17.7	16.0	14.1	20.5	16.6	18.3
Waged	40.9	42.0	42.7	38.9	40.6	40.4
Capitalists	31.6	32.0	31.9	30.8	32.4	31.4
Total	100.0	100.0	100.0	100.0	100.0	100.0
Real consumption (1980 = 100)	100.0	106.2	100.9	95.1	100.4	100.0
Peasants	100.0	98.8	90.7	102.4	108.9	101.8
Laborers	100.0	113.1	113.7	85.3	89.9	97.7
Rentiers	100.0	92.3	80.6	113.0	118.7	103.8
Waged	100.0	113.6	108.7	87.9	93.3	98.6
Capitalists	100.0	100.9	97.1	98.7	103.7	100.7
Savings (1980 = 100)	100.0	100.0	100.0	100.0	100.0	100.0
External	(100.0)	(57.3)	292.3	(170.3)	(433.5)	(89.0)
Public	100.0	103.2	97.5	94.4	108.0	101.6
Firms	100.0	101.3	98.0	97.6	102.3	100.5

Table 3.7 (continued)

		Increased supply		Decreased supply		
	Basic run	Production	Imports	Crop crisis	Exports	Inventory accumulation
Households	100.0	95.4	86.3	107.8	113.8	102.8
Peasants	100.0	90.6	78.0	115.7	121.7	104.3
Laborers	100.0	112.3	107.8	82.6	92.3	98.5
Rentiers	100.0	89.1	74.9	118.5	124.8	105.0
Waged	100.0	107.6	106.9	86.0	93.5	98.7
Capital	100.0	100.5	96.3	99.2	104.4	100.9
Endogenous variables (1980 = 100)						
Food prices	100.0	84.2	74.0	125.5	120.3	104.2
Urban production	100.0	101.3	98.0	97.5	102.3	99.5

Note: The exercise simulates a 10 percent change in global food supply. In the case of stock change (as in cattle), the exercise supposes a 50 percent change. Notice that nominal saving changes only when some factor of the I-S identity shifts (e.g., stock changes).

wages rise enough in response to food price declines to increase real consumption of both groups of wage earners, even though urban output and employment decline.

The question of political economy that these results pose is how strongly food producers may oppose increases in food supply if they recognize the threat it represents to their real income.

Shifts in Distributional Parameters

The solution is strongly influenced by two key nominal prices—the exchange rate and the money wage. Both are determined outside the model by institutional forces; they can be varied exogenously to explore how macroeconomic equilibrium shifts. Table 3.8 shows the model's responses to 10 percent increases in both parameters.

One way of looking at how the wage and exchange rate affect the system is via the saving-investment balance. Nominal devaluation and wage increases raise the price of capital goods, leading ex ante to a shortfall of saving below nominal investment demand. However, on the saving side, devaluation biases the distribution toward classes with high saving propensities so that real consumption declines; wage increases have the opposite effect. The changes in overall saving dominate the outcomes, so that devaluation is usually contractionary while wage increases raise output. However, these results can be affected by government financial decisions. For example, funding a wage increase for public employees with debt might reduce distributional conflict by increasing the level of economic activity.

For detailed analysis we begin with devaluation. A 10 percent increase in the exchange rate raises the cost of investment by about 1 percent of GDP, contracting the real rate of capital accumulation in the long run. In a shorter time frame, activity falls due to the saving response.

The economy generates additional saving through several channels. Devaluation makes export values go up in local currency terms. There is a windfall gain for high-saving rentier classes, leading overall saving to rise by 0.2 percent of GDP. On the other hand, imports fall, causing a current-account improvement (or loss of foreign saving) of 0.3 percent of GDP. The biggest beneficiary is the public sector, with a saving increase of 1.2 percent of GDP in two major components. The first (if the exchange rate increase is not passed through into higher domestic prices) stems from profits that the National Coffee Fund makes by buying cheap at the national price from growers and selling dear at the border price (external

Table 3.8
Changes in distributional parameters

		Devaluation					Urban wages		Rural wages
	Basic run	1	2	3	4	5	6	7	8
Income distribution									
Peasants	3.6	3.5	3.5	3.5	3.5	3.7	3.7	3.5	3.5
Laborers	6.2	6.3	6.2	6.2	6.2	6.1	5.8	5.8	6.8
Rentiers	17.7	17.4	17.5	17.5	17.5	17.9	17.4	17.4	17.4
Wages	40.9	40.8	40.2	40.2	40.2	39.9	42.1	41.9	40.8
Capital	31.6	32.0	32.5	32.6	32.6	32.4	31.2	30.9	31.5
Real consumption	100.0	97.6	98.9	99.0	9.0	99.8	101.4	101.1	100.1
Peasants	100.0	96.8	97.2	97.2	97.2	103.5	98.0	98.1	96.7
Laborers	100.0	99.5	99.1	99.0	99.0	98.2	93.7	95.5	109.1
Rentiers	100.0	95.6	97.8	97.8	97.9	100.8	99.9	99.6	98.4
Wages	100.0	97.8	98.8	97.8	97.9	97.8	104.2	104.0	99.6
Capital	100.0	98.0	101.2	101.3	101.3	102.1	100.1	99.6	100.2
Savings	100.0	101.9	104.2	105.1	105.1	105.1	104.2	104.2	100.0
External	(100)	15.9	(216.5)	(191.5)	(192.1)	(171.3)	(146.2)	(165.7)	(96.6)
Public	100.0	101.1	136.2	137.4	137.4	125.5	95.8	117.8	100.3
Firms'	100.0	98.3	101.7	101.7	101.7	102.5	107.9	100.7	100.1

Households	100.0	98.6	101.5	101.5	101.5	103.8	106.1	105.8	99.6
Peasant	100.0	96.2	97.7	97.7	97.7	105.9	104.5	104.0	96.7
Laborer	100.0	100.5	100.1	100.1	100.1	99.6	97.4	97.6	114.2
Rentier	100.0	96.6	99.8	99.8	99.8	103.6	106.3	105.7	98.2
Wages	100.0	98.8	99.0	99.0	99.0	99.2	113.1	112.4	99.6
Capital	100.0	100.5	104.1	104.2	104.2	105.1	106.5	105.8	100.2
Final variables									
Urban production	100.0	98.3	98.8	98.9	98.9	99.6	101.5	100.7	100.1
Food prices	100.0	98.8	99.6	99.7	99.7	101.1	106.9	106.5	100.1
Urban prices	100.0	102.8	102.8	102.8	102.8	102.8	106.2	106.2	101.0
Price index	100.0	100.1	101.4	101.5	101.5	102.1	106.5	106.4	100.5
Devaluation rents									
Coffee's fund	—	—	0.8	0.8	—	—	—	—	—
Capitalists	—	—	0.5	0.5	0.5	0.5	—	—	—
Rentiers	—	—	0.3	0.3	0.3	0.3	—	—	—
Food	—	—	0.1	0.1	0.1	0.1	—	—	—
Raw materials	—	—	0.2	0.2	0.2	0.2	—	—	—
Substitution	—	—	—	—	0.1	0.1	—	—	—

Note: The exercise simulates the effects of a 10 percent change in certain parameters on base general equilibrium. There are eight types of exercises: (1) pure effect of costs (as an external shock); (2) pure effect of costs and exports; (3) pure effect of costs, exports, and capital goods substitution; (4) pure effect of costs, exports, and capital goods and intermediate goods substitution; (5) pure effect of costs, exports, capital goods and intermediate goods substitution, and transfer of devaluation to internal coffee prices; (6) general increase of urban wages (public wages financed through fiscal deficit); (7) general increase of urban wages (with budget restrictions); and (8) rural wage increase.

price times the exchange rate). Its income rises by 0.7 percent of GDP. Other indirect tax and tariff collections add 0.5 percent.

Along with smaller effects these changes lead to a potential surplus of saving over investment. This disequilibrium is eliminated in the new solution (column 4 in table 3.8) by reduced economic activity, along with higher nonfood prices due to higher import costs, lower household consumption, a more regressive income distribution, and improvement in the public sector balance.

Columns 1 through 3 in the table split devaluation's overall effects into cost and quantity (or substitution) components. The latter make exchange rate increases less contractionary but more inflationary. Column 5 shows what happens when the National Coffee Fund's extra income from higher local currency export sales is dissipated into a higher coffee producers's price. The outcome, which has occurred repeatedly in Colombian economic history, is less recession but sharper price increases throughout the system.

As with devaluation a 10 percent urban wage increase (column 6 of table 3.8) requires higher saving of about 1 percent of GDP. However, the additional requirement is due not only to the higher cost of capital goods but also to a fall in potential saving as the income distribution shifts toward wage earners with high marginal propensities to consume. Prices go up for two reasons: Urban firms transfer their wage cost increases to higher prices via the markup, and food prices rise because of demand pressure. The final real wage increase is only 62 percent of the initial nominal wage jump.

In the new equilibrium aggregate saving increases occur through two main channels. Urban output expands by 1.7 percent in response to workers's consumption demands. The extra profits account for 23 percent of the required finance. The rest comes from increased rural surpluses as food prices rise.

Column 7 shows that expansion is restrained if the public sector cannot meet higher wage demands. With less stimulus to growth, nongovernment wage increases become a more strictly redistributive change. The same observation applies even more strongly to rural wage increases (column 8). The impact is almost neutral with respect to rural consumption of urban goods. Increased food demand by workers is offset by lower saving from rentiers. Food prices adjust to one disequilibrium, and urban activity to the other. To a small extent the rest of society underwrites higher rural workers's consumption.

These outcomes are magnified if partial wage indexation to price increases is added to the specification. The real effects of demand shocks on wage earnings are countered at the cost of faster inflation. Indexation adds to inflationary pressures when there is an external food supply shock, and can underlie explosive price increases when food production falls. This model result may be relevant to periods like 1973–77 and 1979–80 in Colombia when food supply shortfalls together with distributional inflexibility led to sharp bursts of inflation.

The Political Economy of Fiscal Deficit Reduction

Typically economic stabilization programs call for reduction of the fiscal deficit. The different ways in which this goal can be pursued—expenditure and/or public investment cuts, tax and/or tariff increases, higher public enterprise prices, and so on—can have diverse macroeconomic and distributional effects. Table 3.9 illustrates the implications of different strategies aimed at reducing the public deficit by 2.1 percent of GDP, the target in the 1985 stabilization program in Colombia.

The table shows that all approaches cause slower output growth. However, by immediately reducing the volume of production upon which indirect taxes are based, expenditure and investment cuts fail to reach the target increase in public saving. They are far more contractionary than higher tax (compare the first two columns with the latter three).

A second point is that as a strategy to reduce the external deficit, fiscal tightness acts mostly by reducing intermediate imports for urban production. The linkage is weak, implying that if external adjustment is to be attained by fiscal measures alone, enormous sacrifices in the level of economic activity might be required.

Third, distributive effects differ. Expenditure reductions work by redistributing from the private to the public sector a *reduced* saving total because of their contractionary effect on activity. Higher indirect taxes or tariffs redistribute an *increased* nominal level of savings because they drive up prices. Direct taxes operate on a stable level of savings.

One implication is that expenditure cuts are highly contractionary. With indirect taxes, consumption is held down by price rationing as well as real output losses. Income taxes reduce household incomes and firms's retained earnings directly. Since total savings are not much affected, direct taxes are a more purely redistributive tool.

Finally, the classes are affected in different manners. Direct taxes mostly hit capitalists, especially at the level of firms's income. Wage earners suffer less recession than with other measures, and agricultural surpluses are less affected by falling food prices. Expenditure cuts hit employment directly and induce food price decreases via reduced demand. Capitalists are the

Table 3.9
Effects of attempted fiscal adjustment under alternative policies (desired deficit reduction = 2.1 percent of GDP)

	Fiscal strategies[a]				
	Total expenditure cut	Investment cut	Direct taxes increase	Tariffs increase	Indirect taxes increase
Effects on savings (as a proportion of GDP)					
Public savings desired	2.1	2.1	2.1	2.1	2.1
Public savings obtained[b]	1.1	(0.6)	1.8	1.9	1.7
New savings generated	(0.1)	(2.8)	—	(1.0)	0.4
Savings redistribution among institutions	1.2	2.2	1.8	0.9	1.3
Firms	0.4	0.5	1.0	0.1	0.3
External sector	0.3	1.3	0.4	0.6	0.7
Households	0.5	0.4	0.4	0.2	0.3
Capitalists	0.3	0.2	0.2	—	0.1
Rentiers	0.2	0.2	0.2	0.2	0.2
Workers	—	—	—	—	—
Global effects (percent change)					
GDP	(3.0)	(4.0)	(2.0)	(2.1)	(2.5)
Urban production	(5.2)	(6.7)	(3.4)	(3.6)	(4.2)
Household consumption	(4.0)	(3.4)	(3.0)	(2.9)	(4.0)

a. Five alternative extreme policies for fiscal deficit reduction are evaluated in order to identify their differences.
b. Desired savings could have not been obtained. By affecting aggregate demand and economic growth, the fisal strategies affect taxing capacity.

social group touched the least by higher tariffs because their impacts spread over the whole economy.

Some Recent Macroeconomic Scenarios

Macroeconomic policy in Colombia has usually been guided by highly aggregative models of an orthodox hue. Supply limitations and intersectoral complications have been conspicuously lacking. The increasing volatility of the external sector since the 1970s has led policymakers to concentrate on tuning the fiscal balance and real exchange rate. Public investment, the most flexible component of state spending, has been used to compensate for external fluctuations. The real exchange rate has oscillated strongly, depending on the economic authorities's changing perceptions of the scarcity or abundance of foreign exchange. Both investment and exchange rate movements have deeply affected the distributional structure, and hence effective demand. The outcomes have included entirely unexpected changes in prices and quantities in the economy.

Even if our CGE model cannot capture the complexity of all factors underlying the formulation and outcome of demand management policies, it can help clarify the main linkages. For that reason, we have simulated three recent macro scenarios for Colombia, in which distinct types of fiscal policies have been used to try to stabilize external shocks.

In the 1976–82 coffee cycle, public finance management (mainly through changes in public investment) played an active countercyclical role. It was used to counter expansion during the initial boom and to add to demand in the later slowdown or "destorcida" period. In 1983–85 policy concentrated on attempts to use fiscal instruments for macro stimulation of the external sector. The real exchange rate appreciated in the first two periods, and substantially depreciated during the last.

We begin with the 1976–79 coffee boom. The model's simulation of this period appears in the second column of table 3.10. The exercise underlines the differences between specific and general public expenditures as discussed above.

During the initial years of the boom, public investment was cut to offset a sharp increase in growers's income (due to a jump in world market coffee prices caused by frost in Brazil). The policy neither held down inflation nor did it support urban economic growth. It relieved pressure in the food market only insofar as it reduced urban incomes.

In the boom period the fiscal position improved because of expenditure reductions and higher coffee taxes. With increased saving from the public

Table 3.10
Macroeconomic policy scenarios

	Basic run	Coffee boom	Coffee de-boom 1	2	3	4	5
Income distribution							
Peasants	3.6	3.8	3.2	3.3	3.2	3.3	3.3
Laborers	6.2	6.2	6.4	6.4	6.4	6.4	6.4
Rentiers	17.7	18.1	16.9	17.4	16.9	17.5	17.5
Wage workers	40.9	40.5	41.6	41.8	41.5	42.0	42.0
Capitalists	31.6	31.3	31.9	31.2	31.9	30.8	30.9
Real consumption	100.0	99.7	98.3	100.8	98.1	100.7	101.2
Peasants	100.0	105.9	7.1	91.3	86.9	91.2	91.5
Laborers	100.0	99.8	101.7	103.2	101.9	103.3	103.0
Rentiers	100.0	102.1	93.9	99.5	93.7	99.3	99.8
Wage workers	100.0	98.8	100.1	103.2	99.2	103.0	103.5
Capitalists	100.0	99.1	98.4	98.8	98.2	98.6	99.4
Savings	100.0	96.1	100.0	92.4	100.8	93.1	95.1
External	100.0	282.8	158.2	222.7	201.2	261.4	293.5
Public	100.0	105.8	76.3	26.4	76.1	26.4	29.0
Firms'	100.0	98.6	98.4	95.3	97.9	94.9	95.9
Households	100.0	100.9	95.3	95.5	95.1	95.3	96.0
Peasants	100.0	107.0	83.6	87.0	83.4	86.9	87.4
Laborers	100.0	83.4	101.1	100.9	101.2	101.0	100.8
Rentiers	100.0	102.5	92.4	95.5	87.9	95.2	95.8
Wage workers	100.0	98.4	99.6	100.5	99.2	100.2	101.0
Capitalists	100.0	99.1	98.2	94.5	98.0	94.4	95.2
Final variables							
Urban production	100.0	100.4	98.3	99.5	97.8	99.1	100.1
Price index	100.0	99.1	98.7	96.6	98.6	96.5	96.7
Food prices	100.0	98.6	97.0	97.6	96.8	97.4	97.9

Note: We isolate the distinct components of the de-boom period as shown: (1) coffee de-boom, (2) coffee de-boom plus appreciation, (3) coffee de-boom plus imports liberation, (4) coffee de-boom plus imports liberation plus appreciation, and (5) coffee de-boom plus imports liberation plus appreciation plus public expenditure.

sector and rural peasants and rentiers, saving from urban classes had to decline via stagnation of their economic activity and shifts in relative prices against them. After 1978 in the destorcida period, food supply increased and expenditure policy was less restrictive. Urban activity recovered, and the distributional biases of 1976–77 reversed. These outcomes parallel the 1986 coffee boom, during which noncontractionary fiscal policy and a favorable food supply situation led to a situation with low inflation and fast growth.

Columns 1 through 5 under the "coffee de-boom" heading in table 3.10 allow us to evaluate the impacts of several macroeconomic factors during 1978–82: reduction in coffee receipts, liberalization of import control policies, appreciation of the currency, and expansion of public expenditure.

The fall in coffee prices after the boom, partially transmitted to producers (15 percent in real terms between 1980 and 1982), had two major macro effects shown in column 1. First, a rise in external savings as the trade deficit widened *might* have been offset by lower savings from other parts of the economy such as firms, households, or the public sector. In practice, however, the excess saving was eliminated by a 1.7 percent decline in urban activity which also led to slower food price inflation. Real incomes of rural groups fell, while deflation offset the decline in output in allowing urban workers to improve their distributional position.

Liberalization of urban imports (in the magnitude that actually occurred in 1980–82) provided extra foreign saving which was offset by urban contraction (column 3). The combined effects of lower coffee prices and liberalization caused GDP to fall by 2.2 percent, according to the model. The offsetting forces were exchange appreciation and public expenditure expansion, which we take up next.

Since devaluation is contractionary in our model, appreciation can be expected to play an expansionary role. Column 4 suggests that appreciation during the period offset 70 percent of the coffee destorcida. The main beneficiaries were urban workers, whose real incomes rise as internal prices of traded goods fall. On the other hand, appreciation during the period added 1.5 percent of GDP to the fiscal deficit by reducing tax collection.

Column 7 shows the additional effects of public expenditure expansion. It suggests that altogether the coffee destorcida, import liberalization, appreciation, and expenditure expansion had a neutral effect on economic activity. Persistent inflation during the period must then be attributed not to demand pressure, but to inertial mechanisms such as informal indexation of wages and the crawling peg system for exchange rate management.

Finally, we can draw on our previous results to analyze the effects of "orthodox" macro policy such as that applied in Colombia during 1984–85. The simulations point to five main conclusions.[5]

First, the degree of fiscal restraint actually imposed was substantially less strict than the targets that were originally announced. About 90 percent of the total adjustment was achieved via higher taxes, which as we have seen are less contractionary than spending cuts.

Second, the public sector became a more important source of saving while private saving declined because of economic contraction. This sort of outcome is what the model would predict but was not what the economic authorities proposed or apparently had in mind.

Third, devaluation was a key part of the adjustment. It could not offset the contractionary effects of fiscal restraint, given the low response elasticities of exports and import substitution observed in Colombia. Even if tradability improved sufficiently with devaluation to make it expansionary overall, its detailed effects would not compensate for fiscal moves at the sectoral level.

For example, agricultural exports seem more sensitive than others to real exchange rate movements. Further there are always political pressures to transmit devaluation to internal coffee prices and to use quotas to hold down imports. These linkages have different effects on aggregate demand. Saving from agricultural export income is high, so through this channel export price increases do not add strongly to urban activity. However, higher internal coffee prices come at the cost of reduced public saving, so they are expansionary. Nonprice import rationing stimulates urban output. The balance of forces in 1984–85 was such that coffee price increases and import quotas partly offset the contractionary effects of devaluation.

A fourth point is that the fiscal adjustment contributed minimally to external improvement, as pointed out above. On the other hand, devaluation aimed at improving short-run external balance played a major role in deficit reduction.

Finally, food was in relatively short supply. The resulting inflationary pressure reduced the stimulus to exports and real urban wages. This last fact may have contributed to social expressions of the economic conflict implicit in the internal dynamics of the adjustment process.

Notes

Research supported by FEDESARROLLO, Bogota.

1. A complete presentation of the model with its equations, parameter estimates, and solution strategy appears in Londoño (1985). Londoño (1988) contains a more summary version.

2. Savings flows in the SAM are consistent with cross-sectional estimates based on household expenditure surveys and with time series analysis of the national accounts. Using time series for 1950–80, Ocampo, Londoño, and Villar (1985) estimated average propensities to consume of 0.70 from rural rental incomes, 0.71 from urban profits, and 1.02 from wages.

3. For a full presentation, see Londoño (1985, 1988).

4. The estimated equation for the period 1974–82 is

$$\left(\frac{M}{X_n}\right) = 10.2 - 0.106\left(\frac{P_m}{P_n}\right)$$

with a significant coefficient, $R^2 = 0.59$, and $DW = 1.19$.

5. For more detail, see Ocampo and Lora (1987), who base much of their analysis on the model developed here.

References

Clower, Robert (1965) "The Keynesian Counterrevolution: A Theoretical Appraisal." In F. H. Hahn and F. Brechling (eds.), *The Theory of Interest Rates*. London: Macmillan.

Londoño, Juan Luis. 1985. "Agricultura e Industria en el Corto Plazo: Un Esquema IS-FM de Analysis Macroeconomico Aplicado." Bogota: FEDESARROLLO.

Londoño, Juan Luis. 1988. "El Papel Macroeconomico del Mercado de Alimentos." In E. Lora (ed.), *Lecturas de Macroeconomia Colombiana*, Bogota: FEDESARROLLO

Ocampo, Jose Antonio, and Eduardo Lora. 1987. "Country Study: Colombia." Helsinki: World Institute for Development Economics Research.

Ocampo, Jose Antonio, Juan Luis Londoño, and Leonardo Villar. 1985. "Ahorro e Inversion en Colombia." In *Coyuntura Economica*. Bogota: FEDESARROLLO.

Taylor, Lance. 1983. *Structuralist Macroeconomics*. New York: Basic Books.

4 A CGE for Nicaragua

Bill Gibson

Almost a decade after the barricades were torn down and the FSLN turned to the task of building a new Nicaragua, free of *Somocismo*, a number of concrete problems of development policy remain unresolved. This chapter presents a structuralist CGE model of the postrevolutionary period in an effort to explain why the Sandinista regime is now widely considered a failure, not only by its right-wing enemies but by much of the left as well. The chapter argues that Nicaragua's policy options have been far more constrained than the Sandinistas recognized, due not simply to the U.S. backed counterrevolution but also to the structural nature of the economy inherited by the Sandinistas. The broad conclusion is that even though the Sandinistas have been attacked from all points of the political spectrum, the macropolicies they have employed are basically coherent given the necessarily overheated and foreign-exchange-constrained nature of the economy.

The CGE used to derive this conclusion is a relatively straightforward twelve-sector, six-class model, closed by an exogenously given level of foreign exchange.[1] There is no financial sector. The model is drawn for the very short run, so short that the quantity of export agricultural goods, a key parameter of the model, is taken as given. The adjustment mechanism is what is described in chapter 1 as a "forced savings" variant of structuralist macromodels with exports adjusting to balance aggregate supply and demand. This allows for an independent equation for investment while preserving the basically supply-driven nature of the economy.

In step with a number of other socialist countries, the Sandinistas appear to be dismantling much of the apparatus put in place since the revolution, allowing more flexible prices, reducing subsidies and experimenting with a much more flexible exchange rate. Although they have been accused of lapsing into a Fund mentality, certainly the list of viable options is short.

The learning curve, on the other hand, has been long, and now the government has had to shock the economy with magnitudes unprecedented in Latin America. In February 1988 the *córdoba* was devalued from 70 to 10,000 per U.S. dollar. Wages were increased by 500 percent, the size of the state bureaucracy pared back, and the multiple exchange rate scheme, in place since the revolution, eliminated. All were draconian measures probably made necessary by the delay in adopting some policies in the first place.

The following section develops the model with some attention to the policy setting. No attempt is made to be comprehensive here, and the reader is advised to consult numerous excellent sources of recent economic history of Nicaragua.[2]

4.1 Modeling the Political Economy of Nicaragua

The model presented in this section is a twelve-sector, six-class, SAM-based structuralist CGE, following the general outline of the introductory chapter.[3] The base SAM for 1987 is presented in table 4.1, laid out in a form similar to table 1.1. The SAM is an updated version of a social accounting matrix compiled for 1983.[4] The economy is assumed to produce six distinct goods plus a seventh commercial "good" that forms a composite with the others (see table 4.2.).[5]

Productive Processes

Despite the success of Sandinista agrarian reform programs,[6] agriculture in Nicaragua remains dualistic in its essential structure. With the exception of coffee, the agroexport sector (cotton, sugar, beef, sesame seed) is large and relatively modern, while basic grain production (corn and beans) is left to small producers using rudimentary methods. On one end of the spectrum, *campesinos* (peasants) plant *al espeque* (corn), using a wooden handspike to break the crusty soil; at the other extreme, private and state-run cotton plantations spray pesticides from aircraft. Somewhat less than half the labor force is employed in agriculture, but they are responsible for only a quarter of GDP.

In the postwar period cotton and coffee have dominated exports, earning more than 50 percent of revenues until the late 1960s. With the rise of the Central American Common Market, some nontraditional exports, agricultural chemicals, plastics, and so forth, took root but by mid-1969, the "Football War" signaled the end to the Common Market as a source of

Table 4.1
1987 base SAM (billions of 1987 córdobas)

	1-Capital-lists	1-*Cam-pesinos*	1-APP	2-Capital-ists	2-*Cam-pesinos*	2-APP	Petro-leum	4-Capital-ists	4-APP	Basics	*N*-basics	Com-merce	Total
1. Export agriculture	0.00	0.00	0.00	0.00	0.00	0.00	0.00	184.02	119.72	7.51	0.00	0.00	311.26
2. Domestic agriculture	2.91	4.09	1.55	0.72	3.73	0.23	0.00	11.83	38.70	6.94	0.58	0.00	71.29
3. Petroleum	4.56	1.31	2.36	4.41	1.65	3.35	4.72	4.64	9.55	25.94	3.98	2.32	68.79
4. Agricultural process	3.56	3.80	2.08	3.58	9.86	2.26	0.00	22.36	6.39	27.48	9.89	0.72	91.99
5. Basic industry	46.30	28.22	24.91	38.01	40.04	27.35	1.72	14.11	22.90	53.76	37.05	53.08	387.44
6. Nonbasic industry	0.00	0.00	0.00	0.00	0.00	0.00	0.31	5.57	4.34	72.68	19.77	43.02	145.68
7. Commerce	17.17	11.18	9.31	14.55	17.01	10.40	23.16	54.47	46.19	79.37	31.01	35.95	349.78
Total	74.50	48.60	40.20	61.27	72.30	43.60	29.90	297.00	247.79	273.68	102.29	135.09	1,426.22
1. Agricultural capitalists	3.62	0.00	0.00	6.93	0.00	0.00	0.00	0.00	0.00	0.00	0.00	0.00	10.55
2. Urban capitalists	0.00	0.00	0.00	0.00	0.00	0.00	17.66	174.72	0.00	176.71	78.87	0.01	447.97
3. Agricultural workers	69.02	0.00	34.93	25.35	0.00	33.20	0.00	0.00	0.00	0.00	0.00	0.00	162.51
4. Urban workers	0.00	0.00	0.00	0.00	0.00	0.00	1.06	22.25	134.67	159.73	44.92	79.81	442.43
5. *Campesinos*	0.00	68.05	0.00	0.00	151.99	0.00	0.00	0.00	0.00	0.00	0.00	0.00	220.04
6. Petty capitalists	0.00	0.00	0.00	0.00	0.00	0.00	0.00	7.04	0.00	62.51	137.08	363.62	570.25
Total income	72.65	68.05	34.93	32.28	151.99	33.20	18.71	204.01	134.67	398.95	260.87	443.43	1,853.75
Total tax	−12.80	−18.52	−7.54	−28.30	−18.30	−29.83	−263.97	61.78	−6.09	−220.72	−70.21	360.61	−253.88
Indirect tax	1.34	0.02	0.76	1.12	0.08	0.57	0.04	76.79	20.71	47.08	15.79	377.61	541.91
Subsidy	14.13	18.54	8.30	29.41	18.38	30.40	264.01	15.01	26.80	267.80	86.00	17.00	795.79
Savings	0.00	0.00	0.00	0.00	0.00	0.00	0.00	0.00	0.00	0.00	0.00	0.00	0.00
Noncomp. imports	18.02	6.95	10.13	23.95	14.70	18.38	318.07	14.77	19.24	253.78	109.87	4.82	812.68
Totals	152.37	105.08	77.67	89.20	220.68	65.36	102.71	577.56	395.66	705.69	402.81	943.96	3,838.76

Table 4.1 (continued)

	Agricultural capitalists	Urban capitalists	Agricultural workers	Urban workers	*Campesinos*	Petty capitalists	Total	Government	Investment	Net exports	GVP
1. Export agriculture	0.00	0.00	0.00	0.00	0.00	0.00	0.00	0.00	5.59	18.28	335.12
2. Domestic agriculture	0.15	11.26	56.13	144.95	100.91	46.75	360.14	0.60	1.14	−57.93	375.24
3. Petroleum	0.21	15.69	0.00	3.37	0.00	65.16	84.43	20.05	0.19	−70.74	102.71
4. Agricultural process	0.98	75.33	70.43	215.56	67.53	104.30	534.14	3.77	0.47	342.86	973.22
5. Basic industry	0.07	10.83	5.40	23.25	9.71	44.99	94.25	169.77	87.01	−32.78	705.69
6. Nonbasic industry	0.26	15.37	1.89	17.44	3.94	13.68	52.57	180.74	29.96	−6.14	402.81
7. Commerce	0.53	37.83	37.64	116.02	50.17	71.40	313.60	136.44	68.27	75.87	943.96
Total	2.20	166.30	171.50	520.58	232.26	346.27	1,439.12	511.37	192.63	269.42	3,838.76
1. Agricultural capitalists								0.76			11.31
2. Urban capitalists								17.11			465.08
3. Agricultural workers								0.00			162.51
4. Urban workers								73.73			516.17
5. *Campesinos*								0.00			220.04
6. Petty capitalists								0.00			570.25
Total income								91.60			1,945.35
Total tax	4.91	49.22	−9.09	−6.23	−12.22	−25.90	0.69	−40.84	−320.89		−614.92
Indirect tax	6.22	81.47	0.00	26.63	0.00	57.86	172.18				714.09
Subsidy	1.31	32.25	9.09	32.85	12.22	83.76	171.49	40.84	320.89		967.28
Savings	3.40	228.65	0.00	0.00	0.00	171.07	403.12	−1,204.05		1,060.20	259.27
Noncomp. imports	0.80	20.90	0.10	1.81	0.00	78.80	102.41	27.00	387.53		1,329.62
Totals	11.31	465.08	162.51	516.17	220.04	570.25	1,945.35	−614.92	259.27	1,329.62	

Table 4.2
Goods in the Nicaraguan model

1.	Export agriculture
2.	Domestic agriculture
3.	Petroleum
4.	Agricultural processing
5.	Basic industry
6.	Nonbasic industry
7.	Commerce

Table 4.3
Agricultural processes

1.	Capitalist agroexport
2.	*Campesino* agroexport
3.	APP agroexport
4.	Capitalist domestic agriculture
5.	*Campesino* domestic agriculture
6.	APP domestic agriculture

demand. Since the 1979 revolution nontraditional exports have all but disappeared as cotton and coffee have reasserted their dominance.

Immediately after the revolution abandoned and expropriated properties of the Somoza families and their close associates were combined into a system of state-directed agricultural enterprises known as the *Area de Propriedad del Pueblo* (Area of People's Property) or APP. These installations are large, highly mechanized and potentially the most efficient productive units in the country. They have not performed up to expectations, however, due to a host of managerial and other problems. As seen from the base SAM, the state sector produces approximately 23 percent of agroexports and less than 17.5 percent of domestic foodstuffs.

The relatively complex nature of Nicaraguan agriculture requires a substantial degree of disaggregation in the CGE. In order to avoid serious errors of aggregation, separate input–output technologies were compiled for the six subsectors listed in table 4.3. Note that this pattern of disaggregation creates a multiple-process model with a rectangular input–output matrix, inasmuch as the number of processes is no longer equal to the number of goods.

Table 4.4
Nonagricultural sectors

7.	Petroleum
8.	Capitalist agricultural processing
9.	APP agricultural processing
10.	Basics
11.	Nonbasics
12.	Commerce

Although the model is based on annual data, within a year output in the agricultural sectors can vary for several reasons. First, depending upon the crop, there can be up to three plantings per year. During this time changing relative prices can affect output as can changing conditions of labor supply and other problems facing producers. Labor shortages have been particularly severe since the revolution due to growth of the urban informal sector, the educational sector, central government, and the armed forces (Utting 1987, 134). The specific limits on output vary from sector to sector. In cotton, for example, it is clear that a political constraint binds in that cotton producers were the most privileged class prior to the revolution and now feel threatened by the new regime. Yields have fallen, farms have been "decapitalized," and the market for cotton land has disappeared (Colburn 1986, 57). The acreage sown to cotton by the private sector is widely regarded as a political barometer of the relationship between the Sandinistas and the private sector. Even counting the state sector, which faces a different set of barriers to increased production, output has been restored to only a fraction of prerevolutionary acreage levels. Peasant production is limited as well by a myriad of factors, the rate at which the agrarian reform proceeds, cooperative development, credit, technical support and the rate of renovation of Nicaragua's coffee plantations, the oldest in the region.

Because of the political nature of the constraints on agroexport production, supply is taken as exogenously given. The agroexport price is a policy variable, set by the state. In practice, the guarantee price frequently changes with the world price, but it bears no necessary or one-to-one correspondence. The agroexport price defines an "implicit exchange rate" for each crop sold to the government clearinghouse for exports.

The nonagricultural sectors are shown in table 4.4. Petroleum is broken out as a separate sector given the politicized nature of the level of supply. It will be assumed that the total quantity of output is fixed and the private consumption adjusts to bring total demand in line. The output of agricultural processing, on the other hand, is limited by the available raw material that comes from the three production processes for agroexports. The difference between total supply of the agroexport good and domestic demand is available for export. But rather than selling goods directly to the government, the exportable quantity is first sold as an intermediate good to the agricultural processing sectors. As seen, these are divided into two subsectors, corresponding to private producers and the APP. The assumption is that the APP's raw material needs are satisfied first; the private sector gets the residual.

Basic goods are defined both in the model and in practice as goods that have been "prioritized" by the government. In effect, this means that foreign exchange for intermediate requirements are given preference over nonbasics. What constitutes a "basic" is highly politicized and in fact determines much of the character of the Sandinista revolution. Together with a lengthy list of essential consumer goods, medicine, and educational material, basics include intermediates such as agricultural chemicals and implements. The nature of the protected inputs reflects the government's development policies, which attend to the needs of small as well as large growers and are not strictly defined by the needs of the state sector. Prices of basic goods are controlled by the government. Their scarcity, however, provides for a long chain of middlemen, or "speculators" as they are referred to in the (progovernment) press, and final transactions are often at prices substantially higher than the official price.

Conversely, nonbasics enjoy no special foreign exchange allocation. In the model, as in reality, nonbasic intermediate import requirements constitute a residual use of foreign exchange. In other words, output in this market adjusts to satisfy the overall foreign exchange constraint.

Finally, commerce is taken to be a strictly demand-determined market in which the quantity of commercial services rendered depends upon the level

Table 4.5
Commercial margins

Export agriculture	0.20
Domestic agriculture	0.25
Petroleum	0.05
Agricultural processing	0.30
Basic industry	0.30
Nonbasic industry	0.45
Imports	0.07

of economic activity. Commercial margins for each good were estimated and are presented in table 4.5. No distinction was made between wholesale and retail margins.

The Model

In the formal specification of the model, we employ indices i to stand for goods, j for processes, and k for social classes. Consider first the supply-demand balances for the seven goods:

$$q_i = \sum_{j=1}^{12} a_{ij}x_j + \sum_{k=1}^{6} c_{ik} + \frac{I_i + G_i}{p_i} + E_i, \qquad i = 1, 2, \ldots, 7, \tag{1}$$

where q_i is the quantity produced of the ith good, a_{ij} the input–output coefficient describing the amount of the ith good required by process j, x_j the ouput of process j, and c_{ik} consumption of the ith good by the kth class. I_i is the nominally given investment including change in inventories, G_i is the nominally fixed government consumption, E_i is exports (for simplicity, considered to be net of competitive imports), and p_i is the producer price of the ith good.

The seven adjusting variables associated with equations (1) are as follows: For export agriculture, x_8, the residual use of raw materials by capitalist agricultural processing adjusts, as described above. Since output is given, q_1 is simply:

$$q_1 = x_1 + x_2 + x_3. \tag{2}$$

Supply in the second market, domestic agriculture, is assumed to be much less politicized and more flexible than agroexports. Consequently it is assumed to depend upon a simplified schedule given by the relationship between costs and price in the capitalist process 4:

$$x_4 = \bar{x}_4^s \left(\frac{p_2}{B_4}\right)^{\alpha}, \tag{3}$$

where the bar indicates a constant and α is the response elasticity. For the simulations below it is given at 2. Intermediates, import, and wages costs are summarized in B_j which is defined as

$$B_j = \sum_{i=1}^{8} p_i a_{ij} + w_j l_j, \qquad j = 1, 2, \ldots, 12, \tag{4}$$

where w is the wage rate, and l is the labor coefficient. The eighth input–

output coefficient describes the amount of noncompetitive intermediate imports required per unit of output. p_8 is then

$$p_8 = e_m p_m, \tag{5}$$

where e_m is the exchange rate for imports and p_m is the given international price of imports.

For domestic agriculture the supply balance equation is

$$q_2 = x_4 + x_5 + x_6. \tag{6}$$

Adjustment in the market for domestic agricultural goods is through the flexible price, p_2. Prior to 1985 the Sandinistas attempted to control the market for basic grains through ENABAS, the state marketing agency, but since then, internal markets have been increasingly liberalized to the point that it is now appropriate to model the domestic agricultural sector as flex-price market.

The model is designed to reflect petroleum rationing for private use, which has been in place since 1982. Only very recently, in 1988, has the price risen to the point that there are surplus rationing cards. For 1987, however, the appropriate model is to ration consumers at a controlled price. The shortage of petroleum imports has been a brake on Nicaraguan development since immediately after the revolution when the price of oil rose by 137 percent, and petroleum has been as high as 40 percent of the import bill. In the early days of the revolution, Mexico and Venezuela agreed to supply Nicaragua with oil at concessional terms. More recently, Nicaragua has obtained the bulk of its unprocessed petroleum from the Soviet Union. Given the particular nature of petroleum supply, it is taken as given: hence

$$q_3 = x_7. \tag{7}$$

As mentioned above, it is assumed that once intermediate demand, investment, and government demand is satisfied; the residual, C_3,

$$C_3 = \sum_{k=1}^{6} c_{3k}$$

is rationed for private consumption according to

$$c_{3k} = \left(\frac{\bar{c}_{3k}}{\bar{C}_3}\right) C_3, \qquad k = 1, 2, \ldots, 6, \tag{8}$$

where $\bar{c}_{3k}$ and $\bar{C}_3$ are consumption by class and total consumption, respectively, in the base SAM.

The price of refined petroleum products is determined by the state as a policy variable. The rule is that price reflect costs plus an exogenously given markup, γ:[7]

$$p_3 = (1 + \gamma_7)(1 + t_7)B_7, \tag{9}$$

where t is the indirect tax rate.

E_4, in the fourth of equation (1), moves to clear the agricultural processing market with total supply given by

$$q_4 = x_8 + x_9. \tag{10}$$

In this market, as in petroleum, the price level is determined by the state. p_4 is set according to costs in the capitalist process with an exogenously given markup:

$$p_4 = (1 + \gamma_8)(1 + t_8)B_8. \tag{11}$$

The market for basics is initially Keynesian (this is changed below when the recent policies are analyzed). There is only one process, with

$$q_5 = x_{10}. \tag{12}$$

In the model the controlled price of basic goods is determined by an equation of the same form as (10):

$$p_5 = (1 + \gamma_{10})(1 + t_{10})B_{10}. \tag{13}$$

As indicated above, the nonbasic process fends for itself in that there is no guarantee that foreign exchange will be available to support intermediate purchases. There is but one process for nonbasics:

$$q_6 = x_{11} \tag{14}$$

Commerce

The basic SAM is expressed in producers' prices, with the commerce sector explicitly separated out. Conceptually, commerce is treated as a "physical" commodity that forms a composite with other goods. The "price" of commercial services is therefore a coherent concept and is determined in the model by a markup equation:

$$p_7 = (1 + \gamma_{12})(1 + t_{12})B_{12}. \tag{15}$$

The quantity is demand determined and is given by the third of equation (1) with only one process:

$$q_7 = x_7. \tag{16}$$

The commercial expenditure for consumption is simply the commercial margins, ψ_i, times real consumption:

$$c_{7k} = \sum_{i=1}^{6} \psi_i c_{ik} + \psi_m c_{8k}, \qquad k = 1, 2, \ldots, 6. \tag{17}$$

Commercial expenditure for intermediate purchases, investment, government expenditure and net exports is defined analogously, but because these coefficients remain constant, there is not need to define commercial expenditure with an equation such as (17).

Social Classes and Consumption

The Nicaraguan class structure, which is complex in reality, is highly simplified for the purposes of the model. Six social classes are distinguished, as shown in table 4.6. Capitalists are disaggregated into urban and rural. All categories of capitalists save, but workers and *campesinos* do not (table 4.1 gives saving proportions). Agricultural capitalist income, y_1, is given simply by the sum of profits in the two capitalist processes, 1 and 4:

$$y_1 = \sum_{j=1,4} \frac{[pp_j - (1 + t_j)B_j]x_j}{(1 + t_j)}, \tag{18}$$

where pp_j is the price of the good produced by the jth process.[8] Urban capitalist income is earned in processes 7, 8, 10 and 11 and is given by

$$y_2 = \sum_{j=7,\,8,\,10,\,11} \frac{[pp_j - (1 + t_j)B_j]x_j}{(1 + t_j)}, \tag{20}$$

One may reasonably question why capitalists in process 8 are classified as urban capitalists. In reality capitalists in agricultural processing are typically

Table 4.6
Social classes

1. Agricultural capitalists
2. Urban capitalists
3. Agricultural workers
4. Urban workers
5. *Campesinos*
6. Petty capitalists

urban based and share the consumption and savings propensities of their urban rather than rural counterparts. This leaves a small quantity of income for truly agricultural capitalists, however, and creates large percentage changes in the simulations to follow.

Workers and peasants are divided on grounds of access to the means of production. *Campesinos* have land, but workers are landless and derive their income from selling wage labor:

$$y_3 = \sum_{j=1}^{6} w_j l_j. \tag{21}$$

However, urban workers earn

$$y_4 = \sum_{j=7}^{12} w_j l_j. \tag{22}$$

Campesinos are distinguished from agricultural capitalists by landholdings. *Campesinos* have less than 35 hectares which means that the both "rich" and "middle" peasants are considered *campesinos*.[9] Note that any single individual may well be both an agricultural worker and a *campesino*. Their income is determined in a similar way to that of capitalists:

$$y_5 = \sum_{j=2,\,5} \frac{[pp_j - (1 + t_j)B_j]x_j}{(1 + t_j)}. \tag{23}$$

The petty-capitalist class consists of small producers and merchants of the burgeoning informal sector. It is an amalgam of more sociologically defined classes in that the term "capitalist" is not to imply that they are necessarily "rich." Some of course are, but many of this class are nearly destitute and survive by means of sometimes creative, sometimes demeaning strategies. Because this class is the most flourishing in Nicaragua, its savings propensity is high, although not as high as urban capitalists (see table 4.1). For the purposes of the model they are assumed to capture a fixed and given fraction, Φ_j, of private value added in processes 10, 11 and 12:

$$y_6 = \sum_{j=10}^{12} \Phi_j \left[pp_j - (1 + t_j)\left(\sum_{i=1}^{8} p_i a_{ij} \right) \right] x_j. \tag{24}$$

Once incomes are defined, consumption is taken to be linear in expenditure, as discussed in the introduction. The consumption equation is lengthy but straightforward:

$$c_{ik} = \theta_{ik} + \left(\frac{\mu_{ik}}{p_i^*}\right)\left(\varepsilon_k - \sum_{i=1}^{7} p_i^* \theta_{ik}\right), \quad i = 1, 2, 4, 5, 6, 8,\ k = 1, 2, \ldots 6, \tag{25}$$

where θ_{ik} is the consumption intercept and μ_{ik} is the marginal propensity to consume out of supernumerary expenditure ($\varepsilon_k - \sum p_i^* \theta_{ik}$). The latter is total expenditure, ε_k, less expenditure on "subsistence" (or more generally the intercept). Note in the commodity index that petroleum is left out, imports are included, and commerce is not considered a commodity that classes choose to consume. Expenditure depends upon savings rates, s_k, as well as the direct tax rates, d_k:

$$\varepsilon_k = (1 - s_k)(1 - d_k)y_k, \qquad k = 1, 2, \ldots, 6. \tag{26}$$

Finally, p^*, is the *retail* price of good i, and is defined as

$$p_i^* = p_i + p_7\psi_i, \qquad i = 1, 2, \ldots, 6, 8, \tag{27}$$

where p_7 is the price of the physical commercial margin, ψ.

The Closure

Table 4.7 summarizes the details of the variables and equations of the model just described. Variables not listed in the table are taken as given parameters. As presented, the model consists of 107 equations in 108 variables.

To close the model, an additional equation is needed, and this is what endows the model with its character as a foreign-exchange-constrained model:

$$S_f + \sum_{i=1}^{7} p_{ei}E_i = \sum_{j=1}^{12} p_8 a_{8j} x_j + \sum_{k=1}^{6} p_8 c_{8k} + I_8 + G_8,$$

where S_f is foreign savings and p_{ei} is the dollar price of imports.

To summarize, the model is essentially supply determined with agroexports earning the foreign exchange that positions the supply curve for nonbasics. There are three adjustment mechanisms in the model, all discussed in chapter 1, and all working simultaneously: (1) Keynesian: the market for nonbasics is essentially Keynesian in that the supply curve is flat and effective demand determines the level of output. (2) Neoclassical: the market for domestic agricultural goods is price clearing with a traditional supply and demand curve. The market for nonbasics is also flex-price, but with a supply curve that moves to hold foreign savings constant. (3) Tradeflows: in the market for processed agricultural goods, exports less competitive imports adjust to clear the market. Supply is determined by the quantity of raw materials that can be delivered to the agricultural processing sector while demand derives from general economic equilibrium.

Table 4.7
Model summary

Variables	Number	Equation	Number	
q_1	1	2	1	Quantity of agroexports
q_2	1	6	1	Quantity of domestic agriculture
q_3	1	7	1	Quantity of petroleum
q_4	1	10	1	Quantity of agricultural processing
q_5	1	12	1	Quantity of basics
q_6	1	14	1	Quantity of nonbasics
q_7	1	16	1	Quantity of commerce
x_4	1	3	1	Output domestic agric-capitalist
x_8	1	1	1	Output agricultural proc-capitalist
x_{10}	1	1	1	Output basics
x_{11}	1			Output nonbasics
x_{12}	1	1	1	Output commerce
E_4	1	1	1	Agricultural processing exports
p_2	1	1	1	Domestic Agriculture's price
p_3	1	9	1	Petroleum's price
p_4	1	11	1	Agricultural processing price
p_5	1	13	1	Basics price
p_6	1	1	1	Nonbasics price
p_7	1	15	1	Commerce price
p_8	1	5	1	Noncomposite import price
pp_j	8	19	8	Process prices
B_j	12	4	12	Costs
y_k	6	18, 20–24	6	Incomes of classes
c_{ik}	48	8, 17, 25	48	Consumption
C_3	1	1	1	Petroleum consumption
ϵ_k	6	26	6	Expenditures
P_i^*	7	27	7	Retail prices
Total	108		107	

Note: Index i refers to goods, j to processes and k to social classes.

4.2 How the Model Works

The binding foreign-exchange constraint requires that as the model adjusts to parametric changes, imports and exports will change to allow the level of foreign savings to remain constant in dollar terms. As indicated above, the nonbasic sector is the residual user of foreign exchange. Its fixed-proportions technology imposes a rigid relationship between output and its allocation of foreign exchange. While this may strike more neoclassically minded readers as too restrictive, the data do in fact suggest a close relationship, at least recently, between imports and output. Table 4.8 gives a breakdown of the economy as a whole and indicates a stable relationship, especially for manufacturing since 1982.

The first question to arise is how does the model respond to a change in the level of foreign savings? Figure 4.1 provides "characteristic curves" of the model showing how it behaves with respect to this key parameter. The horizontal axis measures the percentage change of foreign savings, running from a 5 percent reduction to a 10 percent increase. Several endogenous variables are plotted on the vertical axis, all measured as a percentage change from the base SAM. The curve labeled GDP is upward sloping in that more foreign exchange causes real GDP to rise. The CPI curve shows how the consumer price index changes. With more foreign exchange, the

Table 4.8
Nicaragua's import coefficients

	1982	1983	1984	1985	1986
Gross domestic product					
Agriculture	5436	5749	5442	5181	4901
Manufacturing	5496	5806	5829	5555	5644
Construction	500	583	634	697	697
Intermediate imports					
Agriculture	34.9	55.6	59.1	74.6	76.5
Manufacturing	187.1	203.8	229.1	213.6	215.3
Construction	26.7	21.9	22	26	25.2
Ratios 2 : 1 (× 1,000)					
Agriculture	6.42	9.67	10.86	14.40	15.61
Manufacturing	34.04	35.10	39.30	38.45	38.15
Construction	53.40	37.56	34.70	37.30	36.15

Source: IMF Mission Report, 1987.
Note: GDP in millions of 1980 córdobas; intermediate imports in millions of U.S. dollars

supply of intermediate imports used in nonbasic production is greater, and consequently the price falls; this pulls down the consumer price index. PCW measures the *share* in total income accruing to *campesinos* and workers as it changes with foreign savings and gives an overall measure of the distribution of income. Finally, TOT plots an index of the agricultural-nonagricultural terms of trade.

Figure 4.1 captures the essence of the macroadjustment of the model, inasmuch as it shows how external strangulation causes forced savings. With a given level of exogenous spending, lower foreign savings requires a shift in the distribution of income favoring higher saving classes, in this case to urban and petty capitalists. This causes the share in total income of workers and peasants to fall as foreign savings is reduced. More foreign savings, on the other hand, causes forced *dis*savings in that incomes earned by the urban and petty-capitalist class in nonbasic industry decline, while output and employment increase.

The foregoing provides an account of the overall macroadjustment process. When the model is disaggregated, however, there emerge some interesting twists in how the adjustment takes place. The left frame of table 4.9, under the heading "I-p_5 fix" shows the impact on the distribution of income for a 2 percent decrease in the level of foreign savings. Here it is clear that the forced savings mechanism is at work: Income is shifted to urban and petty capitalists while workers and peasants suffer a decline in share as well as real purchasing power. The shift in relative prices attenuates the effect somewhat: The price of nonbasics, consumed in larger proportions by the wealthier classes, rises to 1.26, while the price of food, prominent in the market basket of the popular classes, falls by 2 percent.

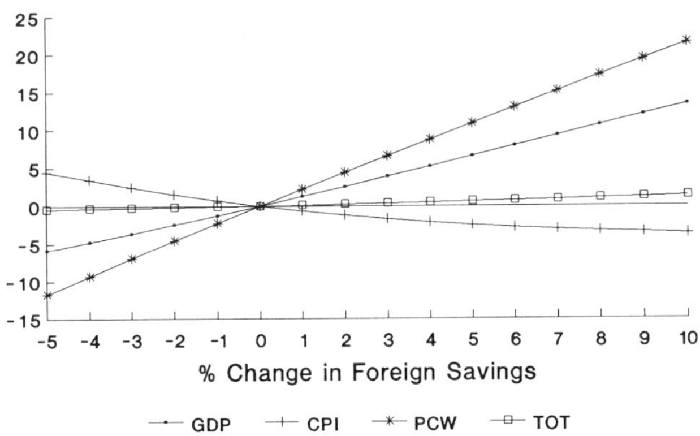

Figure 4.1
Percent change from base SAM when the level of foreign savings varies

Table 4.9
The distribution of income for a 2 percent decrease in foreign savings

	Model I: p_5 fix			Model I: p_5 flex	
	Base share	Share	Δ in income	Share	Δ in income
Agricultural capitalists	0.6	0.3	−51.7	0.1	−91.3
Urban capitalists	23.9	25.5	5.9	26.7	12.3
Agricultural workers	8.3	8.1	−1.7	8.1	−2.0
Urban workers	26.5	25.3	−3.5	25.4	−3.0
Campesinos	11.3	10.7	−3.7	10.6	−5.1
Petty capitalists	29.3	30.2	3.7	29.3	0.5

This terms-of-trade effect is simply the manifestation in the system of relative prices of the adjustment that must take place to increase profits and therefore private savings as foreign savings declines. Note that since three out of four urban sectors have fixed prices, the flexible price must bear the brunt of the adjustment. It is this structure that is to blame for much of the discontent among social classes who consume relatively large proportions of nonbasics.

The explanation for the relatively flat shape of the terms-of-trade locus lies in the supply response in domestic agriculture. With a fall in foreign savings, prices of intermediate inputs rise and domestic agricultural supply falls, putting upward pressure on its price. When the supply of foreign savings increases, however, the increased demand due to higher employment keeps the terms of trade moving in favor of agriculture.

The rest of the macro story following a reduction in foreign savings is easily anticipated. There is stagflation, with real output declining by 3 percent while the CPI rises by 2.5 percent. Exports rise due to the employment effect on food demand, and imports fall due to the general contraction. As we will see in the continuation, the model is symmetrical in that if foreign savings *increases*, these effects are all reversed; exports, for example, fall in a typical "Dutch disease" fashion. The drop in foreign savings does not affect government savings substantially, due to the assumption of fixed nominal government expenditure. The adjustment comes in private savings which increases in nominal terms by 11 percent.

4.3 Policy Dilemmas

One of the thorniest problems the Sandinistas face is how to restart the "formal" economic apparatus that has all but disappeared in the last five years. Wage labor, at controlled wages, has become almost impossible due to the limited control the government is able to exercise over prices and supply of basic goods. Initially, the Sandinistas believed that it would be sufficient to rely on wage and price controls to establish a progressive distribution of income. But with a growing fiscal deficit, due in part to subsidized basics, prices of nonbasic goods have skyrocketed, The net effect has been to create a vacuum in the urban informal sector, drawing labor from formal sector production as well as from the countryside.[10] Contra attacks on rural communities have further intensified the inflow of labor to Managua to the point that more that 50 percent of the economically active population is engaged in informal activities. The constant drain of the war means that the government must invoke nominal wage controls as a means of simply fighting inflation rather than solving more profound policy problems.[11]

The results of the model confirm the conventional wisdom of how the distribution of income has changed under the low-intensity conflict of the Contra war. Simulation results show that an increase in nominal government expenditure has essentially the same effect as a reduction in foreign savings. Increasing government expenditure by 10 percent causes the real GDP to fall by 2.2 percent and the CPI to rise by 5 percent. The terms of trade turn against agricultural producers and urban capital, large and small, are the big winners in terms of both real income and share of the total. Exports and imports fall, and private savings increase to offset the rise in the government deficit.

The model thus supports the widely held perception that the ultimate beneficiaries of the war are the petty bourgeoisie. As Medal (1988) observes,

> ... income redistribution has relatively favored the new "*burguesia de delantal*" [literally, the "apron bourgeoisie" or petty bourgeoisie, shopkeepers, etc.], the informal scetor, some producers and a reduced strata of the state bureaucracy. The expansion in public consumption has run parallel with a reduction in private consumption. (Medal 1988, 113)

Argüello et al. (no date, 10), citing an INEC study, note that in the period 1980–85 basic consumption has increased by an average annual rate of 2.9 percent while nonbasic consumption has declined by 18.1 percent. These data say that in per capita terms, basic consumption has not kept pace, given an annual population growth rate of approximately 3.5 percent.

As the crisis of what the Sandinistas call "speculation" has deepened, they have turned to liberalization of the economy as the solution. Since the early days of the revolution, the Sandinistas have attempted to maintain

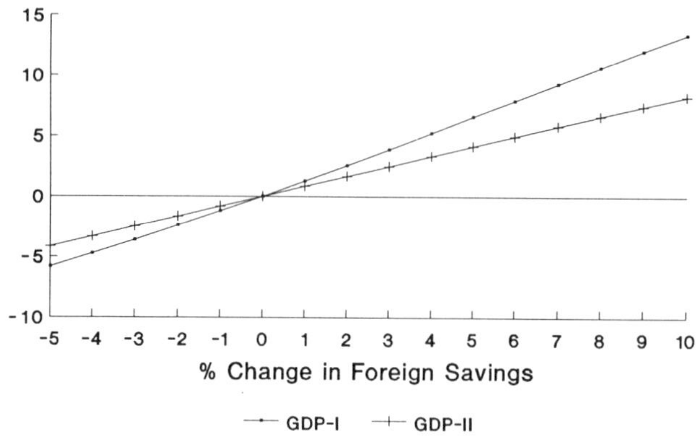

Figure 4.2
Percent change from base SAM when prices of basics are free to fluctuate

basic consumption levels through a series of consumer subsidies and price and wage controls. In a process that began in 1985, but greatly accelerated in February and again in June 1988, the regime has dramatically loosened its control over the economy. Most prices are now free to fluctuate, with the exception of agroexports, petroleum products and a few basic foods, such as sugar, rice, beans, and oil. As of February 1988 wages other than in the public sector are also free to adjust to market conditions. Although not accompanied by the typical privatization effort, these policies amount to a concerted liberalization of the economy implemented as a strategy to confront the crisis.

The pliable nature of structuralist CGEs provides a way to grapple with such "large" changes. The characteristic curves of figure 4.2 compare the model with a second version of the model, labeled II, in which prices of basics are free to fluctuate. In this second setup basic supply is determined by the amount of foreign exchange allocated to that sector under the simplifying assumption that the proportion between basics and nonbasics in the base SAM is maintained. Figure 4.2 shows that the characteristic curve for the model with more flexible prices is flatter and therefore less sensitive to variations in foreign exchange availability. A 10 percent increase in foreign exchange causes almost twice as much growth with price controls on basics as in the alternative model. On the other hand, a reduction in the availability of foreign exchange is not as harmful to the economy in the second more flexible model. This suggests that if the economy is to subsist on a thinner diet of foreign exchange, liberalization is perhaps not an unreasonable strategy from the standpoint of growth in real GDP.[12]

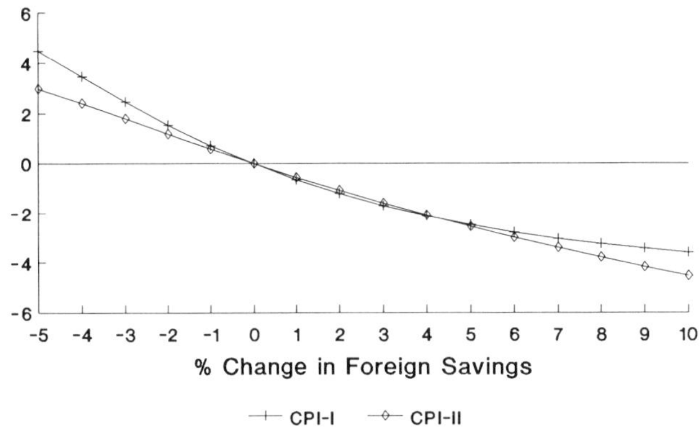

Figure 4.3
Percent change from base SAM comparing versions I and II of the model

Figure 4.3 shows the CPI in both models I and II. Note that inflation is also somewhat less in the first version with more foreign exchange. But again, with a planned contraction in foreign dependence, price controls actually cause *more* inflation than in the partially liberalized economy.

The two right-hand columns of table 4.9 show how the second model compares with the first when foreign savings is falling. Although the share of income accruing to workers and peasants is the same, the fix-price regime imposes less forced savings on *campesinos* and agricultural workers but more on urban workers. On balance, the fix model favors the agricultural sector, but the second is superior for urban workers and capitalists. Petty-capitalist income, however, moves with the agricultural sector, suggesting that the Sandinistas face a basic dilemma if they wish to deter "speculation" while stimulating agroexports. Again, if foreign exchange is contracting, it may not be unreasonable to shift to a more flexible price regime, as long as other policies are adopted simultaneously to ward off agricultural stagnation.

But what of the more heady days in which foreign exchange availability is on the rise? Table 4.10 shows results for a 5 percent *increase* in foreign savings. Here it is clear that price controls protect urban capitalist more than any other class. Their loss in real income under flex-prices is almost twice as great as under fix-prices. Note that the results are the inverse of the case in which foreign exchange availability is falling: The flex-price scheme now strongly favors the countryside while fix-price are better for the urban classes. Petty capitalists lose either way, but less so when P_5 is flexible.

Table 4.10
The distribution of income for a 5 percent increase in foreign savings

	Model I: p_5 fix			Model I: p_5 flex	
	Base share	Share	Δ in income	Share	Δ in income
Agricultural capitalists	0.6	1.2	98.3	1.9	211.2
Urban capitalists	23.9	20.2	−15.7	17.0	−30.3
Agricultural workers	8.3	9.0	2.9	9.1	4.8
Urban workers	26.5	29.7	8.2	29.6	7.9
Campesinos	11.3	12.6	6.1	13.0	10.0
Petty capitalists	29.3	27.4	−9.3	29.5	−1.4

Clearly the conclusion is that price controls are not automatically more progressive than a liberalized regime. If petty capitalists benefit at the expense of the productive sectors, there is a clear incentive to abandon foreign exchange earning (or import-substituting) activities in favor of commerce or the informal sector. With this in mind, the data suggest that the fix-price system is superior when foreign exchange availability is increasing. On the other hand, when foreign exchange is becoming more scarce, it is better to switch to a flex-price regime to prevent the *burguesia de delantal* from capturing the rent associated with dollar scarcity.

Inflation, Devaluation, and Nominal Wages

Now with the 1988 inflation rate expected to be in the neighborhood of 3,000 to 4,000 percent, there is no question that the economy is seriously overheated. By 1986 CEPAL data showed Nicaragua with the highest inflation rate in Latin America, at 747.4 percent (CEPAL 1987, 17).[13] In 1987 inflation again accelerated to 1,225.7 percent. Despite the substantial currency reform in February 1988 in which the overall money supply declined by 19.8 percent, the hyperinflation continues (IHC 1988, 12).

The response of the government has been to progressively relinquish control of the economy to the market. The measures undertaken in February 1988 continue a process begun in February 1985 in which consumer and producer subsidies have been cut, the multiple exchange rate system dismantled,[14] and the enormous state bureaucracy pared back. Then in February 1988 the córdoba was devalued from 70 to 10 *new* córdobas per dollar. New córdobas were simply different colored notes with three zeros deleted. Given the multiple exchange rate system in place, the devaluation amounted to some 3,000 percent, a maxidevaluation by any measure, even compared to the 1985 devaluations of Argentina and Brazil which were 600 percent and 800 percent, respectively (IHC 1988, 13).

Certainly prior to February 1988 the córdoba was hideously overvalued. Medal (1988) observes that while the official rate was 70 to 1, the "parallel rate," that which could be obtained in government sponsored and controlled exchange houses, was 20,000 to 1 and the black market was 55,000 to 1. Medal questions whether a real devaluation is possible, but his argument appears to be based on a "constant markup theory" of price formation.[15] He argues that devaluation trips a vicious cycle of inflation–devaluation–inflation (Medal 1988, 121).

Since under most circumstances a real devaluation implies a reduction in the living standards of those who can least defend themselves, any regime that seeks to represent the popular classes and at the same time effect a real devaluation is in a bind. Rhetorically, the Sandinistas seem to have singled out the petty-capitalist speculators as the social class from which the real transfer must come. In theory this is eminently sensible given the negligible contribution made to the public wealth by these rent-seeking middlepersons. On the other hand, it is the enormously overvalued exchange rate which has been responsible for unbroken flow of labor from the productive sectors—namely, foreign-exchange-earning sectors—to commerce and the informal sector. The Sandinistas can scarcely blame their constituencies for responding to signals of their own making.

Is it therefore possible to conceive of a real devaluation in an economy in which the principal foreign exchange earning capacity is in private hands and the remaining classes rely on the government to defend their interests against the property owners? Zalkin (1987) argues that, despite the agrarian reform, any weak-willed attempt to reorient resources to tradables has come from the pockets of the peasantry. The policies have left all parties unsatisfied; agrarian capital cannot earn premia large enough to offset the perceived risk of expropriation, *campesinos* not directly affected by the agrarian reform join the Contra in increasing numbers, and the urban working class takes refuge in the informal sector. Is it therefore possible, or even proper, to think of a real devaluation? As *Envio* puts it, "From the popular perspective, devaluation is the enemy."[16]

But how does devaluation work in the framework of the model? First, it should *not* be expected that in a foreign-exchange-constrained model, devaluation would be contractionary, as in a typical (Keynesian) structuralist macromodel. Devaluation raises the nominal value of foreign savings, and income must therefore contract to establish macroeconomic equilibrium of savings and investment. Since savings comes primarily from profits, the

Table 4.11
Distribution of income with 10 percent devaluation

	Model I: imports only			Model II: imports and exports	
	Base share	Share	Δ in income	Share	Δ in income
Agricultural capitalists	0.6	0.3	−45.5	1.2	92.0
Urban capitalists	23.9	23.6	−5.3	23.7	−5.6
Agricultural workers	8.3	8.6	−1.2	8.4	−3.6
Urban workers	26.5	27.3	−0.6	26.8	−3.1
Campesinos	11.3	11.7	−0.6	12.1	3.0
Petty capitalists	29.3	28.5	−8.7	27.8	−10.5

mass of profits must fall in order to provide a consistent quantity of savings. In fix-price models this implies a fall in the level of output, but here output is (essentially) given in the short-run by agricultural productivity. In a foreign-exchange-constrained model prices must therefore fall to reduce profits. The reduction in price causes a "forced dissavings" as well as expenditure switching. The fall in income of the well-to-do also reduces demand for imports and thus foreign savings available to support nonbasic production increases.

Table 4.11 gives the data on income distribution for two simulations in which the import price was increased by 10 percent. In the first case, labeled I, there was no complementary increase in the guarantee price for export agriculture. Since the objective of devaluation is to reduce the level of foreign savings, not simply use it more efficiently, real GDP, foreign savings was reduced by 3.5 percent as a zero-real-growth benchmark. In the second, labeled II, p_1 was also increased by 10 percent.

In the first simulation real income of all saving classes falls by substantially more than that of workers. The consumer price index rises by 2 percent, while the guarantee price remains fixed. Real consumption as a whole declines by 3 percent to make way for a 10 percent increase in exports required to meet the lower foreign-exchange constraint. The redistribution of table 4.11 is achieved by a fall in the price of nonbasics by 12 percent; domestic agricultural prices rise by slightly more than 2 percent and petroleum by 9 percent. A real devaluation has occurred, but agricultural capitalists—those responsible for earning the foreign exchange—are nevertheless the big losers.[17]

This simulation parallels the policy package of February 1988, with the exception of a nominal increase in wages (which will be considered below).

Medal (1988) among others has argued that even though the devaluation was gigantic, it did *not* amount to a real devaluation inasmuch as the guarantee price was only doubled while input prices were increased by twenty-sevenfold. Here it is seen that real devaluation can be achieved by increasing the import prices alone inasmuch as macroconsistency requires prices and therefore incomes of nonwage earners to decline. The inconsistency is resolved by noting that in the model, devaluation is considered in isolation. There is no concomitant increase in nominal government expenditure, for example, nor other components of demand that would erode the gains from devaluation.[18]

To achieve a stronger real devaluation, the guarantee price must also increase. Not surprisingly, the effect is to shift resources to agricultural capital and peasants at the expense of everyone else. As the right-hand panel of table 4.11 shows, the real incomes of urban workers fall by 3.1 percent and agricultural workers by 3.6 percent. Urban workers are relatively well organized, and they are the class with perhaps the most access to the power structure. Hence it is not surprising that the Sandinistas have backed away from a policy that reduces their real wages.

But if nominal wages are increased in an effort to recoup the losses of table 4.11, there is little gain and substantial damage is done to the economy as a whole. A 5 percent across-the-board increase in nominal wages increases agricultural workers' income by less than 2 percent and urban income by less than 0.5 percent.[19] Real GDP declines slightly, and a 5 percent increase in nominal wages cause the CPI to rise by 3 percent.[20] The inflation brings precisely the kind of changes in the distribution of income that the economy cannot tolerate. Petty-capitalist incomes rise and even a small increase in nominal wages drives agroexporters into the red. The inflation–devaluation–inflation cycle is serious dilemma inasmuch as nominal wage increases can quickly wipe out any gains from devaluation. A contraction in available foreign exchange implies a reduction in current consumption possibilities, and if the results of table 4.11 are to be believed, the distribution of the pain following a nominal devaluation is not terribly regressive.

A Saint Valentine's Day Massacre

To treat the reforms of February 1988 in the context of the model, consider the stylized package of parameter changes listed in table 4.12. The relative magnitudes of these numbers are not as extreme as the actual package in which the guarantee price was doubled while the exhange rate was raised

Table 4.12
Policy parameters (percent)

Devaluation	10
Wage increase	5
Guarantee price	3
Government spending	−10
Investment spending	−5
Price of basics	Flexible

by twenty-seven times. When run in the model, the actual changes immediately drive agricultural incomes negative, with negative consumption and other meaningless results. Moreover it is highly doubtful that the guarantee price will remain in force until the harvest in late fall 1988. Some adjustments, whether an explicit change in the guarantee price or through the mechanism of credit allocation, will clearly have to be made. The simulation of table 4.12 therefore attempts only to capture the spirit of the reforms rather than their absolute magnitude. It is to be kept in mind, however, that the Sandinista policies are feasible only so long as the guarantee price increases faster than any further devaluation.

The results of the simulation of the measures of table 4.12 show that the package as a whole works. Real output grows by 2.5 percent, and incomes of workers and peasants increase while incomes of urban and petty capitalists fall. There is virtually no increase in inflation; the rise in food prices is balanced by the fall in basic and nonbasic prices. Exports increase as the distribution of income is shifted to the popular classes who consume fewer exportables. The higher level of exports allows greater supply of basics and nonbasics, and consequently prices of basics and nonbasics decline. The reduction in input prices increases the income of agroexporters substantially, and this is perhaps what the Sandinistas had in mind when there was little attempt to redress the huge imbalance created with the semidevaluation. A big boost also comes from the fall in nominal government expenditure and investment. A simulation in which these were maintained fixed in nominal terms shows a percentage point less in real growth, two points more in inflation and the popular share of income falling from 58 to 52 percent.[21]

A proper comparison of the effects of the policy package, however, must include controlling for the effect of foreign savings on the level of output. Again the objective of the measures was to reduce foreign savings, and hence an appropriate benchmark would be the parameter changes in of

Table 4.13
Distribution of income with policies of table 4.12 and a 3 percent reduction in foreign savings

	Base share	Share	Δ in income	Percent Δ relative to base SAM	
Agricultural capitalists	0.6	1.4	107.6	GDP	0.0
Urban capitalists	23.9	15.6	−40.8	CPI	1.0
Agricultural workers	8.3	9.7	5.6	PCW	7.9
Urban workers	26.5	31.0	6.4	TOT	32.4
Campesinos	11.3	13.3	7.1	Exports	9.4
Petty capitalists	29.3	29.0	−11.4	Defense	−2.4

table 4.12 plus a reduction in foreign savings that would leave real growth at zero. A little trial and error shows that a 3 percent cut in foreign savings, together with the other changes, is sufficient to hold output approximately constant. The results of this simulation are presented in table 4.13.

The results show that broadly speaking, the policy initiative would be successful. Agricultural capitalists' income increases substantially, from 0.6 percent of the total to 1.4 percent, as do the incomes of workers and peasants, while incomes of the urban and petty-capitalist classes fall. Detailed results of the simulations show that urban capitalists in agricultural processing suffer virtually no loss in real income. The crash in flexible prices by some 18 percent is responsible for the loss in urban capitalists' income. Due to the shift in the distribution of income and consequent rise in the demand for food, the terms of trade shift markedly in favor of agriculture, as shown in the right panel of the table 4.13. Consumption as a whole falls, but it is better distributed, and this gives a sizable increase in exports. Real consumption of domestic agriculture rises by 2 percent, while the consumption of processed agricultural goods declines by 5 percent.

Figure 4.4 shows how the policies have affected the characteristic curve for the economy. Curve I is the model with only two flexible prices and with none of the measures described in table 4.12. Curve II shows the relationship between real GDP and foreign savings for the model with flexible prices in the three markets, domestic agriculture, basics, and non-basics along with the parametric changes of table 4.12. First, observe that the combination of policies is equivalent to an increase of approximately 2 percent of total foreign savings under the old regime. This shows that, as a whole, a policy package similar to that implemented in February 1988 would stimulate the economy. Equally important is the flattening of the

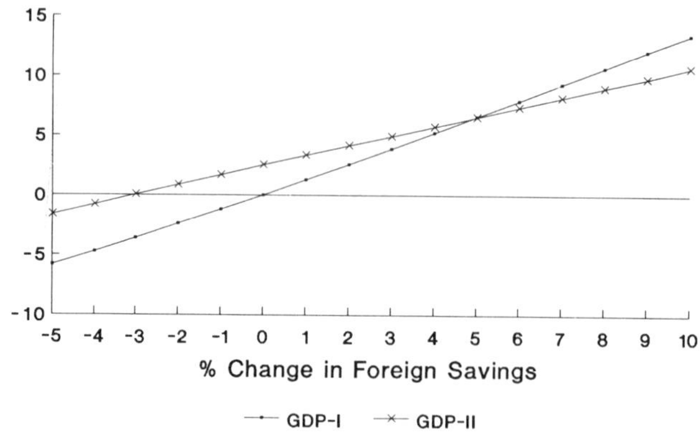

Figure 4.4
Percent change from base SAM under a policy reform package

characteristic curve: The new measures evidently render the economy less sensitive to foreign exchange shortage.

Figure 4.5 charts the change in the share of income in the two different models. I indicates the old regime with none of the policy measures, and II the new Sandinista policies. Here again the policies are shown to be superior to the previous arrangement, so far as the distribution of income measured in terms of shares. Not surprisingly, additional simulations show that nominal wage increases will shift both the curves *down* in an almost parallel fashion. Real incomes of workers increase, but when combined with peasants, the share as a whole declines. As suggested above, nominal wages increases are counterproductive to increases in the real incomes of the popular classes and especially so under the current policy regime.

Observe from table 4.13 that the government deficit falls with the policy package. In fact much of the benefit of the initiatives derives from the assumption on autonomous spending. If there were no reduction in spending, how would the economy fare? Table 4.14 shows the results of a simulation in which the policy parameters are set to the values of table 4.12 but there is no reduction in foreign savings. In model I government and investment spending are at their base values, whereas in model II they are reduced by 10 and 5 percent, respectively. The changes in the distribution of income shown in this table are dramatic in that they clearly show the enormous impact of autonomous spending. In the first case, model I, output rises by 1.7 percent, whereas in the second, the growth rate is 2.5 percent. Inflation is 3 percent higher in the first than in the second, and as the table shows, the percentage of income going to workers and peasants is six

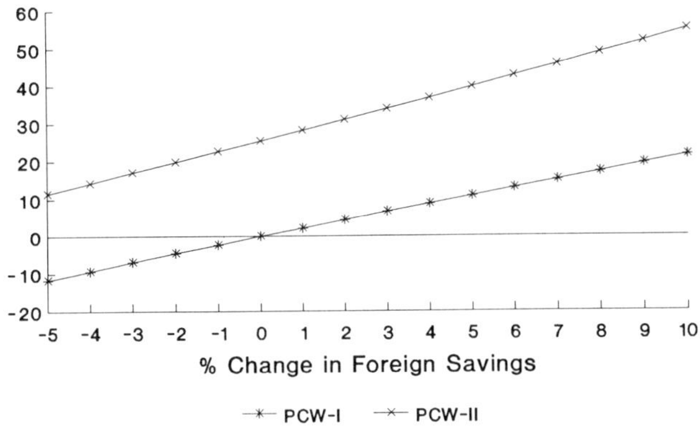

Figure 4.5
Percent change from base SAM when the policy mix changes

Table 4.14
Distribution of income with and without a reduction in autonomous expenditure

	Model I			Model II	
	Base share	Share	Δ in income	Share	Δ in income
Agricultural capitalists	0.6	1.2	91.8	2.1	222.4
Urban capitalists	23.9	17.6	−30.7	10.9	−60.0
Agricultural workers	8.3	9.0	−4.1	10.3	8.3
Urban workers	26.5	29.8	5.8	33.2	11.3
Campesinos	11.3	12.8	6.2	14.4	12.5
Capitalists	29.3	29.4	−6.4	29.1	−12.6

percentage points higher in the second simulation. Agricultural capitalists' income is higher due to the shift in the terms of trade: In the first model basic and nonbasic input prices fall by approximately 10 percent, but in the second they fall by 25 to 30 percent. On balance the nominal government deficit increases by 2.4 percent relative to the base in the first model and *falls* by 3 percent in the second.

4.4 Conclusions

The Sandinistas are not widely considered to be a "model" of development by other Third World nations, and as Noam Chomsky (1985) has observed, this is perhaps the deeper purpose of U.S. involvement in Central America. Nicaragua has been dismissed by the right as a Marxist-Leninist "dungeon," but what is more disconcerting is that much of the left has abandoned the regime as well.[22] Have the Sandinistas grown too rigid? It appears that this not the principal complaint: As suggested by Moises Hassan, the Mayor of Managua until he resigned in July 1988, "its not that the Sandinistas are Stalinists, its that they are incompetent."[23]

The model of this paper suggests that Sandinista policy is not incompetent, with the important exception of the guarantee price for export agriculture. The Sandinistas appear to appreciate the basic nature of the economy as foreign-exchange constrained and overheated by government spending. Policies seem to be designed consistently with this conception of how the economy works. Although recent initiatives have been criticized as *monetarismo sin los reales* (monetarism without the money), the measures taken by the Sandinistas conform to the goal of reducing the rent to scarce foreign exchange appropriated by the informal sector so as to reallocate labor to activities in more productive sectors of the economy. Evidently, the ultra-left view that all that is associated with the market mechanism conflicts with a rational and humane allocation of resources cannot not be taken too seriously. If the Sandinistas wish to maintain a mixed economy, it will be necessary for them to employ mixed policies when confronting the problems that arise.

Clearly the present policy track may not work. But it is important to keep in mind the possibility that *no* set of policies would be sufficient to extricate the Sandinistas from their present set of problems. Given the urgency of the war effort, the commitment to peasants and urban working classes, the resistance of the large growers and powerful urban interests, an aggressive, well-financed internal opposition press, a relatively pluralistic political environment as well as increasing dependence on the Soviet Union and Eastern European countries for trade and aid, it may be that *nothing* the Sandinistas can do from inside the *Casa de Gobierno* will in principle or practice be sufficient to put the economy back on a reasonable growth path.

Three more specific conclusions emerge from the model simulations and are listed here:

1. Price controls are not always progressive in their impact on the distribution of income. The effect of price controls depends upon income and expenditure balances throughout the economy as well as on whether foreign exchange availability is increasing or decreasing.

2. Devaluation is far more progressive than is typically assumed in Nicaragua, even when the foreign savings is declining. In a foreign-exchange-constrained economy real devaluation can more easily be achieved than in standard structuralist models.

3. When foreign savings rises, the income distribution improves; therefore, when foreign resources dry up, not only does the size of the pie decrease, but it is also divided less equally. But this should not be an invitation to protect the popular classes through nominal wage increases or higher government spending. Generally these efforts will be counterproductive and can easily erase the effects of a devaluation.

Notes

1. See Gibson (1985) for a similar model.

2. See, in particular, the books by Corragio et al. (1987), Spalding (1987), and Wheelock (1984). Also see Gibson (1985a). For a right-wing perspective, see Christian (1985). *Envio* is indispensable for recent events.

3. See Gibson (1985) for a simplified version of the present model. The data base is for 1981.

4. The SAM was made consistent with estimates of the 1987 GDP produced by the Secretary of Planning and Budget (SPP) of the central government. One major modification was made: Imports and exports were valued at a uniform exchange rate, that of exports. Both competitive and noncompetitive imports were affected. The details of the methodology are available from the author together with a complete bridge between the data of the SPP and that of the table 4.1.

5. A summary of notation, equations, and parameters is presented in table 4.7.

6. For an analysis of the agrarian reform, see Deere et al. (1985).

7. Keep in mind that there are more processes than goods and thus p_3 is correctly determined by the technological coefficients for process 7.

8. The bridge is given by

$$pp_j = \begin{cases} p_1 & j = 1, 2, 3 \\ p_2 & j = 4, 5, 6 \\ p_3 & j = 7 \\ p_4 & j = 8, 9 \\ p_5 & j = 10 \\ p_6 & j = 11 \\ p_7 & j = 12 \end{cases}$$

9. For more details on the class structure, see Deere et al. (1985).

10. For an excellent discussion of the process, see IHC, "How the Poor Survive," *Envio*, 1986.

11. See FitzGerald (1987) for the most authoritative account of the economic impact of the war.

12. How do we explain the more shallow slope in the second model? In a foreign-exchange-constrained economy a steeper characteristic curve for the growth rate implies that foreign exchange is being used more efficiently. Shifts in demand cause the structure of output to change in a way that uses less intermediate imports per unit of domestic product. Observe that in the base SAM, basic commodities are especially high in import content. Consequently, when their prices are allowed to fluctuate in model II and higher foreign exchange availability causes their prices to fall thereby stimulating demand for basics, imports increase. Moreover, when income shifts toward the petty-capitalists class, imports rise. Since a much greater proportion of income of this class derives from nonbasics than basics, a fall in the price of nonbasics hurts badly; the reverse is true for urban captial, but their propensity to import is not as high.

13. In 1985 it was second after Bolivia.

14. The multiple exchange rate system remains in place, however, in that exporters are required to sell their output to the state at a guarantee price which has seems to have little to do with the rate at which the Central Bank sells dollars. The guarantee price was doubled in February 1988, to the point that the implicit exchange rate is now approximately five new cordobas per dollar.

15. See Medal (1988, 118).

16. IHC (1988a, 16). The author's translation.

17. Both simulations were done in the pre-reform model, the model with nonbasics as a fix-price sector. In the flex-price version devaluation is less effective; a reduction of 2.6 percent in foreign savings is sufficient to return the system to zero growth. The changes in the distribution of income follow the same pattern with differences so slight as not to merit an explicit discussion.

18. Medal's informal estimate that a 10 percent devaluation would lead to a 3 percent increase in prices appears to be somewhat high, but within the same

general ballpark. See Medal (1988, 118). Estimates made at INCAE by Mayorga and Argüello on the basis of a model by Kruger are similar to those of Medal; a threefold increase in the exchange rate leads to an increase in the price level by a factor of 10. As a markup model for all sectors Kruger's scheme requires no consistency between supply and demand and implicitly assumes that the foreign-exchange constraint does not bind. The present model suggests that these estimates are far too pessimistic.

19. The difference is due to the larger proportion of nonbasic consumption in urban workers and the rise in its price (by 3.2 percent) when exports are reduced due to higher food consumption.

20. As the noted by *Envio*, organized workers, typically urban, have become aware of the impact of wages on prices:

... with each nominal rise in salaries, the working class suffered a new deterioration in its living standard. After the third experience of this, the workers began to criticize any new plan to raise their salaries. This seemingly surprising rejection of more wages was a natural reaction to the enormous expansion of money in circulation, in which some income was channeled toward the producers, but much more toward speculators in the commercial sector. (IHC 1986, 19)

21. The data shows further that raising the guarantee price by 5 percent rather than 3 percent has a slightly expansionary effect on output but increases inflation somewhat as well. Overall the effect is neutral on the distribution of income in that employment rises but real wages fall. The share of workers and peasants remains essentially constant.

22. See the July 1988 issue of *Envio*, always a staunch supporter of Sandinista policy, changing course. June 1988 (and again in August 1988) saw a new round of devaluation of which *Envio* was hotly critical:

The second fifteen days of June were marked by a notable lack of confidence by the people in the way the government was managing the economy. The basic difference between the two packages [February and June] is that the first included the people, while the second was an economic package without the people. (*Envio* IHC, 1988a, 11, author's translation)

23. From *La Prensa*, July 1988.

References

Argüello, A. Croes, E., and Kleiterp, N. (no date) "Acumulación, y Transformación: Inversiones 1979:85." Managua: INCAE.

CEPAL. 1987. "Balance Preliminar de la Economía Latinoamericana, 1987." *Notas sobre la Economía y el Desarrollo*. December: 455–456

Chomsky, N. (1985). *Turning the Tide*. Boston: South End Press.

Christian, S. 1985. *Revolution in the Family*. New York: Random House.

Colburn, F. D. 1986. *Post-Revolutionary Nicaragua: State, Class and Dilemmas of Agrarian Policy*. Berkeley: University of California Press.

Coraggio, J. L., and C. D. Deere. 1987. *La transición difícil: la autodeterminación de los pequeños países periféricos*. Mexico: Siglo XXI.

Deere, C. D., P. Marchetti, and N. Reinhardt. 1985. "The Peasantry and the Development of Sandinista Agrarian Policy, 1979–84." *Latin American Research Review* 20: 3.

FitzGerald, E. V. K. 1987. "An Evaluation of the Economic Costs to Nicaragua of U.S. Aggression: 1980–1984." In R. Spalding (ed.), *The Political Economy of Revolutionary Nicaragua*. London: Allen and Unwin.

Gibson, B. 1985. "A macromodel for post-revolutionary Nicaragua." *Cambridge Journal of Economics* 9.

Gibson, B. 1985a. "(de) Stabilization Policy in Nicaragua." Helsinki: UNU, Wider.

Instituto Historico Centroamericano (IHC). 1986. "How the Poor Survive." *Envio* 6 (December): 66.

Instituto Historico Centroamericano (IHC). 1988. "Economic Reform: Taking it to the Streets." *Envio* 7 (May): 82.

Instituto Historico Centroamericano (IHC). 1988a. "Las Medidas de Junio: Paquete Sin Pueblo." *Envio* 7 (July–August): 85.

Medal, J. L. 1988. *Nicaragua: Crisis, Cambio Social Y Política Económica*. Managua: CINASE.

Spalding, R. (ed.). 1987. *The Political Economy of Revolutionary Nicaragua*. London: Allen and Unwin

Utting, P. 1987. "Domestic Supply and Food Shortages." In R. Spalding (ed.), *The Political Economy of Revolutionary Nicaragua*. London: Allen and Unwin.

Wheelock, J. 1984. *Entre la Crisis y la Agresión: La Reforma Agraria Sandinista*. Managua: Communicaciones, MIDINRA.

Zalkin, M. 1987. "Food Policy and Class Transformation in Post-Revolutionary Nicaragua." *World Development*.

5 Resource Mobilization through Administered Prices in an Indian CGE

Manoj Panda and
Hiren Sarkar

The public sector in India has expanded substantially in last few decades and now occupies a significant place in the economy. It now accounts for a quarter of the country's GDP. More important, it accounts for half of gross domestic capital formation. Public sector activities are concentrated in the production of crucial inputs such as electricity, petroleum, coal, fertilizers, minerals, and metals as well as infrastructural services, namely, railways. Most of the public sector production units are managed by public enterprises, though some such as the railways are run directly by government departments. In either mode of management, the pricing policies of these goods and services are under formal or informal administrative control of the government.

5.1 Public Sector Pricing Policy

The pricing policy for these administered price (AP) sectors has historically not been explicitly guided by the profit motive. Most of the public sector enterprises in fact have been either earning only a small profit or losing money. Recently, however, emphasis has shifted toward generating large surpluses in government undertakings. Public enterprises contributed about 17 percent of the total public sector outlay in the sixth Five-Year Plan (1980–85). In the current seventh plan (1985–90) the target has been nearly doubled so that the contribution of public undertakings has been fixed at about one-third of the total public sector outlay. To achieve this, the government may need to resort to increases in administered prices of public sector products in order to avoid raising taxes as a means of financing the plan. Indeed, the prices of petroleum and coal were immediately increased at the start of the seventh Five-Year Plan. Given this background, it would be of considerable interest to examine the implications of increasing administered prices to finance public investment.

In the past some studies in India have attempted to compute the impact of administered price increases on general and sectoral price levels by using cost-based price formation equations (see Rangarajan et al. 1981; Gupta and Srinivasan 1984). Jha and Mundle (1987) extend the analysis by incorporating wage feedback in a simultaneous price-wage system. These studies are confined to inflationary issues only. Since they completely neglect output–price linkages, even the inflationary impact considered by them may be regarded as partial effects. As prices are affected by both cost-push and demand-pull factors, changes in both cost and demand need to be considered in a simultaneous framework to fully reflect the implications of price changes in the administered price sectors. Also when the price of such a sector is increased, the corresponding nominal surplus (profit) is expected to increase. This surplus accrues to government in the form of additional nontax revenue. The government has options for using the extra revenue either to reduce the budget deficit or to incur additional expenditure. These obviously have different macro implications. Government revenue generation and expenditure must be considered jointly in evaluating effects of administered price increases. Dasgupta (1986) examines the macro implications, taking into account the resource use (government wage payments) aspect as well. This attempt has been at an aggregative level and confined to algebra without any practical application.

Clearly the proper framework for analyzing the various implications of changes in administered price is an economywide model in which output, price, income, and expenditure are determined simultaneously and both households and government are considered as agents in the economy with endogenous income and expenditure flows. In this paper we develop a model in this framework and apply it to quantitatively analyze the effects of mobilizing and expending resources generated through increases in administered prices.

In section 5.2 we set up a simple model with two sectors for an easy understanding of both the model's framework and the implications of an administered price rise. This is followed in section 5.3 by the description of an elaborate CGE model developed for empirical use. In section 5.4 we discuss the results of a series of comparative statics on administered price and government investment policies and draw some conclusions about performance of administered prices as instruments for resource mobilization.

5.2 A Two-Sector Model

In this section we consider a two-sector economy with a view toward examining macro implications of financing public investment through the surplus generated by increasing administered prices. The two sectors considered produce manufactured goods and raw materials. The following condition is assumed in order to make the presentation simple: The first sector uses both raw material and labor to produce the manufacturing good, whereas the second sector produces raw material by means of labor alone. One may think of the raw material production as a simple extraction process, such as of coal, requiring only labor.

The second sector is under government control, and its price is administered. The proceeds from the sale of the raw material in excess of wage payment in the sector constitutes the surplus from public sector enterprise. This is the only source of revenue for the government, and it is entirely spent on public investment.

Output levels of both sectors are demand determined. The final demand for the manufactured good is comprised of consumption (private) and investment (private and government). The second sector meets the entire raw material demand of first sector. The raw material output is thus directly linked to the manufacturing output by the input–output coefficient.

The first sector's price is assumed to be cost based determined by applying a constant markup rate on unit prime cost. The latter consists of the raw material's cost and wage bill per unit of output. There are two income classes: wage earners and markup (profit) earners. Wage income is earned in sectors 1 and 2, but private profit originates only in sector 1. The savings propensities of the two classes are assumed to differ.

The above characterization of the simple economy may now be written algebraically as follows:

$$P_1 = (l_1 w_1 + aP_2)(1 + T_1), \tag{1}$$

$$X_1 = C_1 + I_1 + A_1, \tag{2}$$

$$X_2 = aX_1, \tag{3}$$

$$I_1 = \frac{P_2 X_2 - l_2 w_2 X_2}{P_1}, \tag{4}$$

$$Y_w = l_1 w_1 X_1 + l_2 w_2 X_2, \tag{5}$$

$$Y_z = (l_1 w_1 + aP_2) T_1 X_1, \tag{6}$$

$$C_1 = \frac{(1 - S_w) Y_w + (1 - S_z) Y_z}{P_1}, \tag{7}$$

where

P_i = price in sector i (per unit of output),

X_i = output in sector i (real),
l_i = labor output coefficient in sector i,
w_i = money wage rate in sector i,
a = raw material (produced in sector 2) requirement per unit of output in sector 1,
T_1 = markup rate in sector 1,
C_1 = private consumption demand in sector 1 (real),
A_1 = private investment demand in sector 1 (real),
I_1 = government investment demand in sector 1 (real),
Y_w = income of wage earners (nominal),
Y_z = income of profit (markup) earners (nominal),
S_w = savings propensity of wage earners,
S_z = savings propensity of profit earners.

The equations are self-explanatory. They define the price of manufacturing, output levels of the two sectors, real public investment, income accruing to the two classes, and private consumption demand. The raw material price P_2 is assumed to be an exogenous policy variable. Also exogenous are real private investment, markup, and wage rates. The seven variables appearing at the left-hand side of equations (1) through (7) are endogenous. The nominal value of the second sector's output P_2X_2 constitutes the government revenue. Government expenditures consist of wage payment in sector 2 (cost of running public enterprise) and nominal government investment I_1P_1. We consider a "balanced" budget regime so that expenditure equals revenue in the government sector. Thus investment (savings) of public sector is defined by surplus in public enterprise $(P_2X_2 - l_2w_2X_2)$ in equation (4).

In the present model an increase in surplus in the raw material sector would amount to an expansion of public investment. Given technology and wage rate, surplus could be increased by an administrative decision to charge a higher price for the product of sector 2. The macro effects of such a rise in administered price P_2 in the model described by equations (1) through (7) can be explained with the help of a diagram (figure 5.1).

Line P_1P_1' in quadrant 1 of the diagram represents the relationship between P_1 and P_2 and corresponds to equation (1). D_1D_1' in quadrant 2 depicts the implied relationship between output (demand of X_1 and its price P_1 corresponding to a "reduced form" of equations (2), (4), (5), (6), and (7).

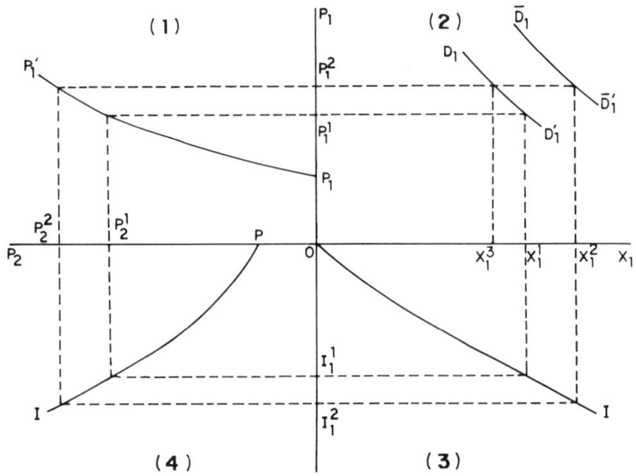

Figure 5.1
Macro effects of increasing administered prices

The line OI in quadrant 3 describes the functional relationship of the government investment I_1 (equal to government surplus) and output (X_1) of the final product. This relationship can be derived from equations (3) and (4). Line IP in quadrant 4 shows the direct dependence of government surplus (investment) on administered price P_2 which is its only source of revenue. This is according to equation (4). To get an equilibrium solution, all of these relationship should be satisfied simultaneously. Accordingly, corresponding to an initial level of P_2 the consistent price of the manufacturing sector is P_1^1, the output is X_1^1, and the government investment is I_1^1. Now, if the administered price P_2^1 is increased to P_2^2, one can work through the diagram to arrive at the new equilibrium set: manufacturing price P_1^2, investment I_1^2, and corresponding output X_1^2. But what will happen to the overall demand schedule $D_1 D_1'$? If the surplus mobilized by increasing P_2 is not spent, one can use the same demand schedule and arrive at the output X_1^3, which is less than initial output X_1^1. An increase in P_2 would clearly lead to inflation and contraction. However, under the present circumstances the contraction in consumption demand, which is indirect, will be more than offset by the direct increase in investment demand activating the usual multiplier. This will result in a shift of the demand schedule $D_1 D_1'$ to $\bar{D}_1 \bar{D}_1'$. The story here is growth and inflation.

The purpose of this section has been twofold: (1) to introduce the linkages of the administered price sector with the rest of the economy and

(2) to examine the macro economic implications of financing public investment by increasing administered price. The main features and adjustment mechanism of this simple model have been used to develop an elaborate computable general equilibrium (CGE) model for India. The CGE model has enabled us to quantitatively analyze the issues associated with resource mobilization through increase in administered prices.

5.3 A Ten-Sector CGE Model

Obviously the Indian economy is far more complex than the two-sector model described in the earlier section. For a realistic description of the economy that also incorporates the relevant linkages of the AP sectors, the following structural features, among others, need to be modeled:

The appropriate sectoral details of economy and differences in sectoral output and price formation mechanisms.

The interindustry linkages among the production sectors of the economy.

Explicit role of the cost-push and demand-pull factors in price formation.

Wage response to price changes.

Income generation processes and savings behaviors of different income recipient groups.

Income generation of the government from both tax and nontax sources and their linkages with output and price.

Government expenditure pattern and its relationship with other macro variables.

The model developed for the present study incorporates these structural features and hence is suitable for analyzing issues related to administered price changes. We now turn to the details of the model. The model considers ten production sectors and three income classes:

1. Food agriculture (cereals, pulses, and vegetables)
2. Other agriculture
3. Basic goods industries (steel, cement, fertilizers, heavy chemicals, petrochemicals)
4. General manufacturing and construction (excluding basic industry)
5. Petroleum refining
6. Coal

7. Electricity, gas, and water
8. Rail transport
9. Other transport
10. Rest of economy

Public administration and defense, which does not have much interindustry linkage with other productive sectors, is considered exogenously. Sectors 5 through 8 are AP sectors. In these sectors all surpluses accrue to government, whereas in others they get divided between private and public sectors.

The three income classes considered in the model are agricultural income earners, nonagricultural wage income earners, and nonagricultural profit (nonwage) income earners. The distinction between wage and profit income is not made in the two agricultural sectors. The reason for considering the entire agricultural income in one class is that Indian agriculture is dominated by the "self-employed" category for which it is not possible to ascertain pure wage and profit components.

The model is build around the consistency framework of a social accounting matrix (SAM). At the core of the model lies a closed-loop version of the input–output model (Leontief 1951) and Kaleckian-type cost-based price formation equations (Kalecki 1971). In AP sectors 5 through 8 prices are exogenously determined by government. In other nonagriculture sectors they are determined by applying a variable markup rate on prime cost. Excess capacity is postulated in all the nonagricultural sectors, and their output levels are demand determined. But on the price front markup rates are assumed to respond to the level of capacity utilization. The production activities generate income that accrues to the three income classes. The private disposable income along with sectoral prices determine the consumption pattern through a linear expenditure system (Stone 1954). The consumption levels in turn influence outputs in the demand-determined sectors.

In the government sector we consider the income and expenditure flows of the government. Government revenue is generated by direct and indirect taxes, market borrowing, and profits of public enterprises. Government expenditure consists of public investment, public consumption, and wages and salaries in public administration and defense. In the external sector we consider exports and competitive and noncompetitive (or intermediate) imports separately.

The equations in the model (glossary given in appendix A) are arranged in six different blocks. We will discuss them one by one.

1. Price, Wage, Markup

Equations (1) and (2):

$$P_j = \alpha_{aj} + \beta_{aj} X_j + \gamma_{aj} Y, \qquad j = 1, 2.$$

Equations (3) through (6):

$$B_j = \sum_{i=1}^{10} a_{ij} P_i + W_j b_j + e a_{0j} P_{0j}^*, \qquad j = 3, 4, 9, 10.$$

Equations (7) through (10):

$$P_j = B_j (1 + T_j)(1 + t_j), \qquad j = 3, 4, 9, 10.$$

Equations (11) and (18):

$$W_j = \alpha_{wj} + \beta_{wj} \text{CPI} + \gamma_{wj} \text{CPI}_{-1}, \qquad j = 3, \ldots, 10.$$

Equation (19):

$$\text{CPI} = \sum_{i=1}^{10} \varphi_i P_i.$$

Equations (20) through (22):

$$T_j = T_j^0 \left(\frac{X_j}{X_j^*} \right)^{\varepsilon_j}, \qquad j = 4, 9, 10.$$

Equations (1) and (2) specify prices of the two agricultural sectors P_1 and P_2 as functions of output of the particular sector and personal disposable income Y. This implies that agricultural prices respond to both supply and demand factors. Among the nonagricultural sectors, prices in four sectors (5 through 8) are administered as already noted. These prices are specified exogenously. In the other four nonagricultural sectors (3, 4, 9, and 10) the prices are determined by applying an appropriate markup and indirect tax rates T and t, respectively, over the unit prime cost B. The latter consists of material inputs $\sum a_{ji} p_j$, the wage bill $b_i w_i$, and imported inputs; these are shown in equations (3) through (6).

Both the wage rate and the markup rate are endogenized in the system. Nonagricultural wage rates W_i are partially indexed to consumer price index (CPI) number of the current year and the previous year. The CPI is estimated as a weighted sum of the sectoral prices. Markup rates of sectors 4, 9, and 10 respond to capacity utilization as indicated by ratio of actual output X_i to a capacity output X_i^*. This mechanism captures the effect of excess demand on price formation.

The international price P_0^* and exchange rate e are exogenously specified. The endogenous variables of this block are prices in the non-AP sectors, wage rates in the nonagricultural sectors, and markup rates in the nonagricultural non-AP sectors.

2. Commodity balance
Equations (23) and (24):

$$\Delta S_i = X_i + M_i - \sum_{j=1}^{10} a_{ij} X_j - C_i - G_i - E_i, \qquad i = 1, 2.$$

Equation (25):

$$X_4 = \sum_{j=1}^{10} a_{ij} X_j + C_4 + G_4 + \Delta S_4 + E_4 - M_4 + PRI + PUBI.$$

Equations (26) through (32):

$$X_i = \sum_{j=1}^{10} a_{ij} X_j + C_i + G_i + \Delta S_i + E_i - M_i, \qquad i = 3, 5, \ldots, 10.$$

In this block we consider the real commodity balance equations for the ten sectors. The commodity supply (output X plus imports M in each sector is equivalent to the intermediate and final demand. Among the final demand elements, public investment *PUBI*, private investment *PRI*, government consumption G, exports E, and competing imports M are exogenous to the model. Private consumption C is endogenous; it is discussed in block 4.

Agricultural output levels are assumed to be exogenous variables since they are weather dependent in the short run. The demand-supply balance in these sectors is achieved by changes in stock. In all other sectors output levels are demand determined. The change in stock ΔS in these sectors is exogenous but endogenous in the agricultural sectors. The fixed investment component of final demand appears only in sector 4 which alone produces investment goods. We distinguish between private and public investment, and both are fixed in real terms.

3. Private income generation
Equations (33) and (34):

$$V_j = P_j - \sum_{i=1}^{2} a_{ij} P_i - a_{3j} P_F - \sum_{i=4}^{10} a_{ij} P_i - e a_{0j} P_{0j}^*, \qquad j = 1, 2.$$

Equation (35):

$$Y_A = V_1 X_1 + V_2 X_2.$$

Equation (36):

$$Y_W = \sum_{i=1}^{10} W_i b_i X_i + W_g L_g + eR + TRANS.$$

Equation (37):

$$W_g = \alpha_{Wg} + \beta_{Wg}\mathrm{CPI} + \gamma_{Wg}(\mathrm{CPI})_{-1}.$$

Equation (38):

$$Y_Z = T_3 B_3 X_3 + T_4 B_4 X_4 + T_9 B_9 X_9 + T_{10} B_{10} X_{10} - GP_3 - GP_4 - GP_9 - GP_{10} + GINT.$$

Equation (39):

$$Y = Y_A + Y_W + (1 - t_Z) Y_Z.$$

In this block we specify income generations of the three income-earning classes. Equations (33) and (34) determine the current price value added per unit of output in the agricultural sectors. The total value added in the two agricultural sectors defines agricultural income Y_A. As already noted, wages and profits are not separated in agriculture. Nonagricultural wage earners receive wages from sectors 3 through 10 and from public administration and defense ($W_g L_g$), remittances from abroad (eR), and transfer payments ($TRANS$) from government. Nonagricultural profit income Y_Z accruing to private individuals is generated from sectors 3, 4, 9, and 10 (for other sectors profits accrue to government only). The total markup income in these sectors less prespecified government profit GP determines the private profit income. The government obtains profits from some of the public enterprises in these sectors. Government interest payments $GINT$ are assumed to be received by profit earners only. It is also assumed that the income tax is paid from profit income alone. The last equation in the block determines private disposable income Y.

4. Private consumption and savings

Equation (40):

$$S_A = \alpha_{SA} + \beta_{SA} Y_A.$$

Equation (41):

$$S_W = \alpha_{SW} + \beta_{SW} Y_W.$$

Equation (42):

$$S_Z = \alpha_{SZ} + \beta_{SZ} Y_Z.$$

Equation (43):

$$D = Y - S_A - S_W - S_Z.$$

Equations (44) through (53):

$$C_i = \theta_i + \frac{m_i}{P_i}(D - \sum_{j=1}^{10} \theta_j P_j), \qquad i = 1, \ldots, 10.$$

Savings S_k of the three classes are specified as linear functions of their respective income levels in equations (44) through (53). Total private consumption expenditure D is then computed by deducting savings from disposable income Y. The LES equations are used to determine sectoral consumption levels C_i as function of total consumption expenditure and all the prices. In equations (44) through (53), the θ_i's denote committed consumption expenditures which are independent of prices. Expenditure in excess of total committed expenditure is distributed among various items depending on marginal propensities to consume m_i and prices. Note that in LES each m_i is restricted to be positive and their sum is unity.

5. Government account

Equation (54):

$$\pi_5 = P_5 - \sum_{\substack{i=1 \\ i \neq 4}}^{10} \left\{ a_{i5} P_i - W_5 b_5 - \left(\frac{\overline{X}_{c5}}{X_5}\right) \overline{P}_{c5} - \left[a_{c5} - \left(\frac{\overline{X}_{c5}}{X_5}\right)\right] eP_{05}^{*} \right\}.$$

Equations (55) through (57):

$$\pi_j = P_j - \sum_{i=1}^{10} (a_{ij} P_i - W_j b_j - ea_{0j} P_{0j}^{*}), \qquad j = 6, 7, 8.$$

Equation (58):

$$GREV = \sum_{i=5}^{8} \pi_i X_i + GP_3 + GP_4 + GP_9 + GP_{10} + t_Z Y_Z$$
$$+ \sum_{i=3,4,9,10} (t_i B_i X_i)(1 + T_i).$$

Equation (59):

$$GEXP = \sum_{i=1}^{10} P_i G_i + W_g L_g + (P_3 - P_F)(a_{31} X_1 + a_{32} X_2)$$
$$+ TRANS + GINT.$$

Equation (60):

$$GBUD = (GREV - GEXP) + (GBDOM + GBEXT - PUBI \cdot P_4)$$

We first compute profit per unit of output in sectors 5 through 8, which are exclusively in the public sector. In sectors 6 through 8 profit is obtained as the difference between the price and the unit's prime cost. In the petroleum refinery sector (sector 5) it is assumed that domestic production of crude petroleum is fixed at $\bar{X}_{c5}$ and that $\bar{P}_{c5}$ is the corresponding unit extraction cost. The rest of crude is imported at international price P^*_{05}. The total cost of crude per unit of refinery output may thus be given as

$$\left(\frac{\bar{X}_{c5}}{X_5}\right)\bar{P}_{c5} + eP^*_{05}\left(a_{c5} - \frac{\bar{X}_{c5}}{X_5}\right),$$

where a_{c5} is coefficient representing the total crude required per unit output of sector 5 and $\bar{X}_{c5}$ the fixed domestic production of crude.

In equation (58) we estimate government current revenue $GREV$ as the sum of government profit from production sectors, direct tax revenue, and indirect tax revenue. Government profit in sectors 5 through 8 are endogenously determined, whereas its level is prespecified for other nonagricultural sectors. Government current expenditure consists of government consumption, the wage bill in public administration and defense, a fertilizer subsidy, and transfer and interest payments. Government capital expenditure consists of public investment expenditure ($P_4 \cdot PUBI$), but capital receipts are composed of domestic and external borrowings. The difference between total (current and capital) expenditure and total revenue constitutes the budget deficit.

6. Other identities

Equation (61):

$$BOP = \sum_{i=1}^{10} P_i M_i + eP^*_{0I} \cdot I_0 + e \sum_{\substack{i=1,\\ i\neq 5}}^{10} a_{0i} \cdot P^*_{0i} \cdot X_i + e(a_{c5}X_5 - \bar{X}_{c5})P^*_{05} - \sum_{i=1}^{10} P_i E_i - eR.$$

Equation (62):

$$GDPN = \sum_{i=1}^{2} V_i X_i + \sum_{i=3}^{10} W_i b_i X_i + \sum_{i=3}^{4} T_i B_i X_i + \sum_{i=9}^{10} T_i B_i X_i + \sum_{i=5}^{8} \pi_i X_i + W_g L_g.$$

Equation (63):

$$GDPR = \sum_{i=1}^{10} VR_i X_i + L_g.$$

Equation (64):

$$GDPPEF = \frac{GDPN}{GDPR}.$$

Equation (65):

$$S_A + S_W + S_Z + (GREV - GEXP) + BOP$$
$$= P_4(PRI + PUBI) + \sum_{i=1}^{10} P_i \cdot \Delta S_i + e \cdot P_{0I}^* \cdot I_0.$$

The import transactions in the external sector relate to competing imports M, capital goods imports I_0, and noncompeting imports linked to sectoral output levels. Foreign receipts accrue from exports and emigrant remittances. Balance of payments on current account *BOP* is determined by total payments and total receipts in external sector. The nominal GDP (*GDPN*) is defined in equation (62) as the sum of all factor payments at current prices including government profits. The real GDP (*GDPR*) is estimated by using real value added–output ratios. Finally, the savings-investment balance is computed in equation (65) which is not an independent entity but can be derived from other equations in the system. By computing total savings and total investment separately, one obtains a numerical check on the income-expenditure balance in the model. In the glossary given in appendix A, we have specified the endogenous variables, the exogenous variables, and the parameters. Given the values of the exogenous variables and parameter estimates, the system of equations has been solved by an interwoven system of Gauss-Siedel iteration routine.

5.4 Simulation Experiments and Results

Using the model developed earlier, we proceed in this section to analyze the short-run macro scenarios corresponding to the situations where the prices of the AP sectors are used as instruments of resource mobilization. This has been done by performing a series of comparative statics experiments. Before describing the simulation experiments and their results, let us briefly comment on the estimation of the model. As pointed out earlier, the present model belongs to the family of social accounting matrix (SAM) based computable general equilibrium (CGE) models. In these models there are two classes of parameters. The first type of parameters are point estimates computed directly from the SAM, and the second type of parameters are behavioral estimates from time series data. For the present model the second set refers to the parameters of the wage rate equations, consumption functions, and the markup rate equations. Details of the construction of SAM for India and related parameters are given in Sarkar and Subbarao (1981a) and Taylor (1983). For this exercise we have used the social accounting matrix of 1983–84. The SAM and the major parameter estimates are given in appendix B. We will refer to the actual 1983–84 macro scenarios as the base run, and the simulations will correspond to scenarios in which some of the exogenous variables of the model are changed from their base (1983–84) values.

Now let us discuss the a priori effects of price rise in an AP sector, say, petroleum. In our model's framework the following chain of events would take place. The price increase in the petroleum sector will be passed on to the non-AP sectors through an increase in the input cost, which will push up their prices. This will reduce private consumption demand, which in turn will translate into a fall in output and income. In AP sectors other than petroleum, production costs will increase, but prices will remain unaltered. As a consequence the surplus from these sectors will decline. However, the surplus in petroleum sector will increase as a direct result of its price rise. This should in general more than offset the indirect decline in surplus of other sectors, leading to an increase in surplus from AP sectors as a whole. Apart from the production costs of AP sectors, other government expenditures like public investment and public consumption will also increase due to inflation. The net effect of changes in government revenue and expenditure arising from the AP increase is likely to be a fall in government budget deficit.

Since markup rates are linked to capacity utilization levels, the effect of the fall in output will be transmitted to prices via a decrease in the markup rates. Thus on the price front for the sectors where prices follow markup pricing, we get an upward cost push through the increase in material cost and wage cost and a downward demand pull through the reduction in the markup rates. The ultimate equilibrium will be determined by the net effect of these two competing forces. The response of the external sector to the domestic petroleum price rise would be in the form of an improvement in BOP situation because of the fall in private and intermediate consumption demand for petroleum. Thus, in a nutshell, the effects of petroleum price increase would be a rise in prices, a fall in output and income, an increase in government revenue, and a decrease in budget deficit and BOP deficit.

Now, if government surplus that accrues due to a price increase in an AP sector is spent by the government for more public investment expenditure, the picture would be different. Expansion in investment will lead to an output increase in the demand-determined nonagricultural sectors. This is in contrast to the output reduction in the previous case. The cost-push inflationary effect would still be felt as earlier, but the demand-pull effect would now act in the opposite direction. In other words, both cost-push and demand-pull effects will exert upward pressure on prices, and so the overall inflation will now be of larger magnitude. In this way we find that the present model is capable of simulating a fairly wide range of alternative economywide effects associated with an increase in administered prices. A flow diagram of the price linkages in AP sectors with other macro variables is shown in figure 5.2.

Now we discuss the results of the comparative statics simulations. First, we examine the pure effects of a price increase in the AP sectors without any other changes. Second, we examine the effects of AP increases when the additional resources are used for expanding public investment expenditure.

Effects of Increasing Administered Prices

Table 5.1 shows the major effects when prices in AP sectors are increased. The levels of the variables corresponding to the base run are given in column 2 of table 5.1. The effects of a 10 percent increase in petroluem price P_5 are documented in column 3 in the form of deviations from base. The next three columns show similar results when the 10 percent price increases are effected in three other AP sectors: coal, electricity, and railways.

A 10 percent rise in P_5 pushes up cost and prices in the petroleum-using non-AP sectors, leading to a general price (as reflected by GDP deflator) rise of 0.55 percent. In the other AP sectors the cost increase leads to a reduction in surplus because the prices do not change. The price rise causes a significant decline in private consumption. This reduces output and income in the demand-determined nonagricultural sectors, leading to a fall in real GDP by a little more than Rs.300 crores (about $250 million). The macro effects of petroleum price increase is clearly stagflationary. We may note that since agricultural prices are linked to the aggregate personal

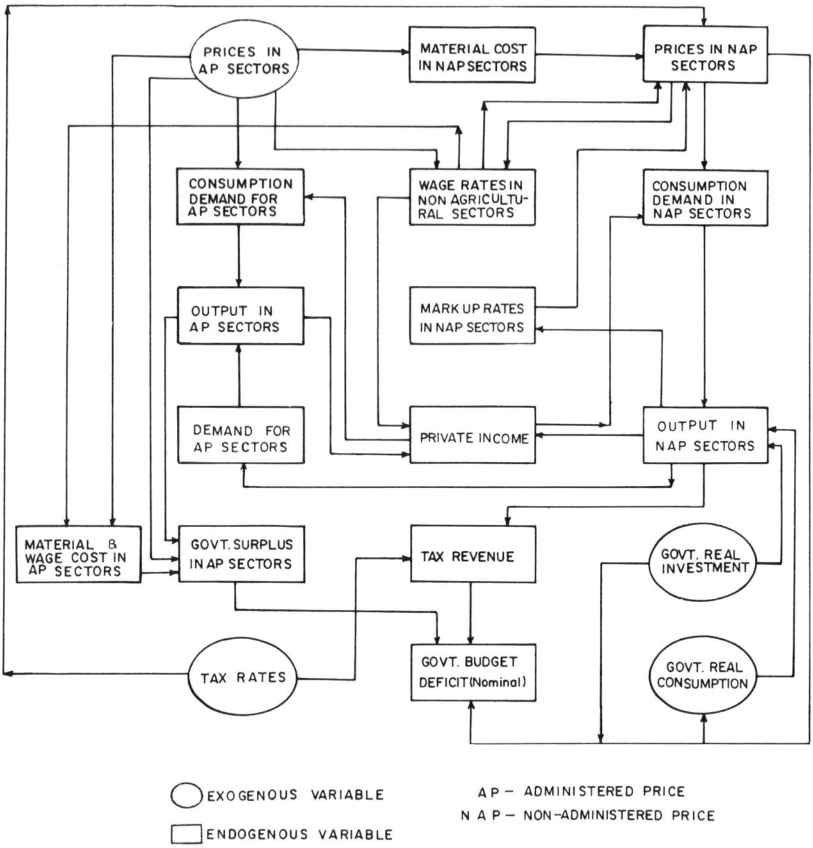

Figure 5.2
Flow chart showing major linkages of administered price with other macro variables

Table 5.1
Effects of increases in administered prices (Rs. crores)

Variables	Level in base run	Deviation from base (increased by 10 percent)			
		Petroleum price P_5	Coal price P_6	Electricity price P_7	Railway price P_8
1. Real GDP at factor cost	173,420	−320	−52	−229	−226
2. GDP deflator	100.00	0.55	0.15	0.44	0.39
3. Real private consumption	135,313	−616	−93	−401	−382
4. Government current expenditure	32,468	182	50	144	145
5. Government investment	20,517	153	54	133	107
6. Government current revenue	42,229	824	209	561	476
7. Government surplus from public enterprises	3,874	668	150	404	356
8. Budget deficit	2,135	−356	−77	−207	−163
9. **Sectoral prices**					
Food agriculture	100.00	−0.04	0.02	0.04	0.02
Other agriculture	100.00	−0.04	0.02	0.05	0.03
Basic industry	100.00	1.09	0.52	1.08	0.56
General manufacturing and construction	100.00	0.75	0.26	0.66	0.53
Petroleum refining	100.00	10.00	—	—	—
Coal	100.00	—	10.00	—	—
Electricity	100.00	—	—	10.00	—
Railways	100.00	—	—	—	10.00
Other transport	100.00	2.54	0.09	0.38	0.31
Services excluding public administration and defense	100.00	0.47	0.10	0.58	0.50

Note: Indices are price variables.

income level, the decline in P_1 and P_2 indicates fall in personal income when P_5 is increased.

The major effects that follow a price increase in other AP sectors are directionwise similar to those of the petroleum price increase (see columns 4, 5, and 6 in table 5.1). In all cases we find the stagflationary story. From the point of view of overall inflationary impact, the petroleum price increase ranks the highest where the GDP deflator increases by 0.55 percentage point from the base. This is followed by electricity (0.44 percent), railways (0.39 percent), and coal (0.15 percent). The fall in real GDP follows similar ranking: the magnitude being 320 crores for the petroleum price increase followed by 229 crores for the increase in electricity price, 226 crores for the railway price, and 52 crores for the coal price. It is to be noted that the impact of both the price and output depends to a great extent on the interindustry linkages as the price increase in one sector is passed on to the other sectors via the input coefficients. In this circumstance when we change one administered price, its effect will be moderated to the extent that prices of other AP sectors are held constant. For example, when the coal price is changed, the effect of this on either the railway or electricity price will not be felt by the user industries and hence will not be transmitted.

The other interesting point to note is that the surplus-generating capacity of the four AP sectors are widely different. It is the highest for petroleum (Rs.668 crores) and the lowest for coal (Rs.150 crores) when the percentage increase in prices is of the same order. This is due to the differences in the extent of (domestic) backward linkages of the AP sectors. For example, when the price of petroleum refining is increased, its own production cost is not affected much because the domestic component of the raw materials used in the production of petroleum is relatively small. As a result profits go up significantly. A formal analysis of this is presented in detail by Sarkar and Kadekodi (1988).

Higher Public Investment Financed by AP Sector Price Increases

We now proceed to evaluate the results when the additional revenue generated by increasing the price in an AP sector is used to finance a public investment increase. The simulations carried out for this purpose are as follows: We increase the real public investment by Rs.500 crores over the base level. As a consequence the budget deficit increases. One of the administered prices, say, that of petroleum, is then iteratively increased until the budget deficit comes back to the base level. This "balanced" budget scenario is repeated for each of the administered prices.

Table 5.2 presents the results for this set of simulation runs. As in table 5.1, this table also shows the estimated absolute levels of the variables in the base run and the deviation from the base run of other runs.

The first and the most important point to note is that the results show real growth and inflation. In all cases both real GDP and the GDP deflator increase from their base value. This result of "growth and inflation" is in contrast to the stagflationary situation noted in the first set of counterfactuals. This difference is a natural consequence of the expansionary fiscal policy considered here.

Next, note that in order to generate the resources for an additional Rs.500 crores of real investment, the prices of the four AP sectors need to be raised by a different amount. The required increase in coal price is as much as 36.9 percent, whereas it is the lowest for petroleum price: only 7.8 percent. This is the result of differences in resource-generating capacity of the AP sectors as noted in table 5.1.

The overall price rise is the highest (0.84 percent) when railways' price P_6 is increased followed by electricity (0.77 percent). The overall price rise in the case of an increase in the petroleum price is the lowest (0.60 percent). At the sectoral level the price effects are relatively stronger for basic industries (sector 3) and general manufacturing (sector 4). These industrial sectors are more intensive users of energy and transport. The petroleum price rise has a significant effect on the price of other transport such as truck transport which is a major user of petroleum. About an 8 percent rise in P_5 leads to a 2 percent rise in P_9. These price changes take into account both cost-push and demand-pull effects in the non-AP sectors. The cost effect is activated directly through the input–output linkages, and the demand-pull effect is captured through the response of markup rates to output changes. Both the changes in GDP and in price influence private consumption; growth in GDP will increase private consumption, whereas a price increase will decrease it. However, it is found that the net effect is a decline in real private consumption by a varying amount ranging between Rs.47 crores for the price of coal to Rs.369 crores for that of railways. At the sectoral level private consumption of the sector whose price is directly increased reduces sharply. This is reflected in the steep fall in output level of the concerned sector in each of the simulation runs. Thus, for example, X_8 falls by Rs.132 crores when P_8 is increased. On the government account we may note that Rs.500 crores additional real investment translates into much larger nominal value. The additional nominal investment turns out to be the highest for coal price (Rs.731 crores) and the lowest for petroleum price (Rs.653 crores). These differences are due to the differences in price increases of the investment goods' sector (sector 4) corresponding to the

Table 5.2
Effects of increasing government investment by increasing administered prices (Rs. crores)

Variables	Level in base run	Deviation from base to finance a Rs.500 crore increase in public investment				
		Price of petroleum P_5	Price of coal P_6	Price of electricity P_7	Price of railways P_8	Indirect tax rate of general industries t_4
1. Real GDP at factor cost	173,420	231	299	173	95	311
2. GDP deflator	100.00	0.60	0.72	0.77	0.84	0.22
3. Real Private consumption	135,313	−195	−47	−252	−369	−48
4. Government current expenditure	32,468	167	209	219	281	110
5. Government investment	20,517	653	731	715	722	725
6. Government current revenue	42,229	835	940	934	1,003	835
7. Government surplus from public enterprises	3,874	525	551	546	618	−49
8. Budget deficit	2,135	—	—	—	—	—
9. BOP	1,512	−78	−10	−34	−59	−22
10. Percentage share of personal income						
Agricultural income	35.75	−0.13	−0.12	−0.14	−0.14	−0.10
Wage income	38.35	−0.02	−0.05	−0.05	−0.06	−0.02
Profit income	25.90	0.15	0.17	0.19	0.20	0.12
11. Sectoral output[a]						
Basic industries	14,855	44	47	43	39	46
General manufacturing and construction	124,399	628	668	617	550	652

	Petroleum refining	8,408	−38	23	13	—	21
	Coal	2,903	10	−15	−1	—	11
	Electricity	7,219	20	22	−69	12	23
	Railways	4,989	13	16	10	−132	15
	Other transport	15,029	−50	33	10	3	31
	Services excluding public administration and defense	80,670	85	139	21	−20	139
12.	Sectoral prices[a]						
	Food agriculture	100.00	0.31	0.44	0.41	0.40	0.34
	Other agriculture	100.00	0.36	0.48	0.45	0.44	0.38
	Basic industries	100.00	0.94	2.00	1.54	1.08	0.45
	General manufacturing and construction	100.00	0.74	1.11	1.03	1.07	1.08
	Petroleum refining	100.00	7.85	—	—	—	—
	Coal	100.00	—	36.91	—	—	—
	Electricity	100.00	—	—	13.56	—	—
	Railways	100.00	—	—	—	17.60	—
	Other transport	100.00	2.10	0.44	0.62	0.64	0.37
	Services excluding public administration and defense	100.00	0.51	0.52	0.91	1.03	0.43

a. Agricultural output are exogenous. Indices are price variable.

price increases in the AP sectors. We may note that in order to achieve investment increases in real terms, it is necessary to take into account the effect of the price rise not only on additional investment but on total investment comprising of both base investment and the additional one. The same logic holds for other components of government expenditure that are held constant in real terms. Another point of interest is that, in each simulation run, an increase in nominal public investment is more than the additional surplus from public enterprises, which implies that part of the increase in investment is financed by an increase in tax revenue. Since tax rates are kept fixed, the additional tax revenue is available due to the buoyancy effect (i.e., the expansion of the tax base associated with economic growth).

The share of the three income classes in total personal income does not show any considerable change. Perhaps the amount of investment increase considered here is not enough to cause significant change. Nevertheless, the direction of change is clear. The relative position of profit income earners increases, whereas that of agricultural income earners and non-agricultural wage income earners falls.

The results presented in this paper can also be used to evaluate the relative performance of the prices of the AP sectors, namely, petroleum, coal, electricity, and railways, as instruments of resource mobilization vis-à-vis alternative instruments such as direct and indirect tax rates. In India direct taxes have never been aggressively used for revenue generation because of a very low base. The whole of agricultural income is exempt from income tax payments. In fact the contribution of direct tax in total tax revenue is only around 15 percent. Indirect taxes levied on products of manufacturing industries constitute bulk of the revenue. Thus from the point of view of the present model, the instrument that can serve as an effective alternative to administered prices for generating resources is an indirect tax rate to the general manufacturing sector (ITGM). The ITGM has much larger base than that of administered prices. Also the commodities under general manufacturing sector are of noninfrastructural noncore type and hence the extent of its forward linkage is weaker compared to the AP sectors. For these reasons one expects that as a resource-generating instrument use of ITGM will be less inflationary. On the other hand, production and distribution of the products of the AP sectors are under direct government control, and as a result the revenue collection system is much more efficient in case of administered prices. However, this aspect can not be quantified in the present exercise but should be kept in mind while evaluating performance of alternative instruments.

For a more purposeful evaluation and comparison, we have repeated the same simulation by using the indirect tax rates of the general manufacturing sector (t_4) as an alternate instrument. The last column of table 5.2 shows the macro scenario when the indirect tax rate t_4 is increased to finance Rs.500 crores of additional real public investments in a balanced budget manner. If the two most important macro indicators of performance —changes in GDP and overall price—are used, the indirect tax increase scenario turns out best where the increase in GDP is highest (Rs.311 crores) and price rise lowest (0.22 percent). Among the administered prices petroleum and coal prices are definitely better instruments than railway or electricity prices. In the case of a petroleum price increase, the GDP is increased by Rs.231 crores and the price by 0.60 percent, but in the case of coal, the magnitudes are Rs.299 crores and 0.72 percent, respectively. Thus there seems to be some trade-off between growth and inflation for these two instruments which can be exploited according to each situation. Our policy conclusion therefore is that the traditional tool of an indirect tax turns out to be a better instrument of resource mobilization in terms of both growth and inflation than increasing the AP sectors' prices. Nevertheless, there may be limitations to the extent to which indirect tax rates can be "efficiently" increased. In our model, when the prices of AP sectors were used as an instrument of investment financing, the prices of petroleum and coal were better instruments than those of the railways and electricity.

Appendix A: Glossary

Endogenous Variables

(1)–(6): P_i = price index, $i = 1, 2, 3, 4, 9, 10$

(7)–(10): B_i = prime cost, $i = 3, 4, 9, 10$

(11)–(18): W_i = wage rate index, $i = 3, \ldots, 10$

(19): CPI = consumer price index

(20)–(22): T_i = markup rate, $i = 4, 9, 10$

(23)–(24): ΔS_i = changes in stock, $i = 1, 2$

(25)–(32): X_i = output level (value at constant price), $i = 3, \ldots, 10$

(33)–(34): V_i = value added–output ratio (at current price), $i = 1, 2$

(35): Y_A = agricultural income

(36): Y_W = wage income in nonagriculture

(37): Y_Z = profit (markup) income in nonagriculture

(38): W_g = wage rate index in public administration and defense

(39): Y = total personal disposable income

(40)–(42): S_K = savings of Kth income class, $K = A, W, Z$
(43): D = total consumption expenditure
(44)–(53): C_i = consumption level, $i = 1, \ldots, 10$
(54)–(57): π_i = surplus per unit output in administered price sector, $i = 5, \ldots, 8$
(58): $GREV$ = government current revenue
(59): $GEXP$ = government current expenditure
(60): $GBUD$ = government budget deficit
(61): BOP = balance of payments
(62): $GDPN$ = gross domestic product at nominal factor cost
(63): $GDPR$ = gross domestic product at real factor cost
(64): $GDPDEF$ = GDP deflator

Exogenous Variables

e = exchange rate
P_{0i}^* = price of noncompeting imports going into ith sectors, $i = 1, \ldots, 10$
T_3 = markup rate in sector 3
T_i^0 = base level markup rate, $i = 4, 9, 10$
CPI_{-1} = consumer price index with one-year lag
X_i = output level, $i = 1, 2$
X_i^* = capacity output level
M_i = competing imports, $i = 1, \ldots, 10$
E_i = exports, $i = 1, \ldots, 10$
G_i = government consumption, $i = 1, \ldots, 10$
ΔS_i = changes in stock, $i = 3, \ldots, 10$
PRI = private real investment
$PUBI$ = public real investment
P_F = price of fertilizers
L_g = real income in public administration and defense
R = remittances from abroad
$TRANS$ = government transfer payments
GPi = government profit in public enterprises in nonadministered price sectors, $i = 3, 4, 9, 10$
$GINT$ = government interest payments
$\bar{X}_{C5}$ = domestic crude production
$\bar{P}_{C5}$ = price (cost) of domestic crude
I_0 = capital imports
P_{0I}^* = price index of capital imports

$GBDOM$ = government borrowing domestic

$GBEXT$ = government borrowing external

Parameters

a_{ij} = input requirement of ith sector's product per unit output production in jth sector

a_{0j} = noncompeting import requirement per unit output in jth sector

b_i = labor output coefficient

t_i = indirect tax rate

t_z = direct tax rate

θ_i = floor level of consumption in LES equations

m_i = marginal budget share in LES equations

φ_i = consumption weight in CPI

ε_i = Response coefficient of markup to excess capacity utilization

VR_i = real value added–output ratio

Appendix B: Social Accounting Matrix for 1983–84 (Rs. crores)

	Food agriculture	Other agriculture	Basic industry	Other manufacturing & construction	Petroleum refinery	Coal
1. Food agriculture	2,769	938	0	168	—	—
2. Other agriculture	844	5,133	25	4,462	—	—
3. Basic industry	3,482	1,282	1,887	7,880	—	—
4. Other manufacturing and construction	742	1,241	2,550	27,742	2,902	25
5. Petroleum refinery	646	213	574	1,790	—	5
6. Coal	2	18	379	977	—	—
7. Electricity, gas, and water	155	98	651	1,827	23	178
8. Railways	26	96	225	1,569	—	15
9. Other transport	41	302	412	4,375	—	7
10. Rest of economy services	1,066	2,077	2,598	21,679	14	536
11. Indirect taxes (less subsidy)	−681	−367	1,591	14,761	—	—
12. Imports	148	112	248	2,302	4,830	—
13. Private income:						
a. wage	—	—	1,950	18,291	223	744
b. markup	—	—	984	15,448	—	—
c. total	28,925	33,732	2,934	33,739	223	744
14. Direct taxes	—	—	—	—	—	—
15. Government income	—	—	781	1,108	416	1,392
16. Gross savings	—	—	—	—	—	—
17. Total	38,165	44,875	14,855	124,399	8,408	2,903

	Electricity, gas, and water	Railways	Other transport	Rest-of-economy services	Private consumption	Government consumption
1. Food agriculture	—	—	—	598	33,904	215
2. Other agriculture	—	—	300	382	31,340	182
3. Basic industry	—	2	58	192	0	0
4. Other manufacturing and construction	255	1,325	2,210	7,780	27,030	3,950
5. Petroleum refinery	304	459	2,792	96	1,216	273
6. Coal	816	277	4	30	193	27
7. Electricity, gas, and water	1,902	112	92	995	1,078	108
8. Railways	167	105	53	904	1,359	470
9. Other transport	141	59	208	2,333	6,189	962
10. Rest of economy services	498	236	2,576	8,905	33,004	5,975
11. Indirect taxes (less subsidy)	—	—	—	10,057	—	—
12. Imports	—	—	—	—	—	—
13. Private income:						
a. wage	1,731	1,753	4,675	21,102	—	8,661
b. markup	—	—	1,849	23,317	—	8,741
c. total	1,731	1,753	6,524	44,419	—	17,402
14. Direct taxes	—	—	—	—	5,433	—
15. Government income	1,405	661	212	3,979	—	—
16. Gross savings	—	—	—	—	34,680	11,184
17. Total	7,219	4,989	15,029	80,670	175,426	40,748

	Gross capital formation						
	Gross fixed investment	Stock changes	Exports	Competitive imports	Indirect taxes	Direct taxes	Total
1. Food agriculture	—	−117	302	−612	—	—	38,165
2. Other agriculture	—	820	1,628	−241	—	—	44,875
3. Basic industry	—	698	337	−963	—	—	14,855
4. Other manufacturing and construction	37,686	5,109	7,181	−3,329	—	—	124,399
5. Petroleum refinery	—	40	—	—	—	—	8,408
6. Coal	—	160	—	—	—	—	2,903
7. Electricity, gas, and water	—	—	—	—	—	—	7,219
8. Railways	—	—	—	—	—	—	4,989
9. Other transport	—	—	—	—	—	—	15,029
10. Rest of economy services	—	—	3,082	−1,576	—	—	80,670
11. Indirect taxes (less subsidy)	—	—	—	—	—	—	25,361
12. Imports	2,981	—	—	6,721	—	—	17,342
13. Private income:							
a. wage	—	—	—	—	—	—	—
b. markup	—	—	—	—	—	—	—
c. total	—	—	3,308	—	—	—	175,426
14. Direct taxes	—	—	—	—	—	—	5,433
15. Government income	—	—	—	—	25,361	5,433	40,748
16. Gross savings	—	—	1,512	—	—	—	—
17. Total	40,667	6,710	17,342	0	25,361	5,433	—

Marginal Savings Rates

$\beta_{SA} = 0.2873,$

$\beta_{SW} = 0.2651,$

$\beta_{SZ} = 0.3331.$

LES Parameters

Sectors	Marginal budget share	Floor consumption
1	0.1855	0.1355
2	0.2256	1.6077
3	0.0	0.0
4	0.2206	1.2105
5	0.0105	0.0506
6	0.0016	0.0085
7	0.0093	0.0449
8	0.0157	0.0297
9	0.0718	0.1331
10	0.2594	1.5454

Wage Indexation Parameters

	α_W	β_W	γ_W
Industry	−0.0272	0.4606	0.6208
Infrastructure	−0.0831	0.4254	0.7202
Services	−0.0723	0.6842	0.4249

References

Chetty, V. K., and D. K. Ratha. 1987. *Inflation, Growth, and Public Sector Price Policy*. New Delhi: Indian Statistical Institute. Mimeo.

Dasgupta, D. 1986. *Reflections on Administered Prices*. Calcutta: Indian Statistical Institute. Mimeo.

Government of India. 1985. *Seventh Five Year Plan—1985–90*. New Delhi: Planning Commission.

Government of India. 1986. *Administered Price Policy—A Discussion*. New Delhi: Ministry of Finance.

Gupta, S. P., and T. G. Srinivasan. 1984. "Inflation and the Role of Administered Prices." *Economic and Political Weekly* 19: 1579–1583.

Jha, S., and S. Mundle. 1987. "Inflationary Implications of Resource Mobilization through Administered Price Increases." *Economic and Political Weekly* 22: 1394–1409.

Kalecki, M. 1971. *Selected Essays on the Dynamics of the Capitalist Economy*. Cambridge: Cambridge University Press.

Leontief, W. W. 1951. *Structure of the American Economy, 1919–1939*. 2d ed. Oxford: Oxford University Press.

National Council of Applied Economic Research. 1981. "A Computable General Equilibrium Model of the Indian Economy: Structure and Sensitivities." New Delhi: NCAER. Mimeo.

Rangarajan, C., R. K. Sah, and K. S. Reddy. 1981. "Impact of Hikes in Prices of Coal and Petroleum Products on the Other Sectors of the Economy." *Artha Vijana* 23: 176–181.

Sarkar, H., and S. V. Subbarao. 1981. "A Short-Term Macro Forecasting Model for India: Structure and Uses." *Indian Economic Review* 16: 55–80.

Sarkar, H., and S. V. Subbarao. 1981a. "A Social Accounting Matrix for India, 1980–81," *Margin* 13: 27–44.

Sarkar, H., and M. K. Panda. 1986. "Quantity-Price-Money Interaction in a CGE Model with Applications to Fiscal Policy." *Margin* 17: 31–52.

Sarkar, H., M. K. Panda, and K. A. Siddique. 1986. *A Macroeconomic Infrastructure Model for India*. New Delhi: NCAER.

Sarkar, H., and G. Kadekodi. 1988. *Energy Pricing in India: Perspectives, Issues, and Options*. New Delhi: ARTEP (ILO).

Stone, R. N. 1954. "Linear Expenditure System and Demand Analysis: An Application to the Pattern of British Demand." *Economic Journal* 64: 511–527.

Taylor, Lance. 1983. *Structuralist Macroeconomics*. New York: Basic Books.

6 Short-Run Energy-Economy Interactions in Egypt

Nazli Choucri and
Supriya Lahiri

The decade of the 1970s produced important political and economic changes in Egypt, many of which have their origins in the economic liberalization policy and the "open door" posture. In particular, five principal factors are responsible for increasing both the level of economic activity and foreign exchange earnings of the country: (1) the expansion of oil production and natural gas resources, in conjunction with the rapid increases in the world price of oil throughout the 1970s; (2) the large inflow of worker remittances due to increasing labor out-migration and apparent growth of confidence in the Egyptian economy; (3) the liberalization policies designed to encourage inflows of foreign capital; (4) the reopening of the Suez canal; and (5) the increase in tourism. Together, these five factors evolved throughout the 1970s, shaping the country's economy and attendant social and political adjustments. By the end of the decade these factors had set in motion a set of economic interactions that will substantially transform the country's economy throughout the 1980s. They are leading to important structural changes in the economy in terms of changes in the structure of demand, role of foreign trade, and allocation of resources. However, these five sources of foreign earnings,—which are the favorable factors for the economy—cannot continue indefinitely into the future.

Recent developments suggest that the Egyptian economy has entered a transitional phase in its growth process undergoing a period of transformation toward a new equilibrium. Processes of adjustment and adaptation are inevitable in being characteristic transitional phases as distinct from the steady state phenomenon which is consistent with and observed in long-run equilibrium. Therefore it is important to understand the short-run adjustment mechanism of the interdependent economic system which would provide reasonable guidelines for appropriate policy measures. There are many countervailing forces in the Egyptian economy, and these five factors differ in their impacts and their overall contribution to growth.

Clearly the most significant contribution to the recent economic upsurge has been provided by the petroleum sector, which is strong, well managed and provides a steady stream of revenue for the government. The petroleum sector does not exist in isolation from the rest of the economy, and analysis of its effects must take into account the strong two-way linkage with the economy. The contribution of the petroleum sector to GDP at factor cost increased from 3 percent in 1975 to 16 percent in 1979 and export earnings jumped almost six times during this period. By 1982 oil exports provided $2.76 billion to the economy.

A major problem arises from the question of whether the increased earnings from the petroleum sector can be maintained in the face of two obstacles: a highly subsidized domestic price of oil which is encouraging domestic consumption and a large degree of uncertainty that prevails in reserve generation and the future production possibilities of oil.

The domestic price of petroleum in Egypt is about one-fifth of the international market price equivalent. Low petroleum prices have led to rapid increases in domestic utilization. Government officials have recently stated that by 1984 both consumption of petroleum products and output will rise by 11–12 percent, and the exportable surplus of domestic petroleum production over consumption may be eliminated completely.[1]

This twofold dilemma has heightened awareness for energy conservation, domestic pricing policy, and better management of energy demand at the national level so that petroleum reserves are not entirely diverted from exports to the domestic market. The crucial policy issue in this context is to change the administered price system of petroleum products toward a more viable domestic price structure that would be more in line with international markets. The problem is whether price-induced conservation is likely to occur and to determine the macroeconomic consequences of an overall reduction in petroleum use.

Among the critical questions to be resolved are the following: What will be the effects of rising energy costs on the other sectors of the economy? Will the economy be able to adapt to this change? To a large extent the adjustments will depend on the flexibility of energy use in the consumption pattern of households and in the production functions underlying industrial sectors. In other words, the structure of energy–economy interactions depends on the role that petroleum plays in the consumption basket and as a factor of production (on the values of the relevant elasticities).

Egypt's energy profile can be characterized as follows: Almost 70 percent of energy use is petroleum based; the remainder is mainly hydroelectric power, with small, but potentially important prospects for natural gas. In a macroeconomic context therefore, if substitution possibilities in production processes (e.g., between petroleum and natural gas), it is important to determine whether the negative macroeconomic impact of rising energy prices can be mitigated through appropriate price policies or if other constraints in the economy will need to be recognized as well. In this context, for Egypt's energy predicament, it is useful to investigate whether the production possibilities in the natural gas sector impose significant constraints on the economy's adjustment process. The effects of the such restrictions can be examined under alternative assumptions regarding how the different sectors of the economy adjust to reach market equilibrium (alternative rules for model closures). For example, price determination differs substantially across sectors and these differences are critical to the overall economic adjustments and to the policy options available for changing domestic price structures. Among issues of concern are the following: If the short-run adjustment to an oil price increase drives down output and puts upward pressure on prices, can the short-run underutilization of production capacity be mitigated through appropriate macroeconomic policies? With this in mind we have formulated a macroeconomic model of the Egyptian economy to trace the short-run energy–economy interactions.

The paper is organized in the following way: Section 6.1 gives a brief overview of the model. Section 6.2 presents the results of alternative simulation runs. Section 6.3 summarizes the results of the analysis.

6.1 Overview of the Model

Despite rapid changes in the Egyptian economy, several features continue to stand out. These include a dominant agricultural sector, a growing construction sector, an expanding industrial base, and a dramatic growth in the petroleum sector. Domestic economic policies—inherited from the revolution of 1952—include extensive subsidies for industrial inputs, energy products, and food stuffs. In agriculture, imports serve to clear the market. Only in construction are prices allowed to adjust to market forces. In all other sectors quantities adjust to demand. The traditional dualism in the economy—agriculture versus the rest of the economy—may well be supplanted by a trilateral structure: agriculture, rest of the economy, and a strong energy sector. With these distinctive features in mind, we have a short-run, ten-sector, macroeconomic model of the Egyptian economy to examine its critical adjustment problems.

The theoretical structure of this model is specified in accordance with the computable general equilibrium models formulated by Taylor (1983), emphasizing the particular structural characteristics of developing countries. Such models are based around the identities of a social accounting matrix (SAM) and incorporate additional technical and behavioral relationships to make the model determinate and represent the distinctive aspects of the specific economy being analyzed. The closure rules behind these models are based on a combination of different schools of thought inspired by Keynes, Kalecki, and the different adherents of the Cambridge school. The model focuses attention on the particular variables that need to adjust to bring about the overall macrobalance of saving equal to investment. Different models can be constructed around the different accommodating variables that would adjust to satisfy the basic macroidentity in the economy. Aggregate demand determined markets of the Keynesian type are included where chronic excess capacities are the essential features of the sectors and price-clearing markets are assumed where bottlenecks and shortages are present. Generalized models of development are not useful for analyzing particular cases. Different structural characteristics are important in case of different countries and the appropriate adjusting variables need to be emphasized accordingly.

The Egyptian macroeconomic model is built around a social accounting matrix (SAM) for the Egyptian economy in the national accounts year of 1977.[2] The model incorporates a complex set of general equilibrium interactions in the price- and quantity-clearing sectors in the commodity market.[3] The model, however, is of a short-run nature and does not incorporate the dynamics of the system. It is designed specifically around a base year to assist in understanding immediate responses to policy changes. Investment has been modeled merely as a component of aggregate demand, and the capital accumulation process of investment has not been considered. It has been specifically designed to explore the short-run adjustment mechanism of the system.

The ten sectors along which the model is built are (1) agriculture, (2) construction and housing, (3) heavy industry, (4) light industry, (5) transportation, (6) sectors in the rest of the economy, (7) Suez, (8) oil extraction, (9) oil refining, and (10) other energy, namely, electricity and a nascent natural gas component.

The overall macrobalance in this structural model is decomposed sectorally. The mechanisms through which excess demand in each sector adjust to zero are the following:

1. The agricultural sector is assumed to have an adjusting "competitive import" level.[4] Both prices and supply are assumed to be fixed in the short run.

2. The construction sector's stability mechanism is built around an adjusting price. Prices are assumed to vary freely to bring about equilibrium because capacity in the construction sector is fully utilized in the short run.

3. For all the other sectors in the economy, adjusting outputs occur due to the prevalence of chronic excess capacities.[5]

Prices in all the quantity-clearing sectors are determined by fixed producers' markup over variable costs as opposed to the neoclassical cost function. The wage rates are assumed to have been determined institutionally (which correspond to the Keynesian assumption of short-run predetermined nominal wages) and the coefficients of production are fixed in the initial version of the model. For purposes of analysis, some of the technological coefficients have been taken as flexible, as reported below, in an alternative version of the model. The model draws upon the well-known linear expenditure system of demand equations to arrive at the sectoral consumption level. Given the different behavioral assumptions and the different identities built around the social accounting matrix, the solution is determined through several adjustment mechanisms, namely, Keynesian output response in the quantity-clearing sectors, a "forced saving" mechanism via the rise in the prices of output relative to wage, adjustments in the trade deficit, and the surplus available in the government current account.

As noted earlier, the formulation of the structural equations for this model are closely related to the model formulation made by Taylor (1983) for India. However, two important extensions to represent the Egyptian case are made, and these extensions may be relevant for other classes of countries with similar macroeconomic features and a strong petroleum sector. These extensions are necessitated by the realities of the Egyptian case.

First, the energy sector is disaggregated in terms of oil extraction, oil refining and other energy (predominantly natural gas and electricity). Egypt has a "mixed" energy portfolio which must be clearly represented.

Second, the pricing equations are reformulated to incorporate the assumption of price responsive technological coefficients in the petroleum intensive sectors. This extension is essential to capture the flexibility of energy use in production processes.

The major macroeconomic consequences that may be evaluated through the model may be classified in the following categories:

1. *Effects on sectoral output.* Since the industrial sectors are characterized by excess capacities, the short-run macro-adjustment takes place in terms of changes in output (capacity utilization);

2. *Effects on sectoral prices.* The changes in relative prices play a key role in the short-run adjustment process and help us to evaluate the inflationary impacts of policy changes;

3. *Impacts on income shares in terms of wages, profits, and government income.* Value added is disaggregated into four categories, namely, agricultural income, wages, government profits and private sector profits. The assumption of fixed wages and markup pricing enables us to arrive at different functional distributions of income (through the "forced savings mechanism");

4. *Impacts on balance of payments.* The effects on balance of payments are evaluated in terms of changes in the level of competitive and noncompetitive imports.

6.2 Empirical Results

An initial set of simulation analyses was undertaken to examine the major macroeconomic adjustments. This section reports the results of the following simulation runs:

1. an increase in the level of aggregate investment demand;

2. an increase in the domestic price of petroleum via changes in the markup rate;

3. the introduction of a fiscally neutralizing policy measure to offset the impact of petroleum-price induced contraction;

4. an increase in the domestic price of oil with flexible technological coefficients in the petroleum-intensive sectors under alternative closure rules for the natural gas sector.

In the initial experiment the total aggregate level of investment demand (in nominal terms) is increased by 10 percent (£E 221.69 million). Our main interest is to examine the responses of the accommodating variables that would give us an improved understanding of the structure of the model.

The largest component of investment demand is met by goods from the construction sector. As a result the variation in the demand for investment goods is mainly reflected in terms of a rise in the aggregate demand for construction sector products. Since the construction sector has fixed capacity in the short run, the increase in aggregate demand will lead to an increase in prices by 15 percent. This, however, will not lead to much of a cost-push inflation in the other sectors of the economy owing to limited sales of intermediate inputs by the construction sector to the other sectors of the economy.

The aggregate level of prices in the economy will increase by 5 percent. The price index of investment goods will increase by a much larger extent (9 percent). This increase will result in a net increase of demand for investment goods in real terms by £E 53.135 million (as against a nominal increase of £E 221.69 million). An increase in prices in the construction sector will lead to a proportionate increase in income generated by the construction sector which will put upward pressure on demand for all commodities.

An increase in aggregate demand for investment goods (in real terms) will also result in an expansion of output and income in the other sectors of the economy. All this will lead to an increase in real value added by £E 149.504 million. The results of this experiment are summarized in column B of table 6.1.

The familiar multiplier and centered arc elasticity measures[6] with respect to shifts in real investment demand are shown in table 6.2. The values of the elasticities show that all of the accommodating variables will respond positively to a change in the real aggregate demand for investment goods in the economy. The high elasticity measure of the construction sector prices (6.24) reveals the sensitive nature of this sector to a change in the economy's level of real investment demand. The sensitivity measure of the competitive level of imports in the agricultural sector is also high (2.59) because of the high demand for the goods in this sector. It also acts as a vehicle to increase foreign savings to meet the rise in investment demand. The elasticity measure of the real value added of 0.82 reveals the limited expansionary impact in real terms of an increase in aggregate investment demand.

We observe a fall in the share of wage income and a rise in the share of profit income resulting from a change in prices brought about by the construction sector. The saving shares also adjust to bring about the new investment-saving equality. The government's share in savings falls from 0.6327 to 0.6102 and that of the households from 0.5904 to 0.5595.

The main burden of adjustment falls in the trade sector (from −0.2231 to −0.1696) because of the rise in the level of competitive imports in the agricultural sector and noncompetitive imports in the other sectors resulting from an expansion in output.

Table 6.1
Results of simulation runs

Sectors	Prices	A	B	C	D
Construction and housing	P2	1.0	1.153	0.983	0.996
Heavy industry	P3	1.0	1.002	1.067	1.068
Light industry	P4	1.0	1.000	1.01	1.01
Transportation	P5	1.0	1.006	1.047	1.048
Rest of the economy	P6	1.0	1.002	1.023	1.023
Suez	P7	1.0	1.000	1.04	1.041
Oil extraction	P8	1.0	1.003	1.076	1.077
Oil refining	P9	1.0	1.003	1.535	1.536
Other energy	P10	1.0	1.002	1.11	1.11
Gross output (in million £E)					
Heavy industry	X3	785.619	794.737	774.598	785.915
Light industry	X4	3,655.81	3,722.97	3,609.49	3,664.79
Transportation	X5	494.243	505. 975	478.732	492.358
Rest of the economy	X6	3,958.58	4,007.50	3,914.80	4,042.32
Suez	X7	185.40	185.492	185.316	185.558
Oil extraction	X8	266.333	267.936	262.311	265.006
Oil refining	X9	287.856	291.522	277.368	284.039
Other energy	X10	116.538	118.665	112.893	115.689
Competitive imports (in million £E)					
Agriculture	M1	568.198	604.188	545.68	578.022

Consumption (in million £E)					
Agriculture	C1	933.667	949.244	925.598	934.449
Construction and housing	C2	156.763	150.514	155.752	157.29
Heavy industry	C3	128.834	132.871	122.267	124.467
Light industry	C4	1,873.40	1,924.72	1,837.63	1,866.74
Transportation	C5	186.453	195.502	173.377	178.82
Rest of the economy	C6	1,132.80	1,171.92	1,094.96	1,117.67
Oil refining	C9	53.4077	54.4938	46.0192	46.44
Other energy	C10	39.4407	40.6239	36.7453	37.373
Sources of saving (in million £E)					
Government savings	GSAV	1,574.54	1,653.44	1,603.01	1,524.64
Household savings	HHSAV	1,469.07	1,515.85	1,461.07	1,485.46
Trade deficit	DEF	−555.144	−459.769	−568.972	−514.969
Agricultural income of households	HYA	1,581.48	1,581.38	1,575.09	1,575.07
Profit income of household	YHP	1,469.05	1,649.45	1,472.11	1,518.86
Wage income of household	YW	2,979.43	3,012.2	2,949.91	3,009.37
Government profit income		1,573.3	1,640.64	1,699.47	1,729.4
Aggregate price index		1.00	1.05	1.028	1.030
Real value added (in million £E)		7,605.22	7,754.724	7,485.17	7,607.3
Nominal value added (in million £E)		7,605.22	7,883.575	7,696.56	7,832.7

Note: A = base case. B = increased investment demand (10 percent). C = increased petroleum markup (200 percent). The markup rate in the petroleum sector has been increased three times to simulate the oil price rise scenario. A threefold increase in the markup of the petroleum sector leads to an increase of approximately 54 percent in the price of petroleum (P9 = 1.535). D = increased fiscal expenditure policy (8 percent).

Table 6.2
Multiplier and elasticity measures of accommodating variables with respect to changes in real investment

Sectors		Multiplier	Elasticity
Gross output			
Heavy industry	X3	0.17	0.48
Light industry	X4	1.26	0.77
Transportation	X5	0.22	0.98
Rest of the economy	X6	0.92	0.52
Suez	X7	0.0017	0.02
Oil extraction	X8	0.03	0.25
Oil refining	X9	0.07	0.54
Other energy	X10	0.04	0.76
Competitive imports			
Agriculture	M1	0.68	2.59
Prices			
Construction and housing	P2	0.003	6.24
Real value added		2.81	0.82
Total value added		5.24	1.51

As Egyptian energy prices have been extremely low, on the average about one-fifth of their international market price equivalent, they obviously have not provided the appropriate price signals to the economy.[7] Our objective in this policy run is to evaluate the short-run macroeconomic impacts and adjustments in the economy that would result from a rise in the price of oil. For purposes of analysis, the domestic price of petroleum has been taken as 20 percent of the international price in the base run of the model.

The rise in the price of petroleum has been simulated by increasing the prespecified markup rate in the petroleum sector by 200 percent. This markup rise increases the price in the petroleum sector by approximately 54 percent, which brings the petroleum prices closer to the international market price equivalent by 10 percent. Although this is a modest increase in the direction of the international market price equivalent, it departs substantially from the current price structure.

The immediate consequence of this price increase is a rise in the variable costs of production in the other sectors of the economy reflected directly in terms of higher prices for their products. The results of changes in the relative prices of the different outputs are depicted in column C of table 6.1. A major effect is a cost-push inflation which occurs in the other sectors of the economy. This is due to the significant role of petroleum as an intermediate input.

The responses of the increases in the sectoral price levels will vary over the different sectors. The price level in the heavy industries, transportation, crude oil, and "other energy" sectors will increase by 7, 5, 8, and 11 percent, respectively. The aggregate level of prices in the economy will increase by almost 3 percent.

The changes in relative prices will lead to a rise in the level of markup income from the petroleum sector. A large proportion of the higher markup income will be going into the hands of the Egyptian government owing to the large share of the government in the petroleum sector and the other sectors of the economy. This will result in higher government savings, leading to leakages in purchasing power. Real wages will fall owing to the assumption of short-run predetermined nominal wages. Thus income will be redistributed from wage to profit recipients. The share of the increased profit-income for the government sector will rise from 0.2071 to 0.22, whereas the wage share of the wage earners will fall from 0.3918 to 0.3818.

The level of consumption will decline as a result of the higher relative prices. All this would generate a downward pressure on the level of aggregate demand. This depression of demand will result in lower prices in the construction sector, lower level of competitive imports in the agricultural sector, and a decline in output in all of the quantity clearing sectors. Thus an increase in the domestic price of oil will lead to a reduction in economic activity of the different sectors of the economy. By far the largest drop in output will occur in the transportation sector. The reasons are the strong input–output linkage between the petroleum sector and the transportation sector and the high value of elasticities in this sector. Real value added will fall by approximately £E 120 million (2 percent) and household consumption of petroleum products will decline merely by £E 7 million (13 percent).

Overall, the rise in domestic petroleum prices will create difficult macroeconomic adjustments for the economy in the short-run involving increased inflation (due to cost-push inflationary pressures originating from the petroleum sector) and contraction of output (brought about by a fall in aggregate demand) leading to underutilization of capacity.

This contraction may be offset through fiscally neutralizing measures, namely, an expansion in the government expenditure policy. We find that if government expenditure is increased by 8 percent this policy might offset the negative impact on real value added and add negligibly to inflation.

The results corresponding to this policy run are presented in column D of table 6.1. This experiment also helps us to separate income effect from the substitution effect by keeping the real value added at its original level. The new consumption basket represented by column D now gives us the demand responses generated by the substitution effect alone. We may also note that the conservation in the uses of petroleum by consumers arises mainly due to the operation of the substitution effect (of a change in price) due perhaps to the small share of petroleum in the consumers budget. In terms of the sectoral responses of output, we find that there is clearly a shift in output, patterns in favor of sectors 4 and 6. This is mainly due to the fact that a large part of the demand for sectors 4 and 6 comes from the government sector, hence they gain more than the others from the policy change.

Much of the demand for petroleum products comes from the industries in the form of intermediate inputs. So far we have assumed that technological coefficients are fixed: that they are used in fixed proportion and no substitution is possible. In fact we know that possibilities exist for substitution away from petroleum input, especially by replacing fuel oil by natural gas. Considerable scope for conversion exists in a number of industries in the Egyptian economy, namely, iron and steel, cement, fertilizers, and cotton textiles. Since most of these industries are aggregated in sectors 3 and 4, we have replaced the constant technological coefficients using petroleum and natural gas in these sectors by making them price responsive. For this analysis we now recognize that substitution possibilities exist between petroleum and natural gas in sectors 3 and 4.

We assume that petroleum and natural gas enter separably into the unit cost function. This enables us to obtain a constant elasticity of substitution (CES)[8] unit cost function corresponding to the use of "aggregate" energy (in terms of petroleum and natural gas) derived from factor demand equations and natural gas in sectors 3 and 4.

The unit cost of "aggregate energy" in sectors 3 and 4 may be represented as follows:

$$EP_i = [(\alpha_9^i)^{\sigma_i}(P_9)^{1-\sigma_i} + (\alpha_{10}^i)^{\sigma_i}(P_{10})^{1-\sigma_i}]^{1/(1-\sigma_i)} \qquad \text{for } i = 1, 4,$$

where

EP_i = price of "aggregate energy" in sector i,

α_9^i = distribution parameter of petroleum used in the CES aggregate energy function in sector i,

α_{10}^i = distribution parameter of "other energy" used in the CES aggregate energy function in sector i,

P_9 and P_{10} = price level in sectors 9 and 10, respectively,

σ_i = elasticity of substitution between petroleum and "other energy" in sector i.

The "fuel shares" or energy coefficients are obtained by using Sheppard's lemma (i.e., the first derivative of the respective cost functions). The relevant price responsive input–output coefficients will take the following form:

$$A9E_i = \left(\alpha_9^i \frac{EP_i}{P_9}\right)^{\sigma_i} \qquad \text{for } i = 3, 4,$$

$$A10E_i = \left(\alpha_{10}^i \frac{EP_i}{P_{10}}\right)^{\sigma_i} \qquad \text{for } i = 3, 4,$$

$A9E_i$ = ratio of petroleum use to "aggregate energy" in sector i,

$A10E_i$ = ratio of "other energy" use to "aggregate energy" in sector i.

The material balance equations for sectors 9 and 10, the pricing and variable cost equations for sectors 3 and 4 will have to be reformulated to incorporate the flexible technological coefficients and the "aggregate prices of energy" in the respective sectors.

Given data constraints at present, no formal econometric estimation of the elasticity of substitution between oil and natural gas has been attempted. There are very few estimates available for the elasticity of substitution even for other developing countries. A recent study by Wood (1983)[9] shows that elasticities of substitution between petroleum oil and natural gas are higher than unity. We have assumed an elasticity of substitution of 1.5 for both the light industry and the heavy industry sectors.

In order to capture the particular characteristics of the Egyptian economy and its unique "distortions," we have made three alternative assumptions (on closures) regarding the natural gas sector:

1. The natural gas sector is assumed to be quantity clearing (which has been the assumption throughout our analysis).

2. The supply of the natural gas sector is taken to be fixed in the short run and the adjustment mechanism is built around flexible prices.

3. The short-run supply response function in the natural gas sector responds positively to changes in its own price and takes the form

$$X_{10} = \bar{X}_{10}\left(\frac{P_{10}}{\bar{P}_{10}}\right)^{\gamma},$$

where

γ = the parameter of the supply response function,[10]

P_{10} = initial price of natural gas,

$\bar{X}_{10}$ = predetermined level of natural gas output,

X_{10} = level of gross output in the natural gas sector.

The results of our analysis are summarized in table 6.3. We observe that the technological coefficients are sensitive to changes in petroleum prices in all three cases. However, the price responsiveness (the resulting induced conservation of petroleum products) varies with the particular assumptions on closures that have been made for the natural gas sector. Given the assumption of excess capacity in the natural gas sector, the substitution away from petroleum to natural gas does not cause any additional increases in the price of the natural gas sector. The flexibility of petroleum use can help to ameliorate some of the contractionary impact on the real value added to the economy.

However, if the supply in the natural gas sector remains fixed, this leads to a substantial rise in the price of natural gas by almost 30 percent. This results in a high rate of inflation in the economy, and the contractionary effect becomes more severe. The results are summarized in column D of table 6.3. This shows that a high elasticity of substitution coupled with fixed supply in the short run may not lead the Eygptian economy to desired long-run results. Hence it is important to capture and analyze the macroimpact of the other restrictions in the economy.

If the short-run supply of natural gas responds to changes in prices, then the upward pressures on the price of natural gas may be offset to a large extent. The price of natural gas increases by only 5 percentage points. The results of this experiment are shown in column E. The solution indicates that if the substitution possibilities between oil and natural gas are high in certain sectors and the supply of the natural gas sector responds accordingly, the negative macroeconomic impact of rising energy prices may be mitigated to a certain extent.

This adjustment illustrates the importance of the implications of the alternative closure rules for determining an appropriate petroleum price

Table 6.3
Results of simulation runs with an increase in markup in the petroleum sector by 200 percent and flexible technological coefficients under alternative closure rules for the natural gas sector

				Flexible technological coefficient		
					Price-clearing natural gas sector	
Sectors		A	B	C	D	E
Heavy industry	Ratio of petroleum use to "aggregate energy"	0.655	0.655	0.532	0.595	0.549
Heavy industry	Ratio of natural gas use to "aggregate energy"	0.344	0.344	0.492	0.409	0.468
Light industry	Ratio of petroleum use to "aggregate energy"	0.561	0.561	0.432	0.497	0.449
Light industry	Ratio of natural gas use to "aggregate energy"	0.439	0.439	0.595	0.509	0.571
Prices						
Construction and housing	P2	1.00	0.983	0.984	0.981	0.985
Heavy industry	P3	1.00	1.067	1.063	1.077	1.058
Light industry	P4	1.00	1.01	1.01	1.012	1.009
Transportation	P5	1.00	1.047	1.047	1.052	1.046
Rest of the economy	P6	1.00	1.023	1.023	1.026	1.022
Suez	P7	1.00	1.04	1.040	1.044	1.039
Oil extraction	P8	1.00	1.067	1.067	1.08	1.074
Oil refining	P9	1.00	1.535	1.535	1.542	1.532
Other energy	P10	1.00	1.11	1.11	1.288	1.051

Table 6.3 (continued)

Sectors		A	B	C	D	E
				Flexible technological coefficient	Price-clearing natural gas sector	
Gross output						
Heavy industry	X3	785.619	774.598	774.96	773.115	775.65
Light industry	X4	3655.61	3609.49	3611.65	3603.18	3614.77
Transportation	X5	494.243	478.732	479.266	477.152	480.032
Rest of the economy	X6	3958.58	3914.80	3915.63	3909.33	3917.93
Suez	X7	185.40	185.316	185.318	185.306	185.334
Oil extraction	X8	266.333	262.311	258.761	259.988	258.334
Oil refining	X9	287.856	277.368	267.417	270.976	266.175
Other energy	X10	116.538	112.893	125.121	116.538	128.561
Competitive imports						
Agriculture	M1	568.198	545.68	546.717	542.696	548.206
Aggregate price index		1.00	1.028	1.0264	1.032	1.0278
Real value added		7605.22	7485.17	7496.89	7472.93	7489.68
Total value added		7605.22	7695.56	7694.78	7710.21	7697.61

Note: A = base case. B = rigid technological coefficient. C = quantity clearing natural gas sector. D = fixed supply of natural gas. E = incorporation of short-run supply response function in the natural gas sector. The markup rate in the petroleum sector has been increased three times to simulate the oil price rise scenario. A threefold increase in the markup of the petroleum sector leads to an increase of approximately 54 percent in the price of petroleum (P9 = 1.535).

strategy. In other words, energy demand management alone cannot bring about the desirable impacts on the economy unless efforts are made to remove cost pressures originating from other structural constraints.

The elasticity measures summarized in table 6.4 help us evaluate the effectiveness of petroleum-pricing policy for the curtailment of energy demand in the short run. We find that the values of the elasticity measures are fairly sensitive to assumptions of flexibility of energy use in the production processes and to the market-clearing assumptions in the natural gas sector.

The elasticity measures under scenario A (− 0.0879) and scenario A′ (− 0.0316) reveal the fact that with rigid technological coefficients, the fall in energy demand mainly takes place through the operation of the contractionary income effect. As expected, the elasticity measures with flexible technological coefficients are relatively larger (−0.1744), and the price effect also seems to be much stronger (as revealed by the elasticity measure of −0.121 under scenario β'). The shift of energy demand to sector 10 is also apparent from the positive elasticity measures in the natural gas sector. The elasticity measure of −0.0676 under the assumption of the price-clearing natural gas sector reveals the ineffectiveness of petroleum pricing as a policy measure for inducing energy conservation under the presence of structural constraints in the natural gas sector. On the whole the short-run elasticity measures seem to indicate the limited effectiveness of the petroleum pricing policy in curtailing energy demand in the short run.

6.3 Conclusions

The above analysis suggests the following points.

First, an increase in the domestic price of oil will encourage the curtailment of petroleum use and induce some amount of conservation of oil resources. This may be redirected to exports or conserved for future use.

Second, the reduction in petroleum use, however, will impose short-run adjustment problems for the economy in terms of an increase in inflation, fall in the share of wage income, and sharp output losses. A concomitant increase in aggregate demand through expansionary government expenditure policies may help to restore some of the lost income and stimulate the economy.

Third, the popular emphasis in macroeconomic policy for counteracting the negative economic effects to date has been effective energy-demand management policies. Since household consumption forms a very small portion of total petroleum demand in Egypt, the demand effects will have

Table 6.4
Elasticity measures of gross output with respect to changes in oil prices

Sector	A	A′	B	B′	C	C′	D	D′
Oil refining	−0.0879	−0.0316	−0.1744	−0.121	−0.1417	−0.0676	−0.1862	−0.1341
Other energy	−0.07527	−0.0173	0.1683	0.2205	[a]	[a]	0.2335	0.2723

Note: A = rigid technological coefficients. A′ = case A with neutralizing fiscal expenditure policy (8 percent). B = quantity clearing natural gas sector. B′ = case B with neutralizing fiscal expenditure policy (7.5 percent). C = fixed supply of natural gas sector. C′ = case C with neutralizing fiscal expenditure policy (9 percent). D = incorporation of short-run supply response function in the natural gas sector. D′ = case D with neutralizing fiscal expenditure policy (7 percent).
a. Undefined.

to operate through interfuel substitution in the industrial sector. Our analysis suggests that a high elasticity of substitution in the production processes between petroleum and natural gas will not bring about the desirable changes in the short run in terms of conservation of petroleum use and amelioration of the negative macroeconomic impacts unless efforts are made to increase the short-run supply of natural gas as well. In other words, for the price of oil to provide the right signal for resource allocation in the economy the other institutional and structural constraints need to be recognized and analysed as well.

Fourth, the results presented in this report stress that the macroeconomic implications of domestic petroleum-pricing strategies in Egypt are extremely important and should be considered carefully. Simply suggesting lifting of domestic subsidies, or increasing domestic energy prices to world prices, will not have the intended effects unless other measures are adopted as well. Treating the energy sector in isolation from the rest of the economy could be counterproductive and lead to adoption of measures that may even have detrimental effects in the short run. An overall energy/economy strategy is required in which adjusting domestic prices toward international prices is only one element.

However, it should be borne in mind that although oil price increases slow down economic activity, these effects may be small and temporary when seen from a long-run perspective as the dynamics of the system are taken into account. For instance, the expansion of government revenue resulting from oil price increases and increase in exports from curtailment of energy consumption can be highly beneficial from a long-run perspective if they are directed toward productive investments. However, in this paper we do not consider the longer run adjustments to short-run interventions.

Notes

This paper reports on aspects of the research project on Resource Development and Policy in Egypt: Petroleum and Natural Gas, undertaken by the Technology Adaptation Program at the Massachusetts Institute of Technology, Cambridge, MA. The authors wish to thank M. Zaki Shafei for useful discussions on the subject. The analysis in this paper benefited greatly from the contribution and collaboration of Lance Taylor. The participation of Desmond McCarthy and Peter Haas at initial stages of this project is appreciated. The authors are also grateful to James Paddock and David Dodd for helpful comments. This paper originally appeared in *World Development* 12: 799–820, 1984.

1. See *Middle East Economic Survey* (28 March 1983).

2. At the time the analysis was undertaken no social accounting matrix or comprehensive data to formulate one for a later date were available. The then existing 1976 matrix did not serve our purpose as it did not incorporate sufficient sectoral detail for energy.

3. The model has been closed in the commodity market in terms of investment-saving equality. Given the paucity of data, an extension of the model to the financial market was not feasible. Hence an implicit assumption of neutrality of money in the short run has been made in our analysis. We are currently considering incorporating a financial market in the model.

4. Imports into the economy which are also produced within the country are labeled as "competitive imports," for example, cotton imports into Egypt.

5. Underutilized capacity has been defined in the sense of firms having excess capacity owing to insufficient demand in an oligopolistic structure.

6. Centred arc elasticity approximations are calculated in the following way:

$$\text{Elast } X_i = \frac{\hat{X}_i - X_i}{\hat{I}_i - I_i} \cdot \frac{\hat{I}_i + I_i}{\hat{X}_i + X_i},$$

where

$\hat{I}_i$ = the perturbed value for I_i,

I_i = the unperturbed value for I_i,

$\hat{X}_i$ = the value calculated for X_i in the perturbed simulation.

7. See J. R. La Pittus, "CDSS Policy Issues Facing Egypt" (USAID/Cairo, 11 February 1982) for a useful discussion of energy price distortions in Egypt.

8. For a description of the CES function, see Arrow et al. (1961).

9. These results have been obtained by an ongoing study conducted by David O. Wood at the Energy Laboratory of MIT. See M. Sehary, R. Villarreal, and D. O. Wood, "Industrial Fuel and Electricity Demand in Mexico," Final Report to the Instituto Tecnologico Autonomo de Mexico (1983).

10. The value for γ has been taken as 2.

References

Arrow, Kenneth J., Hollis B. Chenery, Bagich S. Minhas, and Robert M. Solow. 1961. "Capital-Labor Substitution and Economic Efficiency." *Review of Economics and Statistics* 43: 225–250.

Taylor, Lance. 1983. *Structuralist Macroeconomics*. New York: Basic Books.

7 Continuing the Tradition of Equity in Sri Lanka: Policy Options in a CGE Model

Anne Maasland

Computable general equilibrium (CGE) models have become popular in the 1980s as policy-planning tools in developing countries. They have moved the planning emphasis from optimization of a welfare function, as in linear programming models, toward modeling the market mechanism as it operates with its various institutional features. With their endogenous price determination and feedbacks, CGE models attempt to incorporate the important interrelationships present in an economy.

CGE models can be built to reflect different economic persuasions. They are useful for modeling institutional and structural characteristics of an economy as in the structuralist approach developed by Taylor (1983). Dervis et al. (1982) discuss models based on neoclassical resource allocation theory and Gibson et al. (1983) build a model for Mexico that compares Keynes-Kaleckian and Marxist assumptions. Recent work in CGE model building has stressed the linkages between the financial and real sectors of the economy.

The present paper is an application of a structuralist general equilibrium model as first set out by Taylor (1983) for India. It has been adapted to fit the Sri Lankan context. It is a model in which prices are determined as a Kaleckian markup over costs, with the markup rate adjusting to capacity utilization and to money supply pressures. It is well-suited for this Sri Lankan application where it is felt that various domestic policies have led to high inflation through cost-push and deficit financing effects. The inflation eroded the value of nonindexed food stamp transfers which has had a negative nutritional impact on the poor. Counterfactual exercises show that similar growth rates could have been achieved with policies that would have been less harmful to the poor.

7.1 Background

In 1977, following a change in government, Sri Lanka voluntarily adopted a liberalization strategy to increase free market operations, improve producer incentives, and open up trade. Prior to this, Sri Lanka was an inward-looking economy suffering from a foreign exchange constraint that was restricting necessary imports. Real growth for the years 1970–77 was low at 2.9 percent. Much of the problem was due to bad luck; monsoon rains were poor for three consecutive years, and there was an increase in international prices of imported grain and petroleum. However, bad luck was exacerbated by poor management. Aggressive nationalization caused private sector confrontation, and public investment was in inefficient industrial projects. Domestic policies led to inadequate levels of investment and saving, with investment averaging 16 percent of GDP.[1]

Sri Lanka has a long tradition of trying to achieve a more equitable expenditure distribution through the direct provision of basic needs. Today the country has the best social indicators for its income level of all countries. For many years the government provided an extensive welfare scheme that included free education, free medical care, and highly subsidized food items.[2] These welfare measures became an increasing burden on the government budget; in 1977 social services and gross food subsidies were 42.6 percent of current government expenditures and 10.2 percent of GDP at market prices. By 1977 a situation had developed where domestic resources and foreign inflows were insufficient to meet the recurrent and capital payments of the government and the required import needs.

The initial round of reforms in late 1977 included exchange rate unification and depreciation, price decontrol for most items, import liberalization, interest rate reform, and budgetary reform. These policy reforms came out of discussions with international financial institutions. The International Monetary Fund and the World Bank were instrumental in forming the Sri Lanka Aid Consortium, a group of countries offering sustained financial support. The economic policy shift was undoubtedly a necessary prerequisite for the increased aid inflow. Table 7.1 shows the increase in capital inflows that resulted from these reforms.

The new policy thrust was within the political economic philosophy of the new government. The main policy difference between the international institutions and the Sri Lankan government was the extent of the food subsidy curtailment. The compromise reached was to retain the ration for the poorer half of the population, whereas previously the converage had

Table 7.1
Net capital inflows, including official grants (million U.S.$)

1971	83	1978	218
1972	77	1979	420
1973	75	1980	578
1974	121	1981	570
1975	130	1982	707
1976	122	1983	643
1977	261	1984	525

Source: World Bank.

Table 7.2
Rice imports/production (volume)

1971	36	1978	13
1972	39	1979	17
1973	30	1980	13
1974	28	1981	10
1975	60	1982	11
1976	51	1983	7
1977	49	1984	2

Source: Thorbecke et al. (1985)

been universal. But in late 1979 the government went further and replaced the food subsidy with a nonindexed food stamp program.

Since 1978 Sri Lanka has broken out of the pattern of low investment and low growth. Real GDP increased at an annual rate of 5.5 percent from 1978 to 1984. Growth was particularly strong in the paddy sector which averaged 4.5 percent annual real increases due to improved producer incentives. Table 7.2 reveals the extent of the rice import substitution program. A food stamp scheme that replaced rice rations and food price subsidies, and full cost pricing on imported rice, combined with the devaluation, resulted in significant retail rice price increases. Farm gate prices were thus kept above the government's guaranteed price, and profitable opportunities for the private sector resulted in significant yield increases. Furthermore improved and expanded irrigation increased the area sown.

The second source of growth has been the greatly expanded public investment program which accounts for some 60 to 65 percent of total investment. Total investment as a percentage of GDP rose from 16 percent in the 1970–77 period to 28 percent during 1978–84. Today these two

Table 7.3
Annual average price increases (percent)

	GDP deflator	Colombo CPI	Wholesale	Central bank's CPI
1978	7.8	12.2	15.8	9.1
1979	15.7	10.7	9.5	19.0
1980	18.2	26.1	33.8	37.8
1981	20.5	18.0	16.9	23.7
1982	9.9	10.9	5.5	11.0
1983	15.7	14.0	25.0	11.3

Source: Jayawardena et al. (1986).

sources of growth cannot be expected to continue as self-sufficiency in rice is attained and the ambitious foreign-financed public investment program, dominated by a massive irrigation and power project, is completed.

In 1980 and 1981 there was a large rise in inflation due to several factors: an overly ambitious public investment program financed by both domestic government borrowing and foreign lending, cost-push inflation from import price increases and wage increases, and price subsidy removals (see table 7.3). This inflation reduced the purchasing power of the nonindexed food stamp scheme that replaced food subsidies in 1979. Nutritional studies have subsequently documented that the poorer segments of the population have suffered from current policies.[3]

To carry out counterfactual scenarios, a model was built that could show the effects of different price policies as well as the impact of lower government borrowing on the price level. These scenarios were chosen to try to contain inflation and to suggest policies that would have continued the Sri Lankan concern for equity. The alternatives examined were (1) improved terms of trade scenarios; (2) a continuation of the price subsidy on rice that was replaced by a food stamp scheme in late 1979; (3) a more modest public investment program in 1980 and 1981 to try to reduce the inflation; (4) a combination of food subsidy, lowered investment, and increased consumer tariffs; and (5) input subsidies to oil-using industries and services to allow smoother adjustment to the 1978 oil shock.

7.2 Social Accounting Matrix

A 1981 social accounting matrix (SAM) for Sri Lanka is displayed in table 7.4. The rows are deliveries of commodities or sources of income, and the columns are uses of commodities or incomes. It was constructed using an

Table 7.4
Social accounting matrix for Sri Lanka, 1981 (Rs. million)

	Food and food products	Export agriculture	Manufac- turing and construction	Services	Total	Household	Govern- ment	Invest- ment	Stocks	Exports	Competitve imports	Indirect taxes	Direct taxes	Total	
Food and food products	9,168.6	200.8	1,368.0	1,591.8	12,329.2	26,472.9	265.8	0.0	58.7	2,837.0	−992.0	—	—	40,971.6	
Export agriculture	1,241.7	0.0	139.9	30.9	1,412.5	2,344.4	49.6	0.0	−270.8	7,933.2	0.0	—	—	11,468.9	
Manufacturing and construction	1,448.2	862.2	9,130.4	5,060.8	16,501.6	12,608.2	689.1	12,268.1	100.1	8,088.0	−646.0	—	—	49,609.1	
Services	2,483.7	630.6	5,894.8	2,547.8	11,556.9	21,951.2	3,140.3	3,879.9	443.0	5,915.6	−3,435.0	—	—	43,451.9	
Total	14,342.2	1,693.6	16,533.1	9,231.3	41,800.2	63,376.7	4,144.8	16,148.0	331.0	24,773.8	−5,073.0	—	—	145,501.5	
Wages	12,377.0	3,977.2	8,274.3	23,891.7	48,520.2	—	6,457.8	—	—	3,918.0	—	—	—	58,896.0	88,474.7
Profits and depreciation	9,622.5	0.0	7,238.0	9,575.2	26,435.7	—	3,143.0	—	—	—	—	—	—	29,578.7	
Government income	136.0	1,838.1	−438.0	0.0	1,536.1	—	—	—	—	3,118.0	—	11,863.0	2,029.0	18,546.1	
Value-added at factor cost	22,135.5	5,815.3	15,074.3	33,466.9	76,492.0	—	—	—	—	—	—	—	—	—	
Import duty	189.5	49.6	1,375.6	18.3	1,633.0	1,162.0	—	431.0	—	—	—	—	—	3,226.0	11,863.0
Indirect taxes	2,684.6	3,685.0	878.1	1,389.3	8,637.0	—	—	—	—	—	—	—	—	8,637.0	
Subsidies	−678.2	−375.6	−931.0	−875.9	−2,860.7	0.0	2,860.7	—	—	—	—	—	—	0.0	
Value-added at market price	24,331.4	9,174.3	16,397.0	33,998.6	83,901.3	—	—	—	—	—	—	—	—	—	
Imports	2,298.0	601.0	16,679.0	222.0	19,800.0	6,727.0	2,026.8	6,700.0	—	—	5,073.0	—	—	40,326.8	
Gross savings	—	—	—	—	—	15,180.0	−87.0	—	—	8,517.0	—	—	—	23,610.0	
Direct taxes	—	—	—	—	—	2,029.0	—	—	—	—	—	—	—	2,029.0	
Total	40,971.6	11,468.9	49,609.1	43,451.9	145,501.5	88,474.7	18,546.1	23,279.0	331.0	40,236.8	0.0	11,863.0	2,029.0	—	

input–output table, the national accounts, and information from a household survey on patterns of consumer spending.[4] It is used to calculate parameter values so that the model would reproduce the base-year SAM.

The matrix shows the basic characteristics of the economy. Agriculture accounts for about 37 percent of value added at factor cost and for about 57 percent of merchandise trade. The government tax revenue from export agriculture is 37 percent of that sector's value added at market prices. Sri Lanka can be classified as a small economy that is dependent on its primary products of tea, rubber, and coconut for foreign exchange and government revenue.

The distribution of value added at market prices between wage earners, private profit recipients, and government is about 6:3:1, respectively, although this varies within sectors. In the export agriculture sector these ratios are 43:0:57, reflecting the fact that the government nationalized the tea estates, receives a substantial portion of its tax revenue from them, and is paying low wages to the estate workers.

The services sector is approaching the size of the manufacturing sector. This is due to the growth in tourism and the increasing size of the retail sector which has expanded since import liberalization occurred in 1977. Noncompetitive imports are 31 percent of investment, 11 percent of consumption, and 34 percent of gross output in the manufacturing sector. The latter figure includes crude oil which is refined domestically and then sold to the services sector for transportation purposes and also reexported.

Competitive imports are mostly travel, banking, and insurance in the services sector. The SAM is a one-year snapshot and does not show that competitive agricultural imports have fallen drastically due to significant domestic rice production increases.

The SAM also shows investment and savings behavior. National savings, which here include grants to the government and private remittances, finances 64 percent of investment, and foreign savings is 36 percent of investment. However, excluding remittances and grants yields a domestic savings figure of only 34 percent of investment.

7.3 The Model

As noted earlier, the model is adapted from one constructed by Taylor (1983) for India. It has been reworked to fit the Sri Lankan economic structure. The agricultural sectors have fixed supply and the manufacturing and service sectors have demand-determined output. In the latter sectors the model iterates until supply is equal to the calculated demand.

The model uses markup pricing and allows both a cost-push inflation effect and the effect of inflationary money creation. Cost push comes through the producer variable costs, which include labor and intermediate import costs. The markup rates in the manufacturing and service sectors are positively related both to capacity utilization and to the money supply to capital ratio. This implies that the money supply has both an indirect and a direct effect on prices. Indirectly, the increased money supply leads to increased private credit, private investment, and capacity utilization which then raises markup rates.

The parameters for the markup equation are obtained from time series regressions which show the markup rate increasing with capacity use and the money supply to capital ratio. These results reflect the concern shown in Sri Lanka about the inflationary effects of money growth. Each year in which government borrowing has been high has been followed by stricter government borrowing in subsequent years. In particular the central bank of Ceylon has a high degree of independence and has been known to refuse credit to the government.

In the short run markup rates absorb money supply increases, and in the next year, wages increase as they are indexed to the CPI. This model thus implies that profit recipients are faster at protecting their income from monetary inflation than wage earners.

The formal Sri Lanka model is set up with sixteen blocks of equations and consists of four sectors: (1) food agriculture and processing; (2) export agriculture, (3) manufacturing, mining, and construction; and (4) services, trade, and transport. There are four income classes: agriculture, estate wage earners, nonagricultural wage earners, and nonagricultural profit earners. Also there are two types of consumption classes: poor and rich.

Block I contains real supply–demand balances corresponding to the first four rows of the SAM. Competitive imports adjust to balance sector 1 (agriculture) and exports adjust in sector 2 (agricultural exports). The manufacturing and service sectors (sectors 3 and 4) are demand driven, and so supply adjusts to meet demand. This generally follows the behavior of the Sri Lankan economy.

Block II calculates this year's wages which are indexed to last year's change in the consumer price index.

Blocks III and IV define the price and supply structure of the four sectors. In the agricultural sectors (sectors 1 and 2) output is fixed since supply is generally inelastic in the short run. Final prices are fixed by the government, and the markup rate adjusts to equal the excess of the fixed price over the variable costs. In sector 2, agricultural exports, the discrepancy between the world price and the domestic price accrues to the government which owns most of the tea estates. Taxes on the final good, input subsidies, and intermediate import tariffs are accounted for.

In the nonagricultural sectors (sectors 3 and 4) output is demand determined. Domestic price determination is a Kaleckian markup over variable costs, with the markup rate adjusting to capacity and money supply. An "overall" markup is estimated as a function of capacity and money supply to capital ratio. The markups in sectors 3 and 4 are then adjusted to absorb the difference between markup levels as calculated by the overall rate and the sectoral rates. This markup adjustment is one link from the monetary to the real sector as prices affect real consumption and real exports of manufactures.

Block V contains income equations for the four income classes: agriculture, estate wage earners (sector 2), nonagricultural wage earners, and nonagricultural profits. Government corporation revenues are explicitly accounted for. Each income class can receive remittances from abroad and government transfers.

Block VI specifies the level of consumer spending for the poor and rich classes. The government transfers to nonagricultural wage earners, which are the food stamp transfers, are divided between the poor and rich according to how much leakage is occurring to the upper income class.

Block VII gives consumer spending by the two classes for each of the four sectors' goods as well as for imports. The equations are based on the linear expenditure system which has two sets of parameters: base levels of consumption (ϕ_i) which are independent of price and income, and marginal propensities to consume (δ_i) out of income above the base income needed to attain the base consumption.[5] Note that consumption subsidies and consumer import tariffs are accounted for as part of the consumer price.

Block VIII determines demand for manufacturing exports as a function of the relative world and domestic prices. The exchange rate and export subsidy rate are included in the relative price.

Blocks IX and X yield the government accounts, and blocks XI and XII keep track of the foreign accounts. These blocks determine the government current surplus (SG) and the current-account deficit (SFOR). To maintain consistency in the SAM, the government surplus here includes foreign grant receipts less all foreign interest payments (public corporations and the government hold most of the foreign debt).

Block XIII gives the price of new investment for the private sector, the public corporations, and the government. Real and nominal GDP, the CPI, and the GDP deflator are calculated.

Block XIV contains the monetary accounts. The change in the banking system's government credit is the public sector's borrowing requirement less the government's domestic nonbank borrowing and government's foreign borrowing. The change in reserves is the difference between capital inflows (net of amortization payments) and the current-account deficit. The year-end levels of central bank (CB) government credit and CB reserves is the difference between year-end total government credit and commercial bank government credit, and total reserves and commercial bank reserves, respectively. The money base is the sum of CB reserves, CB government credit, and CB loans to commercial banks, less sundry liabilities. The money supply is a simple multiplier of the money base. Finally, private credit is the residual of the money supply less government credit and reserves, plus nonmonetary commercial and CB liabilities.

Block XV contains equations for investment. Real private investment depends on real private credit, thus establishing a second link between the monetary and real parts of the economy. Real private investment also depends on the change in real GDP as businessmen look at the current state of the economy for their investment decisions. Nominal public corporation investment and government investment are exogenous. The investment by destination is split between sectors 3 and 4 and imports according to the h coefficients which are calculated to ensure that the investment by origin matches figures from the SAM.[6]

Block XVI yields the standard savings-investment identity and is used as a check of the model.

7.4 Simulations

The three years from 1979 to 1981 are examined using the above model. Table 7.5 provides a summary of the percent changes from the base simulations that result under various alternative scenarios.

The base runs come close to replicating what actually happened during the three years. They are used as a comparison for the counterfactual scenarios. The first alternative scenario, lower import price increases, is meant to demonstrate how less adverse terms-of-trade shocks have a strong impact on growth. Sri Lanka has been greatly affected by worsening terms of trade beyond its control.

The second scenario is to keep the food subsidy that was removed. This would continue a food policy that Sri Lanka has had for thirty years and that has contributed to high social indicators. The third scenario is to reduce the public investment program in an attempt to keep the public

Table 7.5
Summary of percent deviations from base runs

	1a 1980	1b 1981	2a 1980	2b 1980	3a 1980	3b 1980	3c 1981	4a 1980	4b 1981	4c 1980	4d 1981	5a 1980
Real GDP	5.1	2.9	0.1	0.8	−1.3	−0.9	−0.2	−0.9	0.4	−1.1	0.2	1.4
Food consumption by the poor	5.6	4.2	15.4	15.2	−1.6	−2.2	−1.5	12.7	14.8	11.9	14.0	2.1
Food imports[a]	143.1	87.9	162.9	126.2	−36.7	−41.7	−22.0	114.8	138.2	100.6	124.4	49.4
CA deficit	−11.6	−17.6	11.6	11.6	−17.7	−19.7	−13.8	−8.6	7.1	−23.7	−16.7	11.7
Total investment	4.3	3.5	−0.7	−0.2	−11.3	−14.8	−10.0	−15.4	−10.7	−15.7	−11.2	2.3
Money supply	12.2	25.9	−2.5	−2.9	−3.5	−16.6	−17.1	−19.1	−20.8	−19.5	−21.7	5.9
CPI	−0.9	−0.7	−5.2	−4.2	−0.9	−1.9	−2.4	−7.1	−6.9	−6.0	−5.3	0.0

Source: Appendix A7.2.
a. Percent deviations are large due to a small base.

sector borrowing requirement down and to contain inflation. Inflation has often been cited as the reason why the poor are worse off today. The fourth scenario combines both the continued food subsidy and reduced investment to show the substantial improvement in food consumption by the poor. The final scenario has an oil price subsidy for a smoother adjustment to the oil shock of the late 1970s.

Base Runs

In the year 1979 there is a rice subsidy scheme in effect, costing the government Rs.1,963 million. The subsidy is intended for the lower 35 percent of the population which consumes 18.2 percent of total expenditure and 30 percent of their expenditure is on rice. However, there is known to be leakage to upper income groups. Edirisinghe (1985) has estimated that about 30 percent of the intended group did not receive benefits. This is captured in the model by reducing the price subsidy to the poor to 21 percent and offering a small subsidy of 6 percent to the rich.

In 1980 and 1981 this subsidy is replaced by a food stamp scheme which is not indexed to inflation. In the model the price subsidy is eliminated, and the government raises transfers to wage earners with the rich once again receiving some of the benefits. The stamps are not indexed and can be deposited in a bank and so can be spent on any good not just food. The effectiveness of food stamps to alleviate malnutrition is thus limited.

This result can be seen in the base runs where total real (1981) consumption of food falls by 5 percent from Rs.26,434 million in 1979 to Rs.25,189m in 1980, with most of this decrease from the lower 35 percent of the population. Their real food consumption falls from Rs.8,773m to Rs.7,644m due to the removal of the free rice ration where rice is 30 percent of their food expenditure. In 1981 food consumption by the poor recovers to Rs.8,301m as general real growth raises incomes. This is still below the 1979 level.

The other feature of this time period is the striking increase in investment from 24 percent of GDP in 1979 to 35 percent in 1980 and 30 percent in 1981. Most of this is generated by larger exogenous government and public corporation investment. Almost all of the increase is financed by foreign savings as national savings remains steady with government savings falling but private remittances rising. The current-account deficit (foreign savings) in the base runs goes from Rs.2,581m in 1979 to Rs.9,287m in 1980 to Rs.8,517m in 1981. Government savings (defined here as government current account surplus + government foreign grants − net inter-

Table 7.6
Foreign trade price indices

	TT	Import prices	Export prices
1978	100.0	100.0	100.0
1979	68.9	154.9	106.8
1980	75.6	214.0	161.8
1981	65.7	263.6	173.1

Source: Department of Census and Statistics.

est payments from BOP data) falls from Rs.2,578m in 1979 to Rs.1,660m to Rs. −87m in 1981, and the public sector borrowing requirement rises from Rs.4,041m to Rs.11,710m to Rs.12,573m.

The effect of this expansionary government investment program is that the money supply rises from Rs.15,194m in 1979 to Rs.19,360m in 1980 to Rs.24,640m in 1981. This occurs because as a result of the higher public sector borrowing requirement, the government credit increase is larger than the reserve decrease. Private credit rises along with the money supply. These monetary occurrences feed back into the real sector in two ways. First, the higher private credit raises real private investment. Second, money supply feeds into the markup rate equation both directly and indirectly via higher capacity utilization. Higher prices then dampen real demand, offsetting the rising real private investment.

The sharp increases in import prices during these three years lead directly to higher sectoral markup prices and provide further fuel to the inflationary process. The CPI rises from 0.62 in 1979 to 0.83 in 1980 to 1.00 in 1981, and the GDP deflator rises from 0.71 to 0.84 to 1.0. This compares with the central bank reported values for the Colombo CPI of 0.67 to 0.84 to 1.0 and for the GDP deflator, 0.70 to 0.83 to 1.0. The GDP deflator compares well, but the Colombo CPI is known to be a downwardly biased indicator of price changes and so the model's CPI is more believable.

Alternative Terms of Trade Experiences

Sri Lanka has suffered significant terms-of-trade deterioration since 1978, as shown in table 7.6. This deterioration can be attributed to rising import costs from the 1978 oil shock and world inflation, both beyond Sri Lanka's control.

The import prices used in the base simulation are given in table 7.7. Simulations 1a and 1b for 1980 and 1981 assume that these prices rise by

Table 7.7
Border prices of imports

	$P_{\text{investment}}$	$P_{\text{intermediate}}$	P_{consumer}
1979	0.6591	0.5638	0.5779
1980	0.8367	0.9099	0.7263
1981	1.0000	1.0000	1.0000

Source: Department of Census and Statistics.

20 percent a year starting from their 1979 values. This is lower than the actual prices, especially for intermediate imports for which the price rise is 61 percent from 1979 to 1980.

The results of slower import price increases are substantial: Real GDP is 5.1 percent higher in 1980 and 2.9 percent higher than in the base scenarios. The effects are stronger in 1980 because the import price rise is much lower in that year compared to the base scenario.

The financial–real links are from the money supply to prices to real demand and from private credit to private investment. Here the lower import price reduces the current-account deficit, although the expansion tends to offset this. The result is higher reserves, and so money supply rises, private credit rises, and private investment expands.

The larger money supply also causes the markup rates in sectors 3 and 4 to increase directly. They are further increased by the higher capacity utilization due to demand pressures from the lowered price. These increased markups show up in income of nonagricultural profit recipients. For example, in situation 1b, sector 4 markup rates are 36 percent compared to 29 percent in the base scenario, and nonagricultural profits are 21 percent higher.

These substantial markup increases affect the relative prices of manufacturing and service sectors. Sector 3 has prices kept down by lower import prices, but sector 4 does not since its import–output coefficient is small. The price level in sector 4 rises much more than sector 3 price. These scenarios point out directions for monetary policy. Sterilization of larger reserves would prevent the large markup increases and the distortion in relative prices.

Continued Food Price Subsidy

The first policy alternative (scenario 2a) is to maintain the 1979 level subsidy of free rice rations to the lower 35 percent of the population. The leakage of rice subsidies to the upper income groups is accounted for by reducing the subsidy to the poor and providing a small subsidy to the rich. With rice consumption about 30 percent of the poor's food expenditure and with about 30 percent not receiving their entitlement, free rice can be approximated by a 21 percent price subsidy to that group. The upper income group receives a subsidy of 6 percent. The food stamp scheme is not implemented and so transfers to households are reduced by Rs.1,614m. As expected, consumption of food by the poor rises dramatically from Rs.7,644m in the 1980 base run to Rs.8,828m in the current 1980 run. This is 0.6 percent higher than in 1979 and is presumably what the trend would have been if the government had not switched from subsidies to transfers. Consumption on all other items by the poor also rises because they are able to achieve their base food necessities more easily. Food consumption by the upper 65 percent rises, but other consumption falls as they lose the benefit of the food stamp transfers.

Normally one would expect a price subsidy to be expansionary as it causes real incomes to rise. Here real GDP in 1980 is almost the same as the 1980 base. This is because the food subsidy is combined with a decrease in transfers to all households. Total consumption of food rises, but total nonfood consumption is unaffected due to the fall in income of the rich. Food supply is fixed in the short run, and so the extra demand does not raise production. Second, the subsidy costs the government Rs.2,502m, which results in a fall in government savings of Rs.925m and thus an increase in government credit of the same amount. Increased real food imports raises the current-account deficit by Rs.1,079m, and so reserves are lower by this amount. Money supply is then lower, private credit is lower, and so private investment falls. This offsets the slightly higher exports.

In simulation 2a the net increase in food consumption results in a one-to-one increase in real food imports as output in food is fixed in the short run. Scenario 2b combines the food subsidy with an increase in producer food prices to provide incentive for increased domestic supplies. A supply elasticity of 0.5 is used, in line with the general success of the actual rice import substitution program that Sri Lanka has been carrying out.[7]

Simulation 2b combines the continued price subsidy with a price rise in food agriculture of 2 percent and a food output increase of 1 percent. GDP now rises 0.87 percent from the base run due to food production rising and also due to increased demand on nonfood sectors as agricultural incomes rise and nonagricultural prices are lower. Prices fall as markups fall due to the lower money supply outweighing the higher capacity utilization in the markup equation. Real food import requirements are Rs.1,828m as opposed to Rs.2,125m in the above simulation. However, the current account deficit is the same as in scenario 2a because increased imports elsewhere, due to higher activity, counter the reduced rice imports.

The price subsidy scheme effectively increases consumption by the poor, especially on food. However the procurement of the extra food is not so straightforward. Unless nonfood imports can be curbed, increased domestic food production does not reduce the foreign savings required.

Reduced Investment

Simulation 3a traces the effects of reductions in investment by the public corporations (irrigation and housing projects) from Rs.7,681m to Rs. 5,681m in 1980. As expected, the effect is contractionary and GDP falls by 1.3 percent. Investment comes from the nonfood sectors and from imports. The nonfood sectors, being demand determined, suffer a loss in output. Consumption demands also fall as the effect of reduced incomes in nonagricultural wage and profit incomes outweighs the effects of reduced prices. Prices fall as markup rates fall with reduced capacity utilization and money supply. With no capital flow changes, there is an improvement in the current-account deficit of Rs.1,644m as consumer imports, intermediate imports, capital imports, and competitive imports all fall. Capital imports fall by Rs.777m. This scenario is deflationary (the GDP deflator falls from 0.8434 to 0.8270) as the borrowing requirements of the government fall and the money supply falls.

It is unrealistic to expect the foreign capital flows to remain the same with reduced investment. A simulation (not reported) in which government foreign borrowing and capital inflows both fall by Rs.2,000m was done. The results for the real economy are identical to simulation 3a because there is no change in the money supply. Government credit rises by Rs.2,000m, but reserves fall by Rs.2,000m, and this perfect offset keeps the money supply unchanged.

Simulation 3b examines the effect of a fall in investment of Rs.2,000m combined with a fall in capital inflows by the same amount and a fall in government foreign borrowing of Rs.1,000m. This would occur if commercial bank and private foreign borrowing fell as a result of the lower investment.

This scenario results in a significant money supply fall as government credit and reserves fall. Government credit will fall since the borrowing requirement falls. Despite the significant improvement in the current-account deficit as the economy contracts, reserves fall because the reduction in capital inflows is larger than the deficit improvement. On subsequent iterations sectoral prices in nonagriculture will fall as their markup rates adjust downward to reduced money supply. Also private credit falls, and so private investment falls; private investment is crowded in by government investment in this model. The reduced sectoral prices increase real consumption demands and real manufacturing exports demand. These effects counter the reduced private and government investment, and nonagricultural output is higher than in 3a. Real GDP is thus not as low as in scenario 3a with reduced investment alone. Also inflation is further contained due to the money supply effect on markup rates. The GDP deflator is 0.8084, down from the 1980 base run value of 0.8434. The CPI (which weights agriculture prices more heavily than the deflator) is 0.8176 down from 0.8334.

These reduced price levels are fed into a 1981 simulation (3c) where public investment is reduced by Rs.1,000m. Capital inflows are reduced by 1,000 and government borrowing is reduced by Rs.500m.

As in 1980 the money supply is lower than in the base year since government credit contracts due to the lowered borrowing requirement and reserves remain steady as the reduced capital inflow offsets the current account improvement. This, combined with a slightly lower capacity utilization, yields lower markup rates. The end result is that nonagricultural prices are reduced sufficiently that consumption demand and manufactured export demand offset the investment demand fall so that final real GDP is Rs.78,989m as compared to the base year Rs.79,164m.[8]

The GDP deflator is 0.97, down from 1.000 in the base run. The CPI is now 0.97 down from 1.000. Over the two-year period of lowered investment, real growth ends up 0.2 percent lower, and inflation has been improved. This shows that excessive public investment has been putting upward pressure on prices in the nonagriculture sectors. The lowered inflation would make the food stamp transfers, which were not indexed to the price level, worth more in real terms. However, because agricultural prices are controlled, they do not respond to the deflationary effect of reduced investment, and so food consumption is not enhanced. This leads us to the next scenario.

Food Subsidy and Lower Investment

The fourth scenario combines the effects of simulations 2a and 3b by both continuing the food subsidy scheme and lowering investment levels and foreign inflows. For the years 1980 and 1981 there are food subsidies of 21 percent to the poorer 35 percent of the population and 6 percent to the wealthier 65 percent of the population (replacing the food stamp transfer of Rs.1,614m in 1980 and Rs.1,321m in 1981), investment is lowered by Rs.2,000m in 1980, and Rs.1,000m in 1981, and foreign inflows are reduced as in simulations 3b and 3c.[9]

In 1980 the lowered investment and the reduced transfers decrease GDP, whereas the subsidies tend to raise it. The resulting real GDP is down by 0.9 percent from the base run. However, the poorer segments of the population are better off as their food consumption rises from Rs.7,644m to Rs.8,615m. The GDP reduction is mainly due to lower investment: a reduction of Rs.2,000m in government investment, as well as a decline of Rs.1,464m in private investment as the money supply and then private credit fall significantly.

Prices are also lower: The GDP deflator is 0.8051 down from 0.8434, and the CPI is 0.7744 down from 0.8334 in the base run. Much of this is due to decreased money supply growth as central bank reserves fall by Rs.1,203m from the base run, due to the lowered capital inflows. Government credit remains about the same as in the base run; the lower investment and transfers are offset by the requirements of the subsidy (Rs.2,457 million) and the lowered government foreign borrowing. The current-account deficit is Rs.8,490m down from Rs.9,287m with the contraction of the economy countering the increased food imports.

These results are fed into a 1981 simulation retaining the price subsidy and decreasing government investment by Rs.1,000m. The results show real GDP as 0.5 percent higher than in the base case. The GDP deflator and CPI are 0.9544 and 0.9314, respectively, instead of 1.0 as in the 1981 base. The lower prices cause real consumption and manufactured exports demand to rise sufficiently to counter the lowered investment.

Food consumption by the poor rises to Rs.9,531m, up from Rs.8,301m in the base run. The food subsidy costs the government Rs.3,099m, and the net effect is that the change in government credit is higher than the 1981 base case by Rs.1,272m. However, reserves fall by Rs.2,809m more than the base due to both the larger current-account deficit as food imports rise and the reduced capital inflows. The result is that the money supply level is greatly reduced from the 1981 base run. This leads to both the low prices and low private investment.

Financing difficulties occur as foreign capital inflows are assumed to fall as capital investment is decreased. The public sector borrowing requirement remains high because the reduced investment is outweighed by the

Table 7.8
Import volumes (1978 = 100)

	Food and drink	Textiles	Other consumption goods	Intermediate goods	Investment goods	All imports
1979	106	173	161	83	112	104
1980	92	170	223	119	153	127
1981	57	194	204	131	147	120
1982	48	159	251	136	192	132

Source: Jayawardena et al. (1986).

cost of the subsidy. The government is forced to resort to expansionary bank financing.

Scenarios 4c and 4d solve the problem of financing the food subsidies by increasing the tariff on consumer imports. As reported by the central bank, and shown in table 7.8, consumer imports other than food and textiles rose faster in volume terms than any other category of imports. This makes consumer import tariffs an attractive revenue source. In runs 4c (1980) and 4d (1981) those tariffs are raised from 0.16 to 0.66 and from 0.17 to 0.67, respectively, while keeping the same changes as in runs 4a and 4b.

Results are similar to scenarios 4a and 4b: The price subsidy and reduced investment lead to lower prices, which encourage consumption and exports, and so real GDP can be sustained at the base levels by 1981. Food consumption by the poor is greatly enhanced. But now the cost of the subsidy program is paid by consumer import tariff receipts of Rs.2,159m in 1980 and Rs.3,222m in 1981. Government savings are significantly improved from 4a and 4b and also from the base simulations. Consumer imports fall substantially, more than the increased imports of food, which gives the added benefit of a lower current-account deficit in both years.

Government credit requirements are reduced due to the extra revenue and reserves are above their base levels. The result is that money supply is kept in line at similar rates as in 4a and 4b, but now this is due to low government credit and high reserves, the opposite of 4a and 4b. Restrained money supply growth again leads to lower prices and increased real demand, and the price subsidies encourage food consumption by the poor. Simulations 4c and 4d successfully continue the tradition of basic needs measures for promoting equity and demonstrate the usefulness of revenue policies that are directed toward certain goods.

Lower Oil Prices

The fifth scenario analyzes how lower national prices for imported oil ease the oil shock adjustment. This was examined by placing an input subsidy on petroleum products going into the manufacturing and services sectors. The manufacturing sector's input of petroleum is 22.6 percent of its total input from manufacturing (refinement of crude oil is done by the petroleum industry). The service sector's input of petroleum is 45.7 percent of total manufacturing inputs.[10] The price of oil doubled from 1979 to 1980, and so a subsidy to manufacturing on the price of manufacturing inputs of 11 percent and a subsidy of 23 percent to the service sector would approximate a constant price of oil to these sectors.

The results is that prices in the manufacturing and service sectors in 1980 go from 0.7870 to 0.7846 and from 0.8197 to 0.8207, respectively. The subsidies reduce the prices, but this effect is offset by the increased markups caused by the bigger government deficit. Real consumption rises due to higher incomes of profit recipients. The subsidies cost the government Rs.1,675m, and this causes government credit to rise. Therefore the money supply rises, private credit rises, and private investment then rises. This contributes to further expansion, and the end result is that real GDP is 1.4 percent higher than the base simulation.

The expansion worsens the current-account deficit as more imports are demanded. The CPI falls, but only marginally. The GDP deflator rises because the calculation of real GDP involves fixed value-added coefficients, whereas the nominal GDP calculation uses the profit rates which have adjusted upward.

Another simulation (not reported) included a second oil facility financed by external sources to cover the cost of the subsidy. As in the investment case, a straight increase in government foreign borrowing by this amount as well as a corresponding increase in capital inflow leaves the money supply unchanged as government credit decreases and reserve increases offset each other. Thus the model solution is the same as above. If the government sterilized the increased reserves, then the money supply would fall as would prices, and an expansion, offset slightly by reduced private investment, would occur.

7.5 Conclusions

Sri Lanka has traditionally been concerned with issues of equity. Studies that debate the relative merits of a basic needs approach to development have typically examined the Sri Lankan experience. The current government has reversed many of the policies that were directly promoting equity. This study has shown that equivalent growth rates could have been achieved while continuing some of these policies.

The specific conclusions for the various policy simulations can be summarized as follows:

1. A continued price subsidy on rice in 1980 instead of food stamps raises food consumption by the poor by 15 percent over the actual base year level. The current account deficit worsens as more food is imported to meet demand. Increased domestic rice production to reduce imports must be accompanied by restraint of nonfood imports in order to get an improvement in the current account.

2. If investment is reduced, the effect is predictably contractionary, with GDP declining and improvements in the external account. The combined effect of a price subsidy on rice and lower investment is to lower prices, which encourages consumption and exports. GDP growth is sustained by 1981 at the same level as in the base scenarios, but food consumption by the poor is substantially increased. Difficulties in financing the subsidy may occur if foreign capital inflows fall as investment is reduced.

3. Directed consumer tariffs can effectively remove the subsidy-financing problems. They can also improve the current account by reducing inessential imports. They are better than deficit financing in that they keep prices low by reducing government credit rather than reducing reserves.

4. Subsidizing imported oil is expansionary but worsens the current-account deficit and the government deficit.

More general conclusions relate to the model itself. Overall the model is a useful tool for examining medium-term effects of various assumptions and policies and for pointing out directions for policy. Different structures could be incorporated in the model. For example, the fast markup rate adjustment and the slower wage adjustment are assumptions of the model. If wages were also allowed to adjust within the period, then the model would be more sensitive to consumption because wage earners have a lower saving propensity.

The financial–real link through the markup rate is a monetarist one generally following the Sri Lankan view of how the economy works. Money raises prices both directly and indirectly through the positive coefficient on capacity utilization. Details of the simulations show that real demand components of sector output are sensitive to the price. It then becomes important to keep prices under control to ensure growth. With the money supply link to prices the government must keep government credit under control and sterilize reserve increases when appropriate. The model is useful for suggesting when this should be done.

Notes

Research supported by the World Institute for Development Economics Research, Helsinki.

1. This figure suggests a high incremental capital–output ratio (5.5 as against 3.5 in the 1960s), but according to the World Bank this is misleading. The ratio of real investment to real GDP would be much lower. Investment imports were valued at the higher of the dual exchange rate, and exports and consumption were understated as they were valued at less than market prices.

2. A large literature has developed on the debate between the "direct" (basic needs) and "indirect" (economic growth) measures of promoting equity. Sri Lanka is often cited as a country that has successfully raised living standards through the direct approach without much cost in terms of reduced growth.

3. Edirisinghe (1985) and Sahn (1985) discuss the falling nutritional status of the poor. Evidence of lower calorie consumption by the poor is found in surveys by both the Central Bank of Ceylon and the Department of Census and Statistics. Jayawardena et al. (1986) summarize these findings and others that demonstrate that real consumption fell in 1980.

4. For applied details on construction of a SAM, see Taylor (1983) or Eckaus, McCarthy, and Mohie-eldin (1981).

5. The original paper on the linear expenditure system by Stone is summarized in Taylor (1979).

6. The h coefficients are equivalent to the elements of Leontieff's B matrix.

7. Log regressions of domestic production on paddy fertilizer use, weighted producer prices, and a time trend yielded price elasticities of 0.1 to 0.41. However, this omits a rainfall variable. To the extent that rainfall is uncorrelated to the explanatory variables, the estimates are not biased. This can be argued since prices and fertilizer issues are controlled by the government and are set by budget considerations prior to the growing season. Thorbecke (1985) reports elasticities ranging from 0.155 to 0.530 for the area sown to the real weighted producer price of paddy. The higher elasticity of 0.5 is chosen because of the emphasis of government policy toward improved agricultural incentives and the success of these incentives.

8. It should be noted that an optimistic export elasticity of 1.5 was used. This can be justified by the large success of the textile industry, which was well below its

U.S. import quota at the time and accounted for a rapidly increasing share of industrial exports. Refined petroleum is the other major share of industrial exports.

9. This scenario revives the debate of whether equity is better promoted by providing basic needs or by encouraging overall growth. To the extent that improved nutrition improves productivity, the argument becomes blurred. Basic needs can then be viewed as an investment in human capital which will promote growth as well as providing direct benefits toward equity.

10. These data come from a twenty-sector input–output table that was aggregated for the four-sector SAM.

References

Central Bank of Ceylon. 1978–84. *Review of the Economy*. Sri Lanka.

Central Bank of Ceylon. 1978–79, 1981–82. *Report on Consumer Finances and Socio Economic Survey*. Sri Lanka.

Department of Census and Statistics. 1985. *Trade Indices 1978–83*. Sri Lanka

Dervis, Kemal, Jaime de Melo, and Sherman Robinson. 1982. *General Equilibrium Models for Development Policy*. Cambridge: Cambridge University Press.

Eckaus, Richard, Desmond McCarthy, and Amr Mohie-eldin. 1981. "A Social Accounting Matrix for Egypt, 1976." *Journal of Development Economics* 9: 182–203.

Edirisinghe, Neville. 1985. "The Food Stamp Programme in Sri Lanka: Costs, Benefits, and Policy Options." Washington DC: IFPRI. Mimeo.

Gibson, Bill, Nora Lustig, and Lance Taylor. 1982. "Terms of Trade and Class Conflict in a Computable General Equilibrium Model for Mexico." Mexico City: El Colegio de Mexico. Mimeo.

Jayawardena, L. R., A. L. Maasland, and P. N. Radhakrishnan. 1986. "Stabilisation and Adjustment Programmes and Policies: Case Study on Sri Lanka." Helsinki: UNU/WIDER. Mimeo.

Sahn, David. 1985. "Food Consumption Patterns and Parameters in Sri Lanka—the Causes and Control of Malnutrition." Washington DC: IFPRI. Mimeo.

Sarkar, H., and M. Panda. 1986. "Quantity Price-Money Interaction in a CGE Model." Delhi: NCAER. Mimeo.

Taylor, Lance. 1983. *Structuralist Macro-Economics*. New York: Basic Books.

Taylor, Lance. 1979. *Macro Models for Developing Countries*. New York: McGraw-Hill.

Taylor, Lance, and Dimitris Diakosavvas. 1983. "Macroeconomic Implications of Alternative Agricultural Price Policies." Rome: FAO. Mimeo.

Thorbecke, Erik, and Jan Svejnar. 1985 "Effects of Macro-Economic Policies on Agricultural Performance in Sri Lanka, 1960–82." Paris: OECD.

World Bank. 1980–85. *Recent Economic Developments and Policies for Growth.* Washington DC.

8 Macro Constraints on India's Economic Growth

Lance Taylor

I never had the fortune to know V. K. Ramaswami, but I understand that he was an economist of parts, combining a lucid mind with a flair for policy advice. It is in the spirit of Ramaswami's blend of analysis with policy that I want to take up a question central to Indian debate—what are the macroeconomic limits to the national rate of growth?

The topic is complex, not least because it is not obvious that one can even *do* macroeconomics for India. In most corners of the world, one can write down a few structural equations, argue on institutional and historical grounds that they make sense, and plug in the numbers to find linkages relevant to the policy issues at hand. In India, with its cross-cutting sectors, regions, classes, and castes, the few equations become many, and they are extremely opaque. One despairs of *a* simple model, but perhaps several models together may shed light on the limiting factors. In this lecture I explore this possibility, using a baker's dozen formulas to circumscribe the rate of growth. Ultimately, its determinants escape the net, but one can see the reasons why. Growth *is* subject to macro limitations, but they are too complicated to set out in equation form. I will take up their political economy at the end of the talk.

The potential constraints fall into five groups—savings limits, the external constraint, agricultural supply, inflation, and internal finance. Their algebra is set out in table 8.1, along with representative numerical solutions. The macro accounts, variables in the equations, and parameters are described in tables 8.2 through 8.4. The data are estimated roughly for 1986–87, mostly on the basis of papers by Minhas (1987) and the National Council of Applied Economic Research (1987). The qualitative implications of the solutions should withstand "reasonable" changes in the parameters, but sensitive numbers will be pointed out as we go along.

8.1 Productivity and Thrift

Since the Second and Third Plans, most discussion of Indian growth has focused on its limits from the side of supply. In the recent period a general savings ceiling on gross investment has been stressed instead of specific constraints such as production capacity of capital goods—the system is said to be driven overall by the forces of productivity and thrift. The first point I want to make is that at the macro level, this way of looking at an economy makes no sense; one has to analyze supply constraints in terms of identifiable limiting factors like food output or foreign exchange. To see why, we can work through a couple of standard growth rate equations.

Equation (1) in table 8.1 sets out a savings constraint: Savings sources as shares of gross output to the left are the current-account deficit f, private sector saving s, and overall public sector saving s_g. *If* output is assumed to be at full capacity and *if* these shares are stable, then their sum fixes total capital formation. Dividing by the incremental capital–output ratio ξ gives the rate of output growth $\hat{X}$. At the far right, the sum of public and private capital formation shares k_g and k_p must equal savings supply.

In the Indian context this accounting is supposed to support two assertions—that the private saving share s is large and has been growing over time, and that the potential benefits of all this saving are nullified because the capital–output ratio ξ is also high.

International comparisons indeed show that s and ξ are empirically large. My quarrel is not with the numbers but with the inferences about growth that (1) as read from with causality running from left to right is alleged to support. As a matter of arithmetic, if s is big and growth $\hat{X}$ is relatively slow, then ξ is bound to be large ex post since it is computed by dividing the sum to the left of the first "equals" sign by the growth rate on its right. The real question is *why* growth is slow, which this computation does not address. Moreover left-to-right causality imposed on the accounting has several problems. I mention just three:

First, more rapid output growth is associated with higher government saving (other parameters unchanged), namely, a more restrictive fiscal stance. In any given period this negative correlation need not (indeed, probably will not) be observed. Second, given saving, higher public investment k_g is necessarily associated with lower private investment k_p. This trade-off flies in the face of fairly good econometric evidence that in India and other semi-industrialized economies, state capital formation crowds private investment *in*, not out. Finally, a numerical value of 4.5 for ξ implies that 1 percent faster output growth will raise the current account deficit by

Table 8.1
Constraint equations

Savings limit on growth

$$f + s + s_g = \xi\hat{X} = k_g + k_p \tag{1}$$

$$0.011 + 0.195 + 0.021 = 4.5 \times 0.0504 = 0.115 + 0.112$$

Total factor productivity growth

$$\hat{X} = \left(\frac{\phi_w}{1 - m}\right)\hat{N} + \left(\frac{i_k}{1 - m}\right)(f + s + s_g) + \rho \tag{2}$$

$$0.0504 = \left(\frac{0.38}{0.936}\right) \times 0.025 + \left(\frac{0.15}{0.936}\right) \times 0.227 + 0.0039$$

Effect of faster capacity growth on current foreign deficit

$$\frac{df}{d\hat{Z}} = [(\alpha m - \beta e - f)\mu_x + \theta]z\xi \tag{3}$$

$$0.493 = [(1.5 \times 0.064 - 1.0 \times 0.054 - 0.011)(1.5) + 0.053](1.1)(4.5)$$

Effect of faster capacity growth on export share (f unchanged)

$$\frac{de}{d\hat{Z}} = [(\alpha m - e)\mu_x + \theta]z\xi \tag{4}$$

$$0.574 = [(1.5 \times 0.064 - 0.054)(1.5) + 0.053](1.1)(4.5)$$

Condition for devaluation to lead to output reduction

$$\eta < \frac{(1 - s_w)m}{e} \tag{5}$$

$$1.0 < 1.126 = \frac{(0.95)(0.064)}{0.054}$$

Increase in ratio of foreign debt to exports

$$\dot{a} = \left(\frac{f}{e}\right) + a(i^* - \hat{E}) \tag{6}$$

$$0.167 = (0.011/0.054) + 1.954(0.031 - 0.05)$$

$\hat{a} = 0.085$ in the base year; $\dot{a} = 0$ when $a = 10.721$

Agricultural capacity growth required for constant terms of trade

$$\hat{Z}_a = \gamma\hat{J} + (1 - \gamma)\hat{N} \tag{7}$$

$$0.04 = 0.6 \times 0.05 + 0.4 \times 0.025$$

Rate of growth of agricultural sector output per capita

$$\hat{Y} = \frac{\gamma(1 + \epsilon)}{\epsilon + \delta}(\hat{J} - \hat{N}) + \frac{1 - \delta}{\epsilon + \delta}(\hat{N} - \hat{Z}_a) \tag{8}$$

$$0.0208 = \frac{0.6(1 + 0.3)}{0.3 + 0.3}(0.05 - 0.025) + \frac{1 - 0.3}{0.3 + 0.3}(0.025 - 0.035)$$

Coefficient on $\hat{N} = [1 - \delta - \gamma(1 + \epsilon)]/(\epsilon + \delta) = -0.133$

Table 8.1 (continued)

Inflation from agricultural demand and nonagricultural costs

$$\hat{P} = \frac{1}{1 - v}\left\{\left[\frac{\gamma(\phi_a + \phi_n v)}{\epsilon + \delta} + \lambda\right](\hat{J} - \hat{N}) + \frac{\phi_a + \phi_n v}{\epsilon + \delta}(\hat{N} - \hat{Z}_a) + \hat{P}_0\right\} \quad (9)$$

$(\phi_a + \phi_n v)/(\epsilon + \delta) = (0.265 + 0.735 \times 0.4)/(0.3 + 0.3) = 0.9317$

$$0.083 = \left(\frac{1}{1 - 0.4}\right)\{[0.6 \times 0.9317 + 1] \times (0.05 - 0.025)$$
$$+ 0.9317 \times (0.025 - 0.035) + 0.02\}$$

Coefficient on $\hat{J} = 2.599$

Equation of exchange

$$HV = PX \quad (10)$$

$13.68 \times 2.234 = 1.0 \times 30.56$

Growth rate of money supply

$$\hat{H} = V\mu_h\psi_h(k_g - s_g) \quad (11)$$

$0.153 = 2.234 \times 3.26 \times 0.2235 \times (0.115 - 0.021)$

$V\mu_h\psi_h = 1.628$

Inflation rate from growth of money supply

$$\hat{P} = [V\mu_h\psi_h\xi(k_g/k) - \pi]\hat{X} - V\mu_h\psi_h s_g \quad (12)$$

$0.076 = (1.628 \times 4.5 \times (0.115/0.227) - 1.5] \times 0.05 - 1.628 \times 0.021$

Coefficient on $\hat{X} = 2.211$

Increase in ratio of internal debt to value of capacity

$$\dot{b} = \frac{\psi_b \tau}{z + b(i - \hat{P} - \hat{Z})} \quad (13)$$

$$0.0452 = \frac{0.838 \times 0.066}{1.1} + 0.253 \times (0.1 - 0.07 - 0.05)$$

$\hat{b} = 0.179$ in the base year; $\dot{b} = 0$ when $b = 2.514$

Note: A "dot" over a variable denotes its increase over time, and a "hat" its rate of growth: $\dot{X} = dX/dt$ and $\hat{X} = \dot{X}/X$.

4.5 percent (from 1.1 to 5.6 percent of output) if national savings rates are fixed. This increase has not been observed in response to observed Indian growth fluctuations in the 1 percent range.

Slow growth and a high capital–output ratio are often rationalized in technological terms. Neoclassical economists start from equation (2), a decomposition of the "sources of growth" into labor force increase, capital stock growth, and a term ρ called *total factor productivity growth* or TFPG. Labor and capital growth are weighted by their shares in total output, and TFPG is computed as a residual. Equation (2) is slightly restated from this simplest version because the output concept we work with includes intermediate imports (output share m) and because the appropriate weighting for the saving share of output in the second term after the "equals" sign is the observed rate of return to capital i_k (set to 15 percent, consistent with an average capital–output ratio of 3.7).

The message of (2) is similar to (1). The low Indian ex post value for ρ (about 0.4 percent) simply says that output growth has been slow in relation to increases in both employment and capital stock. This is a theorem of accounting. Without further evidence the notion that slow TFPG *causes* a low value of $\hat{X}$ does not follow from the equation.

What can take us further, perhaps, is investigation of observed changes in ratios of capital and labor inputs to output separately. Rajaraman (1985) and Ahluwalia and D'Souza (1987) show that labor productivity in both agriculture and manufacturing has been rising over time. Simultaneously, capital productivity in manufacturing has been going down (i.e., excess capacity has apparently been on the rise). The weighted average of these two trends sums to slow TFPG.

Why are the trends observed? More and newer capital stock (along with output growth and humane inputs such as nutrition and education) is typically associated with greater labor productivity, and this linkage appears to be in place. Excess capacity can have at least three causes: First, investment projects may have been undertaken in sectors in which demand has been stagnant. Second, existing capital may be used wastefully. Third, demand expansion may have been slower than capacity formation overall. Which of these three factors explains the numbers in equation (2) is a question we have to take up below, after asking about other potential limits to growth.

8.2 The Foreign Deficit and the External Debt Trap

The problem with equations (1) and (2) is that they implicitly assume that output X is identical to capacity Z. The algebra does not allow aggregate production to fall below the level permitted by available capital stock, meaning that slow growth has to reflect itself into extreme values of parameters like ρ and ξ. If excess capacity is recognized, one can also look into other factors that may hold down output and growth. In this and next section—following Abhijit Sen (1981) and Pronab Sen (1987)—we consider limitations due to shortages of foreign exchange and agricultural supply.

In India as in other countries that have industrialized by import substitution, imports largely take the form of intermediate inputs into current production and capital goods. Even after the trade liberalization experiments of the past few years, foreign commodities directly competitive with national products typically will not cross India's frontiers.

As shown in table 8.2, the current-account deficit F thus is the excess of intermediate (M) and capital (θI) imports and foreign interest payments i^*A over exports E and remittance income Rem. Holding interest and remittances constant, the change in the deficit/output ratio f as the growth rate of capacity $\hat{Z}$ goes up is given by equation (3) in table 8.1.

Capactiy growth requires extra investment in proportion to the capital–output ratio ξ. A share θ will be imported. At the same time output X will rise with a multiplier μ_x—using a multiplier amounts to a short-cut solution to the well-known saving and trade gap equations for output and the trade deficit as functions of capacity growth. Intermediate imports will follow output according to an elasticity α. If capacity is limited, exports may in fact be crowded out by higher domestic demand, but we will assume that they increase with an elasticity β.

Plugging in plausible values for all these parameters (in particular, the multiplier μ_x is set to 1.5, and the elasticities α and β take the values 1.5 and 1.0) suggests that a 1 percent increase in the rate of capacity growth will raise the share of the current-account deficit in output by about 0.05 percent. The increment is large (about Rs. 2,000 crores or $1.5 billion) but one-tenth the amount mechanical application of the savings constraint (1) would suggest. Alternatively, if f is held constant, equation (4) shows that an increase in the capacity growth rate of 1 percent would require the export share of output to rise from 5.4 to 6.0 percent. Export volume itself would have to increase by 13.7 percent.

These are nontrivial changes, but perhaps within the range of plausible discourse. They can be affected by policy. The assumed intermediate import elasticity of 1.5 can be reduced by directed investment in sectors such as oil extraction and fertilizer, as well as sensible quantitative controls. On the other hand, as Singh and Ghosh (1987) emphasize, indiscriminate trade liberalization can drive import propensities rapidly up.

Table 8.2
Base-year flows and stocks

X	Gross output (GDP + intermediate imports)	30.56
X_a	Agricultural output	8.10
X_n	Nonagricultural output	22.46
I	Total investment (including stock changes)	6.94
I_g	Government (public) investment	3.53
I_p	Private investment	3.42
R	Government revenue (taxes, enterprise profits, etc.)	6.29
G	Government purchases of goods and services	3.51
U	Government transfers and subsidies	1.19
A	Government foreign debt	3.25
i^*A	Interest on government foreign debt ($i^* = 0.031$)	0.10
B	Government internal debt	8.5
iB	Interest on government internal debt ($i = 0.1$)	0.85
S_g	Government saving ($R - G - U - i^*A - iB$)	0.64
M	Intermediate imports	1.97
θI	Investment imports ($\theta = 0.053$)	0.37
E	Exports	1.66
Rem	Net foreign remittances	0.44
F	Current foreign deficit ($M + \theta I + i^*A - E -$ Rem)	0.34
S	Private saving	5.96
Z	Overall capacity ($= 1.1X$)	33.62
Z_a	Agricultural capacity ($= 1.05X_a$)	8.51
Y	Agricultural output per capita (P_aX_a/N)	Rs. 1013
H	Money supply (M_3)	13.68
J	Autonomous demand ($I + G + E$)	12.11

Note: Rs.10,000 crores of 1986–87; all base year prices = 1).

Table 8.3
Base year ratio variables

$\phi_a = P_a X_a / PX$	0.265
$\phi_n = P_n X_n / PX$	0.735
ϕ_w (wage payments/gross output)	0.38
ϕ_k (capital income/gross output)	0.556
i_k (capital income/capital stock)	0.15
$k = P_k I / PX$	0.227
$k_g = P_k I_g / PX$	0.115
$k_p = P_k I_p / PX$	0.112
$r = R/PX$	0.206
$g = G/X$	0.115
$u = U/PX$	0.039
i^*A/PX	0.003
iB/PX	0.026
$s_g = S_g/PX\ (= r - g - u - i^*A/PX - iB/PX)$	0.021
$m = P^*M/PX$	0.064
$e = P^*E/PX$	0.054
$f = P^*F/PX$	0.011
$s = S/PX$	0.195
$z = Z/X$	1.1
$a = A/E$	1.954
$b = B/PZ$	0.253

Note: Price variables are P = output deflator; P_a, P_n = sectoral prices; P^* = exchange rate; P_k = cost of capital goods. All prices are set to unity in the base year.

Table 8.4
Parameters

ξ	Marginal capital–output ratio	4.5
$\hat{N}$	Rate of growth of labor force and population	0.025
ρ	Rate of total factor productivity growth	0.0039
α	Elasticity of intermediate imports versus output	1.5
β	Elasticity of exports versus output	1.0
μ_x	Output multiplier versus investment	1.5
θ	Import share of investment	0.053
η	Price elasticity of export demand	1.0
s_w	Saving rate from wage income	0.05
i^*	Average interest rate on external debt	0.031
γ	Income elasticity of demand for agricultural output	0.6
δ	Price elasticity of demand for agricultural output	0.3
$\in$	Price elasticity of supply of agricultural output	0.3
$\hat{Z}_a$	Rate of growth of agricultural capacity	0.035
λ	Elasticity of nonagricultural price versus overall output per capita	1.0
ν	Elasticity of nonagricultural price versus agricultural price	0.4
$\hat{P}_0$	Base rate of inflation of nonagricultural price	0.02
π	Elasticity of money demand versus real output	1.5
V	Velocity of money versus value of output	2.234
μ_h	Multiplier of money supply versus monetary base	3.26
ψ_h	Share of fiscal deficit $(k_g - s_g)PX$ borrowed from the central bank	0.2238
i	Average interest rate on government internal debt	0.1
τ	Output share of government cash deficit net of interest on internal debt $(k_g - s_g - iB)/PX$	0.066
ψ_b	Share of τPX borrowed from domestic sources besides the central bank	0.383

On the side of receipts, one can ask about the implications of more rapid growth of exports and foreign debt. With regard to exports, econometrics for India suggests a volume elasticity of about unity with respect to price. After its effects on the domestic price level are taken into account, a currency devaluation of 15 to 20 percent should stimulate foreign sales enough to support 1 percent faster capacity growth.

The difficulty is that besides feeding into inflation, devaluation is likely to make output contract. Formula (5) is an inequality condition for contractionary devaluation, stating that the expansionary effect of higher sales abroad is more than offset by the demand loss implicit in a weaker exchange rate. With stylized Indian parameters the condition holds, at least for the short to medium run. Potential stagflation from devaluation suggests that other measures to raise exports should be considered—public investment in export "thrust" sectors, subsidies, access to intermediate imports, and directed credits. All these policies are antiliberal, but they stand some chance of generating an export response without devaluation's unfavorable macroeconomic effects. Their potential role in a strategy aimed at more rapid growth is taken up below.

On the borrowing front, India at the moment is in relatively decent shape—its credit rating is as good as any country's in the developing world. The key question is how external debt may evolve over the medium run. A useful criterion is the debt–export ratio a. Equation (6) shows how a increases over time.

The main determinants are the ratio of the current-account deficit to exports (f/e) and the difference between the foreign real interest rate i^* and export growth $\hat{E}$. It is well known that if the interest rate exceeds the growth rate, then the debt–export ratio will go to infinity. India currently seems to be paying about 3 percent interest on its mix of concessional and commercial debt, while exports grow at about 5 percent. The ultimate debt trap is avoided, but not by very much.

On the other hand, if current deficit and export shares of output stay constant, the equilibrium level of the debt–export ratio will be 10.7 as opposed to its current value of 1.9. If the ratio gets anywhere near its long-run value, India will find its interest rate rising or (more likely) its external lines of credit cut off. Evidently, the external debt situation will worsen if the output growth rate increases without import substitution or promotion of exports. Even with an export elasticity β of unity, the deficit/export ratio has an elasticity of 9.1 with respect to capacity growth $\hat{Z}$.

The conclusion is the external constraints may well become severe if the growth rate goes up in the absence of improvements in trade parameters or a decrease in the incremental capital–output ratio ξ. Tradability is more likely to be improved by directed incentive policies and investment rather than devaluation (which has substantial macroeconomic costs) and/or liberalization *tout court*. We return to the question of efficiency improvements after discussing agricultural and financial constraints.

8.3 The Agrarian Constraint

Along with foreign transactions, agriculture is a limiting sector on the side of supply. Its interdependence with the rest of the economy can be captured in part by a "flex price/fix price" macro model. On the "flex" side demand and supply functions for agriculture are price inelastic in the short run. The sector's price P_a must therefore fluctuate (subject to public intervention) to clear the market. To get some feel for the numbers, observe that if its demand (δ) and supply (ε) elasticities both take values of 0.3, then a 5 percent adverse supply shock will force agriculture's relative price to rise by 8.3 percent. By contrast, nonagriculture is likely to have administered (or "fix") prices, with output adjusting to demand.

This simple model can be extended in several ways, for example, as in Rao (1987) to capture the notion that agricultural supply growth is highly dependent on public investment which both adds to infrastructural capacity and crowds private capital formation in. But for present purposes we will focus on the more narrow issue of interactions between the growth rates of agricultural capacity Z_a and an aggregate demand injection (comprising investment, exports, and government spending) denoted by J.

Equation (7) in table 8.1 follows Sen (1987) in asking how fast Z_a has to grow to meet aggregate demand and population expansion at constant terms of trade if the income elasticity of demand for agricultural products is γ. For a value of γ of 0.6, 4 percent supply growth is consistent with demand expansion of 5 percent and population growth of 2.5 percent per year. Without price changes, such a rate of expansion seems unlikely. Hence 5 percent demand growth may require improvement in the agricultural terms of trade.

Suppose state intervention in the form of irrigation projects, provision of new technology, credit, and extension allows the agricultural supply function to shift outward at 3.5 percent per year (a growth rate plausible, bad weather aside, in terms of recent performance). What will happen to the real value in terms of nonagricultural products of the sector's output per head?

Equation (8) answers this question. For the demand and population growth rates and parameter values already mentioned, it shows the value of agricultural output per capita rising at 2 percent per year, made up of an annual favorable shift of the terms of trade of 0.8 percent and an output increase of 3.7 percent (or 1.2 percent per head). The corresponding rate of growth of nonagricultural output is 5.2 percent (or 2.7 percent per head). These rates of increase are broadly compatible with the recent tendency of agricultural and nonagricultural population shares to stay constant since labor productivity rates in the two sectors have been growing about 1 and 2.5 percent per year.

Four implications of these results are worth bringing out. First, slower population growth boosts the value of agricultural per capita output (with an elasticity of 0.13). But suppose that relatively rapid increases in agricultural income cut back on population expansion by bringing on a demographic transition. Then a positive feedback loop can arise, with agricultural income growth retarding population increase and making income grow faster. Such a possibility should not be ignored.

Second, there is a question of rural income distribution. The late Dharm Narain's thesis as refined by several authors in the book edited by Mellor and Desai (1986) is that the poverty head count responds with opposite signs and roughly equal strength to increases in agricultural output and the terms of trade. The numerical results just discussed are consistent with a reduction in poverty since output rises faster than price.

Third, there is the possibility that growth in agriculture's nonagricultural purchases may stimulate private investment and sustain the demand injection that is treated as autonomous in equation (8). A micro question arises as to whether investment will accelerate in response to the goods that agriculturalists usually buy, for example, intermediates and relatively unsophisticated consumer products. If not, then an agriculture-led growth strategy of the type proposed by Chakravarty (1987) may not wash.

Finally, the signs of the numerical results just presented depend on parameters. In particular, if the income elasticity γ is much less than our assumed value of 0.6, the positive trend in the terms of trade and the negative effect of population increase on the growth of agricultural income per capita can easily reverse. The moral is that unless agriculture's product mix is directed toward commodities with relatively buoyant demand, then an agriculture-first strategy can easily run into the terms of trade problems that traditionally bedevil a sector (or an economy) concentrating on primary products.

8.4 Fear of Inflation

Each economy has its own inflation flash point. If price increases go over the critical level, then calls for policies to restrict demand growth inevitably arise (regardless of whether austerity objectively has much impact on the inflation rate).

From my foreigner's perspective, admittedly tainted by some years in Latin America, the Indian polity seems unduly averse to trending prices. Usually social groups opposed to inflation comprise the financial community and net creditors, on the one hand, and, on the other hand, classes whose real income flows are unprotected against price increases along the lines suggested by Dharm Narain. I can't quite fathom how the political powers of rentiers and the rural poor jointly produce an Indian critical inflation rate of not more than around 10 percent, but such a collective preference seems clear. There's no accounting for taste.

With strong public antipathy to inflation, an obvious policy question is how strongly it responds to faster output growth. Economists tend to analyze the causes of inflation from two perspectives. The "structuralist" approach emphasizes distributional conflicts and production costs, while "monetarist" models stress the effects on the price level of money creation in response to the fiscal deficit. Either way, faster demand growth may accelerate inflation. For completeness, I will estimate this linkage's strength in both monetarist and structuralist formulations.

The model just used to discuss interactions between agriculture and nonagriculture easily extends to deal with inflation from a structuralist point of view. The terms of trade or price of agricultural relative to nonagricultural goods is set by the condition that agricultural demand equal supply. Hence the absolute level of P_a will be unit elastic with respect to the nonagricultural price P_n.

Markup pricing typically rules outside agriculture—P_n will be proportional to variable cost as represented by the nominal wage. Wages will rise over time for three reasons. The first is an "inertial" component of inflation P_0. Second, wages can be assumed to respond to the growth of aggregate demand per capita with an elasticity λ (a Phillips curve term). Finally, if P_a goes up, there will be pressure to increase wages more or less in proportion to the share of agricultural products in the consumption basket (say, v).

Solving out these price linkages across the two sectors gives equation (9) in table 8.1. With reasonable parameters ($\lambda = 1.0$ and $v = 0.4$) and 2 percent inertial inflation, the numbers suggest that 5 percent demand growth, 2.5 percent population increase, and growth of agricultural capacity at 3.5 percent per year jointly generate an annual inflation rate of 8.3 percent. Inflation rises about 2.6 percent for each 1 percent increase in the rate of growth of aggregate demand. We will assess the implications of this result after deriving a similar response coefficient from monetarist inflation theory.

The monetarist story begins with (10) in table 8.1, the well-known equation of exchange which defines velocity V. Based on broad money (M_3) and our measure of gross output, V takes a value of 2.234 for India in 1986–87. Because of its convenient dimensions (value of output per unit of money supply), velocity enters into the determination of the money growth rate $\hat{H}$ in (11). Reading the terms from the right, $\hat{H}$ turns out to be the product of the share of the public sector cash deficit (or government investment less saving) in output, the proportion ψ_h of the deficit borrowed from the central bank, the blowup factor μ_h from base money to M_3, and velocity. As the numbers work out, the cash deficit share of output is 9.4 percent, which generates 15.3 percent growth in money supply.

In the monetarist view this M_3 expansion is bound to feed into inflation. To see how much, look at equation (12) based on the ideas that real output growth will raise money demand with an elasticity π ($= 1.5$), and that growth in turn requires investment according to the marginal capital output ratio ξ. The equation gives a 7.6 percent inflation rate, with a response coefficient of inflation to output growth of 2.2. Since they are being applied ex post to the same economy, it is not surprising that structuralist and monetarist inflation formulas produce similar results.

What can we make of these equations? The key parameter is the response of inflation to the growth rate, which takes a value between two and three. Whether the political and distributional costs of an extra two or three points of inflation (which after indexation and other responses might accelerate to five or seven) in exchange for one point of growth are too much to bear is not for an outsider to judge. But it is fair to say that the trade-off would not be considered unfavorable in most developing economies. Is India's distaste for inflation *that* much stronger than what one observes in the rest of the world?

8.5 Financial Fragility and the Internal Debt Trap

Besides borrowing from the central bank, the Indian government also resorts (increasingly in the recent period) to the private financial market to place its liabilities. Two questions arise. Does the state's borrowing presage increased "fragility" of the financial system (i.e., a tendency toward instability)? Second, is the government at risk of running into an internal debt trap?

The second question is more precise, so we take it up first. It is addressed by the final equation in table 8.1, which shows the growth of b, or the ratio of state obligations B to the value of capacity PZ. The algebra is based on the assumptions that increases in public debt are used to pay interest iB and cover a fraction ψ_b of the fiscal cash deficit net of iB. If τ is the share of this deficit concept in the value of output, then equation (13) for b comes out. For 1986–87, ψ_b takes the relatively high value of 0.84, reflecting in part discrepancies between the fiscal and financial accounts. The average nominal interest rate on government debt seems to be about 10 percent, or 3 percent in real terms.

The debt–capacity ratio will become unbounded if the real interest rate exceeds the growth rate of Z. At present, $\hat{Z}$ exceeds $i - \hat{P}$, so fears of uncontrolled debt growth are premature. However, questions of portfolio choice and market stability are worth raising. Recently, the state has paid increasingly high real interest rates to get the private sector to hold its paper. Is this a trend that will continue into the future? If so, is it a symptom of market fragility? We take up these issues momentarily, after discussing growth of debt.

At current rates, b has a stable long-run level about ten times as large as its current value of one-quarter. It presently is rising at the relatively rapid pace of 18 percent (or total debt is growing at close to 30 percent). An issue of starting from a low base is clearly involved, and one should also not forget the potential benefits of having a large stock of national debt. For example, open market operations to control the money supply become a viable (and useful) policy option.

Nonetheless, if b continues to grow rapidly and monetarist fears of inflation rule out an M_3 growth rate of much more than 15 percent, then financial problems may appear. The interest component of fiscal spending—a regressive income transfer to rentiers—will increase and public pressure to cut back on socially useful spending could become intense.

The policy responses—far easier for an expatriate academic to recommend than for a government to implement—should take the form of higher taxes and/or public enterprise prices. Political difficulties aside, tax increases would be contractionary in the short run by reducing the multiplier. However, fiscal drag would be offset in the medium term by two factors. First, the deficit's share of output as measured by $k_g - s_g$ (or τ) would fall, permitting continued demand growth with a reduced financial burden. Second, avoiding interest transfers to high-saving classes would put less downward pressure on the multiplier response.

With regard to public enterprise price increases, one has to offset their short-term inflationary impact against reductions in the cash deficit. Of course, inflationary pressure will be reduced by improvements in efficiency of public sector firms.

Finally, poor revenue collection may go hand in hand with the high interest rate on state debt. Presumably, some share of taxes uncollected becomes black money placed in the booming real estate market and consumer durables. High returns (mostly capital gains) on such assets are the rentier's opportunity cost of holding fiscal debt. The government has to pay dearly to borrow funds it might be raising through taxes in the first place!

More ominously, real estate and other speculation on the basis of anticipated capital gains suggests the existence of large stocks of loanable resources that cannot find outlets the form of productive capital formation. Slow output growth and high marginal capital–output ratios make "white" placements for funds relatively unattractive. Inadequate tax collection and poor revenue performance of public enterprises increase the "black" supply. Speculation in nonproductive assets is a natural result. In both Latin America and the Middle East in recent years, speculation combined with loose financial regulation led to real estate and share booms, followed inevitably by crashes and costly bailouts of the financial system by central banks and the state.

I am by no means predicting such a course of events in India, but to some degree the preconditions exist. They could be explored more fully in a simple three-asset model involving money, private and government debt, and speculative assets. A high apparent elasticity of substitution between speculative and other assets could presage financial fragility.

8.6 Growth in the Medium Run

With what precision have we circumscribed the rate of growth? The equations all cluster around a growth rate of 5 percent and an inflation rate of 7 percent, but that is not surprising since these are more or less the values being observed. The estimates of the effects of expanding 1 percent faster are more interesting. To summarize, 6 instead of 5 percent capacity growth would involve widening the current-account deficit (or increasing the export share) by 0.5 percent of the value of output, a 1 percent trend in the terms of trade toward agriculture, 2 or 3 percent faster inflation, and additional buildup of both external and internal debt.

These estimated costs of faster growth are mild. They point to a strong conclusion. To put it bluntly, the Indian economy does not appear to be supply constrained in any global fashion. This hypothesis is consistent with several observations made in the previous sections.

First, as noted in section 8.1, in neoclassical accounting India's relatively slow growth reflects itself into a high marginal capital–output ratio or slow total factor productivity increase. However, these performance indicators are calculated presupposing an economy operating at full capacity. If the capital stock is not fully utilized, they automatically take on unfavorable values.

Second, excess capacity can arise from both demand and supply factors which require investigation at the micro level. Anecdotes on both sides abound—efficiency of the railroads may have risen in the 1980s due to more imaginative management, while cotton textile industries have chronic excess capacity from lack of demand. What is difficult to assess is whether measured productivity would increase simply if demand grew faster, or whether specific bottlenecks would spill over into significantly higher inflation or an unsustainable trade gap. The macro estimates presented above suggest that both risks are slight.

Third, relative price and financial considerations suggests an absence of demand pressure. The terms of trade are not shifting strongly in the direction of agriculture, the principal supply-constrained sector. On the other hand, interest rates on recently issued government obligations are high—somewhere in the system there are assets with good returns creating large opportunity costs to holding government debt. The obvious alternative forms of wealth are real estate and durable goods, with expected capital gains being the relevant rates of return. Such speculative assets dominate productive capital when profits on real investment are low and potential saving is high. This conjuncture in turn reflects low effective demand and economic rules of the game favoring income flows like black money that are difficult to put into directly productive use. Both causal factors are subject to policy control.

If the economy is indeed demand constrained, the obvious question is how it can be pulled into expanding faster. Four possibilities figure in current debate: direct demand stimulation via government current and capital spending, a strategy aimed at improving agricultural supply and thereby income, industrialization based on consumer durables production aimed at a market made up of the richest few percent of the population, and export-led growth. In closing, I will concentrate on the political economy of these options.

Pure expansion of public spending would create financial problems. With tax and public enterprise receipts not rising faster than the value of output, expansionary policy would widen the share of the fiscal cash deficit in GDP. Currently high interest rates on public debt make borrowing a costly and distributionally regressive proposition. Inflation, which would rise with faster growth whatever the source, would be ascribed to "printing money" and create political backlash. For these reasons straight fiscal expansion is not on the cards.

If it can be managed politically, the alternative of raising both public investment and revenue makes sense. The balanced budget multiplier certainly exceeds zero, and better revenue performance might in fact reduce the rate of interest the government has to pay by slowing the flow of black money toward speculative assets. Output expansion would also raise the return to real capital and presumably induce a portfolio shift in that direction.

Assuming that balanced expansion is feasible, where should additional public investment be directed? One obvious option is investment aimed to breaking internal and external bottlenecks. We have seen that faster growth will involve both inflation and a higher trade gap. At the margin the burdens appear bearable, but they still exist. Trying to lighten them makes sense.

Beyond bottleneck busting, capital formation has to directed to support a self-sustaining economic expansion. The difficulty with public spending as an engine of growth is that it cannot lead into a cumulative process just by itself. A dubious, American-style dependence on technical spin-off from military spending apart, there are no clear feedbacks from a bigger fiscal injection into either increased private investment or accelerated technological advance. This is the point at which sectoral growth strategies enter the picture.

In agriculture, for example, increased public investment is likely to crowd private investment in and lead to an outward shift of the supply function. As discussed above, income growth in the sector may slow the rate of population increase and lead to further increases in real spending power. These can spill over into demand for nonagricultural products and induce urban investment and technical change. The saving counterpart can come from increased output in and of itself.

This sort of growth pattern is desirable on distributional grounds and also would provide insurance against reappearance of the food constraint that plagued the economy until the 1970s. It faces, on the other hand, at least four problems. The first is the specter of falling terms of trade for income-inelastic food products if their supply increases too fast. Both directing investment toward production of relatively income-elastic goods and stimulation of demand via employment-generation programs would be required. However—and this is the second problem—income targeting may not be politically feasible. Food-for-work and similar programs enhance the bargaining position of rural labor. Landowners might resist such interventions, even though they are needed to generate demand to support the prices of the commodities that landowners sell. The third uncertainty is whether consumer demand on the part of agriculturalists for simple industrial products (e.g., fertilizers and cotton textiles) would in fact feed into urban capital formation and technical advance. Middle-class India is conscious of other possibilities and might not countenance such an old-fashioned form of industrialization. Finally, the ecological implications of input-intensive agriculture have to be worked through. The additional need for public investment that they may entail could handicap an agriculture-first approach.

These observations bring in the third strategy—an industrial push based on consumer durables and catering to the upper middle class. Such a process cumulates on the saving side by creating high wage jobs and perhaps generating greater saving flows through income concentration. Demand patterns switch toward cars and consumer durables, which trickle down to the bottom ninety-odd income percentiles through the second-hand market. Luxury consumption induces private and public infrastructural capital formation with a strong accelerator.

This sort of scenario has played out in many corners of the world since World War II (Italy and Brazil are only two examples), and sooner or later spills over into enhanced export capacity. In parts of India, it is well underway. Bombay will start building freeways within a decade and Delhi is not far behind.

Can this process with its demonstrated dynamic capacity be stopped? Should it be? In the Indian context, such questions hinge around employment generation and the alternative agriculture-led strategy. One obvious difficulty with the middle-class scenario is its dependence on a high minimum income level on the part of its participants—say, a few thousand dollars per person or upward of $10,000 per household per year. In India only people in the top few income percentiles have such purchasing power, as opposed to the upper one or two deciles in Brazil when it began its transition in the 1950s. The absolute numbers are about the same. Five million households can support a durables-based industrial push capable of taking advantage of economies of scale (e.g., a few hundred thousand cars per year). The difference is that the *share* of the population enjoying the fruits of such a miracle would be one-tenth the size in India as it was in Brazil.

In the Indian context the numbers and characteristics of the jobs that growth based on cars and TV casettes can create become key questions. Social disruption is the risk if enough acceptable positions do not materialize. Young men not finding employment with their expected levels of income and work content can spread chaos far beyond the invisible borders of Khalistan.

Given the size of the subcontinent and its regional diversity, both the industrial and agricultural roads may be taken—freeways in Bombay and tubewells in eastern Uttar Pradesh. Or the regions may bifurcate with associated political turmoil. The stress to the social fabric that contemporaneously unfolding dual development processes would create should not be underestimated.

Finally, export-led growth is a theoretical possibility. Recent experience seems to show that miracles occur after a period of import-substituting industrialization supported by substantial capital inflows. Exports respond to directed policies such as cheap credit and explicit subsidies, overall price incentives like devaluation, and supportive public investment. Their rapid growth may further require pure luck, as in the surge of demand for Turkish products resulting from the Middle East's oil boom and the Iran–Iraq war.

To a degree these preconditions exist in India. However, one also has to weigh the short-term costs of policies aimed at export promotion (e.g., stagflationary effects of devaluation). In a longer run it is also clear that export miracles such as in South Korea, Brazil, and Turkey involved substantial public intervention in a controlled economy—trade liberalization played no essential role. In the Indian context these considerations suggest that liberalization as propagandized and (to an extent) pursued in recent years is not likely to lead to much in the way of enhanced sales abroad. Indeed, if the elasticity of the trade gap with respect to growth is as high as the equations in table 8.1 suggest, further liberalization could create external difficulties in the short run. This observation is only strengthened by the realization that middle-class industrialization will necessarily draw in imports of the corresponding capital goods. If this strategy is followed, export capacity can ultimately be nurtured in selected thrust sectors, so long as policy is directed to this end.

Internally, any of the four growth strategies will have a better chance to succeed if steps to enhance industrial competition, while at the same time guarding against the risk of a speculative financial boom-*cum*-crash, are pursued. The need for directed intervention to improve public sector productivity and increase the human capital base is also clear. Neither high tech farmers nor mechanics who can deal with modern car engines are going to be plentiful in a population with a literacy rate well less than 50 percent.

The saving grace perhaps is that apparent inefficiencies will be squeezed out of the system if capacity utilization increases in response to demand, but the process will not be painless. The risk is that India will linger at its accustomed leisurely rate of growth because no one dares to try a more expansionary strategy line.

Note

Revised version of the V. K. Ramaswami Memorial Lecture presented at the Institute of Economic Growth on 4 February 1988. I am grateful to Isher Ahluwalia, Sukhamoy Chakravarty, Asim Dasgupta, P. N. Dhar, Vijay Kelkar, V. Pandit, Indira Rajaraman, Mihir Rakshit, C. R. Rangarajan, Hiren Sarkar, Shekar Shah, Ajit Singh, and Suresh Tendulkar for conversations on the topic, and to the Ford Foundation for support while I was Visiting Professor at the Delhi School of Economics. This paper originally appeared in the *Indian Economic Review* 23 (1988): 145–165.

References

Ahluwalia, Isher, and Amita D'Souza. 1987. *Productivity Growth in Indian Manufacturing*. Delhi: ICRIER.

Chakravarty, Sukhamoy. 1987. *Development Planning: The Indian Experience*. Oxford: Clarendon Press.

Minhas, B. S. 1987. "The Planning Process and the Annual Budgets: Some Reflections on Recent Indian Experience." *Indian Economic Review* 22: 115–149.

Mellor, John W., and Gunvant M. Desai. 1986. *Agricultural Change and Rural Poverty*. Oxford: Oxford University Press.

National Council of Applied Economic Research. 1987. "Macro Scenario for 1987–88." New Delhi: NCAER.

Rajaraman, Indira. 1985. "Returns to Labor in Developing Country Agriculture: India." Geneva: ILO.

Rao, J. Mohan. 1987. "Distribution and Growth with an Infrastructure Constraint." Boston: Boston University, Department of Economics.

Sen, Abhijit. 1981. *The Agrarian Constraint in Economic Development: The Case of India*. Cambridge: University of Cambridge, Faculty of Economics and Politics.

Sen, Pronab. 1987. "Indian Experience with Orthodox Stabilization." Delhi: ICRIER.

Singh, Ajit, and Jayati Ghosh. 1987. "Import Liberalization and the New Development Strategy." Delhi: ILO/ARTEP.

9 Conflicting Claims and Dynamic Inflationary Mechanisms in India

Jørn Rattsø

The recent economic history of India shows experiences of inflation related to agricultural droughts and external terms of trade shocks. The present study is based on an understanding that such real factors are important for the inflationary process. In addition it is assumed that income inequalities and struggle for income shares stimulate any inflationary process. The economic system and the social structure lay the foundation for a bias toward inflation in the economy.

A macrodynamic model for India is taken into use to analyze the real dynamic adjustment mechanisms generating inflation. The model is put together on the basis of existing empirical evidence and structuralist macroeconomic theory. The distribution of the national income between the agriculturalists, the wage earners, the profit recipients, the government, and the foreigners reflects the social structure that is built into the model economy. The market situation in agriculture and the cost-plus-price formation in the nonagricultural sectors determine the sectoral price adjustments. The overall macroeconomic setting decides how the interactions between production sectors and income groups work out. The applied general equilibrium framework allows a detailed study of the adjustment process.

The theoretical and empirical background for the analysis is discussed in section 9.1. The model is presented in section 9.2 and documented in the appendix. The model is implemented to reproduce the sixth Five Year Plan and the plan projection discussed in section 9.3 serves as the reference path. Five experiments are presented in section 9.4 to show how each of the economic sectors and groups interact with the macroeconomy and inflation.

9.1 Inflationary Mechanisms

The emphasis on structural inflationary pressures in the analysis of Chile by Sunkel (1960) has influenced later work. The agricultural supply bottleneck is the key structural aspect generating inflation. A permanent bias to inflation is embodied in the system when the growth of food production is inadequate to meet the growing demand under industrialization and economic growth. Structural changes like land reform and investments in irrigation and infrastructure are needed to improve the conditions for agricultural productivity growth. This kind of agricultural bottleneck is the foundation for our model formulation of the situation in India.

In addition to the market rigidities and imbalances in agriculture, Sunkel (1960) draws the attention to propagation mechanisms that generate ongoing inflation and inflationary spirals. The main argument is that the struggle between economic sectors and social groups to control economic resources transmits price shifts into an inflationary process. It shows up in issues such as the financing of the public sector, access to foreign exchange, and the wage–profit nexus. The permanent public sector deficit observed in many developing countries is the result of the combination of a tax problem and demands for public expenditures. It seems to be hard to avoid. The public sector consequently contributes to inflation through overall demand and the monetary system. The permanent foreign exchange shortage is another bottleneck. Both import controls and depreciation of the currency tend to stimulate inflation. Finally, the conflicting claims between industrial labor and capitalists represent the most visual struggle for income shares. The development of real wages and profit margins reflects social and political forces in the economy.

A wide literature on structural aspects of inflation is summarized by Kirkpatrick and Nixson (1976). The relevance for India was shown in an early contribution by Warren (1972). He spelled out the static interactions between food prices and nominal wages, and the spillover to nonagricultural prices through cost push. Some empirical support of this hypothesis can be documented. Pandit (1978) has worked out a comprehensive analysis of Indian inflation. Concerning the real factors, he concludes that the fluctuations in the rate of growth of agricultural output have been important in determining the variations in the rate of inflation. It is shown that the agricultural market situation influences both food prices and raw material prices and that the raw material prices are an important cost element in the manufacturing price equation. The intersectoral transmission process has been focused by Sarkar and Sarkar (1980–81). The relationship that they find between the agricultural prices and the overall price level leads the authors to conclude that markup pricing prevails in the industrial sector. The industrial costs are seriously influenced by raw material prices and nominal wages that are assumed to follow food prices. Lahiri et al. (1984) supply more evidence for such industrial pricing.

The econometric evidence has encouraged a model formulation including the interaction between agriculture and the rest of the economy, where flexible food prices feed into the cost element of nonagricultural markup price equations. Agricultural inflation and profit inflation can be understood in this Warren-type framework. Real side macroeconomic adjustments are added to enable us to capture foreign inflation and public inflation. The role of imported inflation in India is documented by Bhalla (1981). He extends the menu of structural factors compared to Pandit (1978) to define the importance of international fluctuations. The inflationary pressure from public sector expansion is treated through monetary variables in the studies mentioned above. Monetary and fiscal policies are clearly part of the inflation story, but the channeling of effects is controversial. Demand effects of public consumption and investment at domestic markets are emphasized in this study.

Inflation is essentially a time-consuming process, and the dynamic adjustment mechanisms must be understood. The analysis of wage formation and capital accumulation is included to discuss medium-run experiences. the formalization of dynamic structuralist stories is of recent vintage, and not many general conclusions have been reached. The interplay between food inflation and wage indexation is analyzed by Cardoso (1981) in an attempt to handle the structuralist arguments rigorously. The main ingredients consist of the dual model framework to include the agricultural price formation and the income distribution aspect necessary to understand the wage growth. The dynamics are based on excess demand adjustments at the agricultural market, however, and it follows that the time perspective is rather short. Taylor (1982) assumes that the food prices adjust within a temporary equilibrium, and the capital accumulation process is added to a model of steady state dynamics. Consequently he is able to study the long-run interactions among investments, production capacities, and real wages. The theoretical foundation for the dynamic model applied for India is presented in Rattsø (1988). The analytics of medium-run adjustments including food inflation, wage formation, and capital accumulation in a dual framework are worked out. The analytical results call for an applied model formulation to decide the importance of the different factors in the determination of the inflation rate.

The empirical foundation for the medium-run adjustments consists of estimated wage and investment functions. They can be found in a number of econometric models that are constructed to analyze macroeconomic issues in India. The recent models of Ahluwalia (1979), Bhattacharya (1984), Krishnamurty (1984), and Pandit (1984) have inspired the formulations chosen here. Some consensus seems to have been reached regarding wage formation. Imperfect indexation to a consumer price index with heavy weight for food prices is a realistic explanation of the time series available. It also fits well with the assumption of agricultural bottleneck. The investment behavior is not that well understood. We have decided to link up private agricultural investments to the domestic terms of trade, and the private manufacturing investments to their profits, according to the results of Krishnamurty (1984). The agricultural bottleneck thereby is affected by short-run price response through capacity buildup in agriculture.

9.2 The Macrodynamic Model

The macrodynamic model is based on a static macromodel for India documented by Taylor (1983, ch. 4) and Taylor, Sarkar, and Rattsø (1984). The static macromodel is an extension of a closed Leontief model constructed at the National Council of Applied Economic Research (NCAER) in New Delhi, as documented by Sarkar and Subbarao (1981). The static macromodel can be described as structuralist development macro theory as formulated by Taylor (1983, ch. 3) integrated into a Johansen-type applied general equilibrium framework. Another application of this type of static model for India with emphasis on agricultural markets and agricultural policies is made by de Janvry and Subbarao (1985).

The model is built around a Sraffa-Leontief input–output matrix with five production sectors and three income groups. The agricultural production is divided between cereal and noncereal agriculture. The rest of the economic production is separated into three sectors representing manufacturing and construction, infrastructure (energy and transportation), and services. The dynamic formulation of the model is in accordance with the sequential temporary equilibrium system outlined by Dervis, de Melo, and Robinson (1982). Consequently we will separate between each temporary equilibrium (the static part of the model) and the time-essential adjustments between each equilibrium (the dynamic part of the model).

The model equations and the implementation of the model are shown in the appendix. The main assumptions of the analysis are as follows:

1. The supplies of agricultural products are determined by the development of the production capacities. The agricultural price levels are allowed

to fluctuate to clear the agricultural markets in the short run, and several policy instruments for government interventions in the agricultural markets are specified.

2. The outputs of the nonagricultural production sectors are determined by the demand for nonagricultural consumption and investment goods. The price levels of the nonagricultural products are determined by cost plus rules.

3. The income distribution is important for savings, investments, and consumption.

4. The main dynamic adjustment mechanism is related to the capital accumulation. The private agricultural investments react to changes in the domestic terms of trade and the public investments in agriculture. The private manufacturing investments are related to the real profits of the sector in terms of the investment goods and the total public investments. In the nonagricultural sectors production capacities are built up even when the capacity utilizations are low.

5. The other important dynamic adjustment mechanism is represented by wage indexation. The nominal wage level is indexed to the development of the consumer price index for nonagricultural income earners.

6. Strong rigidities are built into the foreign trade specification. Imported intermediate and investment goods are determined by fixed coefficients, whereas competitive imports and exports are exogenous. The world market prices are taken as given, and the exchange rate is fixed.

7. The interplay between agriculture and nonagriculture has several channels: The agricultural sectors deliver raw materials to the nonagricultural production, and the agricultural prices consequently influence the costs of production. The demand linkages related to the consumption system represent Engel effects. The agricultural surplus is the basis for savings generation to finance investments. Agricultural inflation affects the wage level of the nonagricultural sector through the wage indexation.

The macroeconomics of the model are described by the mechanisms that equilibrate total investments and savings. The real investments in all sectors, both private and public, are determined in the dynamic submodel dependent on the past performance of the whole economy. The macroeconomics then is a question of how the savings adjust in each temporary equilibrium to the investments fixed by the dynamic submodel. In the closure of the model presented in the appendix, the following savings generation mechanisms are jointly at work:

1. The agricultural savings in the short run are determined by the fluctuations in the agricultural price levels given the agricultural production capacities.
2. A Keynesian multiplier response in the nonagricultural sectors implies an output adjustment in the short run to create nonagricultural savings.
3. The adjustments in the agricultural prices and the nonagricultural outputs affect the income distribution among agriculturalists, profit recipients, and workers. A kind of forced savings is at work since the three income groups have different savings ratios.
4. The imported intermediate inputs are sensitive to the adjustments in nonagricultural outputs and affect the foreign savings.
5. Both government revenues and expenditures react to adjustments in agricultural prices and nonagricultural outputs, and the government savings are consequently affected.

The combined adjustments of all the five savings mechanisms determine the macroeconomic performance of the economy in the short run. The flexible prices at the agricultural markets are central to any adjustment process. Weather-related shifts in agricultural supply are a constant threat to stabilization. In addition all kinds of factors influencing overall demand tend to spill over into the agricultural price response. Since nominal wages are imperfectly indexed and the markup rates are fixed, shifting agricultural prices will have income distribution effects. The markup pricing outside agriculture carries agricultural price fluctuations to an overall price adjustment in the short run.

Nominal wage indexation influences the dynamics of inflation. Increased nominal wages represent both a cost push in nonagricultural sectors and higher nominal demand affecting agricultural market balance. An inflationary spiral may follow if the degree of indexation is high. The capacity buildup in agriculture may help avoid such a spiral. A shift in the domestic terms of trade toward agriculture is assumed to stimulate agricultural investment, thereby reducing the supply bottleneck. The agricultural investment contributes to balanced growth between sectors and turns out to be an important policy parameter to avoid inflationary bias in the system.

9.3 India's Sixth Five Year Plan: The Reference Path

The benchmark approach to economywide modeling requires a consistent data set for the base year based on the national accounts, and a development path for the reference solution. We have chosen to establish a stable growth scenario as the reference path to investigate the inflationary mechanisms. The model is calibrated to simulate the economic development proposed by the sixth Five Year Plan in India 1980–85 (Government of India, Planning Commission 1980). The macroeconomics of the sixth plan is discussed in Rattsø (1986). Rattsø (1987) shows how the model can be used to evaluate the economic development 1980–85 ex post.

The data base for the static model is developed by the National Council of Applied Economic Research (NCAER 1981) in New Delhi. A social accounting matrix (SAM) is constructed of the preliminary national accounts for 1980–81, and an estimated consumption demand system is added to it. The SAM is published by NCAER (1981) and can be found in Taylor (1983). The main parameters are reproduced in the appendix.

In addition the implementation of the dynamic model is based on the estimated elasticities of the dynamic investment and wage equations by Krishnamurty (1984). The dynamic assumptions regarding the capital accumulation and the wage indexation in the econometric model of Krishnamurty (1984) represent a consistent foundation for the between-period submodel. His approach regarding sectoral disaggregation and linkage effects between production sectors is similar to our specification. The equations are estimated for the period 1962 to 1980 by the ordinary least squares method based on data from national account statistics. The investment functions of the estimated study are somewhat modified to fit the model. The lag structure is defined so that the investment demand for period t depends on variables describing the economic situation in period $t-1$. The trend coefficients of the investment functions are determined so that the investment path is equal to the development described by the sixth plan, assuming that the dependent variables develop according to the plan. The private investments in infrastructure and services are determined exogenously in the model. The total private investments and the exogenous total government investments are allocated to the five production sectors in accordance with the plan, which has equivalent disaggregation of gross investments by destination sectors.

The sixth plan represents an ambitious program for growth. The economic development projected in the reference path is presented in tables 9.1 through 9.6. The overall economic growth is projected to 5.2 percent per year during the plan period. A growth in real gross investments of 9.3 percent per year assumed to be necessary to reach the growth target. The total investments are divided in half between the private and the public sector. The plan gives a breakdown of the gross investments by destination

Table 9.1
Growth rate of consumer price index: deviations from the reference path (percent)

	Reference path	Wage inflation	Profit inflation	Agricultural inflation	Foreign inflation	Government inflation
1980–81 to 1981–82	10.4	+1.5	+3.0	+1.0	+0.6	+0.9
1981–82 to 1982–83	10.2	+3.0	+4.5	+2.0	−0.3	+2.0
1982–83 to 1983–84	9.7	+4.0	+5.0	+3.0	−0.5	+3.5
1983–84 to 1984–85	8.8	+5.0	+4.5	+3.0	−0.2	+4.0

Table 9.2
Growth rate of gross domestic product: deviations from the reference path (percent)

	Reference path	Wage inflation	Profit inflation	Agricultural inflation	Foreign inflation	Government inflation
1980–81 to 1981–82	5.1	+0.2	−0.2	−0.1	−0.3	+0.3
1981–82 to 1982–83	5.2	+0.4	+1.0	+0.2	−0.3	+0.7
1982–83 to 1983–84	5.3	+0.7	+1.0	+0.4	−0.2	+1.0
1983–84 to 1984–85	5.3	+1.0	+1.0	+0.5	−0.2	+1.5

Table 9.3
Growth rate of real foreign trade deficit in rupees: deviations from the reference path (percent)

	Reference path	Wage inflation	Profit inflation	Agricultural inflation	Foreign inflation	Government inflation
1980–81 to 1981–82	5.9	+2.0	+3.0	0.0	−18.0	+3.0
1981–82 to 1982–83	5.9	+5.0	+9.5	+0.2	−4.0	+6.0
1982–83 to 1983–84	5.5	+7.0	+8.5	+4.5	−3.0	+8.5
1983–84 to 1984–85	4.3	+9.0	+8.5	+6.0	−3.0	+10.0

Table 9.4
Growth rate of real wage: deviations from the reference path (percent)

	Reference path	Wage inflation	Profit inflation	Agricultural inflation	Foreign inflation	Government inflation
1980–81 to 1981–82	1.5	−0.6	−3.0	−0.1	−0.6	−0.9
1981–82 to 1982–83	1.8	−1.0	−2.5	−1.5	+0.6	−1.5
1982–83 to 1983–84	2.2	−1.5	−2.0	−1.5	+0.3	−2.0
1983–84 to 1984–85	2.8	−2.0	−2.0	−1.5	0.0	−2.0

Table 9.5
Labor income share: deviations from the reference path (actual shares; percent)

	Reference path	Wage inflation	Profit inflation	Agricultural inflation	Foreign inflation	Government inflation
1980–81 to 1981–82	37.0	−0.3	−1.0	−0.4	+0.1	−0.4
1981–82 to 1982–83	37.2	−0.8	−2.0	−1.0	+0.4	−1.0
1982–83 to 1983–84	37.6	−1.5	−3.0	−2.0	+0.5	−2.0
1983–84 to 1984–85	38.2	−2.5	−4.0	−2.5	+0.6	−2.0

Table 9.6
Domestic terms of trade (base year = 100)

	Reference path	Wage inflation	Profit inflation	Agricultural inflation	Foreign inflation	Government inflation
1981–82	100	102	100	103	98	103
1982–83	100	105	107	106	97	107
1983–84	100	108	111	109	96	110
1984–85	100	111	114	111	93	113

sectors. About 20 percent are directed to agriculture and other primary production. About 35 percent are allocated to mining, manufacturing, and construction. Half of the public sector investments are made in infrastructure such as electricity, water supply, railways, communications, and other transports. This leaves about 20 percent of the gross investments to service sectors, including public administration and real estate. The model results imply that the capacity growth in agriculture will follow the plan projection of about 4 percent per year. In the other sectors the production growth is determined by the growth of demand. The nonagricultural production growth is projected to about 6 percent per year.

The government sector in India will play an increasing role in the economy according to the plan. The public sector investments are mentioned above. In addition the public consumption is assumed to grow at annual rate of 7.5 percent. The government sector controls a number of policy variables. Among the most important the rates of taxes and subsidies are assumed to stay constant. The government interventions in the agricultural markets through procurement and food distribution are assumed to stay at the real level of the base year. The real value of government transfers also is held constant during the period.

The government sector is given a detailed specification in the model. The key role of the government sector in the macroeconomic setting is represented by the government demand for goods and labor. The sectoral structure of the government demand is assumed to stay constant throughout the plan period, and both the demands for goods and labor are assumed to grow at a rate of 7.5 percent per year. The growth of the government sector set by the plan will stimulate a considerable growth of aggregate demand. In addition the government sector gives important contributions to the national savings. The public enterprises in the model are specified as a part of the manufacturing sector.

The foreign trade in India is important for the macroeconomic performance since the balance of payments position may restrict the economic policy and since the foreign savings can contribute to necessary financing of the ambitious investment program. The exports of goods and services are assumed to grow at 9 percent a year in the plan. About one-third is produced in agriculture. The imports are calculated on the basis of import requirements. The deficit on the trade balance will grow somewhat during the plan period since the growth rate is slightly higher for imports than for exports. Invisibles, especially remittances from workers abroad, played an increasing role in the current account in the 1970s. No real growth of invisibles is expected 1980–85, however. Both the agricultural exports and the manufacturing exports are assumed to grow close to the overall growth rate of exports. The international prices are assumed to grow at a constant rate representing some deterioration of the international terms of trade.

Since the plan concentrates on the real economy, the nominal variables have been determined by assumption to generate an inflation rate of about 10 percent per year. The international prices and the nominal wage growth are essential for the price path. In addition the growth of private savings rate has been determined to have overall demand growing consistent with 10 percent agricultural inflation.

The implementation of the sixth plan during the 1980–85 period is known by now, and at the macroeconomic level it must be described as successful. The overall growth target of about 5 percent per year was reached, and the inflation rate stayed below 10 percent. The growth rate fluctuated strongly, however, related to the shifts in agricultural production and private investment. The composition of the growth was different from the plan, implying that manufacturing growth was weaker than expected. The ex post experiences are summarized by Rattsø (1987). We have used the trend growth of the plan as the basis for our experiments.

9.4 A Model Analysis of Five Types of Inflationary Pressures

Five economic groups and sectors with conflicting claims are built into the model. The income groups related to agricultural production, work effort in nonagricultural industries and profits outside agriculture represent the social structure of the economy. The struggle for income and social position is reflected in the adjustment mechanisms of the model. The urban capitalists receive markup income and their strength is shown in the profit margin for nonagricultural goods. The nominal wages seem to follow the consumer prices with a lag, and the strength of the wage earners is reflected in the indexation rule. The purchasing power of the agriculturalists is determined by their production capacity, external factors that may disturb the actual production, and the market situation. They may be able to influence their position through the Agricultural Prices Commission and the government policies. But the policy side is assumed to be kept constant in the experiments below to emphasize the adjustment mechanisms embodied in the economic structure.

The government and the foreign sector may strongly affect the volume and the distribution of the national income. The government controls an important part of the labor force and the investment goods to its own purposes. The tax problem common to most developing countries may give less than desired financing of government expansion. The foreign sector can increase its real income by turning the foreign terms of trade against the country. The international trade cannot be overlooked in an analysis of the distribution of the national income.

The role of each of the five economic groups and sectors in the inflationary process is investigated in five model experiments. They show how each of them may contribute to higher overall inflation. Profit inflation is defined as a situation when profit recipients increase their markup rates and the national inflation rate goes up. It will soon come clear that the interactions of the economy imply that all of the five are involved in any story of inflation. The five experiments each assumes a shift in a central economic variable. The results of higher growth of nominal wages, higher markup rates, lower growth of agricultural supply, higher growth of international prices, and higher growth of public investments are discussed below.

Wage Inflation

Econometric studies in India usually point to the fact that increases in the nominal wage level in the nonagricultural sectors must be understood in relation to the growth of the overall price level, and in particular to the growth of food prices. The nominal wages are imperfectly indexed to the consumer prices in the short run. Over time the wage earners catch up the gap, though during the 1970s the real wage on average had a slow positive growth. Based on the result of Krishnamurty (1984), we assume that the nominal wages are compensated by 50 percent of the consumer price increase during one year. When the overall inflation is 10 percent per year, a real wage growth of 2 percent per year is achieved when the wage indexation is supplemented by an autonomous growth rate of 7 percent per year in the nominal wages. The wage earners try to strengthen their position by pushing up the nominal growth rate. The wage inflation story below is based on an increase in the autonomous growth rate by 1 percent per year.

The nominal wages in the model serve as a cost factor for the nonagricultural sectors, and as a source of consumption demand and savings. The cost effect of increased nominal wages is carried forward to the nonagricultural prices through a fixed markup rate. The demand effect stimulates the demand for agricultural goods. Together the agricultural inflation and the cost push inflation add up to considerable overall inflation according to tables 9.1 through 9.6. The domestic terms of trade are moved in favor of agriculture under our assumptions, and the real profits go up because of the nonagricultural output expansion. It follows that the growth of private investments in both agriculture and manufacturing is increased, and the demand effect of higher investments contribute to continued inflation above the reference path. The supply effect in agriculture following higher investments will tend to reduce the inflation over time.

The higher growth of nominal wages produces a backfire for the wage earners. The agricultural inflation that follows the shift in wage growth reduces the real wages compared to the reference path. Also the labor share of the national income is reduced. The wage earners obviously are interested in some sort of control of the agricultural prices. The agriculturalists end up as the winners of a wage-induced inflation spurt. Other macroeconomic effects include higher GDP growth and a worsening of the balance of payments position.

Profit Inflation

Markup rates on nonagricultural goods are closely related to the share of profits in total income. It is usually assumed that the oligopolistic market structure of nonagricultural industries leads to a cost-plus-type price behavior. The markup rates are assumed to stay constant in the short and medium run since no simple rule for the markup adjustment can be based on the existing econometric evidence. The results of Rattsø (1987) indicate that this is not a bad assumption for the manufacturing sector during the 1980s, but the markup rates of the infrastructure and service sectors seem to have been fluctuating more. Lahiri et al. (1984) show that markup rates for the industrial sector have shifted over time, but they cannot offer a simple adjustment rule.

Profit inflation will be started up when the capitalists increase their markup rates to improve their position. The adjustment mechanisms in this situation are investigated by assuming a positive shift in the markup rates of 5 percent in the first year of the plan period. The results are reported in tables 9.1 through 9.6 together with the other experiments.

The immediate effect of the higher markup rates and the higher nonagricultural prices is to shift the income distribution from wage labor and agriculturalists to profit earners. The purchasing power of agricultural incomes and labor wages goes down and the consumption demand is shifted away from the nonagricultural goods. The demand for agricultural goods is increased and the agricultural prices adjust upward. Consequently the higher inflation follows both from the direct effect of higher profit margins and the indirect effect of higher agricultural prices. But the immediate effect on the economic growth is contractionary. The income distribution shift gives a fall in the demand for nonagricultural goods and the production goes down.

The dynamics of the profit inflation story relate to the response of nominal wages and private manufacturing investments when the prices and profits go up. The wage indexation drives up labor costs and contributes to continuing cost-push inflation in the nonagricultural sectors. The growth of private investments in manufacturing capacity is stimulated by the higher profits, and they give a demand effect that strengthens the agricultural inflation.

The increase of the inflation rate goes on all through the plan period when both the wage adjustments and the investment response are activated. The economic growth also goes up after the first-year contraction because of higher investments. The income distribution shifts against the wage earners, while the profit recipients and the agriculturalists strengthen their positions hand in hand. The terms of trade between agriculture and the rest of the economy is kept constant in the first year. But when the shift in the markup rates has made its way through to the agricultural inflation, the domestic terms of trade turn in favor of agriculture.

Agricultural Inflation

Often is started up by droughts or other factors shifting the agricultural supply down. The shortage of agricultural goods in such situations leads to a normal market response of higher output prices. The government may intervene in bad years to regulate the market by imports or government procurement policies. But the agricultural inflation may also result from a more long-run structural bias against agriculture. The development of the production capacity in agriculture does not keep pace with the growth of demand for food generated by the urban expansion. This kind of inflationary pressure is analyzed by assuming that the capacity growth of agricultural production is reduced compared to the sixth plan's assumptions. The growth of agricultural supply goes down about 0.5 percent per year. The results of the experiment compared to the reference path are shown in tables 9.1 through 9.6.

The agricultural price level goes up as an immediate market reaction to the lower supply of agricultural goods. The higher costs of agricultural inputs to the manufacturing sector are transmitted to nonagricultural prices. But the agricultural inflation is dominating and the terms of trade go in favor of agriculture.

The dynamics of this story consist of somewhat contradicting forces as regards the inflation. The higher food prices push up the nominal wage growth and induce cost inflation in the nonagricultural sector. The shift of the terms of trade toward agriculture stimulates private agricultural investments, and they have two effects on the agricultural inflation. On the one hand, they increase the demand for investment goods and the following multiplier expansion of nonagricultural production leads to demand inflation. On the other hand, higher investments in agriculture means a higher growth of production capacity and the agricultural supply effect contributes to a fall in the agricultural inflation. The total effect of all the dynamic forces are shown in table 9.1 to increase the inflation rate over time compared to the reference path.

The fall in the productivity growth in agriculture reduces the overall economic growth in the first year. But the higher private investments in agriculture turn the contraction into expansion starting in the second year of the plan period. The negative shift in agricultural supply growth therefore ends up like a general expansion with higher inflation, higher economic growth, and higher growth of the trade deficit. The income distribution is turned against labor, as usual when food inflation is important. The agriculturalists in fact increase their relative income share because of the price effect.

Foreign Inflation

Transmission of external price increases into inflation can take place even in India where the foreign sector is relatively small. The role of international raw material prices in the Indian inflation in the early 1970s is best documented by Bhalla (1981). The world market prices directly influence the costs of imported intermediate goods to the nonagricultural production sectors. This is the main channel of inflationary effects. In addition the imports of investment goods and fertilizer are an important part of the outlays of foreign exchange. Foreign inflation has not only a negative impact on the economic situation of the country. It must be expected that the export prices also are affected by a general rise in the international price level. This kind of a general positive shift in the world market prices is assumed in the experiment reported below.

Detailed foreign exchange markets and international capital flows are not represented in the model. The nominal exchange rate is assumed to stay constant. No mechanism puts restrictions on the development of the balance of payments over time or leads to automatic responses to close the trade deficit. The international prices affect the domestic economy because the relative prices between foreign and domestic goods are changed.

All international prices influencing the Indian economy are assumed to shift upward by 15 percent in the first year of the plan period 1980–81, and they return to the reference growth rate of 10 percent per year thereafter. The positive shift in the international prices works like a 15 percent devaluation in the model. It is shown that a devaluation is stagflationary in the short run, and contractionary with lower inflation thereafter. The dramatic shift strongly affects the situation in India as shown in tables 9.1 through 9.6.

The higher foreign inflation gives a cost push for the production sectors using imported intermediate inputs and the growth of the purchasing power of the national income is reduced. The price response consequently is different between the agricultural and the nonagricultural sectors. The nonagricultural price growth is increased due to the dominating cost-push effect. The agricultural inflation is reduced because of the lower growth of consumption demand. The net effect in the first year is higher domestic inflation. The real wage is reduced when the wage indexation is imperfect. The shift in the terms of trade against agriculture and the fall in the real profits lead to a reduction of the investment growth in agriculture and manufacturing. The contractionary effects are stengthened over time. It follows that the agricultural price growth is reduced even more and the overall inflation is brought down compared to the reference path already in the second year. Even the nonagricultural price growth is reduced when the costs of raw materials from agriculture, and the nominal wages go down. The fall in private investment growth implies a negative overall growth effect that lasts for some years. Both the agricultural and the nonagricultural production growth goes down.

The composition of the national savings is affected when the relative price between domestic and foreign goods is changed. The direct effect of higher international prices is a positive shift in the foreign savings when the trade balance is in a deficit position. The adjustments of the economy turn the foreign savings down, however. The imports of intermediate goods are reduced together with lower nonagricultural production. The income distribution effects are small. The reduced agricultural inflation is to the disadvantage of agriculturalists. Both wage earners and profit recipients improve their relative positions. But they all loose from the lower economic growth.

Government Inflation

The government may create pressure for inflation by extending the public investment program. The public investments are a source of demand for manufacturing and imported investment goods. And they add to the production capacity especially through energy production and transportation, but also as agricultural infrastructure and public manufacturing industries. The private and the public sector divide the total investment budget of the sixth plan in half and the growth rate of real investments are 9.3 percent per year. The consequences of government expansion are investigated in an experiment assuming a positive shift in the annual growth rate of public investments from 9.3 to 11.7 percent. The allocation between production sectors is assumed to be kept constant.

The positive shift in the growth of government expenditures to investment goods produces a dominating demand effect in a five-year period. The demand pressure in the manufacturing sector generates multiplier response in the nonagricultural sectors. The higher inflation results from a demand pressure in the economy that creates an excess demand situation at the agricultural markets. The demand inflation is started up through the response of agricultural prices. But it will show up also in the industrial prices since higher costs of agricultural inputs are allowed to influence the price level through the markup mechanism.

The higher growth rate of public investments means a continuing demand pressure compared to the reference path. In addition two mechanisms transmit the inflationary push into the future. The higher public investments stimulate private investments in the model. The multiplier expansion raises manufacturing profits and the growth of the private investments in industrial capacity goes up. The domestic terms of trade are shifted toward the agricultural sector by the agricultural inflation and the demand for investments in agriculture rises. The private investment response means a strengthening of the demand inflation. But the increased capital accumulation in agriculture reduces the supply bottleneck, and thereby reduces the agricultural inflation. The other dynamic inflationary mechanism relates to the nominal wage indexation. The higher agricultural inflation fuels the nominal wage growth. The higher wages represent a cost factor of the nonagricultural sector and they induce a cost push inflation.

Higher public investments lead to an increase in the inflation rate, higher economic growth and a worsening of the balance of payments situation. This is the typical result of any expansionary government policy. In this case the economic growth is strengthened by the capacity effect of higher investments in agriculture. The income distribution shifts against wage earners when agricultural inflation is allowed to take place and the real wage growth goes down. The domestic terms of trade develop in favor of agriculture and signal the improved position of agriculturalists.

9.5 Concluding Remarks

No simple Phillips curve relationship emerges since the price response depends on the particular shock or policy in effect. But some trade-off between inflation and growth is found. Demand expansion increasing the economic growth by 1 percent point per year in the medium run tends to increase the inflation rate by about 3 to 5 percentage points. The trade-off is somewhat less favorable than suggested by other studies (e.g., Bhattacharya 1984). But then agricultural policies have been assumed constant here. In practice agricultural drought always is stabilized through stock adjustments and imports.

The conflicting claims between different economic sectors easily lead to overall inflation. The model analysis has shown that different factors may start up an inflationary process, but the dynamic mechanisms are common to all alternatives: Income distribution shifts or other changes generating higher demand stimulate demand inflation through the price adjustments at the agricultural markets. Shifts in the factor costs related to labor or imported intermediate inputs are transmitted into cost inflation in the nonagricultural prices. If the nominal wages are not starting up the inflationary process, the wage indexation will carry the inflation into the future anyway. The response of private investments in agriculture and manufacturing contributes to dynamic demand inflation.

The model experiments offer some important lessons for policy formulation. The problem of demand inflation is based on imbalances at the agricultural market. The short-run answer to excess demand pressure at food markets can imply the building down of government food stocks or higher imports of agricultural goods. In some time perspective, however, the public investment policy must guarantee the growth of the production capacity in agriculture to be in balance with the growth of demand for agricultural goods generated in the rest of the economy.

The cost inflation is always related to the agricultural inflation since some of the manufacturing industries are based on the processing of agricultural inputs. The tendencies for cost inflation may be cured by squeezing profit margins. The social basis of the government may be a limiting factor against such interventions. The economic argument in defense of a suitable fund of profits is related to the investment activity. Too low profits may hurt the investments in manufacturing capacity and consequently the economic growth.

Cost inflation also may be cured by government regulation of the cost factors like labor and foreign inputs. The wage formation is already a complicated system of government control in India and a reasonable income policy against wage inflation may succeed. The government must balance its actions toward the possibilities of social unrest. The costs of imported intermediate inputs for Indian industries can be influenced by a proper exchange rate policy. But it is hard to do in practice.

The recent economic history in India shows that inflation has been under control. The government regulation of agricultural markets is a key to understanding this record. When food price inflation is moderate, growth of nominal wages and industrial costs are limited also. Investment priority to agriculture is essential to arrange for macroeconomic stability in the future. Such an allocation also may give room for more expansionary fiscal policies. Macroeconomic room for higher capacity utilization will mean a lot for the growth performance.

Appendix: Documentation of the Model

The Static Part of the Model

The static within-period model includes equations (1) through (19) in table 9.7. The symbols are defined below. Equation (1) states the input–output balances. Government purchases, exports, imports, and stock changes are all exogenous. Only the manufacturing sector delivers investment goods. The production of fertilizer in the manufacturing sector is not necessarily equal to the input of fertilizer in the agricultural sectors.

Table 9.7
The static part of the model

$$X_i(t) = \sum_{j=1}^{5} a_{ij}X_j(t) + C_i^a(t) + C_i^n(t) + dS_i(t) + G_i(t) + E_i(t) + J_i(t) - M_i(t) + X_i^f(t) + GP_i(t) - FA_i^a(t) - FN_i^n + GS_i(t) \quad \text{for } i = 1,5 \tag{1}$$

$$Y_a(t) = P_1^*(t)GP_1(t) + P_1(t)[X_1(t) - GP_1(t)] - \left[\sum_{i=1}^{2} a_{i1}P_i(t) + a_{31}P_f(t) + \sum_{i=4}^{5} a_{i1}P_i(t)\right]X_1(t) + [P_2(t) - \sum_{i=1}^{2} a_{i2}P_i(t) - a_{32}P_f(t) - \sum_{i=4}^{5} a_{i2}P_i(t)]X_2(t) \tag{2}$$

$$Y_w(t) = \sum_{i=3}^{5} w_i(t)b_i(t)X_i(t) + w_g(t)L_g(t) + e(t)R(t) + Tr(t) \tag{3}$$

$$B_i(t) = \sum_{j=1}^{5} a_{ji}P_j(t) + w_i(t)b_i(t) + a_{0i}e(t)P_{0i}^*(1 - t_{0i}) - \text{sub}_i P_i(t)a_{ii} \quad \text{for } i = 3,5 \tag{4}$$

$$P_i(t) = \frac{[(1 + t_i)(1 + tt_i)]}{[1 - (1 + t_i)(1 + tt_i)a_{ii}(1 - \text{sub}_i)]}[B_i(t) - a_{ii}P_i(t) + \text{sub}_i P_i(t)a_{ii}] \quad \text{for } i = 3,5 \tag{5}$$

$$Y_z(t) = \sum_{i=3}^{5} [tt_i B_i(t)X_i(t) - GR_i(t)] - (1 - \phi)\text{DEP}(t) + \text{GINT}(t) \tag{6}$$

$$D_a(t) = [1 - s_a(t)]Y_a(t) \tag{7}$$

$$D_n(t) = [1 - s_w(t)]Y_w(t) + [1 - s_z(t)](1 - t_z)Y_z(t) - e(t)P_{0c}^*(t)C_o(t) \tag{8}$$

$$C_i^j(t) = \theta_i^j(t)FA_i^j(t) - FN_i^j(t) + \left[\frac{m_i^j}{P_i(t)}\{D_j(t) + P_1(t)FA_1^j(t) - [P_1(t) - \bar{P}_1(t)]\cdot FN_1^j(t) - \sum_{k=1}^{5} P_k(t)\theta_k^j\}\right. \quad \text{for } i = 1,5,\ \text{j} = a,n \tag{9}$$

$$T^{\text{ind}}(t) = \sum_{i=3}^{5} t_i(1 + tt_i)B_i(t)X_i(t) \tag{10}$$

$$GREV(t) = t_z Y_z(t) + T^{\text{ind}}(t) + \sum_{i=3}^{5} GR_i(t) \tag{11}$$

$$\begin{aligned} GEXP(t) = {} & P_1(t)FA_1^a(t) + [P_1(t) - \bar{P}_1(t)]FN_1^n(t) + P_5(t)GS_5(t) + \sum_{i=1}^{5} P_i(t)G_i(t) \\ & + [P_3(t) - e(t)P_{0f}^*(t)]X_3^f(t) + [e(t)P_{0f}^*(t) - P_f(t)][a_{31}X_1(t) + a_{32}X_2(t)] \\ & + w_g(t)L_g(t) + Tr(t) + \phi DEP(t) + GINT(t) + \text{sub}_3 a_{33}X_3(t) \\ & + \sum_{i=1}^{5} [P_1(t) - e(t)P_{ei}^*(t)]E_i(t) + \sum_{i=1}^{5} a_{0i}e(t)P_{0i}^*(t)X_i(t)t_{0i} \\ & + [P_1(t) - P_1^*(t)]GP_1(t) \end{aligned} \tag{12}$$

$$\begin{aligned} DEF(t) = {} & \sum_{i=1}^{5} P_i(t)M_i(t) + e(t)P_{0c}^*(t)C_0(t) + \sum_{i=1}^{5} e(t)P_{0i}^*(t)a_{0i}X_i(t) + e(t)P_{0i}^*(t)J_0(t) \\ & + e(t)P_{0f}^*(t)[a_{31}X_1(t) + a_{32}X_2(t) - X_3^f(t)] - \sum_{i=1}^{5} e(t)P_{ei}^*(t)E_i(t) - e(t)R(t) \end{aligned} \tag{13}$$

$$Z(t) = \sum_{i=3}^{5} tt_i B_i(t)X_i(t) - GR_i(t) \tag{14}$$

Table 9.7 (continued)

$$VA_i(t) = X_i(t) - \sum_{j=1}^{5} a_{ji}X_i(t) - a_{oi}X_i(t) \quad \text{for } i = 1, 5 \tag{15}$$

$$GDP(t) = \sum_{i=1}^{5} VA_i(t) + L_g \tag{16}$$

$$P(t) = \sum_{i=1}^{5} \{VA_i(t)/[\sum_{i=1}^{5} VA_i(t)]\} P_i(t) \tag{17}$$

$$CPI(t) = \sum_{i=1}^{5} \{[P_i(t)C_i^n(t)]/D(t)\} P_i(t) \tag{18}$$

$$P_a(t) = \sum_{i=1}^{2} \{VA_i(t)/[VA_1(t) + VA_2(t)]\} P_i(t) \tag{19}$$

Equations (2) through (6) define the income creation. Agricultural income $Y_a(t)$ consists of value added in the two sectors plus a subsidy for procurement of cereals. The wage income, $Y_w(t)$, includes private wages, government wages, remittances from abroad and transfers from the government. The variable costs per unit of output in the three nonagricultural sectors $B_i(t)$, $i = 3, 5$, include wages, intermediate deliveries and imported inputs. The markup rate is fixed in all the three urban sectors. The private profits $Y_z(t)$ consist of the markups less government profits and depreciation plus government interest payments.

The consumption system is presented by equations (7) through (9). Consumption expenditures from agricultural incomes $D_a(t)$ follow when we know the savings ratio. Consumption spending for domestic goods from nonagricultural incomes $D_n(t)$ takes into account the savings, the profit tax, and imported consumer goods. In the linear expenditure system the spending for floor level consumption is determined exogenously in real terms for each product. The marginal propensities to consume out of income are given, and they are assumed different between rural and urban incomes. The subsidies on food distribution add effectively to consumer incomes.

The government sector is defined by equations (10) through (12). Government revenues consist of profit tax, indirect taxes, and government profits. The indirect taxes are applied for the nonagricultural sectors only. Government expenditures include different sorts of subsidies like food distribution, procurement of cereals, fertilizer, intermediate imports, and subsidies covering the differential between world and domestic prices of exports. In addition government demand for commodities, government wages, transfers, depreciation, and the development budget add to the expenditures.

The foreign sector is specified by equation (13). Foreign exchange earnings come from exports and remittances, while the outlays are divided between competitive imports, imports of consumer and investment goods, intermediate goods, and fertilizer.

Equations (14) through (19) define some variables needed in the dynamic part of the model. Equation (14) defines the nominal profits relevant for the motivation of private manufacturing investment demand. The gross product in the sectors and in the total economy are calculated by (15) and (16). Three price indexes are needed for deflation. Equation (17) represents the price index relevant for the gross domestic product, and the consumer price index for nonagricultural incomes is defined by (18). The average price level of agricultural production comes out of (19).

The within-period model determines the forty endogenous variables:

$P_i(t)$, $C_i^a(t)$, $C_i^n(t)$, $VA_i(t)$ $(i = 1, 5)$,

$X_i(t)$, $B_i(t)$ $(i = 3, 5)$,

$Y_a(t)$, $Y_w(t)$, $Y_z(t)$, $D_a(t)$, $D_n(t)$, $T^{ind}(t)$, $GREV(t)$, $GEXP(t)$, $DEF(t)$,
$VA(t)$, $Z(t)$, $P(t)$, $P_a(t)$, $CPI(t)$.

The Dynamic Part of the Model

The dynamic between-period model is given by equations (20) through (34) in table 9.8. The capital accumulation represents the central dynamic interactions of the model by equations (20) through (32). First, the investment goods produced in sector 3 and imported are allocated to the accumulation of sectoral capital stocks. The investment demand is separated between three groups: private agricultural investments, private nonagricultural investments, and public investments. The three groups of investments are allocated to the five production sectors by equations (20) and (21). The two agricultural sectors acquire fixed shares of the private agricultural investments according to the base year, and the same apply for a part

Table 9.8
The dynamic part of the model

$IS_i(t) = ISH_i^P J_a^P(t) + ISH_i^g J^g(t)$ for $i = 1, 2$	(20)
$IS_i(t) = J_i^P(t) + ISH_i^g J^g(t)$ for $i = 3, 5$	(21)
$K_i(t+1) = K_i(t) + IS_i(t) - d_i K_i(t)$ for $i = 1, 5$	(22)
$DEP(t+1) = \sum_{i=1}^{5} d_i P_3(t) K_i(t)$	(23)
$\bar{X}_i(t+1) = [1/COR_i(t+1)] K_i(t+1)(1 + pg_i)$ for $i = 1, 5$	(24)
$X_i(t+1) = \bar{X}_i(t+1)$ for $i = 1, 2$	(25)
$J_a^P(t+1) = A_0[P_a(t)/P(t)]^{e_1}[(ISH_1^g + ISH_2^g)J^g(t)]^{e_2}[1 + e_3)^t$	(26)
$J_3^P(t+1) = B_0[Z(t)/P_3(t)]^{f_1}[J^g(t)]^{f_2}(1 + f_3)^t$	(27)
$J_i^P(t+1) = J_i^P(t)(1 + pig_i)$ for $i = 4, 5$	(28)
$J^g(t+1) = J^g(t)(1 + gig)$	(29)
$J(t+1) = J_a^P(t+1) + J_3^P(t+1) + J_4^P(t+1) + J_5^P(t+1) + J^g(t+1)$	(30)
$J_0(t+1) = k\,J(t+1)$	(31)
$J_3(t+1) = J(t+1) - J_0(t+1)$	(32)
$w_i(t+1) = w_i(t)\{(1 + wg) + w[(CPI(t) - CPI(t-1))/CPI(t-1)]\}$ for $i = 3, 5$	(33)
$w_g(t+1) = w_g(t)\{(1 + wg) + w[(CPI(t) - CPI(t-1))/CPI(t-1)]\}$	(34)

of the total public investments. The three nonagricultural sectors receive both private investments and fixed parts of the total public investments. Second, the investments allocated to the production sectors contribute to increased capital stocks in period $t + 1$ when the depreciation is taken into account with fixed coefficients in (22) and (23). Third, the capital stocks in period $t + 1$ determine the production capacities in the same period through fixed capital output ratios. A coefficient representing productivity growth is included in the capacity-determining equations (24). The actual production levels in the two agricultural sectors are set equal to the production capacities as shown by (25).

The private investment demand functions are shown in (26) through (28) and are based on the econometric study by Krishnamurty (1985). The private demand for agricultural investments is dependent on the relative price of agricultural products and the public investments in agriculture. The elasticities e_1 and e_2 in equation (26) are fixed, and a trend coefficient e_3 is included.

The private demand for manufacturing investments is dependent on the real profits in terms of investment goods and the total public investment. The elasticities f_1 and f_2 of the investment demand function (27) are constant, and a fixed trend coefficient is assumed. A constant growth rate is defined in (28) for the private investments in sectors 4 and 5. The public investment demand is exogenously determined, and a fixed growth rate is assumed by (29). The total investment demand in period $t + 1$ is added up in equation (30). The total investments of the period are distributed between imported and domestically produced investment goods. A fixed share of the total investment demand is assumed to be imported in each period and the rest is delivered from sector 3, as shown by (31) and (32).

The other central dynamic mechanism of the model is the wage indexation shown in (33) and (34). The wage indexation functions also are in accordance with the econometric study by Krishnamurty (1984). The consumer price index is a weighted average of the sectoral price levels where the weights are defined by the sectoral shares of the consumption expenditures from nonagricultural incomes in each period. The wage growth is determined by an autonomous growth rate and an index mechanism. The system of indexation is based on the lagged growth of the urban consumer price index. The degree of indexation is regulated by the parameter w. Both private wages and government wages follow the same indexation rule.

Constant trend growth is assumed for a number of variables mainly representing the government sector and the foreign trade.

The Data Base of the Model

The social accounting matrix forming the benchmark of the model is worked out by the National Council of Applied Economic Research (1981). The dynamic model is based on the sixth Five Year Plan (Government of India, Planning Commission 1980) and most of the assumptions come clear from the text. The main parameters of the model are as follows:

1. Savings rates in the base year:

$s_a = 0.12, \quad s_w = 0.1482, \quad s_z = 0.2223.$

2. The markup rates in the base year:

$tt_3 = 0.1455, \quad tt_4 = 0.3066, \quad tt_5 = 0.50158.$

3. The consumption demand from agricultural income:

	Income elasticity	Direct price elasticity
Sector 1	0.62	−0.52
Sector 2	1.17	−0.64
Sector 3	1.65	−0.89
Sector 4	0.64	−0.33
Sector 5	1.30	−0.72

4. The consumption demand from nonagricultural income:

	Income elasticity	Direct price elasticity
Sector 1	0.75	−0.44
Sector 2	1.22	−0.67
Sector 3	1.25	−0.76
Sector 4	0.78	−0.41
Sector 5	0.95	−0.69

5. Tax rates in the base year:

$t_3 = 0.1243, \quad t_4 = 0.10157, \quad t_5 = 0.06987, \quad t_z = 0.10936.$

6. Capital–output ratios:

$COR_1 = COR_2 = 2.7, \quad COR_3 = 7.0, \quad COR_4 = 10.0, \quad COR_5 = 2.5.$

7. Agricultural investment demand:
Elasticity with respect to relative price of agricultural products = 1.7; public investments in agriculture = 0.6.

8. Manufacturing investment demand:
Elasticity with respect to real profits in terms of investment goods = 1,6; total public investments = 0.3.

9. Wage indexation:
Elasticity with respect to the consumer price index = 0.5; trend growth rate = 7 percent per year.

Definition of Symbols of the Model

Sectors

1 Cereal agriculture
2 Noncereal agriculture
3 Manufacturing industries
4 Intermediate production (energy and transportation)
5 Services

Endogenous Variables of the Within-period Submodel

$X_i(t)$	Sectoral output levels, $i = 3, 5$
$VA_i(t)$	Sectoral value added, $i = 1, 5$
$P_i(t)$	Sectoral price levels, $i = 1, 5$
$C_i^a(t)$	Sectoral consumption levels based on agricultural incomes, $i = 1, 5$
$C_i^n(t)$	Sectoral consumption levels based on nonagricultural incomes, $i = 1, 5$
$B_i(t)$	Variable costs per unit output, $i = 3, 5$
$Y_a(t)$	Agricultural income
$Y_w(t)$	Wage income
$Y_z(t)$	Markup income
$D_a(t)$	Consumption spending from agricultural income
$D_n(t)$	Consumption spending from nonagricultural income
$T^{ind}(t)$	Indirect taxes
$GREV(t)$	Government revenue
$GEXP(t)$	Government spending
$DEF(t)$	Trade deficit
$VA(t)$	Gross national product
$Z(t)$	Total gross private profits
$P(t)$	Price index of the national product
$P_a(t)$	Price index of the agricultural value added
$CPI(t)$	Urban incomes consumer price index

Endogenous Variables of the Between-period Submodel

$IS_i(t)$	Investment goods allocated to sector i, $i = 1, 5$
$K_i(t)$	Stock of real capital in sector i, $i = 1, 5$
$DEP(t)$	Total depreciation
$\bar{X}_i(t)$	Production capacity in sector i, $i = 1, 5$
$X_i(t)$	Sectoral output levels, $i = 1, 2$
$JP_a(t)$	Private demand for investment goods in agriculture, sectors 1 and 2
$JP_i(t)$	Private demand for investment goods in sector i, $i = 3, 5$
$J^g(t)$	Total government investment
$J(t)$	Total investment demand
$J_o(t)$	Demand for imported investment goods
$J_3(t)$	Demand for investment goods delivered from sector 3
$V(t)$	Total investment demand
$w_i(t)$	Nominal wages in sector i, $i = 3, 5$
$w_g(t)$	Nominal government wages

Endogenous Variables Determined by Trend Growth

$b_i(t)$	Labor productivity in sector i, $i = 3, 5$
$G_i(t)$	Government purchases of goods from sector i, $i = 1, 5$
$L_g(t)$	Government employment
$Tr(t)$	Government transfer payments
$GINT(t)$	Government interest payments
$GR_i(t)$	Government profits from enterprises in sector i, $i = 1, 5$
$E_i(t)$	Exports from sector i, $i = 1, 5$
$M_i(t)$	Competitive imports in sector i, $i = 1, 5$
$R(t)$	Remittances
$P_{ei}^*(t)$	Border price of sectoral exports, $i = 1, 5$
$P_{oi}^*(t)$	Border price of intermediate imports, $i = 3, 5$
$P_{oI}^*(t)$	Border price of imported investment goods
$P_f(t)$	Subsidized price of fertilizer from sector 3
$P_1(t)$	Issue price
$P_1^*(t)$	Procurement price
$X_i^f(t)$	Domestic production of fertilizer, sector i, $i = 1, 5$
$S_a(t)$	Savings ratio for agricultural income
$S_w(t)$	Savings ratio for wage income
$S_z(t)$	Savings ratio for profit income

Exogenous Variables and Parameters

$GP_1(t)$	Procurement of cereals at prespecified price P_1^*
$GS_5(t)$	Government demand for services on development budget
$dS_i(t)$	Change in sectoral stocks, $i = 1, 5$
$FA_1^a(t)$	Food distribution under rural food-for-work program
$FN_1^n(t)$	Food distribution in ration shops, "issue"
$C_0(t)$	Consumption of imported goods
$e(t)$	Exchange rate
t_{0i}	Subsidy rates on intermediate imports, $i = 3, 5$
sub_3	Subsidy rates for manufacturing industries
tt_i	Markup rates in sector i, $i = 3, 5$
t_i	Indirect tax rates, $i = 3, 5$
φ	Share of depreciation for government capital
d_i	Depreciation rates, $i = 1, 5$
t_z	Tax rate on profit income
ISH_{ig}	Share of government investments allocated to sector i, $i = 1, 5$

ISH_ip	Share of private agricultural investments allocated to sector i, $i = 1, 2$
$COR_i(t)$	Capital output ratio of sector i, $i = 1, 5$
gig	Growth rate of government investments
pig_i	Growth rate of private investment demand of sector i, $i = 4, 5$
a, i, j	Sectoral input–output coefficients, $i, j = 1, 5$
k	Share of imported investment goods in total investments
a_{0i}	Input coefficients for intermediate imports, $i = 1, 5$
m_i^a	Marginal propensity to consume from agricultural income, $i = 1, 5$
m_i^n	Marginal propensity to consume from nonagricultural income, $i = 1, 5$
θ_i^a	Floor level consumption from agricultural income, $i = 1, 5$
θ_i^n	Floor level consumption from nonagricultural income, $i = 1, 5$

References

Ahluwalia, I. 1979. "An Analysis of Price and Output Behavior in the Indian Economy." *Journal of Development Economics* 6 (3).

Bhalla, S. 1981. "India's Closed Economy and World Inflation." In W. R. Cline (ed.), *World Inflation and the Developing Countries.* Washington: Brookings Institution.

Bhattacharya, B. 1984. *Public Expenditure, Inflation and Growth: A Macro-Economic Analysis of India.* Oxford: Oxford University Press.

Cardoso, E. 1981. Food Supply and Inflation. *Journal of Development Economics* 8: 269–284.

de Janvry, A., and K. Subbarao. 1985. "Agricultural Price Policy in India." *Economic and Political Weekly* (December 22–29): A166–A178.

Dervis, K., J. de Melo, and S. Robinson. 1982. *General Equilibrium Models for Development Policy.* Cambridge: Cambridge University Press.

Government of India, Planning Commission. 1980. *Sixth Five Year Plan.* New Delhi.

Government of India, Planning Commission. 1981. *A Technical Note on the Sixth Plan of India.* New Delhi.

Kirkpatrick, C., and F. Nixson. 1976. "The Origins of Inflation in Less Developed Countries: A Selected Review." In M. Parker and G. Zis (eds.), *Inflation in Open Economies.* Manchester, England: Manchester University Press.

Krishnamurty, K. 1984. "Inflation and Growth: A Model for India. *Indian Economic Review* 19: 16–111.

Lahiri, A., et al. 1984. "The Industrial Sector in India." *Economic and Political Weekly* 19: 1285–1306.

National Council of Applied Economic Research. 1981. *A Computable General Equilibrium Model of the Indian Economy: Structure and Sensitivities.* New Delhi.

Pandit, V. 1978. "An Analysis of Inflation in India 1950–75. *Indian Economic Review* 13: 89–115.

Pandit, V. 1984. "Macroeconomic Adjustments in a Developing Economy: A Medium Term Model of Outputs and Prices in India." *Indian Economic Review* 19: 112–156.

Rattsø, J. 1986. "The Macroeconomics of India's 6th Five Year Plan." *Economic Modelling* 3: 269–282.

Rattsø, J. 1987. "The Macroeconomic Performance in India 1980–85: An Applied General Equilibrium Model Analysis." *Journal of Quantitative Economics* 3: 225–258.

Rattsø, J. 1988. "Macrodynamic Adjustment Mechanisms in a Dual Semi-industrialized Economy." *Journal of Development Economics,* forthcoming.

Sarkar, H., and S. V. Subbarao. 1981. "A Short-Term Macro Forecasting Model for India—Structure and Uses." *Indian Economic Review.*

Sarkar D., and G. Sarkar. 1980–81. "Inter-sectoral Linkages and Price Movements in India." *Indian Journal of Economics*: 173–182.

Sunkel, O. 1960. "Inflation in Chile: An Unorthodox Approach." International Economic Papers, 10.

Taylor, L. 1982. "Food Price Inflation, Terms of Trade and Growth." In M. Gersovitz et al. (eds.), *The Theory and Experience of Economic Development.* London: Allen and Unwin.

Taylor, L. 1983. *Structuralist Macroeconomics.* New York: Basic Books.

Taylor, L., H. Sarkar, and J. Rattsø. 1984. "Macroeconomic Adjustment in a Computable General Equilibrium Model for India." In M. Syrquin et al. (eds.), *Economic Structure and Performance.* New York: Academic Press.

Warren, B. 1972. *Inflation and Wages in Underdeveloped Countries.* London: Frank Cass.

10 Portfolio Effects in a CGE Model: Devaluation in a Dollarized Economy

William Easterly

The tradition of computable general equilibrium (CGE) models with only real variables has limited in important ways the analysis of the current problems of less developed countries' economies. The CGE framework is unmatched for capturing differential effects on consumer classes and isolating the role of the consolidated public sector. However, many of the urgent issues facing LDC's, particularly in Latin America, involve financial variables such as external debt and flight capital. Thus, for example, the relationship between exchange rate devaluation and external debt has seldom been explored in a CGE framework. Devaluation clearly has a different meaning when a large share of liabilities (and even assets) in the economy are denominated in foreign currency, a situation often referred to as "dollarization." Yet most CGE models confine themselves to treatment of the relative price of tradables and nontradables, leaving money and debt for simplified aggregate portfolio models which themselves slight the real side of the economy. Many of the obvious linkages between debt and devaluation thus tend to fall between two stools.

A related issue that traditional CGE models do not treat adequately is the role of the public sector. Certainly CGE models are well suited for analysis of a wide variety of fiscal issues—such as the effects of taxes and subsidies on income distribution and resource allocation. However, the exclusion of financial relations leaves out a large part of the story since foreign and domestic interest payments bulk large in the public sector accounts. The fiscal effects of devaluation, for example, must surely take reflect the changed valuation of interest payments, as well as the usual effects on import taxes, public sector exports, and so on. Once the financial balances are incorporated into a CGE framework, interesting linkages between fiscal and financial effects become evident.

The current paper attempts to partially remedy the lacunae in the CGE literature by utilizing a CGE model incorporating portfolio balances for one case of a highly indebted economy—Mexico—to analyze the effects of devaluation both through the usual real channels and via the real level of financial stocks. This is intended to serve as an example of how CGE models with portfolio balances can dramatize real–financial linkages in the economy.

10.1 The Classical Tradition

Some of the flavor of how financial balances in the CGE give a different view of devaluation can be gained by drawing on the "classical" tradition of devaluation. The essential element of this tradition is to focus on changes in the real value of financial stocks induced by the devaluation or by accompanying price movements. This approach is in the spirit of the monetary approach to the balance of payments such as that of Dornbusch (1980, 1973) or the International Monetary Fund (1977). These approaches typically assume complete purchasing power parity, so relative prices are unchanged but the real value of money balances changes with a devaluation. Holders of real balances are then induced to save more to rebuild them back to the desired level. Depending on whether full employment is assumed, this affects either the composition or the level of output. The monetary approach to the balance of payments builds on a long classical tradition of analyzing devaluation and more generally price level changes via their effect on the real stock of money. The clearest example is of course the real balance effect cited by Pigou in his controversy with Keynes on the effectiveness of wage deflation in curing unemployment. But as Tobin (1980) has ably pointed out, both Pigou and his successors among modern monetarists have been too narrow in focusing exclusively on real balances. The changes in real valuation of the corresponding liabilities must be considered as well. Indeed, there is an even longer classical tradition that considers devaluation and inflation primarily in terms of the wealth redistribution occasioned by the changed valuation of all financial assets and liabilities. As Adam Smith himself put it, "such operations (devaluation) have always proved favorable to the debtor and ruinous to the creditor."

Keynes was actually more in the classical tradition than Pigou in this matter, since he followed the emphasis of the *Wealth of Nations* on wealth redistribution. He specified a three-class structure of investors (holders of financial assets), businessmen (holders of physical capital and financial debts), and wage earners (no financial assets or debts) and hypothesized that devaluation "redistributes wealth in a manner very injurious to the investor, very beneficial to the businessman, and probably, in modern industrial conditions, beneficial on the whole to the wage-earner.[1]

If the propensity to spend from wealth differs between the first two classes, then there could be effects on the level of investment or on overall output. Keynes made clear elsewhere that for these reasons revaluation and deflation were worse evils than devaluation: "Revaluation is liable in these days of huge national debts expressed in legal tender money, to overturn the balance so far ... in the interests of rentier, that the burden of taxation becomes intolerable on the productive classes of the community ... it is worse, in an impoverished world, to provoke unemployment than to disappoint the rentier.[2]

As Tobin (1980) points out, Keynes' contemporary Irving Fisher had much the same concerns. He felt that the deflation of the 1930s was imposing a burden on debtors—corporations, farmers, and homeowners—which was worsening the Depression. He recommended reflation through a combination of devaluation and monetary expansion as a first step to recovery.

10.2 Dollarization in Latin America

Of course neither modern monetarists nor classical economists have been dealing with economies where debts and even the money stock may be partially denominated in foreign currency. In many Latin American countries, however, foreign debt is more than half of total financial liabilities. For example, in 1981 the following ratios of foreign debt to financial liabilities held in key Latin borrowers:[3] Argentina, 30 percent, Brazil, 66 percent, Mexico, 37 percent, Peru, 59 percent, and Venezuela, 32 percent.

Foreign currency assets are also highly significant in many countries because of extensive capital flight in recent years and because of the institution of foreign currency deposits in many countries' banking systems. In Mexico in 1981, for example, cumulative capital flight was equivalent to 40 percent of the foreign debt, while foreign currency deposits in the domestic banking system accounted for 24 percent of all financial savings.[4] The existence of simultaneous borrowing and lending points up the need for a multiagent portfolio framework. The portfolio diversification motives behind the holdings of foreign assets, and liabilities then become clear. More important, the possibility that different classes account for the borrowing and lending can be explicitly taken into account. Thus in Mexico in 1981 it was evident that the foreign debt was owed by corporations, both public and private, while the foreign assets were held by private individuals. Because of the limited liability of corporations, it could have even been profitable for the owner of a business to finance the purchase of foreign assets to his own account with funds from his externally indebted business. As the Mexican president bitterly phrased it after the crisis of 1982: "One meets with the contradictory case of partners in businesses which owe dollars, who also have personal accounts in dollars here or abroad and/or own real estate abroad, in amounts whose total value far exceeds the private sector's entire debt. Rich businessmen; poor businesses."[5]

In such circumstances, if the effect of devaluation on the real exchange rate and real financial stocks is sufficiently large, devaluation will worsen the real burden of debtors, while asset holders will gain if dollars figure prominently enough in their portfolios. Ironically, devaluation in highly indebted countries could have much the same effect that Keynes and Fisher foresaw for revaluation and deflation during the Depression.

10.3 A CGE Model of Mexico: Social and Financial Accounting

To capture this effect of devaluation in one highly indebted country—Mexico—the approach used is to construct a CGE model with financial portfolio balances and then to simulate the effects of devaluation with this model. In keeping with the emphasis on redistribution, the model places more emphasis on distinctions between economic agents (or classes) than between sectors. Moreover, since the focus of the model is on short-run stabilization rather than long-run resource allocation, the real part of the model is a Leontief-type quantity-clearing macro model.[6] This is chosen over the neoclassical CGE models, since the latter can only consider real variables and so are unable to address the real balance effects being considered here. The neoclassical specification also forces some of the key variables of interest for stabilization purposes to be exogenous—the current-account balance, for example. The Leontief/Keynesian real model thus seems the more promising suitor to join with the financial portfolio model. For the latter the obvious candidate is the system first proposed by Tobin (1969) and since elaborated by him and others (e.g., Backus et al. 1982).

The basic structure of the model can be given as follows. There are four productive sectors:

1. Petroleum sector
2. Nonpetroleum sector: controlled-price goods and uncontrolled goods
3. Financial services
4. External goods and services: goods and services

Petroleum is broken out separately to capture its unique position in both the fiscal and external accounts in Mexico. Financial services are broken out separately because of the emphasis of the model on financial transactions. The separation of external goods and services as a separate good assumes an Armington-type structure for the economy in which domestic goods are imperfect substitutes for foreign ones. These five basic sectors are subdivided further in the consumption relations. For sector 2 a distinction is made between those goods subject to price controls and those not, while for sector 4 the existence of tariffs on goods requires that they be distinguished from foreign services.

Economic agents who participate in goods and asset markets are classified into eight classes:

1. Rentiers—household recipients of dividend, rental, and interest income
2. Proprietors—owners of unincorporated small businesses
3. Private corporations—autonomous limited liability enterprises
4. Nonfinancial public sector—consolidated, including the national government and state enterprise
5. Rest of the world—external income and expenditure flows
6. Banking system
7. Central bank (Banco de Mexico)
8. Wage earners

The breakdown of classes reflects the objective of capturing redistributional effects of wealth and income. Keynes' three class distinction of investors/businessman/wage earners becomes here rentiers/corporations/wage earners. Proprietors are considered separately because of the importance in Mexico of the informal sector which they represent. The public, external, and banking sectors are considered separately because of the importance of the corresponding macro relations.

The financial assets available to these agents are classified into three types. Because of the emphasis on the revaluation effects of exchange rate changes, the classification is by currency denomination:

1. Peso assets
2. Mexdollar assets (a hybrid assets, in that it was held internally but denominated in dollars)
3. Dollar assets (dollar-denominated assets that were an asset or liability of foreigners).

The existence of Mexdollars in the Mexican financial system (prior to

August 1982) adds another interesting wrinkle, since the exchange rate change will affect the valuation of internal as well as external instruments.

The real and financial flows based on these classifications can be shown for the Mexican economy for a given year (1981) in the familiar Social Accounting Matrix, shown in table 10.1. The first nine lines of the SAM give a conventional input–output and final demand breakdown for the four-sector economy, with expenditure on each sector's goods differentiated by class (profit earners, proprietors, corporations, wage recipients, and the government). The first four columns of the SAM show the conventional breakdown of income received by class directly from production activities. The more unconventional part of the SAM is the remaining lower rectangle, which shows the financial income and expenditure flows between classes and the banking system (as well as taxes and subsidies). The financial payments and receipts are broken down by currency denomination. Thus, for example, in column 14, lines 12–15, is shown the interest payments made by the banking system to profit earners, who hold peso and Mexdollar deposits. In column 9, line 43, the interest payments by the government to external lenders are given.

The balancing item for all expenditures and revenues by class will be the saving shown in line 54. To capture the corresponding financial flows, the saving flow by class is divided between accumulation of physical capital (investment) and net financial accumulation, which is further subdivided into flow by each of the three types of assets. This is a version of the Tobin (1969) matrix, which summarizes intersectoral financing flows by type of instrument.

Some important information is left out of the SAM, however. In order to evaluate the revaluation effects of exchange rate changes, it is necessary to know the stocks of financial assets and liabilities. Moreover, to capture the redistribution induced, it must be clear who owes what to whom. This is captured in table 10.2 by creating a stock counterpart to the SAM called a financial accounting matrix (FAM). Just as the SAM shows income flows by spender and by recipient, the FAM shows financial stocks by creditor and debtor. The creditors are shown in the rows, while the debtors are given at the head of the columns. For example, row 1, column 5, shows that the external sector owed rentiers 553 billion pesos at the end of 1981, representing the peso equivalent of the U.S.$21 billion in foreign assets held by rentiers. The "balancing item" for each agent is their net claims on the financial system, shown as a liability in row 8. As would be expected, rentiers and external sector are net creditors, while proprietors, corporations, and the public sector are net debtors. The banks have net worth close to zero in financial terms.

Table 10.1
Social accounting matrix (billion Mexican pesos)

	1	2	3	4	5	6	7	8	9
	Intermediate goods and services								
Expenditures (down)/ Income (across)	Petroleum sector	Nonpetroleum sector	Financial services	External sector	Total	Profit recipients	Proprietors	Corporate	Government
1 Petroleum sector	28.5	73.0			101.5	15.5	6.7		0.9
2 Nonpetroleum sector	87.7	2978.7			3066.4	739.0	679.7		137.3
3 Controlled-price goods						73.5	58.9		
4 Uncontrolled goods	87.7	2978.7			3066.4	665.5	620.8		137.3
5 Financial services		94.9			94.9				
6 Total domestic intermediates	116.2	3146.7			3262.9	754.5	686.4		138.2
7 Goods imports	7.2	337.3			344.5	7.8	7.1		25.5
8 Services imports		43.1			43.1	36.1	32.9		
9 Total imported intermediates	7.2	380.4			387.6	44.0	39.9		25.5
10 Profit-earners		210.5			210.5			1253.7	5.5
11 Profits		210.5			210.5				
12 Interest									
13 Pesos									
14 Mexdollars									
15 Dollars									
16 Distributed profits								1253.7	
17 Transfers									5.5
18 Proprietors		857.5			857.5				
19 Profits		857.5			857.5				
20 Interest									

Table 10.1 (continued)

Expenditures (down)/ Income (across)	1 Intermediate goods and services: Petroleum sector	2 Nonpetroleum sector	3 Financial services	4 External sector	5 Total	6 Profit recipients	7 Proprietors	8 Corporate	9 Government
21 Corporations		1969.7			1969.7				
22 Profits		1969.7			1969.7				
23 Interest									
24 Pesos									
25 Mexdollars									
26 Dollars									
27 Public sector	196.7	392.8			589.5	43.2	13.8	233.8	0.6
28 Profits	−56.0	52.3			−3.7				
29 Indirect tax	252.7	340.5			593.2	1.0	1.0		0.6
30 PEMEX	232.4				232.4				
31 Gasoline	20.3				20.3				
32 Tariffs		46.9			46.9	1.0	1.0		0.6
33 Other		293.7			293.7				
34 Direct tax						42.1	12.8	160.1	
35 Social security								73.7	
36 Interest									
37 Banking									
38 External sector				798.1	798.1			60.1	88.8
39 Remitted profits				798.1	798.1			14.7	
40 Interest								45.4	88.8
41 Pesos									

42	Mexdollars									
43	Dollars								45.4	88.8
44	Banking sector			35.0		35.0	90.5	94.7	176.8	216.1
45	Interest						90.5	94.7	176.8	216.1
46	Pesos						88.3	85.7	137.9	112.8
47	Mexdollars						2.2	9.0	38.9	103.3
48	Dollars									
49	Profits			35.0		35.0				
50	Banco de Mexico									
51	Wage earners	34.8	1579.2	59.9		1673.9				514.8
52	Subsidies							−12.3	−56.8	191.3
53	Financial intermediation						−23.7	−24.8	−46.4	
54	Saving						965.8	60.5	390.7	−14.4
55	Capital						285.7	116.0	536.2	764.8
56	Net financial assets						680.1	−55.5	−145.5	−779.2
57	Pesos						343.9	−33.6	−31.1	−231.3
58	Mexdollars						84.8	−21.9	−43.3	−322.1
59	Dollars						251.4		−71.1	−225.8
60	Profits	−56.0	3090.1	35.0		3069.1				
61	Value added	231.5	5009.8	94.9		5336.2	1.0	−11.3	−56.8	706.7
62	Total	354.9	8536.9	94.9	798.1	9784.8	1874.2	858.3	2011.9	1166.3

Table 10.1 (continued)

		10 Exports	11	12	13	14	15	16	17
Expenditures (down)/ Income (across)		External total	Public exports	Private goods exports	Private service exports	Banking	Banco de Mexico	Wage earner	Private consumption
1	Petroleum sector	351.5	351.5					12.6	34.8
2	Nonpetroleum sector	350.1	30.9	86.2	233.0			1928.6	3347.3
3	Controlled-price goods							297.4	429.8
4	Uncontrolled goods	350.1	30.9	86.2	233.0			1631.1	2917.5
5	Financial services								
6	Total domestic intermediates	701.6	382.4	86.2	233.0			1941.1	3382.0
7	Goods imports							20.1	35.0
8	Services imports							93.0	162.0
9	Total imported intermediates							113.0	197.0
10	Profit earners	45.7				358.9			
11	Profits								
12	Interest	32.7				342.1			
13	Pesos					302.2			
14	Mexdollars					39.9			
15	Dollars	32.7							
16	Distributed profits					16.7			
17	Transfers	13.0							
18	Proprietors					0.6			
19	Profits								
20	Interest					0.6			

21	Corporations	42.2		
22	Profits			
23	Interest	42.2		
24	Pesos	34.1		
25	Mexdollars	8.1		
26	Dollars			
27	Public sector	5.4	145.3	4.8
28	Profits			
29	Indirect tax		2.7	4.8
30	PEMEX			
31	Gasoline			
32	Tariffs		2.7	4.8
33	Other			
34	Direct tax		113.1	
35	Social security		29.5	
36	Interest	5.4		
37	Banking			
38	External sector	92.8		
39	Remitted profits			
40	Interest	92.8		
41	Pesos	0.5		
42	Mexdollars	3.1		
43	Dollars	89.2		
44	Banking sector			

Table 10.1 (continued)

	10 Exports	11	12	13	14	15	16	17
Expenditures (down)/ Income (across)	External total	Public exports	Private goods exports	Private service exports	Banking	Banco de Mexico	Wage earner	Private consumption
45 Interest								
46 Pesos								
47 Mexdollars								
48 Dollars								
49 Profits								
50 Banco de Mexico								
51 Wage earners	5.3					5.5		
52 Subsidies								
53 Financial intermediation					94.9			
54 Saving	287.3				18.3	−5.5		
55 Capital								
56 Net financial assets	287.3				18.3	−5.5		
57 Pesos	−0.3				23.2	−70.8		
58 Mexdollars	12.9				253.0	36.6		
59 Dollars	274.7				−257.9	28.7		
60 Profits								
61 Value added	5.3					5.5	2.7	4.8
62 Total	1039.9	382.4	86.2	233.0	613.1	0.0	2199.5	3583.8

Table 10.1 (continued)

		18 Investment	19	20	21	22	23	24	25
Expenditures (down)/ Income (across)		Profit recipients	Proprietors	Corporate	Government	Total	Final demand	Price differential	Total
1	Petroleum sector				0.9	0.9	388.1	−134.7	354.8
2	Nonpetroleum sector	285.7	92.7	428.2	707.2	1513.7	5348.3	122.2	8537.0
3	Controlled-price goods						429.8	122.2	552.0
4	Uncontrolled goods	285.7	92.7	428.2	707.2	1513.7	4918.5		7984.9
5	Financial services								94.9
6	Total domestic intermediates	285.7	92.7	428.2	708.1	1514.6	5736.4	−12.5	8986.7
7	Goods imports		23.4	108.1	56.7	188.1	−344.5		593.0
8	Services imports						−43.1		205.1
9	Total imported intermediates		23.4	108.1	56.7	188.1	−387.6		798.1
10	Profit earners								1874.3
11	Profits								210.5
12	Interest								374.8
13	Pesos								302.2
14	Mexdollars								39.9
15	Dollars								32.7
16	Distributed profits								1270.4
17	Transfers								18.5
18	Proprietors								858.2
19	Profits								857.5
20	Interest								0.6

Table 10.1 (continued)

	18	19	20	21	22	23	24	25
	Investment							
Expenditures (down)/ Income (across)	Profit recipients	Proprietors	Corporate	Government	Total	Final demand	Price differential	Total
21 Corporations								2011.9
22 Profits								1969.7
23 Interest								42.2
24 Pesos								34.1
25 Mexdollars								8.1
26 Dollars								
27 Public sector						5.4	134.7	1166.3
28 Profits							134.7	131.0
29 Indirect tax						5.4		598.6
30 PEMEX								232.4
31 Gasoline								20.3
32 Tariffs						5.4		52.2
33 Other								293.7
34 Direct tax								328.2
35 Social security								103.2
36 Interest								5.4
37 Banking								
38 External sector								1039.8
39 Remitted profits								812.8

40	Interest								227.0
41	Pesos								0.5
42	Mexdollars								3.1
43	Dollars								223.4
44	Banking sector								613.1
45	Interest								578.1
46	Pesos								424.7
47	Mexdollars								153.3
48	Dollars								
49	Profits								35.0
50	Banco de Mexico								
51	Wage earners						520.1		2199.5
52	Subsidies							−122.2	0.0
53	Financial intermediation								0.0
54	Saving								1702.7
55	Capital								1702.7
56	Net financial assets								0.0
57	Pesos								0.0
58	Mexdollars								0.0
59	Dollars								0.0
60	Profits							134.7	3203.8
61	Value added						525.5	12.5	5874.2
62	Total	285.7	116.0	536.2	764.8	1702.7	5874.2		

Table 10.2
Financial accounting matrix: financial assets and liabilities by economic agent (billion Mexican pesos, end 1981)

Liabilities (down)/assets (across)	1 Rentiers	2 Proprietors	3 Corporations	4 Public sector	5 External	6 Banks	7 Banco de Mexico	8 Total
1 Rentiers				41.8	553.1	1398.2	281.7	2274.8
2 Proprietors						29.7		29.7
3 Corporations						300.9		300.9
4 Public sector						261.8		261.8
5 External sector			375.2	793.9		823.6		1992.7
6 Banks	275.0	296.5	626.5	893.2	26.8		786.7	2904.7
7 Banco de Mexico				900.0	132.1	46.5		1078.6
8 Net financial assets	1999.8	−266.8	−700.8	−2367.1	1280.7	44.0	10.2	0.0
9 Total	2274.8	29.7	300.9	261.8	1992.7	2904.7	1078.6	8843.2

The sparseness of the FAM reflects the relative simplicity of the financial sector in Mexico. There is little direct marketing of paper assets between productive agents so that virtually all financing takes place through the banking system or through external lending. The only direct financing is through the purchase of a small amount of government securities by rentiers. The extent of dollarization of the financial system can be seen through the importance of foreign assets and liabilities in domestic portfolios, as well as by the large Mexdollar component of bank assets and liabilities (shown in parentheses for each entry where applicable).

10.4 Structure of the Model

The structure of the model based on these matrices is set out in the appendix. A comprehensive discussion appears in Easterly (1985). Here only a brief description will be given. The production technology for the three domestic sectors is Leontief, with the exception of sector 2 which nests a CES function for imported and domestic intermediate goods into an otherwise Leontief structure. The expenditure functions for rentiers, proprietors, and wage earners are specified as a linear expenditure system (LES), like that described by Taylor (1979). Total consumption by economic agent is a standard consumption function (linear in disposable income), with a real balances term added. Investment is a function of cash flow by economic agent, which is gross profits less taxes, interest payments, and capital losses on debt. Portfolio behavior is a modified form of Tobin's system: Net position in each asset (in this case currency denomination) is a linear function of net financial wealth and a logistic function of rates of return by asset. Gross stocks in cases where agents hold both assets and loans of the same type are determined by stock-flow behavioral coefficients, such as a fixed ratio of peso deposits to operating costs for proprietors and corporations.

Some of these relations need to be detailed further because of the central role they play in the debt/devaluation story. The consumption function for each class will have a real balances term which will be net financial assets deflated by the consumer price index for that class. It is straightforward that devaluation will lead to an increase in "real balances" if the share of dollar assets in total financial holdings exceeds the elasticity of the aggregate consumer price deflator to the exchange rate. The latter depends not only on the share of imported goods in the consumption basket but also on the extent to which prices and wages under the control of the authorities are adjusted in response to devaluation. In Mexico these included the price of petroleum products, certain other basic products such as bread, tortillas, and public transport, and the minimum wage, which is thought to be an indicator for most wage contracts. Since workers do not have dollar income, there is clear distributional trade-off involved in wage adjustments. These raise the inflationary response to devaluation and lower real balances of rentiers while preserving real incomes of wage earners. On the other hand, suppressing price increases in the other items tends temporarily to benefit both rentiers and wage earners, although at the expense of the fiscal deficits that ensue from greater subsidies. A similar analysis would apply in flow terms to interest income from financial assets by rentiers (i.e, financial real income will increase if the share of the dollar-denominated assets exceeds the elasticity of the consumption deflator to the exchange rate).

Financial flows also enter into the investment function because of the cash flow specification assumed. This specification reflects fragmented capital markets in which internal self-financing of enterprises as well as credit rationing predominate, which seems to be the case in Mexico as well as in many other underdeveloped economies. The nominal cash flow of enterprises is deflated by the replacement cost of capital. Since cash flow is gross profits (including export profits) less interest costs, taxes, and capital losses, it is clear that the effect of devaluation will depend on the relative shares of exports in total sales, of dollar-denominated loans in total debt, and of imported goods in total investment. The condition for the outcome of devaluation on investment is complicated, but it can be broken down into its component parts. The nonfinancial effect can be isolated by assuming no indebtedness, in which case devaluations' effect on real cash flow can be shown to be negative if the ratio of export revenues to gross profits is less than the import share of investment expenditure. The "debt burden" effect of devaluation, on the other hand, will be a negative factor if the following holds:

$$\mathrm{FSH} > \mathrm{PI} * (1 - \mathrm{QSH}) + \mathrm{QSH},$$

where FSH is the share of dollar loans in the total, QSH is the share of imported capital goods in investment, and PI is the price elasticity of the domestic price with respect to the exchange rate. It is clear from this expression that the effect of devaluation depends on the domestic price response and on the extent of financial "dollarization," in roughly the opposite way to the effect on consumption. In the limit, if there is purchasing power parity and PI is unity, then the debt burden will be reduced by devaluation. If PI is low and the share of dollar debt is high, on the other hand, it will be increased. Not surprisingly, the interests of indebted corporations are opposed to those of asset-holding rentiers. More novel is the way in which the interests of corporations and their employees could coincide. Since any domestic price increase—including a wage increase—lowers the debt burden, an economywide wage hike could benefit corporations if debt is sufficiently high. From the political economy point of view, this could present the interesting spectacle of business managers lobbying the government for minimum wage hikes, of which there was some evidence in the wake of the 1982–83 devaluations in Mexico.

The other key relations in a financial stocks' view of devaluation are the portfolio demand equations themselves. For fixed rates of return, these come down to simple linear functions of net financial wealth for each currency denomination. For rentiers, devaluation will both raise the share of the dollar-denominated assets in the total portfolio and increase their total net financial wealth. The increase in wealth will lead them to hold a higher nominal value of all assets. Thus the increase in the value of dollar assets will be shared out among both dollar and peso assets through converting some dollars into pesos. This is just the effect predicted by the monetary approach to devaluation—when the real value of domestic currency drops below the desired level due to devaluation, actions are taken to rebuild them back up. However, here the action is a simple portfolio shift rather than increased saving—indeed, as was seen above, saving may fall if wealth increases in real terms. This approach of including dollar assets is thus much more general than the usual empirical models of devaluation.

On the liability side, a similar adjustment is taking place for debtors. Devaluation causes an unwanted increase in the share of dollar debt in the total, so some dollar loans are retired and replaced by peso debt. Thus overall the interesting result is obtained that devaluation tends to reduce the dollarization of the financial system on both the asset and liability sides.

The model also has important implications for the fiscal response to devaluation, especially taking the financial balances into account. The government can influence its own real balances through its control over the key nominal benchmark—the exchange rate. Even if there is full pass-through of devaluation into wages and controlled prices, the government's position will improve through the fall in the real value of its external debt. This is the conventional "classical" view of the effect of devaluation on debt and the fiscal balance, reiterated in many modern writers (e.g., see Buiter 1985, p. 27). It is evident in this model, however, that the dollarization of the government debt makes more difficult this remedy for the budget so that a higher rate of devaluation (and inflation) would be required for a given fiscal improvement. This may give a hint as to why devaluation was so drastic in 1982 in Mexico when it finally came.

Of course the government is also affected by changes in the real exchange rate, as its dollar deficit becomes more burdensome, which may or may not offset its net export income. Contrary to neoclassical models, the public authorities can essentially choose the desired result in this model, as their control over the nominal values of the exchange rate, public sector wages (which function as a price leader for private wages in the formal sector), and the price of subsidized goods allow them to target the real exchange rate in the short run.[7]

So far, the effects considered here are viewed in isolation. In solving the model, naturally they all operate in conjunction. The way in which they affect the results is determined by the model closure, which, as seen above, places the model on the continuum of neoclassical versus Keynesian and short run versus long run. Here the model closure is short run and Keynesian (i.e., quantity adjustment in all sectors is assumed). Thus both the overall level of output and the level of the current-account balance are determined endogenously. On the financial side, the equilibrating variables are the level of foreign exchange reserves and the foreign debt of the nonfinancial public sector. All interest rates are fixed, as well as the exchange rate. The operative assumption for this closure is that the country faces an "open window" in foreign capital markets where it can borrow all it needs to finance external deficits (as was certainly true for pre-1982 Mexico, hard as it is to conceive of today). The monetary authority makes no attempt to control the quantity of money, instead fixing the domestic peso interest rate. However, because of imperfect substitutability of foreign and domestic assets and positive expectations of devaluation, domestic interest rates are not equal to foreign ones.

10.5 Results of the Simulations

The model is used to simulate the effect of a 50 percent devaluation on the Mexican economy, as it was structured in 1981. Table 10.3 shows the results of the simulation, which presumes partial indexation of wages and controlled prices. To be more precise, the wage will be increased by half the precentage amount by which the CPI rises, domestic petroleum prices will be increased by half the amount by which the peso-equivalent world price increases, and controlled nonpetroleum prices will be raised half as fast as their noncontrolled counterparts. As shown in table 10.3, the effect of the devaluation is highly contractionary, leading GDP to drop by about

Table 10.3
Results of model simulation for 50 percent devaluation (partially indexed wages and prices)

	Percent change	Percent change from base for constant output
GDP	−4.2	
Private consumption	−8.2	
Rentier	−5	−0.99
Proprietor	−5.4	−0.81
Wage earner	−10.5	−7.29
Private investment	−7.4	
Rentier	0.3	1.86
Proprietor	−5.4	−2.81
Corporate	−11.9	−10.41
CPI	18.6	
Replacement cost of capital	24.1	
Foreign assets of profit earners (U.S.$)	−23.1	
Foreign debt of corporations (U.S.$)	−14.9	

4 percent. This is partially a consequence of several of the effects of several of the effects detailed in the "contractionary devaluation" literature, to wit:

1. The redistribution of income from wage earners with high propensity to consume to high-saving recipients of export profits (cf. Díaz-Alejandro 1964).
2. The revaluation of the large initial dollar current-account deficit in peso terms, increasing foreign saving (cf. the "Hirschman effect" in Krugman and Taylor 1978).
3. The increase in government saving because of the higher peso income from oil exports by the publicly owned oil company and taxes on foreign trade (the "fiscal effect," cf. Krugman and Taylor 1978).

In addition to these contractionary effects, this model captures the impact of the fall in investment induced by the increased "debt burden" on corporations. As the second panel of table 10.3 shows, the fall in investment is sharp, even removing the output effect by calculating the fall for constant total output. As would be expected from the far greater dollar indebtedness of corporations, they experienced the sharpest drop in investment. Their cash flow actually declines by 28 percent in the simulation, as a result of the capital losses on dollar debt, while the replacement cost of capital rises by 24 percent. The squeeze on proprietor investment is much less because of their modest indebtedness in dollars. Rentiers, on the other hand, can actually increase their investment because of their net asset position in dollars. (This would imply a sectoral shift in investment since rentier capital spending is concentrated in construction and real estate.)

The different asset positions of the consuming agents also greatly affects the distribution of the decline in consumption. Although consumption by rentiers and proprietors does fall, the second panel of table 10.3 shows that this was mainly due to the fall in output. The asset holdings of these classes, especially their dollar-denominated component, limits the consumption impact for them. For wage earners, on the other hand, there is no asset cushion to soften the blow.[8] Thus taking the asset holdings into account shows that the contractionary impact of devaluation is unequally distributed.

The portfolio effects of devaluation also show up in this simulation. The revaluation of their dollar holdings induces rentiers to reduce the actual dollar amounts by 24 percent compared to the base. This does not mean that there are capital inflows but simply that capital flight is less severe than it was in the base, being cut in half from U.S.$10.2 billion to $5.6 billion. This is purely a valuation effect, holding constant the expected rates of return. Similarly corporations wind up with a lower rate of dollar debt than in the base. This is a consequence of both the lower level of investment and a valuation-induced shift toward peso debt.

10.6 Conclusions and Policy Implications

The showing of a contractionary effect of devaluation is in line with other works in the structuralist tradition. Here, however, the emphasis is on the contraction of investment, which means that the impact of the contraction extends to the medium term because the loss in physical capital formation will have to be made up later if the economy is to stay on its long-run growth path.

This is not to suggest that devaluation is an ill-advised policy in a situation of external imbalance. Indeed, the "dollarization" that leads to the severe effects on investment often will have resulted from an overvalued exchange rate through high current-account deficits and capital flight. The lesson from this model is thus more the inadvisability of postponing devaluation rather than the wisdom of avoiding it. As the model results show, devaluation will induce a portfolio shift away from dollar-denominated assets, which will make it possible to reduce dollar external debt as well.

What the model does make clear, however, is the very high cost of an "overshooting" exchange rate when the adjustment does take place. By the time the "overshooting" is eliminated, a substantial cost will have been paid in loss of physical capital formation and new productive capacity. This is another argument for devaluing sooner rather than later, as well as for creation of dual foreign exchange markets in which speculative pressures can be confined to one segment of the market, while a simply competitive rate can be applied for goods transactions and debt payments.

The results of the model also illustrate the futility of systems that attempt to cure capital flight by making available foreign currency instruments in the domestic banking system. The Mexdollar debt is just as much a burden on firms as the dollar debt after the devaluation. Although Mexdollars could be valued at a lower rate than dollars to limit the damage—as the Mexicans in fact did in 1982—this is a one-time measure that destroys the confidence in Mexdollars in the future. Indeed, the possibility of this happening makes the Mexdollar holdings highly vulnerable to speculative attack in the first place, as was demonstrated in the 1982 crisis in Mexico.

Appendix: Description of the Macro-Financial CGE for Mexico

The model is based on the social accounting and financial accounting matrices given in tables 10.1 and 10.2. This annex describes the equations for the variables in the SAM, going column by column. Table 10.4 gives the variable and parameter definitions for the model.

Production Technology and Price Determination

Production in the petroleum sector is based on a Leontief technology in petroleum and nonpetroleum goods, labor, and imported intermediates. Both domestic and international output prices are fixed, the former by government decree, the latter by international market forces. Thus, instead of a markup equation, profits in the petroleum sector are the residual:

$$\begin{aligned} UP1 = {} & P1 * (XR1 - XER1) + E * PF1 * XER1 - W * B1 * XR1 - P1 * A11 * XR1 \\ & - P3 * A31 * XR1 - E * PF * A41 * XR1 \\ & - \left(\frac{TIG1}{1 + TIG1}\right) * P1 * (XR1 - XER1). \end{aligned}$$

Table 10.4
Parameter and variable names in the model

UP1	Petroleum profits
P1	Domestic price of petroleum
XR1	Total production of petroleum
XER1	Export volume of petroleum
E	Exchange rate pesos/dollar
PF1	Dollar export price of petroleum
W	Wage rate
Bi	Labor input coefficient in sector i
Aij	Input coefficient of good i by sector j
P3	Price of aggregate nonpetroleum goods (uncontrolled)
PF	International dollar price index
TIG1	Gasoline tax rate
P7	Aggregate price index of imported and domestic intermediates for sector 2 production
RHO	Substitution parameter between imported and domestic intermediates in sector 2 production
TIM2	Tariff on intermediate imports, sector 2
TIO2	Indirect tax on sector 2 goods
RPi	Markup rate by class i on its share of sector 2 production costs
SHi	Share of class i in sector 2 production costs
P6	Price index of financial services
Cij	Consumption of good i by class j
CBij	Basic consumption of good i by class j
CMij	Marginal consumption share of good i for class j
CEj	Total consumption expenditure by class j
SAi	Marginal savings rates, class i
TTDi	Total direct taxes, class i
CKi	Propensity to consume out of wealth, class i
FNAi	Net financial assets, class i
CPI	Consumer price index
CEOi	Intercept of consumption function, class i
FIPi	Financial interest payments, class i
RILPi	Interest rate on peso loans, class i
FLPi	Stock of peso liabilities, class i
EM	Exchange rate, pesos/Mexdollar
RILMi	Interest rate on Mexdollar loans, class i
FLMi	Stock of Mexdollar liabilities, class i
RILDi	Interest rate on dollar liabilities, class i

Table 10.4 (continued)

FLDi	Stock of dollar liabilities, class i
G	Current government spending
GSHi	Share of good i in government spending
GR	Real government spending
TMC4	Tariff rate applied to government imports
Z4	Government labor force
PDIF2	Government expenditure (subsidy) to cover price differential between controlled price and uncontrolled nonpetroleum goods
P2	Price of subsidized nonpetroleum goods
XE	Domestic currency value of total exports
XER2G	Volume of exports on nonpetroleum goods by public sector
H2PM	Base volume of nonpetroleum goods exports
A2PM	Price elasticity of supply of nonpetroleum exports
H2PS	Base volume on nonpetroleum service exports
A2PS	Price elasticity of demand for service exports
PDIF6	Profits or losses of banking system
X62	Value added in financial services sector
RIAPi	Interest rate on peso assets, class i
FAPi	Peso assets of class i
FAMi	Mexdollar assets of class i
RIAMi	Interest rate on Mexdollar assets, class i
QRi	Real investment expenditure, class i
QRiO	Intercept of investment function, class i
Si	Saving of class i
Vi	Net capital gains/losses on financial assets/liabilities, class i
PKi	Price of new capital goods, class i
QELi	Elasticity of investment with respect to cash flow, class i
QSHij	Share of sector i goods in investment by class j
P1O	Base level of domestic petroleum price
P1I	Coefficient of indexation of domestic petroleum price
EPF1O	Base level of peso value of foreign petroleum price
P20	Base level of controlled price index
P2I	Coefficient of indexation of controlled-price goods
P3O	Base level of uncontrolled price of nonpetroleum goods
CSHi	Share of good i in consumer price index basket
FMPi	Cross-elasticity of Mexdollar asset demand to peso rate, class i
EEM	Expected rate of devaluation of Mexdollar exchange rate
FMMi	Elasticity of Mexdollar asset demand to Mexdollar rate, class i

Table 10.4 (continued)

FMDi	Cross-elasticity of Mexdollar asset demand to dollar rate, class i
EE	Expected rate of devaluation of dollar exchange rate
FDPi	Cross-elasticity of dollar asset demand to peso rate, class i
FDMi	Cross-elasticity of dollar asset demand to Mexdollar rate, class i
FDDi	Elasticity of dollar asset demand to dollar interest rate, class i
FLBDP7	Reserves against peso deposits
FLBDM7	Reserves against Mexdollar deposits
HP6	Reserve ratio, peso deposits
Hm6	Reserve ratio, Mexdollar deposits

The profits include the differential between internal and external sales (the latter at a higher price), but they do not include the gasoline tax going to the government, which is the last term subtracted here.

In the aggregate nonpetroleum sector, a combination of Leontief and constant elasticity of production functions is assumed. Imported goods can be substituted for domestic intermediates, but their aggregate is used in fixed proportions, as are petroleum, services, and labor. The "price" of the aggregate intermediate good would be the following:

$$\mathrm{P7} = ((\mathrm{A32} * \mathrm{P3}) ** \mathrm{RHO} + (\mathrm{A42} * (1 + \mathrm{TIM2}) * \mathrm{E} * \mathrm{PF}) ** \mathrm{RHO}) ** \left(\frac{1}{\mathrm{RHO}}\right).$$

The output price of the aggregate nonpetroleum sector is then determined in a standard markup equation as follows:

$$\mathrm{P3} = (1 + \mathrm{TIO2}) * [1 + \mathrm{SUM}(\mathrm{RPi} * \mathrm{SHi})] * (\mathrm{P1} * \mathrm{A12} + \mathrm{P7} * \mathrm{A72} + \mathrm{PF} * \mathrm{E} * \mathrm{A52} + \mathrm{P6} * \mathrm{A62} + \mathrm{B2} * \mathrm{W}).$$

This equation reflects a different markup for each of the classes (rentiers, proprietors, corporations, and the government) involved in this sector's production.

Consumption Expenditures

Each group of consumers (rentiers, proprietors, and wage earners) is assumed to have demands based on the linear expenditure system, first introduced by R. A. Stone. This implies that each consumer has demands for some minimum levels of each good. The sum of expenditure on these minimum levels will be basic consumption expenditure. The excess of consumption expenditure over the basic level will then be shared out among the alternative goods. This implies individual demand functions like the following:

$$\mathrm{Cij} = \mathrm{Pi} * \mathrm{CBij} + \mathrm{CMij} * [\mathrm{CEj} - \mathrm{SUM}(\mathrm{Pi} * \mathrm{CBij})].$$

The consumption expenditures of the classes are determined very differently. Workers are assumed to simply consume all of their income, which is an exaggeration but not by much. Rentiers and proprietors save some proportion of their aftertax income, after allowing for some basic level of consumption (by analogy with the linear expenditure system). There is also the additional wrinkle of a "real balances" effect of liquid financial net assets on consumption. This will prove important in assessing the effects of exchange rate induced asset valuation changes on the level of demand. The consumption equations for rentiers and proprietors are thus

$$CEi = (1 - SAi) * (Yi - TTDi) + CKi * FNAi + CPI * CEOi.$$

Outlays for Interest Obligations

Rentiers, proprietors, corporations, and the government borrow from the banking system and aborad, in pesos, Mexdollars, and dollars. Thus they incur interest costs, which can be given as follows for class i:

$$FIPi = RILPi * FLPi + EM * RILMi * FLMi + E * RILDi * FLDi.$$

Note that each class has its own interest rate since the type of borrowing will vary from one class to another, even with the same currency type. There is also a different exchange rate for the Mexdollar loans compared to dollar loans, to allow for the possibility of dual exchange rates.

Government spending is assumed to be fixed in real terms so that nominal spending is determined by prices:

$$G = P1 * GSH1 * GR + P3 * GSH3 * GR + (1 + TMC4) * E * PF * GSH4 * GR + W * Z4.$$

The size of the government labor force Z4 is also assumed to be fixed so that the public wage bill is determined by the wage rate W. The government also incurs expense by subsidizing the consumption of some nonpetroleum goods. The amount of the subsidy is determined by the amount of expenditure on these goods times the rate of subsidy:

$$PDIF2 = \frac{P3 - P2}{P2} * (C21 + C22 + C28).$$

Export behavior is different across sectors. The volume of petroleum exports are a residual, given by the difference between domestic consumption and exogenously determined production. Exports of nonpetroleum goods depend on the external price relative to the domestic one, assuming a standard small-country export supply function. The domestic currency value of these exports (as well as those of the exogenously determined other government exports XER2G) are given by their international prices times the exchange rate. Exports of services, on the other hand, reflect mainly sales to tourists and border purchases, and so these carry the same price as other domestic goods. The volume of these service exports will also depend on the relative price of international versus domestic goods, but now viewed from the demand side. The total domestic currency value of exports will then be as follows:

$$XE = E * [PF1 * XER1 + PF * (XER2G + H2PM * \left(\frac{E * PF}{P3}\right) ** A2PM)]$$
$$+ P3 * H2PS * \left(\frac{E * PF}{P3}\right) ** A2PS.$$

The banking system has both interest expenditure on its deposit obligations and external loans and interest receipts from the outstanding loans in its portfolio. It must meet the requirement that interest receipts less interest costs equal the output of financial services (i.e., valued added in the financial sector). Since sudden changes in exchange rates and asset valuations can disrupt this equality, a residual balancing item is defined:

$$PDIF6 = X62 + SUM(RIAPi * FAPi + EM * RIAMi * FAMi)$$
$$+ E * RILD6 * FLD6 - SUM(RILPi * FLPi + EM * RILMi * FLMi).$$

This residual can be thought of as the amount necessary to give normal profits to the owners of the banking system. Thus in time of banking crisis induced by asset and liability valuations, PDIF6 could represent the amount of expenditure by the public sector necessary to keep the banking system afloat.

Real investment levels will be determined by investment functions for each class except the government, whose investment is assumed to be set by an exogenous policy decision. The general form of the investment function for the first three classes is the following:

$$QRi = QRiO * \left(\frac{Si + Vi}{PKi}\right) ** QELi.$$

The term in parentheses is the surplus of income over current expenditure (i.e., saving) for each class, including also the net capital gains on financial assets and liabilities, deflated for the price of capital goods for that class. The price of capital goods will differ from one class to another because of differing compositions of imported versus domestic goods. Investment responds to this real saving with an elasticity QELi. This is a generalization of the "cash-flow" approach to investment, appropriate for an economy where there is widespread credit rationing and self-financing of investment predominates.

Once the real level of investment by class is given, the expenditure on different types of capital goods is determined in fixed proportions. The price of capital is thus a weighted average of the sectoral prices for each class:

$$PKj = SUM(Pi * QSHij * QRj).$$

Incomes by Class and Commodity Balances

To close the real side of the model, there are two types of identities needed. One is that income must equal expenditure and saving for each class, and the other is that the supply of each good must equal demand. On the income side it is not necessary to go into the algebraic details since the SAM (table 10.1) shows the expenditure flows that will show up as income to the different classes. Rentiers derive income from their share in production (mainly real estate services) as well as remittances from corporations and interest. Proprietors' income is made up largely of value added earned in production. Corporations also derive their income from production profits. The public sector gets income from oil exports, from the domestic sales of public enterprises, and from direct and indirect taxes. Foreigners receive income from sales of imported goods and services and from interest payments on the foreign debt of residents. The banks receive interest income on their outstanding loans, along with the profits in the provision of financial services. Wage earners get income from their sales of labor serivces, both at home and abroad.

The sectoral supply and demand equations clear via quantity adjustment. In the petroleum sector the quantity of exports is the balancing item, as noted earlier. In the nonpetroleum and financial services sectors, output is demand determined. The assumption is that supply is perfectly elastic over the relevant region. The gap between foreign expenditure and income (the current-account balance) is also demand determined, presuming that the country can borrow any amount necessary on world capital markets. This was a reasonable assumption in the pre-1982 world.

Price Indexation

Before presenting details about the financial side of the model, it is necessary to discuss the price variables that affect both the real and financial sides. The domestic prices of petroleum and controlled nonpetroleum goods are set by the government. Policy makers can also control the domestic nominal wage rate to some extent through determination of public sector wages and the minimum wage for formal sector workers. The nominal exchange rate is also set by the authorities. It is assumed that the government follows partial indexation rules in setting these various nominal quantities. The degree of indexation will be set exogenously in the model, and then the nominal prices will adjust endogenously in response to changes in the respective benchmarks.

The domestic petroleum price is indexed to the domestic currency value of the dollar export price:

$$\mathrm{P1} = \frac{\mathrm{P10} + \mathrm{P1I} * \mathrm{P10} * (\mathrm{E} * \mathrm{PF1} - \mathrm{EPF10})}{\mathrm{EPF10}}.$$

The controlled price of nonpetroleum goods will be partially indexed to the uncontrolled price of these goods:

$$P2 = P20 + P2I * P20 * (P3 - P30).$$

The wage rate is indexed to a cost of living index CPI defined as follows:

$$CPI = CSH1 * P1 + CSH2 * P2 + CSH3 * P3 + CSH4 * E * PF * (1 + TMC) + CSH5 * E * PF,$$

$$W = WO + WI(CPI - 1).$$

Financial Markets

The first step in describing financial markets is linking the real and financial sides by determining the stocks of net financial assets held by each class. This will be determined by the savings less investment of each class, adjusted for capital gains:

$$FNAi - FNAi(-1) = Si - Qi + Vi.$$

The FNA variables will play the role of wealth in Tobin-like portfolio demand equations. The assumption is that agents decide their wealth composition in two stages: First they decide the amount of physical capital they wish to hold; then they decide the makeup of the implied stock of financial assets or liabilities.

The net position of each class in each type of asset (peso, Mexdollar, and dollar) is given by a logistic function of relative rates of return, with linear shares of financial wealth. The peso net assets are determined as a residual:

$$FAMi - FLMi = \{1 - 1/[1 + EXP(FMi + FMPi * RIAPi + FMMi * (RIAMi + EEM) + FMDi * (RIADi + EE))]\} * FNAi/EM,$$

$$FADi - FLDi = \{1 - 1/[1 + EXP(FDi + FDPi * RIAPi + FDMi * (RIAMi + EEM) + FDDi * (RIADi + EE))]\} * FNAi/E,$$

$$FAPi - FLPi = FNAi - EM * (FAMi - FLMi) - E * (FADi - FLDi).$$

These equations determine only net positions in each asset. To determine the amounts of gross assets and liabilities, it is necessary to assume various stylized rules for financial behavior. For example, rentiers are assumed to hold an amount of peso and Mexdollar loans proportional to their stock of physical capital (mainly real estate) and no dollar loans. Proprietors and corporations hold deposits proportional to their variable production costs for working capital purposes. The government holds deposits proportional to its consumption expenditures.

The banking system has liabilities corresponding to the asset choices made by the other agents in the economy. On the asset side banks may take positions in each currency. For example, they play the role of intermediary between foreign lenders and domestic borrowers, which leads them to be short in dollars and long in Mexdollars. The net holdings of each currency are modeled to be independent of the small amount of bank net financial assets in order to avoid instability in the solution.

Once the banks decide the level of net assets to have in each currency, they need to place these loans with domestic borrowers. One kind of loan is obligatory, and that is the reserves they must deposit at the central bank against their peso and Mexdollar deposits. These are determined as a ratio to the deposits:

$$FLBDP7 = HP6 * SUM(FAPi),$$

$$FLBDM7 = HM6 * SUM(FAMi).$$

Other loans are made by the banking system according to the demands of the borrowers. To equilibrate the system, either interest rates must adjust, or there must be quantity adjustment. The latter is chosen here in view of the fixed interest rates prevailing during this period. The quantity adjustment takes the form of the government passively absorbing all of the loans that are left over after the demands of the other classes have been satisfied. The government will resort to external borrowing for any residual financing needs.

The central bank is the other major agent in financial markets. Its liabilities are determined by the currency holdings of the private sector, which are determined as a fixed share of peso assets, and bank reserves against deposits. The credit extended to the government will be fixed as a policy variable. The balancing item for the central bank will then be foreign exchange reserves.

The last element of the financial side to present is the calculation of capital gains and losses. These are very complicated to determine since the entire paths of the exchange rate and the relevant financial stocks must be know. Here the simplifying assumption is made that any exchange rate change will be made only at the beginning of the period. The revaluation of each financial stock is then simply the change in the exchange rate times the stock left over from the previous period. The total net capital gain will be the sum of its capital gains and losses on all instruments:

$$Vi = [EM - EM(-1)] * (FAMi - FLMi) + [E - E(-1)] * (FADi - FLDi).$$

Model Closure

On its nonfinancial side possible adjusting variables to close the model are total output, investment, the exchange rate, the price level, the interest rate, and the current-account balance (capital inflow). At least two of these variables must adjust so that external and internal balance obtains. On the financial side the possible endogenous variables are the peso and Mexdollar interest rates, high-powered money, foreign exchange reserves, foreign debt, and the exchange rate. Quantity adjustment on the real side will imply quantity adjustment in the financial model. For example, if output and the current-account deficit vary to ensure equilibrium, then the quantity of foreign debt and foreign exchange reserves should be endogenous in the financial model. The fixing of interest rates and exchange rates means both real and financial flows adjust in quantity terms. This corresponds to the "Keynesian" type of model closure (using Taylor's terminology) in the literature described in note 6.

Notes

1. Keynes (1931), p. 30.

2. Ibid., p. 32.

3. Easterly (1985), p. 30.

4. Ibid., pp. 31–32.

5. Ibid., p. 16

6. See Ahluwalia and Lysy's (1979) article which classifies CGE models as neoclassical (capital and labor fully employed), Keynesian (only capital fully employed), and Leontief (neither fully employed). As Taylor (1983) points out, it is actually more historically accurate to call the last "Keynesian."

7. Even in a neoclassical model where the private sector labor market clears at an endogenous real wage, the real exchange rate can be changed through a nominal devaluation since the government budget is not homogeneous in prices. The government can still achieve a fiscal improvement through the lower internal real debt and lower real wages to its own employees (which only devaluation can achieve due to downward rigidity in nominal wages). The increased government saving then supports a relative price shift through lower demand for nontradables.

8. Although the assumption that wage earners do not save and have no financial assets is a bit extreme, it may not be far from reality. A 1978 income-expenditure survey showed that the bottom 60 percent of the income distribution had no net saving.

References

Ahluwalia, M., and F. Lysy. 1979. "Welfare Effects of Demand Management Policies: Impact Multipliers under Alternative Model Structures." *Journal of Policy Modelling* 3: 317–342.

Armington, P. 1969. "A Theory of Demand for Products Distinguished by Place of Production." *IMF Staff Papers* 16: 159–178.

Backus, D., W. Brainard, G. Smith, and J. Tobin. 1980. "A Model of U.S. Financial and Nonfinancial Economic Behavior." *Journal of Money, Credit, and Banking* 12(2): 259–293.

Buiter, W. 1985. "A Guide to Public Sector Debt and Deficits." *Economic Policy* (November).

Díaz-Alejandro, C. 1964. *Exchange Rate Devaluation in a Semi-industrialized Economy.* Cambridge: MIT Press.

Dornbusch, R. 1973. "Devaluation, Money, and Non-traded Goods." *American Economic Review.* 63(5).

Dornbusch, R. 1980. *Open Economy Macroeconomics.* New York: Basic Books.

Easterly, W. 1985. *A Computable General Equilibrium Model of Mexico with Portfolio Balances.* Ph. D. dissertation. Massachusetts Institute of Technology.

International Monetary Fund. 1977. *The Monetary Approach to the Balance of Payments.* Washington: IMF.

Keynes, J. M. 1931. "The Consequences to Society of Changes in the Value of Money." In *Essays in Persuasion.* London: Macmillan.

Krugman, P., and L. Taylor. 1978. "Contractionary Effects of Devaluation." *Journal of International Economics* 8: 445–456.

Taylor, L. 1983. *Structuralist Macroeconomics.* New York: Basic Books.

Tobin, J. 1969. "A General Equilibrium Approach to Monetary Theory." *Journal of Money, Credit, and Banking* 1: 15–29.

Tobin, J. 1980. *Asset Accumulation and Economic Activity.* Chicago: University of Chicago Press.

11 Devaluation, Capital Flows, and Crowding-out: A CGE Model with Portfolio Choice for Thailand

Jeffrey A. Rosensweig and Lance Taylor

There is a long tradition in economics of theorizing about markets for goods and financial assets in general equilibrium: Tobin's (1982) Nobel lecture is a lucid review. More recently, the use of numerically based computable general equilibrium models for research and policy simulation has grown rapidly. However, few numerical models explicitly include financial markets and portfolio choice.[1] In this paper we present an initial attempt at filling this gap, in the context of fiscal and monetary policy formation for Thailand.

The model developed here focuses on short-term macroeconomic adjustment. The data base is a social accounting matrix (SAM) integrating national income and flow of funds accounts for the year 1980. Originally constructed by Chaipravat and Ganjarerndee (1983), the SAM is reviewed in a format different from theirs in section 11.2 (after a preliminary reconnaissance of the Thai economy in section 11.1). The SAM distinguishes four production sectors, eight major types of assets, and eight classes of economic actors.

A general equilibrium model consistent with the accounting categories of the SAM is described in section 11.3, and its parameterization (taking the SAM as a base solution) in section 11.4. Several comparative static experiments with the model are discussed in section 11.5. They concentrate on potential crowding-out or crowding-in of private investment by expansionary fiscal and monetary policies, on how capital movements may offset monetary policy initiatives to an extent, and on the real and financial effects of devaluation. Conclusions appear in section 11.6.

11.1 Thailand

Thailand is "lower-middle-income" economy in the World Bank's classification, with a per capita GNP of $790 in 1982 and an average per capita growth rate of 4.5 percent over the period 1960–82. Inflation during the 1970s averaged about 10 percent per year.

As described by Cole, Chunanuntathum, and Loohawenchit (1984) and the World Bank (1982), the Thai financial system centers around commercial banks. Historically, few barriers have been raised against foreign capital flows. Though individuals are forbidden to hold foreign assets or liabilities, both banks and national enterprises borrow and lend abroad. The exchange rate is pegged, and the central bank (the Bank of Thailand) has traditionally maintained substantial exchange reserves. As discussed below, one question that immediately arises under Thailand's capital market regime is the extent to which capital movements may offset attempted monetary interventions.

Supplies of money and credit are regulated by changes in rediscount and reserve requirements. Commercial banks are encouraged to hold government securities, and the ratio of such holdings to their deposits is treated as a policy instrument below. The banks' principal assets besides credit to the government are loans to firms and reserves (usually in excess of requirements). Their chief liabilities are deposits and net loans from abroad. In the model the banks base their loan supply function on available domestic resources (deposits + rediscount − credit to government − required reserves) and resort to foreign net borrowing to generate resources on the margin.

The major liabilities of firms are shares and loans from domestic banks and foreign sources. The equity market is price clearing in the model, while the interest rate adjusts (in practice under policy control) to clear the credit market by reducing firms' demand for loans and increasing the banks' supply. When the domestic interest rate rises, firms divert part of their credit demand abroad. These alternatives are explored below.

Households hold physical capital (housing and the capital of nonincorporated enterprise), currency, deposits, shares, and securities issued by the government. Their portfolio choice depends on interest rates and an average rate of profit of firms as a measure of the expected return to holding shares. In the model household asset choice takes a role secondary to interactions among banks, firms, the government, and the rest of the world.

The analysis in this paper is based on the financial market entities and instruments just discussed. It is fair to add that the actual Thai market structure is much more complex, incorporating informal transactions such as an active trade in rice merchants' bills and a variety of officially recognized nonbank financial intermediaries (consolidated with the banks here). This detail is simply omitted from the SAM—its accounting is self-consistent but not complete. The conclusions reached here probably would not be affected if the analysis were based on more inclusive data. However, the real and financial incidence of policy changes on different groups in the economy could be analyzed more faithfully with fuller accounting. This reservation should be borne in mind.

11.2 The Social Accounting Matrix

The main accounting categories of the SAM appear in table 11.1, and a schematic in figure 11.1. The matrix itself is too large for presentation here, although its main flows are described in this section. The SAM incorporates financial linkages explicitly by feeding saving by different groups into their flows of funds, and then adding changes in financial stocks to initial asset and liability holdings to generate excess demand equations for end-of-period asset choice. The accounting period is one year, and the units are millions of baht.[2]

Interindustry transactions, income flows, and generation of final demand are set out in the northwest section of figure 11.1 (rows 9–37 and columns 1–13 of the full matrix). The arrangement of this section of the SAM is standard.[3]

Extensions begin with accounting balances linking saving by different participants in the economy to portfolio changes. Savings flows are the left-most entries in rows 38–43 (we take up their relationships with the real side of the economy below). As an accounting convention, *positive* saving in the SAM must equal the sum of accumulation of assets (with a *negative* sign) and increases in liabilities (*positive*).

For example, entries in row 38 with their corresponding column headings appear in the full matrix as

5	14	15	16	17	18	56
74,433	−10,898	−6,684	−45,805	−1,735	−9,311	0

Households, to whom the row refers, split their saving of 74,433 among 10,898 in physical capital (column 14), 6,684 of currency holdings (column 15), 45,805 of net deposits with commercial banks (column 16), 1,735 of new holdings of Thai government securities (column 17), and 9,311 of new corporate shares (column 18).

Similar accounting shows that firms in the model's three producing sectors (details below) undertake net capital formation, which their own saving is inadequate to finance. To raise funds, they issue new shares and

Table 11.1
Accounting categories

Sectors or commodities
Nontraded goods (1)
Traded goods (2)
Goods from state enterprises (3)
Composite of traded goods and imports (4)
Factors of production
Labor (*L*)
Capital (*K*)
Market participants
Households (*h*)
Nontraded sector firms (1)
Traded sector firms (2)
State enterprises (3)
Government (*g*)
Bank of Thailand (4)
Commercial banks (5)
Rest of world (*f*)
Payment flows
Wages (*w*)
Operating surpluses (*OS*)
Dividends
Interest payments (*INT*)
Taxes, tariffs, subsidies
Transfers (*TRAN*)
Depreciation
Assets and liabilities
Physical capital (*K*)
Currency (*CURR*)
Deposits at commercial banks (*DEP*)
Government securities (*GSEC*)
Equity of firms (*Z*)
Loans from commercial banks (*BLN*)
Loans from central bank (*BTLN*)
Loans from abroad (*FLN*)
Foreign exchange reserves (*BTNIR*)
Commercial bank balances at the central bank (*DEPBT*)
Advances from central bank to commercial banks (*RDSCNT*)
Required reserves of commercial banks at central bank (*RESCB*)
Net worth (*NW*)

Row numbers \ Column numbers	1–4	5–11	12–13	14–19	20–34	35–39	40–42	43–48	49–55	56
1–8				Household's initial portfolio	Enterprises' initial portfolios	Govern-ment's initial portfolio	Rest of world's initial portfolio	Central bank's initial portfolio	Commercial bank's initial portfolio	
9–12	Interindustry flows	Final current demand	Gross capital formation							Gross value of production
13–14	Factor payments									Total factor payments
15–19	Household's sources of income									Total sources of incomes
20–26	Enterprises' sources of income									
27–31	Government's sources of income									
32–36	Rest of world's sources of income									
37	Depreciation									Total depreciation

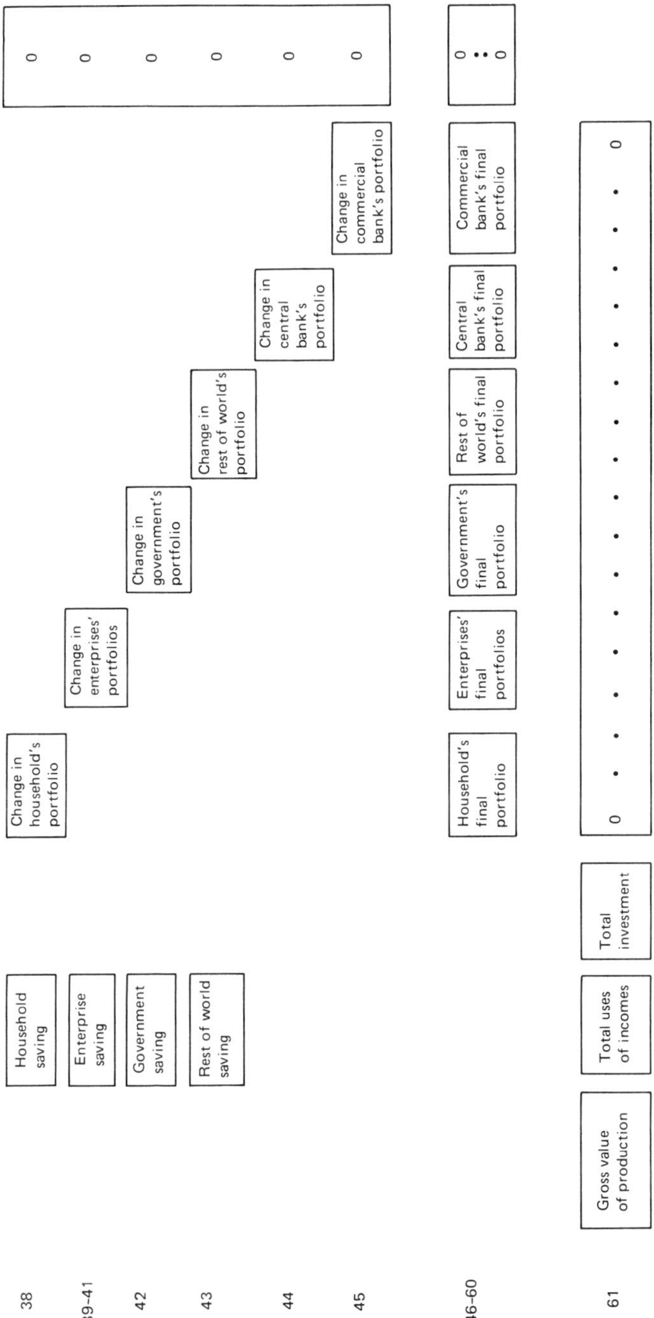

Figure 11.1
Schematic for the Thailand SAM

take loans from commercial banks and abroad. In a typical accounting discrepancy, the original data have net worth of state enterprises declining by 6,758. In keeping with the SAM's double entry bookkeeping, net worth of the Bank of Thailand is assumed to increase by the same amount.

The government's flow of funds is set out in row 42. Its investment of 23,681 (column 35) and acquisition of state enterprise shares (4,202 in column 36) exceed its saving of 4,424 (column 9). Hence it borrows 7,051 from abroad (column 37) and issues domestic liabilities of 16,408 (column 38) to cover its deficit. In row 38, column 17, we have seen that households take up only 1,735 of this new government debt. The rest is absorbed by the banking system.

In row 43, saving of the rest of the world (44,587 in column 10) is just offset by new loans to Thailand (54,287 in column 40) net of increased foreign reserves held by the central bank (9,700 in column 41).

Rows 44 and 45 show the accounts of the Bank of Thailand and commercial banks, respectively. Neither component of the banking system does any saving—the sums of changes in banks' assets and liabilities must be equal.

Beginning with commercial banks, their only increase in liabilities is 45,805 in net deposits from households (column 54). A second liability item—loans from abroad in column 53—declined by 8,940 in 1980. A third—advances from the Bank of Thailand of column 54—declined by one million baht.

Commercial bank asset increases were 9,351 of credit to the government (column 49), 1,579 in balances or reserves at the Bank of Thailand (column 50), and 25,934 in loans to corporations (column 52). It is easy to verify that these changes in banks' assets and liabilities just offset each other.

There is still 5,322 of new domestic credit to the government to be accounted for. In row 44, column 43, the residual deficit is unsurprisingly financed by the Bank of Thailand. The central bank also reduces its advances to commercial banks (column 44), acquires foreign reserves (column 45), accepts more deposits from commercial banks (column 46), issues currency (column 47), and picks up the accounting discrepancy of the state enterprises as net worth in column 48.

With description of the flow of funds now complete, the next step is to bring in accumulation of assets and liabilities. As shown in figure 11.1, initial compositions of portfolios appear in the top rows 1 through 8 of the SAM. Like the flows of funds, initial asset stocks have a negative sign and liability stocks a positive one. Also, in line with the periodization of the model below, beginning stocks are valued at end-of-period prices. Thus households enter the period with physical capital $K_h(t-1)$. In their net worth statement it is valued at the end-of-period capital goods price $P_h^k(t)$. Since $P_h^k(t)K_h(t-1) = P_h^k(t-1)K_h(t-1) + [P_h^k(t) - P_h^k(t-1)]K_h(t-1)$, capital gains are automatically included in net worth by the price accounting.

Columns 14 through 55 show how asset positions change. For example, in column 14 households initially hold physical capital worth 154,568 in current prices (row 1). Their net investment is 10,898 (row 38), and they end up with a capital stock of 165,466 (row 46). As a final accounting convention, assets have a positive sign and liabilities a negative sign in rows 46 through 60. These rows represent end-of-period excess demand relationships for assets and liabilities. As such, they enter as market-clearing conditions in the model.

Running through the list rapidly, the row 47 balance shows that currency is demanded by households and issued by the central bank. Households hold net deposits at commercial banks in row 48. In row 49 government domestic liabilities are held by households and the banks, and households hold equity in enterprises in row 50. Banks lend money to the three types of firms in row 51; firms, the government, and commercial banks borrow from abroad in row 52. In row 53 the government holds state enterprise shares, and the Bank of Thailand holds foreign reserves in row 54. In row 55 the central bank makes advances ("rediscount") to commercial banks; they in turn hold reserves at the central bank in row 56. Rows 46 and 57 through 60 complete the accounting by recording values of capital stock held by households, enterprise and government.

Some variables will have to adjust endogenously to permit the accounting balances for assets to hold—for example, the interest rate on bank loans might vary to make the demand for loans equal the supply in row 51. These interest rate shifts will in turn affect the real side of the economy portrayed in the northwest part of the SAM, and in this way there is a general equilibrium system.

On the real side of the economy, briefly note that three domestic producing sectors are distinguished—nontraded goods (sales accounted for in row 9), traded goods (row 10), and goods produced by state enterprises (row 11). Intermediate purchases of the producing sectors appear in rows 9 through 12 and columns 1 through 4. Traded goods have only two destinations of sale—exports in column 10 (subject to a tax in column 11) and as an input into a "composite" commodity used domestically to satisfy intermediate and final demands. The composite's cost structure appears in column 4 and sales in row 12. In the model imports enter with traded goods in creating the composite according to an elasticity of substitution

σ_4^{Fin}. This specification of imperfect substitution between traded goods and imports in satisfying domestic uses follows Armington (1969) and has been adopted in previous models for Thailand (e.g., Grais 1983).

Payments to labor and capital are given in rows 13 and 14—they come from enterprises (columns 1 to 3) and the rest of the world (column 10). Wages, profits, taxes, transfers, subsidies, depreciation allowances, and interest payments are distributed in rows 15 through 37 among the different groups of income recipients. The details are not reviewed here. Suffice it to note that depreciation charges are treated as a separate payment category in row 37, and that interest payments from government and households accrue to nontraded sector firms in row 20 (columns 9 and 5, respectively).[4]

Spending flows are recorded in columns 5 through 13. Total net investment "by origin" appears in column 12, as does depreciation in column 13. Net capital formation "by agents," or as undertaken by different groups in the economy, appears in the flow of funds. The entry in row 10, column 11, of the SAM is an export tax.

Current uses of income flows appear in columns 5 through 10. For example, households in column 5 consume goods and services (nontraded in row 9, from state enterprises in row 11, and the composite in row 12), pay interest (row 20) and direct taxes (row 27), make transfers to the rest of the world (row 35), and save (row 38). As is usual in SAM's, total household uses of income in column 5 is equal to total receipts in row 19.

Similar accounting applies to the other market participants. Outlays of corporations in the three sectors appear in columns 6 through 8. They pay dividends (row 16) and direct taxes (row 27), and save (rows 39 through 41). The government in column 9 buys goods (rows 9, 11, and 12), makes transfers (rows 18 and 35), pays interest (row 20) and subsidies (row 24), and saves (row 42). Foreigners in column 10 make several sorts of payments to Thailand besides buying exports in row 10, and their "saving" or the current account deficit appears in row 43. The bulk of saving comes from households (74,433 million baht) and abroad (44,587). The rest of the SAM is devoted to showing how saving flows are mediated in financial terms. Since the details have already been discussed, we now turn to the real/financial model.

11.3 Specification of the Model

The model for Thailand partially decomposes into real and financial submodels, linked by flows of funds and the interest rate on bank loans. There are rising supply curves on the real side of the system, since sectoral capital stocks are fixed in the short run. Levels of demand by sector depend on income flows (dependent on output levels in the usual fashion), prices, the interest rate, and exogenous elements such as government spending.

Within-period savings flows add to entering asset and liability stocks to determine end-of-period portfolio balances as discussed in the previous section. Since end-of-period excess demands for stocks are assumed to be zero, both stock and flow considerations affect financial equilibrium, in line with the usual view of market participants in most countries. The financial markets clear through both quantity and price adjustments. One of the clearing variables is the interest rate which (as just discussed) affects aggregate demand. Overall, the "closure" of the model is Keynesian with its equilibration involving both price and quantity changes.[5]

The 131 equations of the model appear in table 11.2, arranged in a dozen blocks. We begin by describing household portfolio choice in section I. Equation (1) states that households' end-of-period net worth is the sum of initial assets—currency, bank deposits, shares of private firms, securities from the government, and physical capital—plus their flow of saving $S_h(t-1)$ within the period. As discussed above, entering shares $Z_h(t-1)$ are valued at end-of-period prices to account for capital gains.

Equation (2) defines household financial assets as net worth less their end-of-period capital stock (computed from this period's investment in equation (12) below). How do households allocate this financial wealth among the available menu of assets? Equations (3) through (11) set out one practical way of modeling portfolio choice, based on the algebra of the well-known CES production function.

We assume that each asset has a well-defined yield or rate of return— i_d or the interest rate on bank deposits, r or the average corporate rate of profit for equity, and i_g or the interest rate on government securities. Currency is assumed to have no measurable yield.[6]

Equation (3) defines a CES-type harmonic mean return q_h on household assets. The main parameter is an elasticity of substitution σ_h. The parameters $\bar{i}_{dh}$, $\bar{i}_{gh}$, and $\bar{r}_h$ can be taken as "normal" yields on bank deposits, corporate capital, and government securities, respectively, and the A_i^h resemble distribution parameters in the standard CES formulation. Shares of different assets in the total QA_h are defined by equations (4) through (7). It is easy to verify that the sum of the ϕ_i^h is one so that desired asset holdings equal QA_h. This adding-up property can be taken as the practical justification for using the harmonic mean q_h.

A second justification can be derived from an optimizing model. Suppose there are only two assets for simplicity, currency C and deposits D. Their

Table 11.2
Equations for the Thailand model

I. Household portfolio

$$NW_h(t) = CURR_h(t-1) + DEP_h(t-1) + P_z(t)Z_h(t-1) + GSEC_h(t-1) + P_h^k(t)K_h(t-1) + S_h(t) \quad (1)$$

$$QA_h(t) = NW_h(t) - P_h^k(t)K_h(t) \quad (2)$$

$$q_h = A_1^h(i_d/\bar{i}_{dh})^{\sigma_h - 1} + A_2^h(r/\bar{r}_h)^{\sigma_h - 1} + A_3^h(i_g/\bar{i}_{gh})^{\sigma_h - 1} + A_4^h \quad (3)$$

$$\phi_1^h = A_1^h \frac{(i_d/\bar{i}_{dh})^{\sigma_h - 1}}{q_h} \quad (4)$$

$$\phi_2^h = A_2^h \frac{(r/\bar{r}_h)^{\sigma_h - 1}}{q_h} \quad (5)$$

$$\phi_3^h = A_2^h \frac{(i_g/\bar{i}_{gh})^{\sigma_h - 1}}{q_h} \quad (6)$$

$$\phi_4^h = A_4^h(1/q_h) \quad (7)$$

$$DEP_h = \phi_1^h QA_h \quad (8)$$

$$ZZ_h = \phi_2^h QA_h \quad (9)$$

$$GESC_h = \phi_3^h QA_h \quad (10)$$

$$CURR_h = \phi_4^h QA_h \quad (11)$$

$$K_h(t) = K_h(t-1) + I_h(t) \quad (12)$$

II. Enterprise portfolios

$$DEF_i = P_i^k I_i - S_i, \quad i = 1, 2, 3 \quad (13)\text{–}(15)$$

$$Z_i(t) = Z_i(t-1) + \alpha_i + \beta_i[DEF_i(t)/P_i^k(t)], \quad i = 1, 2, 3 \quad (16)\text{–}(18)$$

$$QL_i(t) = FLN_i(t-1) + BLN_i(t-1) - P_z(t)[Z_i(t) - Z_i(t-1) + DEF_i(t), \quad i = 1, 2 \quad (19)\text{–}(20)$$

$$QL_3(t) = FLN_3(t-1) + BLN_3(t-1) - P_z(t)[Z_3(t) - Z_3(t-1)] + DEF_3(t) + FUDGE_3(t) \quad (21)$$

$$q_i = A_1^i(\bar{i}_{Li}/I_L)^{\sigma_i - 1} + A_2^i(\bar{i}_{Fi}/i_F)^{\sigma_i - 1}, \quad i = 1, 2, 3 \quad (22)\text{–}(24)$$

$$\phi_1^i = A_1 \frac{(\bar{i}_{Li}/i_L)^{\sigma_i - 1}}{q_i}, \quad i = 1, 2, 3 \quad (25)\text{–}(27)$$

$$\phi_2^i = A_2^i \frac{(\bar{i}_{Fi}/i_F)^{\sigma_i - 1}}{q_i}, \quad i = 1, 2, 3 \quad (28)\text{–}(30)$$

$$BLN_i = \phi_1^i QL_i, \quad i = 1, 2, 3 \quad (31)\text{–}(33)$$

$$BLN_5 = BLN_1 + BLN_2 + BLN_3 \quad (34)$$

$$FLN_i = \phi_2^i QL_i, \quad i = 1, 2, 3 \quad (35)\text{–}(37)$$

$$K_i(t) = K_i(t-1) + I_i(t), \quad i = 1, 2, 3 \quad (38)\text{–}(40)$$

III. Government portfolio

$$FLN_g(t) = FLN_g(t-1) + e(\Delta FLN_g^\$) \quad (41)$$

$$QL_g = P_g^k(t)I_g(t) + P_z(t)[Z_3(t) - Z_3(t-1)] - e(\Delta FLN_g^\$) - S_g(t) + FLN_g(t-1) + GSEC_h(t-1) + BTLN_g(t-1) \quad (42)$$

$$BLN_g = \alpha_g^5 + \beta_g^5(DEP_5) \quad (43)$$

Table 11.2 (continued)

$$BTLN_g = QL_g - BLN_g - GSEC_h \tag{44}$$

$$K_g(t) = K_g(t-1) + I_g(t) \tag{45}$$

IV. Commercial banks' portfolio

$$DEP_5 = DEP_h \tag{46}$$

$$RESCB = \mu_1 + \mu_2(DEP_5) \tag{47}$$

$$QL_5 = DEP_5 + RDSCNT - BLN_g - RESCB \tag{48}$$

$$i_L = \bar{i}_{L5}\left[\frac{BLN_5(i_5/\bar{i}_{F5})^{\epsilon_5}(i_R/\bar{i}_{R5})^{\phi_5}}{\alpha_5 QL_5}\right]^{1/\delta_5} \tag{49}$$

$$DEPBT = RESCB\,[1 + \theta_5(i_L/\bar{i}_{L5})^{-\gamma_5}] \tag{50}$$

$$FLN_5 = BLN_g + DEPBT + BLN_5 - DEP_5 - RDSCNT - NW_5 \tag{51}$$

V. Central bank's portfolio

$$FLN = FLN_1 + FLN_2 + FLN_3 + FLN_g + FLN_5 \tag{52}$$

$$RDSCNT = RDSBAR - \theta_4(FLN_5 - FLNBAR) - \gamma_4(DEPBT - RESCB) \tag{53}$$

$$CURR_4 = CURR_h \tag{54}$$

$$NW_4(t) = NW_4(t-1) + FUDGE_3(t) \tag{55}$$

$$BTNIR(t) = FLN(t) - FLN(t-1) - S_f(t) + BNTIR(t-1) \tag{56}$$

VI. Central bank's portfolio balance

$$NWRES = BTLN_g + RDSCNT + BTNIR - CURR_4 - DEPBT - NW_4 \tag{57}$$

VII. Other financial balances

$$P_z = ZZ_h/(Z_1 + Z_2) \tag{58}$$

$$INT = (A_5^h + i_L BLN_5) + (A_5^g + i_L BLN_g) \tag{59}$$

VIII. Production and price formation

$$P_i^k = \xi_1 P_1 + \xi_4 P_4, \quad i = 1, 2, 3, h, g \tag{60)–(64}$$

$$P_i^* = [(\theta_{1i})^{\sigma_i^{\text{Int}}}(P_1)^{1-\sigma_i^{\text{Int}}} + (\theta_{3i})^{\sigma_i^{\text{Int}}}(P_3)^{1-\sigma_i^{\text{Int}}} + (\theta_{4i})^{\sigma_i^{\text{Int}}}(P_4)^{1-\sigma_i^{\text{Int}}}]^{1/(1-\sigma_i^{\text{Int}})}, \quad i = 1, 2, 3 \tag{65)–(67}$$

$$a_{ji}^* = \left[\frac{P_i^*\,\theta_{ji}}{P_j}\right]^{\sigma_i^{\text{Int}}}, \quad j = 1, 3, 4; \quad i = 1, 2, 3 \tag{68)–(76}$$

$$P_i^c = [(\theta_{Li})^{\sigma_i^{\text{Fin}}}(w_i)^{1-\sigma_i^{\text{Fin}}} + (\theta_i^*)^{\sigma_i^{\text{Fin}}}(P_i^*)^{1-\sigma_i^{\text{Fin}}} + (\theta_{Ki})^{\sigma_i^{\text{Fin}}}[(r_i + \delta_i)(P_i^k)^{1-\sigma_i^{\text{Fin}}}]^{1/(1-\sigma_i^{\text{Fin}})}, \quad i = 1, 2, 3 \tag{77)–(79}$$

$$L_i = (P_i^c \theta_{Li}/w_i)^{\sigma_i^{\text{Fin}}} X_i, \quad i = 1, 2, 3 \tag{80)–(82}$$

$$r_i(t) = \frac{1}{P_i^k(t)}\left[P_i^c(t)\theta_{Ki}\left[\frac{X_i(t)}{K_i(t-1)}\right]^{1/\sigma_i^{\text{Int}}}\right] - \delta_i, \quad i = 1, 2, 3 \tag{83)–(85}$$

$$r(t) = \frac{r_1(t)P_1^k(t)K_1(t-1) + r_2(t)P_2^k(t)K_2(t-1)}{P_1^k(t)K_1(t-1) + P_2^k(t)K_2(t-1)} \tag{86}$$

$$X_{ji} = a_{ji}^*\left[\frac{P_i^c \theta_i^*}{P_i^*}\right]^{\sigma_i^{\text{Fin}}} X_i, \quad j = 1, 3, 4; \quad i = 1, 2, 3 \tag{87)–(95}$$

$$P_4 = [(\theta_{04})^{\sigma_4^{\text{Fin}}}[e(1 + t_0)P_0]^{1-\sigma_4^{\text{Fin}}} + (\theta_{24})^{\sigma_4^{\text{Fin}}}[P_2^c(1 + t_2)]^{1-\sigma_4^{\text{Fin}}}]^{1/(1-\sigma_4^{\text{Fin}})} \tag{96}$$

Table 11.2 (continued)

$$M = \left[\frac{P_4\theta_{04}}{e(1+t_0)P_0}\right]^{\sigma_4^{\mathrm{Fin}}} X_4 \quad (97)$$

$$X_{24} = \left[\frac{P_4\theta_{24}}{P_2^c(1+t_2)}\right]^{\sigma_4^{\mathrm{Fin}}} X_4 \quad (98)$$

$$P_i = P_i^c(1+t_i), \quad i = 1, 3 \quad (99)\text{–}(100)$$

IX. Income generation and saving

$$W = w_1L_1 + w_2L_2 + w_3L_3 + W_{fh} - W_{hf} \quad (101)$$

$$\Pi_i(t) = r_i(t)P_i^k(t)K_i(t-1) + \Pi_{fi} - \Pi_{if}, \quad \Pi = 1, 2, 3 \quad (102)\text{–}(104)$$

$$OS_1 = INT + (1 - v_1)\Pi_1 \quad (105)$$

$$OS_2 = (1 - v_2)\Pi_2 \quad (106)$$

$$OS_3 = \Pi_3 + SUB \quad (107)$$

$$S_i = (1 - d_i - t_i^{\mathrm{Dir}})OS_i, \quad i = 1, 2 \quad (108)\text{–}(109)$$

$$S_3 = (1 - t_3^{\mathrm{Dir}})OS_3 \quad (110)$$

$$Y_h = W + d_1OS_1 + d_2OS_2 + v_1\Pi_1 + v_2\Pi_2 + TRAN_{gh} + TRAN_{fh} \quad (111)$$

$$D = D_0 + (1 - s)[Y_h - TRAN_{hf} - t_h^{\mathrm{Dir}}Y_h - (A_5^h + i_LBLN_5)] + \gamma_hNW_h \quad (112)$$

$$S_h = Y_h - TRAN_{hf} - t_h^{\mathrm{Dir}}\, Y_h - (A_f^h + i_LBLN_5) - D \quad (113)$$

$$Y_g = t_1P_1^cX_1 + t_2P_2^cX_{24} + t_3P_3^cX_3 + et_0P_0M + t_h^{\mathrm{Dir}}Y_h + t_1^{\mathrm{Dir}}OS_1 + t_2^{\mathrm{Dir}}OS_2 + t_3^{\mathrm{Dir}}OS_3 + t_2^{\mathrm{Exp}}P_2^cE_2 + TRAN_{fg} \quad (114)$$

$$S_g = Y_g - P_1G_1 - P_3G_3 - P_4G_4 - TRAN_{gh} - (A_5^g + i_LBLN_g) \quad (115)$$

$$S_f = \Pi_{1f} + \Pi_{2f} + \Pi_{3f} + W_{hf} + eP_0M + TRAN_{hf} + TRAN_{gf} - (1 + t_2^{\mathrm{Exp}})P_2^cE_2 - W_{fh} - \Pi_{f1} - \Pi_{f2} - \Pi_{f3} - TRAN_{fg} - TRAN_{fh} \quad (116)$$

X. Final demand determination

$$\tilde{D} = \theta_1^{\mathrm{Dem}}P_1 + \theta_3^{\mathrm{Dem}}P_3 + \theta_4^{\mathrm{Dem}}P_4 \quad (117)$$

$$C_i = \theta_i^{\mathrm{Dem}} + (\alpha_i^{\mathrm{Dem}}/P_i)(D - \tilde{D}), \quad i = 1, 3, 4 \quad (118)\text{–}(120)$$

$$I_i(t) = [I_{0i} + h_i(r_i(t) - i_L(t))]K_i(t-1), \quad i = 1, 2, 3 \quad (121)\text{–}(123)$$

$$I_h = I_{0h} - h_hi_L + g_h(Y_h/P_h^k) \quad (124)$$

$$I_g = I_{0g} \quad (125)$$

$$E_2 = E_{02}\left[\frac{eP_f^E}{(1 + t_2^{\mathrm{Exp}})P_2^c}\right]^{\eta} \quad (126)$$

XI. Commodity balances

$$X_1 = X_{11} + X_{12} + X_{13} + C_1 + G_1 + \xi_1(I_1 + I_2 + I_3 + I_h + I_g) = \rho_1[\delta_1K_1(t-1) + \delta_2K_2(t-1) + \delta_3K_3(t-1)] \quad (127)$$

$$X_2 = X_{24} + E_2 \quad (128)$$

$$X_3 = X_{31} + X_{32} + X_{33} + C_3 + G_3 \quad (129)$$

$$X_4 = X_{41} + X_{42} + X_{43} + C_4 + G_4 + \xi_4(I_1 + I_2 + I_3) + \rho_4[\delta_1K_1(t-1) + \delta_2K_2(t-1) + \delta_3K_3(t-1)] \quad (130)$$

XII. Saving-investment balance

$$SIRES = S_1 + S_2 + S_3 + S_h + S_f - (P_1^kI_1 + P_2^kI_2 + P_3^kI_3 + P_h^kI_h + P_g^kI_g) \quad (131)$$

expected yields are z_c ($= i_c/\bar{i}_c$) and z_d ($= i_d/\bar{i}_d$). The representative household maximizes utility from expected total earnings from the two assets,

$$\text{Max } U(z_c C, z_d D) = [A_1(z_c C)^\rho + A_2(z_d D)^\rho]^{1/\rho}$$

subject to the wealth constraint

$$C + D = QA.$$

On the usual interpretation, incomes from holding the assets are not perfect substitutes, for reasons of convenience, risk, and so forth. Instead, they trade off at some elasticity of subsitution σ, where $\rho = (\sigma - 1)/\sigma$.

Solving the maximization problem shows that asset demands are

$$C = \frac{A_1^\sigma z_c^{\sigma-1} QA}{q}$$

and

$$D = \frac{A_2^\sigma z_d^{\sigma-1} QA}{q},$$

where

$$q = A_1^\sigma z_c^{\sigma-1} + A_2^\sigma z_d^{\sigma-1}.$$

These equations are of the same form as (3) through (11) in table 11.2—the Thailand model just considers more assets (and also nominal share-holding ZZ in (9), with the share price following from (58) below). Finally, note that this specification makes sense only when the elasticity of substitution σ_h exceeds 1. Otherwise, an increase in an asset's rate of return will cause its desired share in wealth to fall. High substitutibility among assets rules out such an occurrence.

Returning to the equations, we next take up portfolio behavior for the three types of corporate firms—producing nontraded goods (sector 1), traded goods (sector 2), and the regulated products of state enterprises (sector 3)—in section II. As opposed to the specification for households, a mix of stock and flow equations is adopted. Equations (13) through (15) state that each type of enterprise has a current excess of net investment $P_i^k I_i$ over saving S_i, or a deficit DEF_i which must be financed. Equations (16) through (18) state that some part of the deficit will be offset by equity emission—in the model the α_i parameters are given negative values so that equity is an elastic function of the deflated deficit DEF_i/P_i^k. Equations (19) through (21) give levels of required borrowing QL_i by enterprises after equity is accounted for. Total borrowing this period will be the sum of last period's loans from abroad and from banks (FLN_i and BLN_i, respectively), less the increase in outstanding equity valued at end-of-period prices, plus the deficit DEF_i. (Equation (21) has an extra term FUDGE_3 for the accounting discrepancy mentioned last section).

Total borrowing is split between bank loans (interest rate i_L) and foreign loans (interest rate i_F). We use the same CES specification as for households, except that firms minimize a utility function based on capitalized borrowing costs (e.g., $(\bar{i}_F/i_F)FLN$ for foreign loans FLN) instead of maximizing the utility of expected returns.

For firm i its average rate of capitalized interest is defined in (22) through (24), and loan shares by type in (25) through (30). Equations (31) through (33) give demands for bank loans by type of firm (BLN_i), and (34) is their sum (the subscript 5 labels commercial banks). Equations (35) through (37) give foreign loan demands (FLN_i) by firms, and (38) through (40) their end-of-period capital stocks.

Government portfolio behavior is set out in section III. It receives an exogenous quantity of new loans in dollar terms from abroad ($\Delta FLN_g^{\$}$)—the baht value follows after multiplication by the exchange rate e. Total foreign loans in baht terms are given in (41). Government demand for domestic credit (QL_g) follows in (42). It is equal to government investment $P_g^k I_g$ plus new shares acquired from state enterprises (valued for simplicity at the private sector share price index P_z), less new foreign loans and government saving, plus initial levels of borrowing from commercial banks (BLN_g), outstanding securities held by the private sector ($GSEC_h$) and loans from the Bank of Thailand ($BTLN_g$).

In equation (43) bank credit to government BLN_g is made a function of total deposits DEP_5. In effect the government is assumed to have a prior claim to a certain share of commercial banks' available resources. Dumping government liabilities on the banking sector occurs frequently in most countries that lack complex financial markets; (41) amounts to algebraic recognition of this policy maneuver. The parameter β_g^5 is often called a "statutory liquidity ratio" or something similar.

Equation (44) gives the government's borrowing from the Bank of Thailand ($BTLN_g$) as its balance sheet residual. The quantities QL_g and BLN_g have already been determined in (42) and (43). Households' holding of government securities ($GSEC_h$) comes from (10) if their yield i_g is set exogenously as a policy variable. In effect, the market for the sort of government paper held by private citizens is assumed to be quantity clearing.

Commercial banks supply loans on the basis of their available resources. With a fixed deposit rate i_d, they accept in equation (46) the volume of deposits forthcoming from households (another quantity-clearing financial market). Required reserves *RESCB* are given in (47). Bank's available domestic resources QL_5 in (48) are deposits plus advances from the central bank (*RDSCNT*) less enforced loans to the government (BLN_g) and required reserves.

A simple loan supply function can be written as

$$BLN_5 = \alpha_5 QL_5 \left(\frac{i_L}{\bar{i}_{L5}}\right)^{\delta_5} \left(\frac{i_F}{\bar{i}_{F5}}\right)^{-\varepsilon_5} \left(\frac{i_R}{\bar{i}_{R5}}\right)^{-\phi_5},$$

where i_L is the interest rate banks receive on their loans, and i_F and i_R are the rates they pay for foreign loans and rediscount, respectively.

The demand for bank loans by firms is given by (34). The interest rate i_L is assumed to clear the market; hence it can be calculated from the inverse supply function (49). In (50) commercial banks always hold reserves at the central bank (*DEPBT*) greater than the amount required (*RESCB*)—the excess reserve ratio declines as the loan rate i_L goes up. Finally, (51) shows that the residual item in the banks' balance sheet is the total of their foreign loans FLN_5. At the margin the banks adjust their foreign exposure in response to changes in domestic conditions. Such behavior appears plausible for Thailand.

Now we come to the central bank. Roughly speaking, its role in the model is to set the reserve ratio and the volume of rediscount, and accommodate the market. To verify this latter function, observe that most demand-supply balances for assets are now specified. Currency demands by households will be met automatically by the Bank of Thailand in equation (52). Household deposits flow to commercial banks in (46), and central bank credit to the government comes from (44). The demand-supply balance for domestic bank loans determines the interest rate in (49). In (58) the price of equity P_z adjusts to equate households' nominal share demand ZZ_h to the real supply from firms, $Z_1 + Z_2$.

The remaining portfolio transactions are between banks, and between Thailand and the rest of the world. In (52) foreign loan supply *FLN* automatically meets demand from firms, the government, and commercial banks. Equation (53) gives a behavioral rule for the central bank in setting the volume of rediscount. It can specify a level (*RDSBAR*), cut back on advances to commercial banks when they have taken a large volume of foreign loans ($\theta_4 > 0$), or "mop up liquidity" when excess reserves are high ($\gamma_4 > 0$). Finally, Bank of Thailand reserves (*BTNIR*) rise with increased foreign lending and decline with the current account deficit or foreign saving S_f in (56). As always, central bank reserves balance the foreign accounts.

The financial bookkeeping is now complete, except for the balance sheet of the Bank of Thailand. Is it an independent constraint on the system, now that we have specified demand-supply balances for all assets and portfolio balances for all market participants besides the central bank? The answer is clearly in the negative, so a residual check *NWRES* is defined in equation (57). It will be "small" (e.g., less than 10^{-3} times central bank total assets) in an equilibrium solution to the model.[7]

The rest of the equations describe the real side of the economy in standard fashion, and we review them quickly.

Price indexes for each sector's capital stock are defined in (60) through (64). Capital goods come from the nontraded sector (number one) and the composite good (number four). For simplicity, the composition of the capital stock is assumed to be the same in all uses.

The three domestic producing sectors have constant elasticities of substitution σ_i^{Int} among intermediate inputs. Cost indexes P_i^* for sectoral intermediate uses and input-output coefficients a_{ji}^* (defined with respect to the intermediate aggregate) follow in (65) through (76) from the algebra of the CES specification.[8]

Labor, each sector's intermediate aggregate, and its fixed initial capital stock are inputs into its gross value of output. The corresponding CES cost functions (with elasticities of substitution σ_i^{Fin}) are given in (77) through (79). Levels of employment follow in (80) through (82) and intermediate flows (using the a_{ji}^* coefficients) in (87) through (95). Sectoral rates of profit r_i are determined by output levels X_i and incoming capital stocks $K_i(t-1)$ in (83) through (85). The average rate of profit r used for household portfolio decisions is defined in (86).

A CES cost function for the composite between traded goods and imports is given in (96), including tariffs at rate t_0 and a domestic sales tax at rate t_2. Corresponding derived demands for imports and "intermediate" inputs from sector two appear in (97) and (98). Aftertax prices for sectors one and three are defined in (99) and (100).

Rules for income generation are set out in section IX of table 11.3. Wage and profit income flows are in (101) through (104), where the W and Π variables represent transfers to and from abroad. Operating surpluses of enterprise (OS_i) are in (105) through (107). In sectors one and two unincorporated household productive activities get shares v_1 and v_2 of total profits, and firms get the rest. Nontraded firms get interest payments *INT*

Table 11.3
Key parameters and base year shares

Household portfolio	
Elasticity of substitution (σ_h)	1.4
Deposit share (ϕ_1^h)	0.533
Equity share (ϕ_2^h)	0.302
Government security share (ϕ_3^h)	0.031
Currency share (ϕ_4^h)	0.134
Enterprise portfolios	
Equity issue response coefficients (β_i)	
Sectors 1–3	0.20
Equity issue intercepts (α_i)	
Sector 1	−2.364
Sector 2	−1.277
Sector 3	−0.619
Elasticities of substitution (σ_i)	
Sectors 1–3	1.4
Domestic loan shares (ϕ_1^i)	
Sector 1	0.641
Sector 2	0.827
Sector 3	0.342
Foreign loan shares (ϕ_2^i)	
Sector 1	0.359
Sector 2	0.173
Sector 3	0.658
Exchange rate (e)	20.63
Government portfolio	
"Statutory liquidity ratio" (β_g^5)	0.25
Commercial bank portfolio	
Marginal reserve requirement (μ_2)	0.035
Loan supply interest rate elasticities ($\delta_5, \epsilon_5, \phi_5$)	0.2
Loan supply intercept (α_5)	1.551
Excess reserve interest rate elasticities	0.2
Central bank portfolio	
Rediscount response parameters (θ_4, γ_4)	0.0
Supply parameters	
Capital stock composition	
Nontraded good (ξ_1)	0.583
Composite good (ξ_4)	0.417
Elasticity of substitution among intermediate inputs (σ_i^{Int})	
Sectors 1–3	0.25

Table 11.3 (continued)

Elasticity of substitution among factor inputs (σ_i^{Fin})	
Sectors 1–2	0.667
Sectors 3	0.5
Depreciation rates (δ_i)	
Sector 1	0.065
Sector 2	0.066
Sector 3	0.092
Elasticities of substitution in generating composite (σ_4^{Fin})	0.25
Tariff and indirect tax rates (t_i)	
Imports	0.095
Sector 1	0.059
Sector 2 (to composite)	0.061
Sector 2 (to exports)	0.021
Sector 3	0.040
Income generation	
Household shares in profit incomes (v_i)	
Sector 1	1.143
Sector 2	0.674
Direct tax rates (t_i^{Dir})	
Sector 1	0.391
Sector 2	0.381
Sector 3	0.622
Households	0.017
Demand generation	
Marginal propensities to consume	
From income $(1 - s)$	0.85
From wealth (γ_h)	0.05
Marginal consumer budget shares (α_i^{Dem})	
Sector 1	0.388
Sector 2	0.016
Sector 3	0.596
Enterprise investment parameters (h_i)	
Sectors 1–3	0.05
Household investment parameters	
Interest rate (h_h)	10.0
Income (g_h)	0.02
Export elasticity (η)	1.5
Sectoral composition of depreciation (ρ_i)	
Nontraded good	0.538
Composite	0.462

in (105) and state enterprises benefit from a government subsidy *SUB* in (107).

Savings flows by firms after dividend payouts (rates d_i) and direct taxes (rates t_i^{Dir}) appear in (107) through (110). Household saving is given in (113), from income Y_h and consumption spending D. The marginal propensity to consume from income is $(1 - s)$, and from wealth γ_h. Direct taxes (rate t_h^{Dir}), transfers, and interest payments also enter the accounting. Government income and saving are set out in (114) and (115). The current-account deficit appears in (116)—it is in foreign terms (converted at the official exchange rate) since an export tax at rate t_2^{Exp} is included.

Final demand equations appear in section X. Consumer demands for the three sectors follow a linear expenditure system in (117) through (120). In (121) through (123) investment demands by firms depend positively on profit rates r_i and negatively on the loan interest rate i_L. Household investment in (124) is a function of the interest rate and household real income. In (126) exports respond to the ratio between the price of foreign similars and Thai border prices with an elasticity η.

Material balance equations are set out in section XI. Sectors one, three, and four (the composite) sell to intermediate uses, private consumption and government; one and four also satisfy net investment and depreciation on existing capital stock. Sector two supplies only an intermediate to sector four, and exports.

The material balances (127) through (130) complete the accounting for the system. Overall macroeconomic equilibrium requires that saving equal the value of investment, but like the central bank's balance sheet this condition is not an independent restriction on the system. Hence a residual check on the difference between saving and investment is included as equation (131).

11.4 Calibration of the Model

Following the usual practice, the 1980 SAM is taken as a base-year solution of the model, and its parameters are chosen so that solving the equation set with exogenous variables at 1980 levels replicates the SAM. This sort of calibration boils down to setting key "slope" coefficients such as elasticities of substitution or income elasticities of demand, and using marginal conditions and accounting identities to compute intercepts, distribution parameters in the CES, and so on.

Table 11.3 gives the main parameters for the model. One sees first that elasticities of substitution among components of the portfolios of households and firms (σ_h and $\sigma_1 - \sigma_3$) were set to 1.4—the number is not supported econometrically but generates plausible "offset coefficients" in portfolio shifts, as discussed below. The firms' equity response coefficients (β_i) take a value of 0.2, consistent with Thai historical data. As noted above, the corresponding intercepts (α_i) are negative, so issue of new equity is an elastic function of firms' deficits in equations (16) through (18).

The government's statutory liquidity ratio or marginal "credit requirement" against commercial bank deposits (β_g^5) takes the value 0.25, consistent with recent history. The central bank's marginal reserve requirement (μ_2) is 0.035. Elasticities of commercial banks' loan supply with respect to interest rates are 0.2. The intercept α_5 in the loan supply function takes the value 1.551, reflecting the fact that Thai banks borrow heavily abroad to generate resources to lend at home. (Recall that the loan supply function is based on domestic resources alone.)

The supply parameters take values consistent with Thai data and stylized facts. The elasticity of substitution between traded goods and imports in generating the composite (σ_4^{Fin}) is set at 0.25, so the two types of goods are close to being complementary. Tax and tariff rates are computed from 1980 flow data. The same is true of the household shares in profit incomes (υ_i). The value 1.143 for υ_i is consistent with the SAM—firms in the nontraded sector make money from interest, not profits.

The marginal propensities to consume from income and wealth are consistent with historical data. The marginal budget shares in the linear expenditure system (α_i^{Dem}) correspond to income elasticities of 0.926 for nontraded goods, 1.20 for state enterprise products, and 0.953 for the composite. Investment parameters show modest responsiveness to profits, and the export elasticity of 1.5 is plausible for the medium term.

11.5 Solutions to the Model

We used the model in comparative static fashion to explore how the economy might respond to fiscal and monetary initiatives, and devaluation. A summary of the results from eight runs appears in table 11.4, with the base run in column 1.[9]

In solution 2 real public consumption is increased by 5 percent, or 4.101 billion baht. In nominal terms government saving declines from 4.423 to 1.156. Unsurprisingly, the effect is expansionary. Real GDP rises by 6.721, to give a multiplier of 1.53. Price indexes rise by about 0.5 percent and (with a nominal peg) the real exchange rate appreciates. As a consequence real exports fall by 0.6 from their initial level of 164.346.

Table 11.4
Variant solutions to the Thailand model (flow values in billions of 1980 baht)

		1	2	3	4	5	6	7	8
		Base run	Raise real government consump-tion by 0.05	Reduce rediscount by 0.50	Raise minimum reserves ratio by 0.01	Raise government loan ratio by 0.02	Runs 2 and 5 combined	Devaluation of baht by 0.10	Run 7 with low export elasticity
1	Nominal GDP	684.927	694.433	676.002	682.995	681.324	690.822	719.775	697.212
2	Real GDP	684.927	691.198	678.617	683.564	682.385	688.667	707.275	691.325
3	GDP deflator	1.0	1.0047	0.9961	0.9992	0.9984	1.0031	1.0177	1.0085
4	Consumer price index	1.0	1.0028	0.9970	0.9994	0.9988	1.0016	1.0393	1.0325
5	Nominal exchange rate	20.63	20.63	20.63	20.63	20.63	20.63	22.69	22.69
6	Real exchange rate	20.63	20.53	20.71	20.65	20.66	20.57	22.30	22.50
7	Equity price index	1.0	1.0138	0.9911	0.9981	0.9973	1.0112	1.0419	0.9994
8	Loan interest rate	0.1500	0.1489	0.1709	0.1544	0.1588	0.1576	0.1479	0.1506
9	Average profit rate	0.1273	0.1295	0.1243	0.1266	0.1261	0.1283	0.1332	0.1260
Sources of saving									
10	Nontraded sector firms	5.834	5.671	8.044	6.314	7.040	6.876	5.642	6.033
11	Traded sector firms	5.742	5.847	5.630	5.718	5.697	5.802	6.457	6.002
12	State enterprises	2.598	3.032	2.562	2.590	2.583	3.017	2.663	2.577
13	Households	74.433	75.706	72.555	74.026	73.678	74.950	79.096	75.708
14	Government	4.423	1.156	4.048	4.346	3.919	0.655	7.327	4.932
15	Rest of world	44.587	47.144	41.830	43.991	43.478	46.036	42.140	45.870
16	Nominal net investment	137.617	138.556	134.669	136.985	136.395	137.336	143.325	141.122

Table 11.4 (continued)

	1 Base run	2 Raise real government consump-tion by 0.05	3 Reduce rediscount by 0.50	4 Raise minimum reserves ratio by 0.01	5 Raise government loan ratio by 0.02	6 Runs 2 and 5 combined	7 Devaluation of baht by 0.10	8 Run 7 with low export elasticity
17 Real net investment	137.617	138.160	135.128	137.088	136.587	137.134	138.477	137.313
18 Real exports	164.346	163.746	164.948	164.475	164.588	163.986	181.141	173.546
19 Real imports	204.591	206.943	202.038	204.038	203.564	205.917	204.543	199.388
20 Interest payments	17.122	16.917	21.618	18.098	19.604	19.395	16.996	17.494
21 Government receipts	103.518	105.342	104.027	103.629	103.987	105.806	109.194	106.331
22 Government current outlays	99.095	104.186	99.979	99.283	100.068	105.151	101.867	101.399
Central bank's balance sheet								
23 Loans to government	41.884	45.006	42.242	41.757	38.613	41.718	38.432	41.046
24 Loans to commercial banks	16.537	16.537	8.269	16.537	16.537	16.537	16.537	16.537
25 Foreign reserves	52.256	49.242	59.906	54.069	55.376	52.480	56.232	53.175
26 Currency	47.387	47.564	47.263	47.360	47.349	47.527	48.079	47.613
27 Commercial bank reserves	5.905	5.932	5.876	7.920	5.895	5.922	6.009	5.939
28 Net worth	57.282	57.282	57.282	57.282	57.282	57.282	57.282	57.282
29 Total assets	110.577	110.785	110.417	112.363	110.526	110.735	111.301	110.758
Commercial banks' balance sheet								
30 Loans to government	53.648	53.823	53.525	53.621	57.366	57.557	54.334	53.873
31 Reserves at central bank	5.905	5.932	5.876	7.920	5.895	5.922	6.009	5.939

32	Loans to enterprises	225.438	225.893	217.682	223.715	221.954	222.407	227.841	226.610
33	Deposits	187.933	188.636	187.442	187.826	187.784	188.488	190.677	188.832
34	Loans from central bank	16.537	16.537	8.269	16.537	16.537	16.537	16.537	16.537
35	Loans from abroad	18.667	18.623	19.519	19.039	19.040	19.008	19.117	19.198
36	Net worth	61.853	61.853	61.853	61.853	61.853	61.853	61.853	61.853
37	Total assets	284.991	285.648	277.083	285.256	285.215	285.886	288.184	286.422
Loans from abroad									
38	Loans to firms	125.723	125.410	129.864	126.668	127.461	127.156	126.297	126.789
39	Loans to government	30.265	30.265	30.265	30.265	30.265	30.265	30.970	30.970
40	Loans to commercial banks	18.667	18.623	19.519	19.039	19.040	19.008	19.117	19.198
41	Total loans	174.655	174.298	179.648	175.972	176.766	176.429	176.384	176.957

All these responses are to be expected in an expanding economy. The financial linkages are more interesting. Nominal household net worth as defined in equation (1) rises with augmented savings flows and capital gains from higher commodity and share prices. Deposits go up, the banks' loan supply schedule shifts outward, and the interest rate falls eleven basis points from its initial value of 0.15. Profit rates rise with higher output; together with the lower interest rate they stimulate investment by 0.54, adding to the expansion. In run 2 increased government spending accommodated by the central bank crowds investment in, not out.

The government principally finances its increased spending by borrowing 3.122 from the Bank of Thailand (the goverment loan ratio from the commercial banks β_g^5 is not altered). At the same time, imports rise by 2.352 in real terms, and firms reduce their borrowing abroad as the internal interest rate falls. These current and capital account changes cause the Bank of Thailand to lose 2.914 in reserves. If the government finances a fiscal expansion by borrowing from the central bank, the ultimate outcome in the open Thai economy is an almost equal reserve loss.

Table 11.5 shows changes in assets of the banks and the rest of the world in more detail. In the terminology of Kouri and Porter (1974) the reserve loss "offset coefficient" to the government's extra borrowing from the central bank is 2.914/3.122 = 0.93. We will see below that capital flow offsets to other monetary interventions are substantially lower. The reserve loss with central bank-financed expansion is high because the Thai economy's marginal propensity to import (with respect to real GDP) takes the relatively large value of 0.375.

Runs 3 through 5 show the effects of different kinds of restrictive monetary policy. In run 3 central bank advances to the commercial banks are cut in half, from 16.537 to 8.269. The banks' loan supply schedule shifts inward, and the interest rate rises to a new equilibrium value of 0.1709. Real private investment contracts by 2.479, and real GDP by 6.21 (an investment multiplier of 2.505).

With higher interest payments, saving by nontraded sector firms rises 2.21; the increase is more than offset by a reduction of 2.757 in the current account deficit. Price indexes fall by about 0.5 percent as the economy contracts.

In run 3 the central bank loses 8.269 in assets when the volume of "rediscount" is reduced. It gains 7.75 in reserves. Part of the gain comes from a lower current-account gap; the bulk comes from capital inflows of 4.993. Firms add 4.141 to their foreign borrowing as the domestic loan rate rises, and banks go abroad for 0.852 to compensate for a reduction in

Table 11.5
Changes in assets of banks and the rest of the world (billion of 1980 baht)

	Bank of Thailand				Commercial banks				Rest of the world			
Number of runs	Loans to govern-ment	Redis-count	Inter-national Reserves	Total	Loans to govern-ment	Reserves at Bank of Thailand	Loans to firms	Total	Loans to govern-ment	Loans to firms	Loans to banks	Total
2. Government's real consumption increased 5 percent	3.122		−2.914	0.208	0.175	0.027	0.455	0.657		−0.313	−0.044	−0.357
3. Rediscount	0.358	−8.269	7.750	−0.161	−0.123	−0.029	−7.756	−7.908		4.414	0.852	4.993
4. Bank reserve ratio increased by 0.01	−0.127		1.913	1.786	−0.027	2.015	−1.723	0.265		0.945	0.372	1.317
5. Government's loan ratio increased by 0.02	−3.271		3.220	−0.051	3.718	−0.010	−3.484	0.224		1.738	0.373	2.111
6. Runs 2 and 5												
A. As in table 11.4	−0.166		0.324	0.158	3.909	0.017	−3.031	0.895		1.433	0.341	1.774
B. With σ_i set to 1.2	−0.167		0.308	0.141	3.895	0.014	−2.733	1.176		0.866	0.672	1.538
C. With σ_i set to 1.6	−0.166		0.336	0.170	3.918	0.019	−3.257	0.680		1.863	0.088	1.951
D. With δ_5 set to 0.1	−0.122		0.263	0.141	3.894	0.014	−3.876	0.032		1.885	−0.047	1.415
7. Devaluation by 10 percent	−3.452		4.176	0.724	0.686	0.104	2.403	3.193	0.705	0.574	0.45	1.729
8. Devaluation by 10 percent with export elasticity of 0.75	−0.838		1.019	0.181	0.225	0.034	1.172	1.413	0.705	1.066	0.531	2.302

deposits. The capital flow offset coefficient to the reduction in rediscount is 4.993/8.269 = 0.604. Thai monetary authorities in their open economy have some room for independent policy action, but capital flows in the case of rediscount reduction undo about 60 percent of what they try to achieve.

Similar outcomes occur when the marginal reserve requirement for commercial bank deposits (μ_2) is increased by 0.01 in run 4, and the "statutory liquidity ratio" (β_g^5) by 0.02 in run 5. In the former case a reserve increase of 2.015 is offset by 1.317 in capital inflows; in the latter, an additional 3.718 in bank lending to the government draws in 2.111 of foreign loans. In both cases firms account for three-quarters of the new borrowing, the domestic interest rate rises, and investment is crowded out.

Recall from solution 2 that an expansion of public consumption initially financed by borrowing from the central bank is strongly expansionary; indeed, private investment is crowded in. Run 6 shows what happens when government spending is financed principally by borrowing from commercial banks (the increase in β_g^5 is the same as in run 5). Bank loans to the government rise by 3.909, and are partially financed by 1.774 in new capital inflows. The offset is not sufficient to undo all the credit contraction to domestic firms, and the interest rate rises to 0.1576. Real investment falls by 0.483, or 12 percent of the increase in real public consumption. The conclusion is that there will be modest crowding-out of private capital formation if the government taps the banks to finance a fiscal expansion. However, capital inflows hold the investment loss to a fairly small value.

All these results are of course contingent on the parameter values assumed in table 11.3. Table 11.5 shows three variations around run 6. In 6B firms' borrowing patterns are made less responsive to interest rate changes—the elasticities of substitution σ_i are reduced from 1.4 to 1.2. The capital offset coefficient to new government borrowing from commercial bank falls from 0.454 to 0.395, and the domestic interest rate rises 13 basis points in comparison to run 6A. Private investment falls by 0.638, or 15.5 percent of the increase in real public consumption.

In run 6C the σ_i are raised to 1.6, and the foreign offset coefficient likewise rises to 0.498. The domestic interest rate falls 9 basis points between runs and the investment reduction is only 9 percent of extra government spending. Finally, in run 6D the commercial banks' loan supply elasticity δ_5 in equation (49) is reduced from 0.2 to 0.1. The interest rate becomes 0.1599, and real investment falls by 0.751, or 18 percent of the public spending increase. The foreign capital offset coefficient falls to 0.363 as banks cut back domestic lending enough to lead to a decline in their foreign exposure.

The directions of change in this set of runs are mutually consistent, and magnitudes are easy to understand in terms of shifts in elasticities. The conclusion is that in an economy open to capital flows, monetary innovations are partly offset by foreign borrowing, and effects on investment demand are correspondingly moderated.

Runs 7 and 8 show the effects of a 10 percent nominal devaluation of the baht, with the export elasticity η set to values of 1.5 and 0.75, respectively. The results reported in tables 11.4 and 11.5 do not take into account capital losses on Thailand's foreign liabilities from exchange depreciation. That is, foreign base period liabilities $FLN_h(t-1)$, $FLN_g(t-1)$, etc., and central bank reserves $BTNIR(t-1)$ are held constant in baht terms after devaluation by unspecified central bank interventions. Flow foreign borrowing by the government, $e(\Delta FLN_g^{\$})$ is assumed to rise with e.

In run 7 the real devaluation after domestic price increases is 8.1 percent. Real exports rise by 10.2 percent and real GDP by 3.3 percent—the effect is strongly expansionary. As in run 2 higher household net worth provides more deposits to banks, loan supply increases, and the interest rate falls. The resulting increase in investment adds to the expansion.

Despite higher aggregate demand, substitution against imports because of the devaluation is strong enough to hold their real level nearly constant. Increased exports lead foreign saving to fall by 2.447 in baht terms. Firms and banks borrow more abroad, so Bank of Thailand reserves rise by 4.176.

In run 8 exports rise by 5.6 percent and real GDP by 0.09 percent—devaluation is close to being contractionary when the export response is weak. The trade deficit declines in real terms, but the current-account gap widens by 1.283 in baht. The price of capital goods rises with devaluation and puts enough pressure on loan markets to cause the interest rate to rise to 0.1506 (as opposed to falling to 0.1479 in run 7). Feedbacks through investment demand are expansionary in run 7 and contractionary in run 8.

A next step is to bring in capital losses on foreign loans. In equations (19) through (21), the terms $FLN_i(t-1)$ become $eFLN_i^{\$}(t-1)$, and an increase in e causes initial dollar liabilities $FLN_i^{\$}(t-1)$ to rise in terms of baht. Pressure is placed on loan markets, with the following results:

	Real GDP	Loan interest rate	Real investment
Run 7			
No capital loss	707.275	0.1479	138.477
With capital loss	705.178	0.1533	137.810
Run 8			
No capital loss	691.325	0.1506	137.313
With capital loss	688.989	0.1561	136.622

Unless countered by central bank intervention, capital losses on foreign liabilities after devaluation can crowd out domestic capital formation and cancel expansionary export and import changes.

11.6 Conclusions

Further runs could be described, for example, a set performed that shows that the "automatic" policy responses in equation (53) with θ_4 and γ_4 nonzero go in the expected directions. However, we have already discussed enough variations to show that the model behaves "sensibly" and can help quantify how the economy might respond to monetary, and fiscal policy, and exchange rate interventions. Such calculations are the practical justifications for computable models. Our results show that general equilibrium systems can be extended successfully to deal with fiscal and monetary questions. Particularly with the spread of microcomputers around the world (the present model could easily be solved on such a machine), real-financial general equilibrium models should become a standard tool for policy analysis in developing economies. This conclusion is especially strong for the majority of poor countries in which lack of time series data precludes econometric approaches to the issues discussed here.

Notes

Research supported by the World Bank, which is not responsible for the views expressed here. We are grateful to Wafik Grais for advice and collaboration on all phases of the research.

1. On computable models for developing countries, see Davis, deMelo, and Robinson (1982), Bell and Srinivasan (1984), and Taylor, Sarkar and Rattsø (1984); on those for developed countries, see Shoven and Whalley (1984). Tobin and associates have a long-running project for constructing an econometrically based real and financial model of the U.S. economy. Aside from that and several models for developing countries which do flow-of-funds calculations posterior to the real solution, there seem to be few examples in the literature of computable models that integrate markets for goods and assets. Feltenstein (1980) and Slemrod (1983) are isolated exceptions.

2. In taking the basic data for the SAM over from Chaipravat and Ganjarerndee (1983), we made simple scaling adjustments to eliminate inconsistent accounting in the interindustry balances and flow of funds. Initial asset holdings were inferred from capital-output ratios and similar parameters. One dollar sold for 20.63 baht in 1980.

3. For detail on how the national accounts/interindustry portion of the social accounting matrix is set up, see Taylor (1983).

4. Since households only hold assets in the portfolio data, why they pay interest is not clear. The problem stems from the fact that the SAM records their *net* position vis-à-vis the banks—in practice households both make deposits and take interest-bearing loans. Fuller accounting (as in official Thai flow of funds accounts) reveals this fact.

5. On different aspects of model closure, see Sen (1963), Tobin (1982), Taylor (1983), and Marglin (1984).

6. These rates of return can in turn be linked to expected asset prices—again see Tobin (1982)—but we drop this extension for simplicity.

7. In passing, we should mention that initially we did try to impose (57) with $NWRES = 0$ as an independent relationship. The model's equation set would reproduce the original SAM, but would not converge back to the original solution when perturbed. What else can you expect from an overdetermined system?

8. For a review, see Taylor (1979), app. D.

9. The model was solved using the Newton nonlinear equation routine in the TROLL simulation package at MIT. New solutions in response to the perturbations described here were found after a dozen iterations or so.

References

Armington, Paul S. 1969. "A Theory of Demand for Products Distinguished by Place of Production." *IMF Staff Papers* 16: 159–78.

Bell, Clive, and Srinivasan, T. N. 1984. "On the Uses and Abuses of Economywide Models in Development Policy Analysis." In M. Syrquin, L. Taylor, L. Westphal (eds.), *Economic Structure and Performance: Essays in Honor of Hollis B. Chenery*. New York: Academic Press.

Chaipravat, Olarn, and Siri Ganjarernjee. 1983. "A Manual for Financial Data Compilation in the Social Account Matrices III of Thailand." Bangkok: Siam Commercial Bank and Bank of Thailand. Mimeo.

Cole, David, Supote Chunanuntathum, and Chesada Loohawenchit. 1984. "Modelling of Finanical Markets in Thailand in an Asset-Demand and Institutional Framework." Paper presented at the 14th Pacific Trade and Development Conference. National University of Singapore.

Dervis, Kemal, Jaime deMelo, and Sherman Robinson. 1982. *General Equilibrium Models for Development Policy*. Cambridge: Cambridge University Press.

Feltenstein, Andrew. 1980. "A General Equilibrium Approach to the Analysis of Trade Restrictions with an Application to Argentina." *IMF Staff Papers* 27: 749–784.

Grais, Wafik M. 1983. "Coping with a Drop of Energy Prices: Macroeconomic and Income Distribution Effects in Thailand." Paper presented at a Conference on the

SIAM Project on Macroeconomic Management of the Thai Economy. Pattaya City, Thailand.

Kouri, Pentti J. K., and Michael G. Porter. 1974. "International Capital Flows and Portfolio Equilibrium." *Journal of Political Economy* 82: 443–467.

Marglin, Stephen A. 1984. *Growth, Distribution and Prices.* Cambridge: Harvard University Press.

Sen, Amartya K. 1963. "Neo-Classical and Non-Keynesian Theories of Distribution." *Economic Record* 39: 54–64.

Shoven, John B., and John Whalley. 1984. "Applied General Equilibrium Models of Taxation and International Trade." *Journal of Economic Literature* 22: 1007–51.

Slemrod, Joel. 1983. "A General Equilibrium Model of Taxation with Endogenous Financial Behavior." In M. Feldstein (ed.), *Behavioral Simulation Methods in Tax Policy Analysis.* Chicago: University of Chicago Press.

Taylor, Lance. 1979. *Macro Models for Developing Countries.* New York: McGraw-Hill.

Taylor, Lance 1983. *Structuralist Macroeconomics: Applicable Models for the Third World.* New York: Basic Books.

Taylor, Lance, Hiren Sarkar, and Jørn Rattsø. 1984. "Macroeconomic Adjustment in a Computable General Equilibrium Model for India." In M. Syrquin, L. Taylor, and L. Westphal (eds.), *Economic Structure and Performance: Essays in Honor of Hollis B. Chenery.* New York: Academic Press.

Tobin, James. 1982. "Money and Finance in the Macroeconomic Process." *Journal of Money, Credit and Banking* 14: 171–204.

World Bank. 1982. "Thailand: Perspectives for Financial Reform." Report No. 4085-TH. Projects Dept., East Asia and Pacific Regional Office.

12 Medium-Term Growth Projections for Kuwait from a Dynamic CGE

Motaz Khorshid

At the beginning of the 1980s, the Kuwaiti economy was suffering from several structural imbalances, particularly, (1) an undiversified productive base and limited absorptive capacity of the domestic market; (2) a heavy reliance on the outside world, especially regarding oil revenues, investment income, imports, and foreign labor; and (3) distortion in the population structure and low productivity of national labor.

These imbalances were aggravated by new unfavorable internal and external conditions that may lead to further structural distortions and a decline in the tempo of growth unless appropriate policy measures are undertaken. The drop in oil prices, the "Al-Manakh" financial crisis and the Gulf War are examples of such conditions.

Against this background the government of Kuwait formulated and implemented a five-year development plan for the period 1985–86 to 1989–90 in recognition of the need to reevaluate its development strategy. In 1989 the Kuwaiti government will begin preparing the next five-year plan. Given the present problems facing the Kuwaiti economy, the new development plan will probably sustain the same long-term goals and directions with some adjustments and fine tuning. These objectives include (1) improving the productivity of Kuwaitis and their participation in economic activities, and achieving a more balanced population structure and labor force profile; (2) restructuring the economy by diversifying the productive base and raising the level of satisfaction of domestic demand through domestic production, particularly, in sectors of strategic importance; and (3) maintaining the present level of social welfare for Kuwaiti citizens in the future and taking the necessary measures for preserving national security and independent decision making.

The purpose of this paper is twofold: first, to outline the economic rationale and structure of an aggregate oil-non-oil general equilibrium model for the Kuwaiti economy, and, second, to use the model in evaluating the medium-term performance of the economy under different development scenarios and policies. The model captures the major structural features of the Kuwaiti economy and can address a set of policy issues such as

- the medium-term effects of probable scenarios on oil production and prices,
- the impact of different investment levels on sectoral growth and external balance,
- the outcome of specific fiscal and public expenditure policies,
- the effect of increasing the productivity and participation ratio of the Kuwaiti population,
- the sensitivity of macroeconomic performace to variations in external conditions.

12.1 Model Structure and Rationale

A dynamic computable general equilibrium (CGE) model is determined by three factors: (1) the independent decisions of the agents intervening in the economy; (2) the rules that ensure the consistency of all such decisions; and (3) the interperiod variations that drive the model dynamically. The first two factors are required to obtain a within-period general equilibrium solution, whereas the last factor ensures the dynamic behavior of the model. The data base of the model is an aggregate social accounting matrix (SAM) for the year 1983, developed in a joint project undertaken by the Kuwait Institute for Scientific Research (KISR) and the Ministry of Planning (Khorshid et al. 1988; Khorshid and Al-Sabah 1987).

The within-period model is derived by a set of exogenous variables coupled with various behavioral assumptions that reflect the major linkages within the economy and its mode of functioning. Assumptions of the model include the following: (1) The labor markets consist of government and nongovernment labor, each divided into Kuwaitis and expatriates. In these markets all prices are exogenous, and demands for non-Kuwaiti labor clear the markets. Markets for capital services are only modeled for the non-oil sector. Given exogenous oil production, capital income is computed as a residual after excluding other input. (2) In product markets, production of the non-oil sector is demand determined, and crude oil production is supply driven. In the oil sector supply is fixed, and exports clear the market. (3) On the macroeconomic level the model is investment driven. Here investment expenditure is exogenous, households and companies savings are determined as a fixed share of their nominal income, and government savings are estimated as the difference between income and current expenditure. The difference between domestic savings and investment is channelled to the rest of the world in the form of net capital outflows (foreign savings).

The mechanisms and behavioral rules of the Kuwaiti model can be explained by four major modules: income generation and demand for factors of production, income distribution, foreign trade, and price relations.

In figure 12.1 gross output of the oil sector is exogenously determined. Output of the non-oil sector is determined by the level of demand for goods and services. Given the production function of each sector, labor demand is estimated. In the oil sector a Leontief production function is used. Given the particular nature of the sector, the gross operating surplus is computed as a residual after considering demand for labor and for intermediate input. In the non-oil sector a two-level production function is adopted. The first divides gross output between value added and intermediate input, using Leontief technology. The second allocates the value added between labor and capital, using a constant elasticity of substitution (CES) function. Given the exogenous government wage bill, demand for labor in both government and non-government sectors can be estimated. The demand for labor is later divided between Kuwaitis and non-Kuwaitis by planning the supply of Kuwaiti labor (in government and nongovernment sectors) as an exogenous variable in the within period model.

Figure 12.2 shows distribution of national income to domestic institutions. The national wage bill is allocated to households (both Kuwaitis and non-Kuwaitis). Operating surplus of the oil sector is directed to government. The operating surplus generated in the non-oil sector is distributed to three institutions according to the pattern of ownership of the productive assets. Similarly, Kuwaiti and non-Kuwaiti households and companies are assumed to allocate their total receipts on different outlays as a fixed share of nominal income. After netting current transfers between institutions, they are left with disposable income that is allocated between final consumption and domestic savings. Government transfers and final consumption are exogenous. However, public final consumption, including the government wage bill, is fixed in real terms to permit analysis of the price effects. Kuwaiti and non-Kuwaiti private consumption is estimated as a function of their income that, in turn, depends on wage income, operating surplus of unincorporated business and other transfers.

Figure 12.3 sets out the linkages between the Kuwaiti economy and the outside world. It computes exports of domestic origin, reexports, imports, and the balance of trade. In the oil sector, given exogenous output and

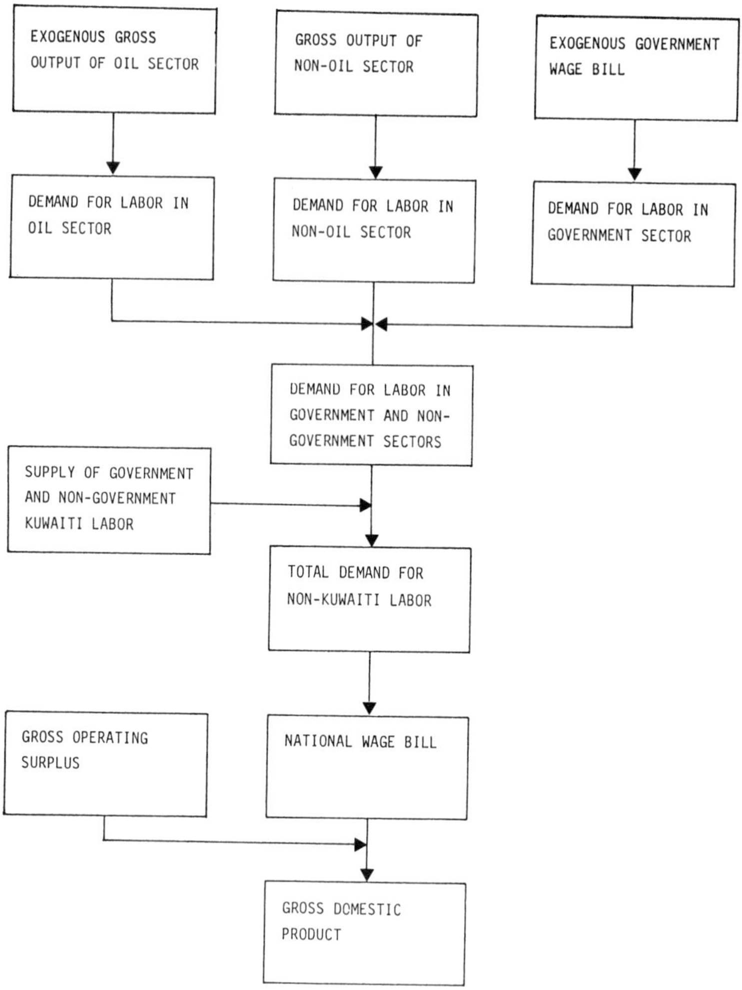

Figure 12.1
Income generation and factor income

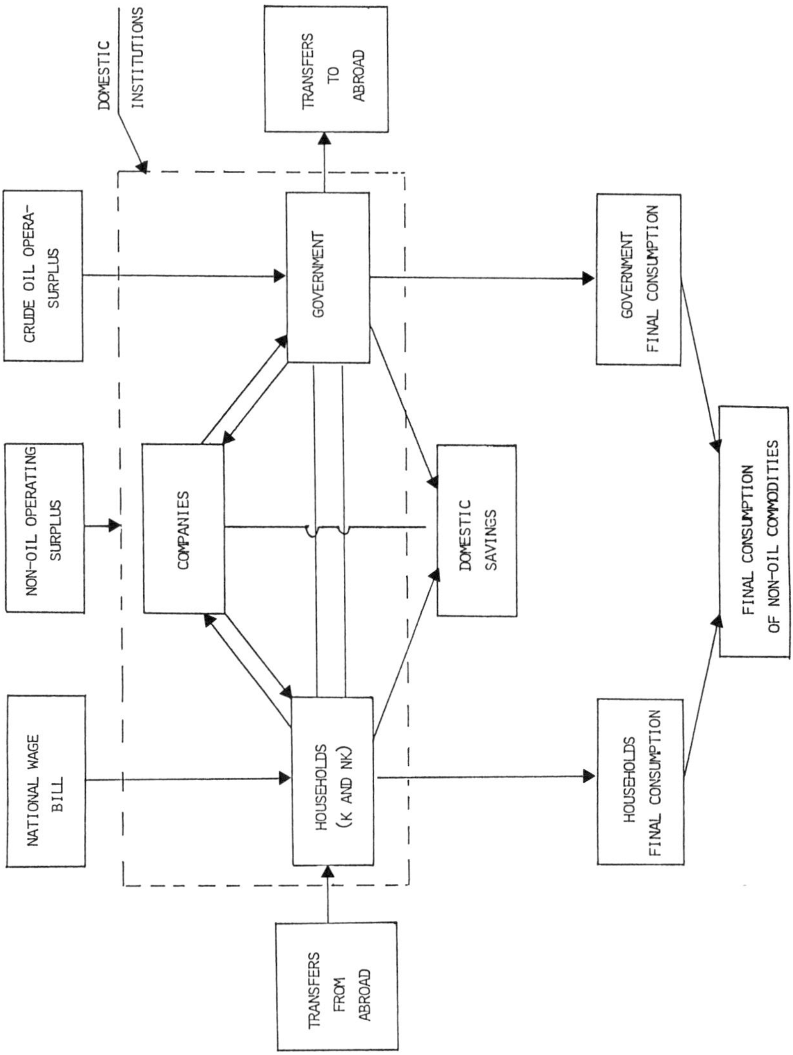

Figure 12.2
Income distribution module

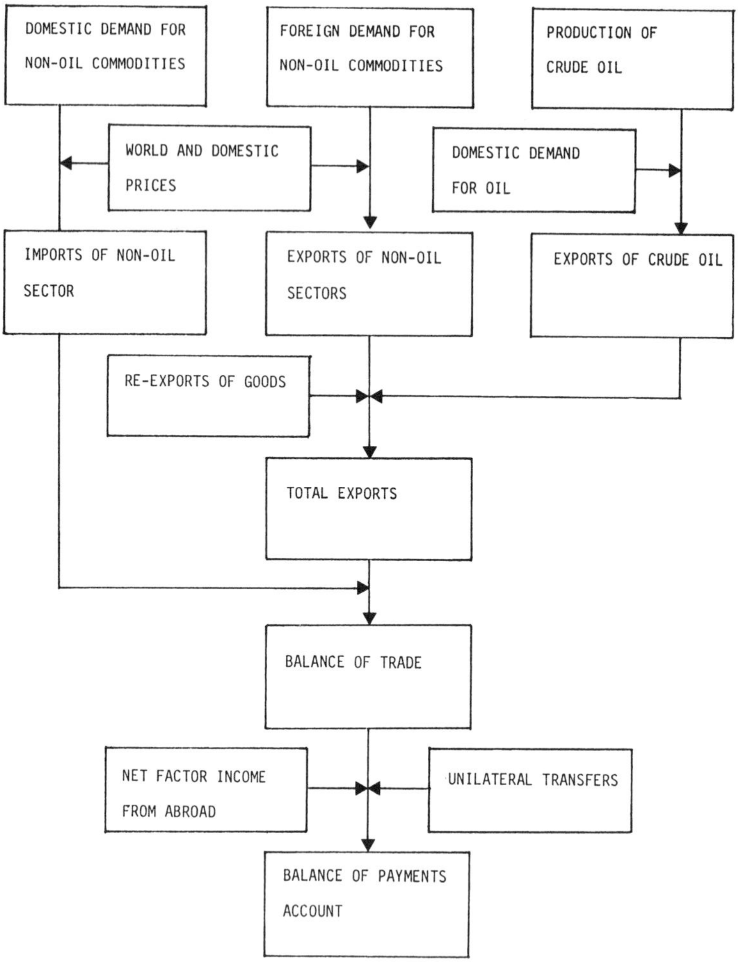

Figure 12.3
Foreign trade relations

domestic demand for crude oil, exports are estimated as a residual. In the case of the non-oil sector, imports, exports, and production for domestic use are determined by combined constant elasticity of substitution (CES) and constant elasticity of tranformation (CET) functions. First, composite demand for non-oil commodities is determined. It consists of final consumption, intermediate demand and investment expenditure. The demand for composite non-oil commodities is then separated into domestically produced and imported goods using a cost minimization function subjected to a CES constraint. Similarly gross output of the sector is distributed to domestic markets and exports using profit maximization subjected to a CET function. The results of this process are imports, exports and production for domestic use in the non-oil sector. Demand for reexports is estimated as a function of world prices in domestic currency, supply price of reexports, and elasticity of trade.

The block diagram in figure 12.4 shows the price relations of the non-oil sector. The price of unit value added is determined as a function of the rate of return on capital and the average wage rate of the sector. Price of composite goods is estimated using prices of the domestic and imported commodities. Given prices of composite goods and unit value added, output price of non-oil commodities can be determined. This price is evaluated at cost of production. When we add to it taxes and subtract subsidies, we obtain producer price of non-oil output. Again, when adding trade and transportation margins, purchaser price of non-oil commodities is determined. Similarly landed prices of non-oil imports is determined as the sum of world prices in local currency plus import duties. When trade and transportation margins are added, we get purchaser price of imported goods and services.

The intertemporal model comprises interperiod relations. The Kuwaiti interperiod model is used to update the capital stock of the non-oil sector, population size, and government general reserves and future generation funds from one period to another. The capital stock in the non-oil sector is updated using the capital stock of the previous period, investment expenditure, and the depreciation rate. In figure 12.5 the population size of Kuwaitis is adjusted between periods assuming a fixed annual growth rate. The interperiod growth of the non-Kuwaiti population is estimated by the model as a function of the percentage changes in demand for non-Kuwaitis and their participation rate. Figure 12.6 shows rules for updating state assets: the "future generation" and "general reserve" funds. Accumulation in the future generation fund is determined by adding 10 percent of government revenues plus the interest received on its investments abroad.

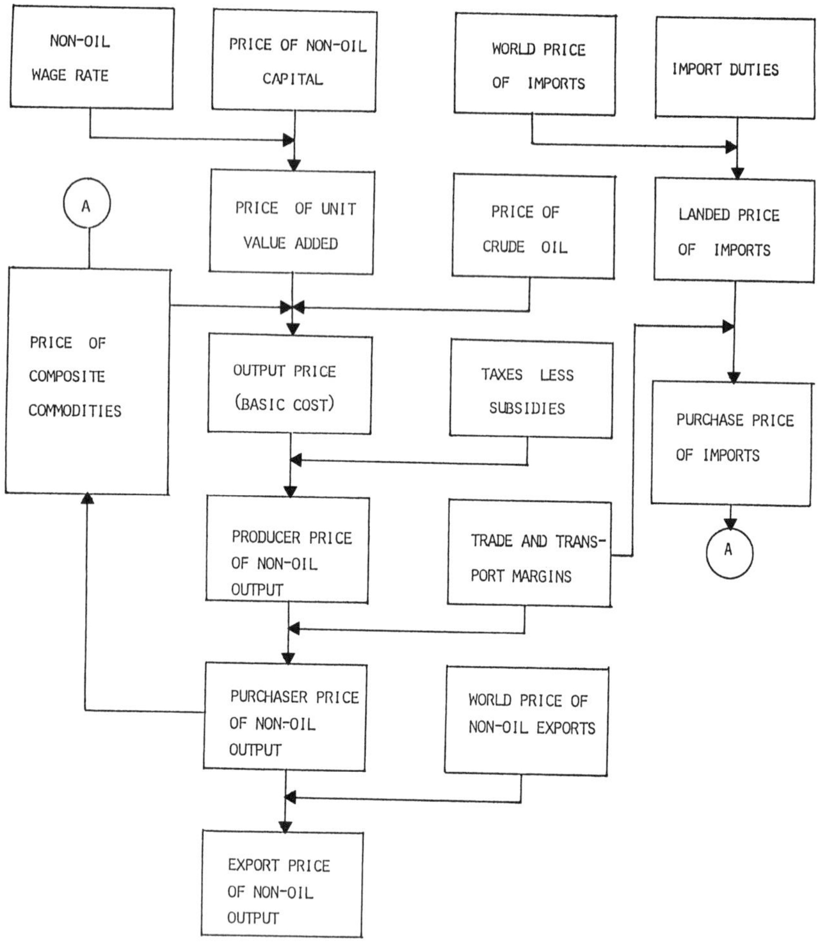

Figure 12.4
Price relations of non-oil sector

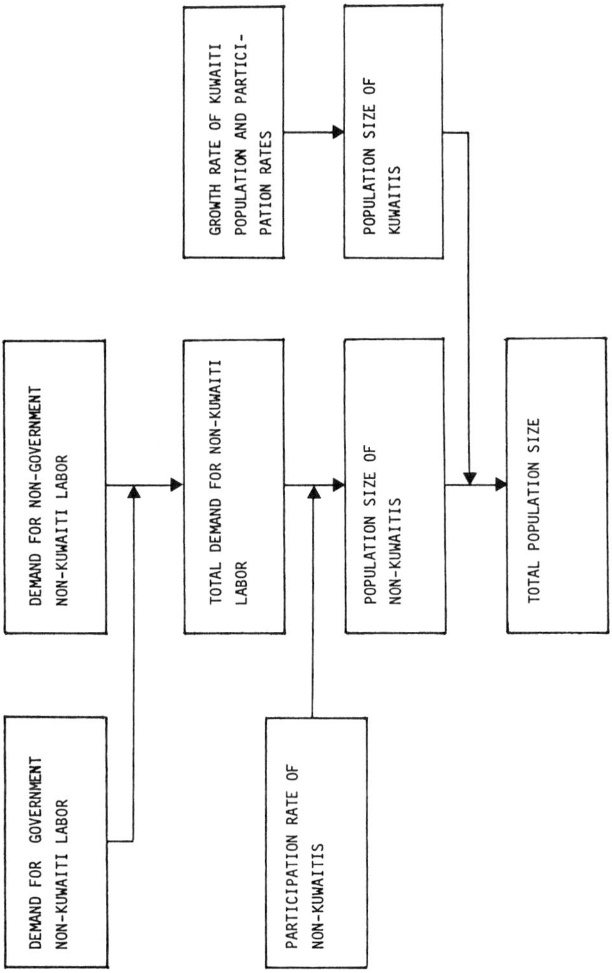

Figure 12.5
The interperiod model for updating population structure

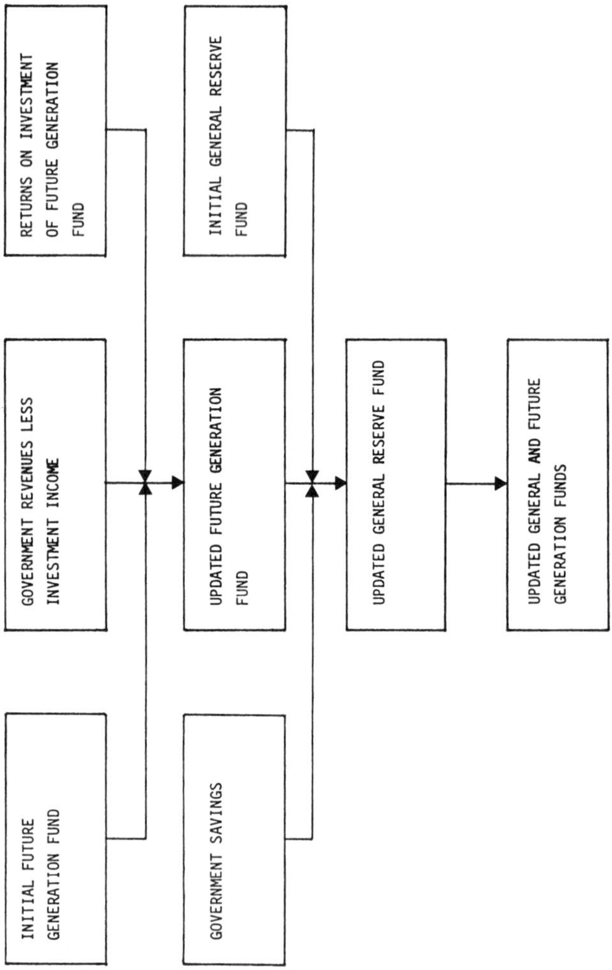

Figure 12.6
The interperiod model for updating government funds

By subtracting the change in the future generation fund and government investment expenditure from government savings, we obtain the incremental change in the general reserve fund. When adding the incremental changes in these funds to their initial values, we get an estimate of the overall assets held abroad by the Kuwaiti government.

12.2 The Medium-Term Path of the Economy

The CGE model was used to estimate the "reference path" of the economy during the period 1986–95. The purpose is to generate the most probable future changes in the development path of the economy assuming the continuation of the same policy instruments applied during the first part of the 1980s. This reference path forms the basis for comparing different scenarios and policy measures and is intended to show the implications of continuing the current path on growth and welfare targets.

Assumptions of the Reference Path

Following the considerable drop in oil prices in 1986, they increased by 35 percent in 1987 and then decreased by 12 percent in 1988. After 1988 prices are assumed to increase by about 3.7 percent a year on average. Similarly, the base case assumes that crude oil production will grow by 5 percent in 1990–93 and then by zero percent till 1995. Following the probable development in the international financial markets, investment income from abroad is expected to grow by 3 to 5 percent a year. Gross fixed capital formation in real terms is also assumed to grow by 3 percent a year, which is a relatively low percentage compared wth the 1970s. However, government revenues and savings have fallen since the beginning of the 1980s. The government wage bill in real terms is assumed to grow between 2 to 3.5 percent, and the supply of Kuwaiti government labor is also assumed to grow by 3 to 3.5 percent. This increase reflects the continuation of government policy to absorb most Kuwaiti graduates and to substitute foreign labor by national labor. The Kuwaiti labor supply in the private sector will also grow by 1 percent until 1990 and then by 2 percent until 1995. This low growth rate is explained by the tendency of managers in the private sector to engage non-Kuwaiti labor due to their lower wages and higher productivity. However, the base scenario assumes that the 1990s will witness an increase in the rate of growth from 1 to 2 percent to reflect government efforts to encourage the increase in participation of Kuwaiti labor in nongovernment activities. Government purchase of goods and services is assumed to increase by 3.5 percent a year to be consistent with the rate of growth of the government wage bill and investment expenditure. The base scenario also assumes a 3.5 percent annual increase in government transfers to households to indicate the continuation of government welfare measures for Kuwaitis. However, government transfers to companies will be subjected to two reductions in 1988 and 1992. This reflects the government's intention to gradually reduce its financial support to indebted and insolvent companies. Finally, government loans and transfers to the rest of the world will be around KD 120 million during the planning period, which represents the average value of official transfers during 1982–86.

Results of the reference path are summarized in table 12.1. If the assumptions of the reference path hold, the Kuwaiti economy will witness modest growth. During the projection period GDP increased from KD 6,607 million to KD 8,346 million, with an average annual growth of 2.9 percent. Non-oil GDP grew by 3.2 percent a year, and by 28.9 percent over the period. The growth in non-oil GDP was accompanied by an increase in both imports and private consumption. Their overall growth reached 15.7 percent and 7.8 percent, respectively. This lower growth rate of private consumption and imports compared with non-oil GDP is explained by a decrease in the growth rate of household income. Exports grew by 25.5 percent over the projected period and by 2.8 percent per annum. With respect to the per capita indicators, the table presents some interesting results. First, per capita GDP as a measure of the social welfare of Kuwaiti society witnessed an overall growth of 1.78 percent. This can be explained by the fact that the lower growth rates of investment and government consumption reduced the demand for foreign labor compared with the previous period. If we add to this the substitution effect, the outcome is lower demand on non-Kuwaiti labor. This in turn leads to a reduction in overall population growth and consequently to a slight increase in per capita GDP. Second, household income and consumption per Kuwaiti dropped by 3.37 and 15.4 percent, respectively. This drop can also be explained by the choice of Kuwaiti population size as the denominator. A major assumption of the reference path is that the public and private sectors of the economy have to absorb the increase in the labor supply of Kuwaitis. Labor supply of Kuwaitis then witnessed constant growth ranging from 3.5 to 4 percent per annum. With a relatively smaller growth rate of Kuwaiti household income and consumption, the per capita estimates will fall compared with the initial year. Third, the general reserve fund per Kuwaiti fell from KD 11,053 to KD 2,130 in the period 1986–95, which

Table 12.1
Results of the reference path

Economic indicator	Indicator 1986	Indicator 1995	Growth rate (percent) Total	Annual
Economic aggregates[a]				
GDP	6,607.110	6,346.595	26.33	2.93
Non-oil GDP	3,255,840	4,196.000	28.94	3.22
Private consumption	2,753.497	2,967,717	7.76	0.86
Imports	2,849.000	3,298.000	15.76	1.75
Exports	4,089.031	5,133.719	25.55	2.84
Per capita indicators				
Per capita GDP (real)	3,926	3,996	1.78	0.20
Household income/Kuwaiti[b]	2,694	2,603	(3.38)	(0.38)
Household consumption/Kuwaiti	2,011	1,700	(15.46)	(1.72)
GENF/Kuwaiti[b]	11,053	2,130	(80.73)	(8.97)
Population				
Kuwaiti share (percent)	42.90	48.40	12.82	1.42
As percent of GDP				
Non-oil GDP	49.28	50.30	2.07	0.23
Imports	43.12	39.51	(8.37)	(0.93)
Exports	61.89	61.51	(0.62)	(0.07)
Private consumption	41.67	35.56	(14.68)	(1.63)
Current surplus (nominal)	38.00	41.50	9.21	1.02
Household Kuwaiti revenue (nominal)	42.80	38.90	(9.11)	(1.01)

a. In real terms, KD million.
b. In nominal terms, KD.

indicates a 80.7 percent decline compared with 1986. This dramatic drop can be explained by the mechanism that links the future generation fund to government revenues. This fund accumulates 10 percent of government revenues plus the interest income received on its own investments abroad. As government revenues have been declining since the early 1980s, the addition to the general reserve fund has been decreasing accordingly. The sluggish growth in the fund coupled with the 3.5 percentage growth rate of the Kuwaiti population resulted in this dramatic drop in per capita fund estimates. The opposite movement of these social welfare measures stresses the need to carefully select the indicators that appropriately signify the preference of Kuwaiti society.

Finally, since achieving a more balanced population structure is a major target of Kuwait's development plan, an important indicator is the percentage share of Kuwaitis in the total population size. In the reference path the percentage share of Kuwaitis relatively increased from 42.9 to 48.4 percent. This relative increase could be explained by the increase in participation rate of Kuwaitis, particularly in the government sector, and the lower demand for non-Kuwaiti labor created by the moderate growth of GDP.

12.3 Alternative Development Scenarios

The analysis of the medium-term performance of the Kuwaiti economy, given the assumptions of the reference path, underlined three major problems. First, the continuation of the current trends and policies would lead to a lower growth rate of the main economic indicators compared with the 1970s and the early 1980s. They grew in real terms by 1 to 3 percent a year, which is less than the projected growth rate of the Kuwaiti population. Second, the current standard of living cannot be maintained at the present oil production level and the projected population growth rate without additional policy interventions. In the reference path per capita household income and consumption dropped at the end of 1995. The wealth of Kuwaitis measured by per capita government foreign assets also considerably decreased. Third, the results of the base run suggest that improving the Kuwaiti population ratio depends on the growth of GDP and government policies. Growth of GDP would increase the demand for non-Kuwaiti labor and then worsen the ratio in the absence of appropriate policy adjustments. Govenment can affect this ratio by increasing the participation rate of Kuwaitis or affecting the demand for foreign labor in some sectors of the economy.

In conclusion the continuation of the present trends and policies will lead to a modest growth of the economy, a reduction in the Kuwaiti per capita income and wealth and a slight improvement in the population ratio. Accordingly, the Kuwaiti government needs to reevaluate its development strategy to attain a balance between sustainable economic growth, a better living standard and a more balanced population structure.

Productivity Growth versus Reducing Economic Activity

Against this background Kuwait is facing two main development options. The thrust of the first one is directed at reducing the level of economic activity as a means of decreasing the demand for foreign labor. Since the government is a dominant economic agent in Kuwait, it can affect the demand for non-oil commodities and foreign labor by reducing the current levels of both development and current expenditure. This policy might also lead to an increase in government savings and foreign assets per capita. However, this option will affect the productive capability and growth of the economy. The second option aims primarily at enhancing the overall productivity of the non-oil sector through improving the productive efficiency of employed factors of production. This option necessitates higher levels of investments in human resources, physical capital, and organizational and managerial capabilities. The outcome of this scenario is affected by two factors. On one hand, higher investment and efficiency gains will increase GDP and then the demand for foreign labor, given the limited supply of Kuwaitis, particularly in the nonservice sectors. This might increase the population ratio (at least in the medium term). On the other hand, improving the efficiency of Kuwaitis will gradually reduce the dependence on foreign labor through the increased substitution possibilities, the improved labor structure and, finally, the reduced number of labor per unit output.

To investigate these possibilities, the model was used to test the medium-term impact of three development scenarios:

1. Reducing the tempo of growth of the economic activity.
2. Increasing productivity of the non-oil sector by 0.5 percent a year.
3. Increasing productivity of the non-oil sector by 1 percent a year.

The first scenario assumes a 3 percent annual decrease in investment expenditure until 1990 followed by 4 percent until 1995, which amounts to an overall reduction of 30 percent over the projection period. Government current expenditure is also subjected to a reduction compared with the reference path. The government wage bill (in real terms) is assumed to grow by only 1 to 2 percent until 1995. Similarly government purchase of goods and services and transfers to companies are reduced relative to the reference path assumptions. However, the scenario assumes that the government will keep the same level of expenditure with respect to transfers to Kuwaiti households and to the rest of the world. Finally, a slight decrease in the supply of Kuwaiti labor is assumed. This point reflects the negative impact of the drop in economic activity and government transfers to companies on the possibility of creating more jobs for Kuwaitis.

The two productivity scenarios based on increasing the efficiency of the non-oil sector by 0.5 and 1 percent, respectively, are the second development option. To increase the productivity of Kuwaiti labor, the government needs to undertake a higher level of investments in human resources. This includes restructuring the educational system to satisfy development requirements, adopting a policy for intensive training and retraining of Kuwaiti employees, and providing direct and indirect incentives to companies for raising the efficiency of production. At the same time additional development effort should be directed toward improving the organizational and managerial capabilities of the production units. These measures will be reflected in the scenario by a higher investment expenditure compared to the reference path, an increase in government wage bill, purchase of goods and services, and transfers to companies. The increase in those items will depend on the aspired level of productivity growth. Finally, the productivity scenario assumes that beginning from 1990, the supply of Kuwaiti labor in government and nongovernment sectors will slightly increase compared to the reference path. This was undertaken to reflect the positive effect of productivity growth on reducing the dependence on foreign labor and increasing substitution possibilities.

12.4 Results of the Development Scenarios

Tables 12.2 and 12.3 show the impact of various development scenarios on the main economic and social indicators. Table 12.2 compares the performance of different scenarios with the reference scenario at the end of year 1995. Table 12.3 estimates the annual and total percentage change of the economic indicators during the planning period.

As expected, the medium-term impact of each scenario depends on the selected indicator. In general, the 1 percent productivity increase comes on top of the list with respect to GDP growth and household per capita

Table 12.2
Results of the development scenarios for 1995

Economic indicators	Reference path, 1995	Reducing economic activity		Increasing productivity (0.005)		Increasing productivity	
		Indicator	Percent change	Indicator	Percent change	Indicator	Percent change
Economic aggregates[a]							
GDP	8,346.595	7,825.808	(6.24)	8,830.446	5.80	9,134.130	9.44
Non-oil GDP	4,198.000	3,673.205	(12.50)	4,685.849	11.62	4,992.466	18.92
Private consumption	2,967.717	2,745.599	(7.48)	3,377.904	13.82	3,704.319	24.82
Imports	3,298.000	2,692.843	(18.35)	3,672.460	11.35	3,928.753	19.13
Exports	5,133.719	5,071.480	(1.21)	5,373.113	4.66	5,624.915	9.57
Per capita indicators[b]							
Per capita GDP (real)	3,996	4,205	5.23	3,912	(2.10)	3,906	(2.25)
Household income per Kuwaiti	2,603	2,467	(5.22)	2,725	4.69	2,822	8.41
Household consumption per Kuwaiti	1,700	1,656	(2.59)	1,833	7.82	1,957	15.12
GEHE per Kuwaiti	2,130	6,463	203.43	72	(96.62)	(959)	(145.02)
Population							
Kuwaiti share (percent)	48.400	55.100	13.84	43.200	(10.74)	40.400	(16.53)

a. In real terms, KD million.
b. In nominal terms, KD.

Table 12.3
Impact of development scenarios on growth rates of the major economic indicators, 1986–95 (percent)

Economic indicator	Indicator in base year 1986	Reference path		Reducing economic activity		Increasing product, 0.005		Increasing product, 0.01	
		Total	Annual			Total	Annual	Total	Annual
Economic aggregates[a]									
GDP	6,607.110	26.33	2.93	18.45	2.05	33.65	3.74	38.25	4.25
Non-oil GDP	3,255.840	28.94	3.22	12.82	1.42	43.92	4.86	53.34	5.93
Private consumption	2,753.497	7.78	0.86	(0.29)	(0.03)	22.68	2.52	34.53	3.84
Imports	2,849.000	15.76	1.75	(5.49)	(0.61)	28.90	3.21	37.89	4.21
Exports	4,089.031	25.55	2.84	24.03	2.67	31.40	3.49	37.56	4.17
Per capita indicators[b]									
Per capita GDP (real)	3,926	1.78	0.20	7.11	0.79	(0.36)	(0.04)	(0.51)	(0.06)
Household income per Kuwaiti	2,694	(3.38)	(0.38)	(8.43)	(0.94)	1.15	0.13	4.75	0.53
Household consumption per Kuwaiti	2,011	(15.46)	(1.72)	(17.65)	(1.96)	(8.85)	(0.98)	(2.69)	(0.30)
GEHF per Kuwaiti	11,053	(80.73)	(8.97)	(11.53)	(4.61)	(99.35)	(11.04)	(108.68)	(12.06)
Population									
Kuwaiti share (percent)	42.900	12.821	1.425	28.436	3.160	0.699	(0.04)	(0.51)	(0.06)

a. In real terms, KD million.
b. In nominal terms, KD.

income and expenditure. However, the scenario of reducing economic activity is the best with respect to the Kuwaiti population ratio and general reserve fund per Kuwaiti. As shown in table 12.2, the option of reducing economic activity resulted in a deterioration in the performance of non-oil GDP compared with the base run. The relative decrease is estimated to be 12 percent at the end of 1992. On the contrary, the productivity scenarios substantially improved non-oil GDP growth. At the end of 1995 the 0.5 and 1 percent productivity scenarios achieved overall improvement accounting for 11.6 and 18.9 percent, respectively. The average annual growth rates of the same indicator for the three development scenarios were, respectively, 1.4, 4.8, and 5.9 percent. Table 12.3 also shows that private consumption, imports and exports in real terms follow the same pattern of non-oil GDP.

A slowdown in economic activity through lower investment and public expenditure levels would result in a decrease in the growth rates of non-oil GDP that in turn affect the income of households and their consumption. The slowdown of investment and final consumption would lead to a reduction in the demand for goods and services and then imports.

Both productivity scenarios generate opposite effects on GDP components compared with the slowdown scenario. Raising overall efficiency results in an increase of output per unit labor, capital, and intermediate input. This would contribute to a growth in non-oil GDP, private income and expenditure, imports, and exports. The annual percentage changes in the GDP indicators reflected this economic rationale. Growth rates of GDP indicators were around 2.5 to 4.8 percent for the case of a 0.5 percent increase in productivity and reached 4.1 to 5.9 percent for a 1 percent productivity growth.

Although the effect of different scenarios on GDP components is clear, their impact on selected per capita indicators is not a direct exercise and needs particular attention. Figures 12.7 to 12.9 compare performance of the three scenarios with respect to per capita GDP in real terms and per Kuwaiti household income. The slowdown scenario improved the per capita GDP relative to the reference path. The per capita gain was 5.2 percent at the end of 1995 and the overall growth during 1986–95 was 7.1 percent. The impact of the productivity scenarios on per capita GDP was in the opposite direction. Compared with the reference path, per capita GDP dropped by 2.2 percent in 1995 with a negative overall growth rate accounting for 0.5 percent. The per capita GDP is affected by two factors: GDP and population size of Kuwaitis and expatriates. The growth of these factors exerts an opposite effect on per capita GDP. In the case of the

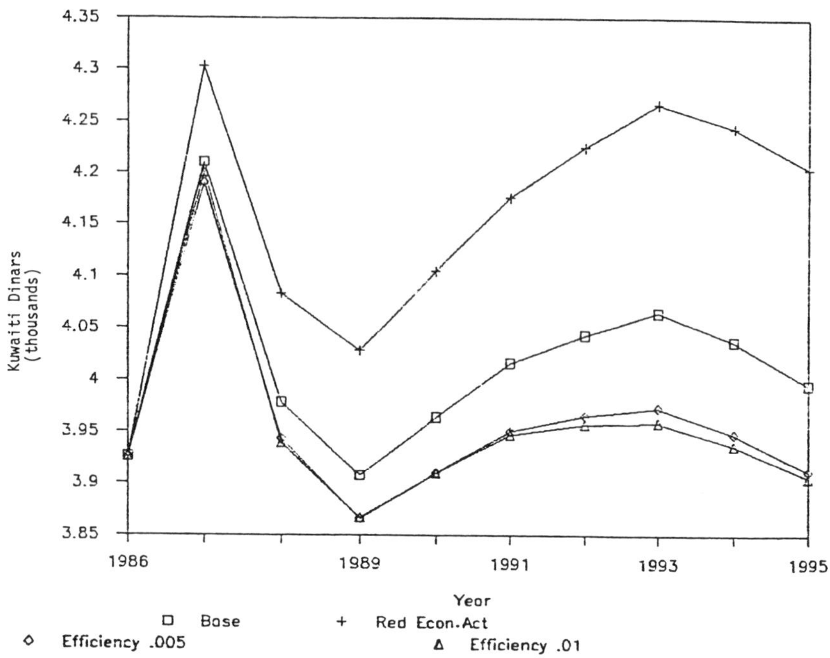

Figure 12.7
Impact of development scenarios on per capita GDP

slowdown scenario, the decline in GDP has a negative effect, whereas the drop in population size has a positive effect. The increase of per capita GDP associated with this scenario can be attributed to the magnitude of the positive effect of reducing population size. In the case of the productivity scenarios, the significant growth in non-oil GDP is accompanied by a similar increase in demand for labor and then a growth in population size. Given that the growing population size was greater than the increase in GDP, the per capita GDP deteriorated relative to the base case scenario. The pattern of the per capita GDP for the three scenarios varied during the forecasting period. Until 1989, the per capita indicator fluctuated. The period 1989–93 witnessed a gradual increase in its value, however, the per capita GDP, dropped after 1993 until 1995.

Household income per Kuwaiti is another indicator of the living standard of the Kuwaiti population. Figure 12.8 shows that the slowdown scenario negatively affected the indicator compared with the reference path. The per capita loss attained 5.2 percent 1995, and the overall drop in the forecasting period was 8.4 percent. On the contrary, both productivity scenarios

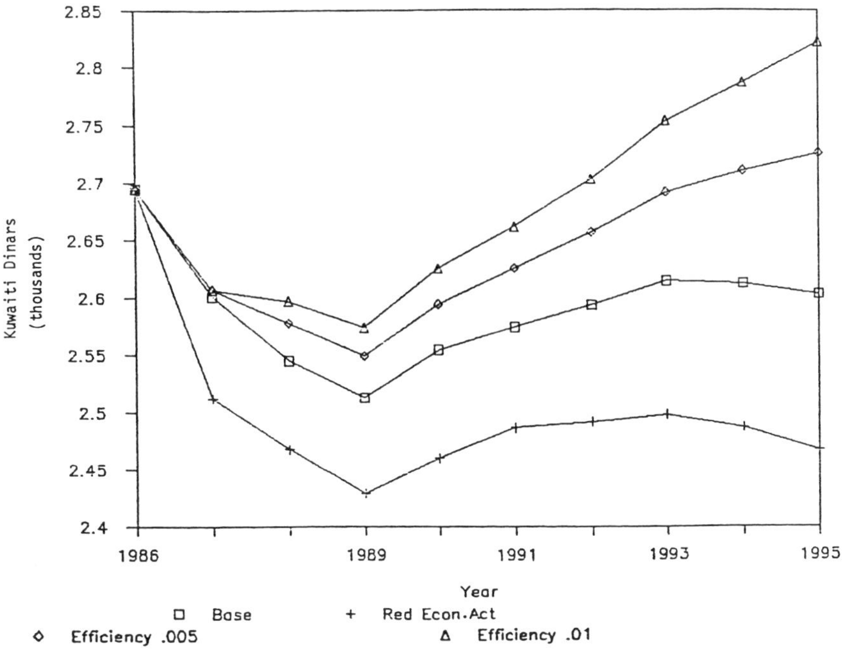

Figure 12.8
Impact of development scenario on Kuwaiti household income

improved the performance of the per capita Kuwaiti household income. The increase reached 4.6 and 8.4 percent, respectively. An annual increase of 1 percent in productivity led to an overall growth of 4.7 percent in the indicator during the period 1986–95. Here again, the per capita indicator depends on the estimated household income and the Kuwaiti population size. The Kuwaiti population size for each period is determined by an exogenous growth rate and is not affected by the selected scenario. The change in the per capita Kuwaiti income depends on the behavior of the household disposable income. In the case of the slowdown scenario, the deterioration of the non-oil GDP has a negative effect on household income and expenditure, which is not the case for the productivity scenarios. Figure 12.8 shows that the per capita Kuwaiti income decreased substantially in 1986–89. The period 1989–91 witnessed an improvement in the performance of the indicator for all scenarios. This recovery, however, continued only for the productivity scenarios until 1995. This point confirms the superiority of the productivity scenarios with respect to the impact on per capita Kuwaiti household income.

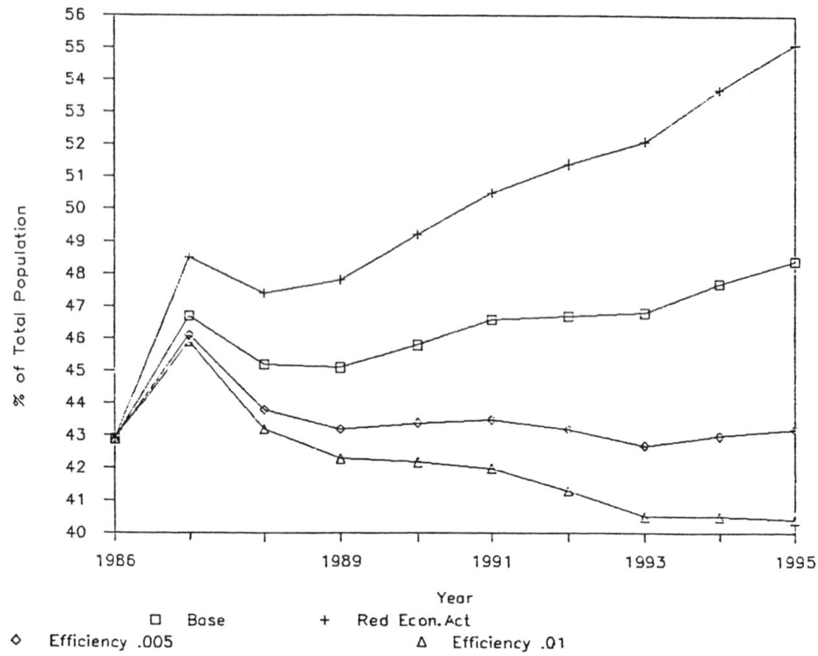

Figure 12.9
Impact of development scenarios on Kuwaiti population ratio

The per capita Kuwaiti general reserve fund reflects the share of Kuwaitis in the foreign assets held by the Kuwaiti government. The slowdown scenario increased the per capita Kuwaiti general fund compared with the reference path from KD 2,130 to KD 6,463 at the end of 1995. The reduction in government development and current expenditure, associated with this scenario contributed to the increase in public savings and then the accumulation of foreign assets. Since the productivity scenarios require heavy investment expenditure and increased government transfers to companies, it was expected that government surplus and then net change in the general reserve fund would deteriorate with time. The general reserves in the third scenario turned negative and became an external debt. According to the productivity scenario, general fund per Kuwaiti witnessed an overall reduction of 108 percent during the planning period.

Finally, figure 12.9 shows the performance of the Kuwaiti population ratio in the proposed development scenarios. The first observation is that the slower growth of GDP associated with the slowdown scenario improved the Kuwaiti/non-Kuwaiti balance. The slowdown of the economy reduced the demand for foreign labor and then improved the population ratio from 48 percent in the base run to about 55 percent. The productivity growth deteriorated the performance of the Kuwaiti ratio over the planning period. When the two productivity scenarios were applied, the Kuwaiti population ratio dropped in 1995 to 43.3 and 40.4 percent, respectively. This result can again be explained by the positive correlation between the growth of GDP and the demand for labor, as well as the limited supply of the Kuwaiti labor force. Figure 12.9, however, indicates that the last three years of the planning period will witness a relative improvement of the population ratio resulting from the productivity scenarios. Although a long-term analysis is required to confirm such a positive trend, this result provided empirical evidence that increasing productivity of factors would gradually reduce the dependence on foreign labor and increase the possibility of substituting expatriates by Kuwaitis.

12.5 The Need for a Combined Policy Package

None of the proposed scenarios succeeded to provide a medium-term path for the economy that satisfies Kuwait's development priorities and objectives. The productivity scenario improved GDP growth and per capita Kuwaiti household income and expenditure but lowered Kuwaiti population ratio and the per capita general fund. The slowdown scenario, on the contrary, improved the Kuwaiti/non-Kuwaiti balance and the share of Kuwaitis in government assets held abroad but substantially deteriorated the growth prospects of the economy and the personal income of Kuwaiti households. The results of our simulation experiments strongly point to the need for a combined policy package that provides the means for achieving sustainable economic growth, a better living standard for Kuwaitis and a more balanced population structure.

Developing the elements of this combined scenario goes beyond the scope of this paper. A more detailed sectoral analysis is required to achieve this purpose. However, the present simulation experiment can provide general guidelines or directions that can be useful to the scenario formulation process.

The first direction is to reduce the economic activity and the demand for foreign labor in some activities that, by nature, do not seriously affect the overall structure, the productive capability of the economy. This might include sectors such as business services, domestic servants, and some unincorporated commercial and industrial activities.

The second direction aims at increasing the productivity of the national factors of production by investing in human resources, physical capital, and the organizational and managerial capabilities of society. Here also a selection between economic activities would be required in view of maximizing the gain from increasing productivity. However, this direction should be accompanied by a national training and reorientation program and an overall evaluation of the educational system to efficiently satisfy the development needs of Kuwaiti society.

The third directon needs to consider restructuring the economy in view of giving more emphasis to the activities in which Kuwait can have a comparative advantage in future. These activities might include the contracting sector, financial services, and information sciences. Kuwait can also use its foreign assets to diversify the productive base of the economy by direct investment abroad in the type of activities requiring intensive labor techniques. This strategy will provide the means for satisfying part of domestic demand and reducing the dependence on foreign labor inside Kuwait.

The fourth direction requires the continuation of government support to the activities of strategic importance for national security purposes. These include, for example, agriculture and food beverage sectors. The government of Kuwait also needs to provide direct and indirect incentives for encouraging the private sector to be involved in such activities and select the appropriate technologies needed to reduce the dependence on foreign labor.

These directions should only be considered as guidelines toward the development of a comprehensive socioeconomic plan for Kuwait. To test these directions and evaluate their medium-term impact on the path of the economy requires the availability of a more elaborate, multisector, SAM-based model.

Note

The research for this study was supported by the Kuwait Institute of Scientific Research.

References

Dervis, K., J. de Melo, and S. Robinson. 1982. *General Equilibrium Models for Development Policy*. Cambridge: Cambridge University Press.

Durd, A., W. Grais, and G. Pyatt. 1985. "An Approach to Macroeconomic Model Building Based on Social Accounting Principles." Report No. DRD 150. Washington: The World Bank.

Khorshid, M. 1986. "National Accounts and Social Accounting Matrices—The Case of Kuwait." *Finance and Industry* 7: 41–86.

Khorshid, M., M. Al-Sabah, and J. Dahdah. 1988. "Social Accounting Matrix for Kuwait: Structure Documentation and Analysis." Kuwait Institute for Scientific Research, Report No. KISR 2630. June.

Khorshid, M., and M. Al-Sabah. 1987. "An Aggregate SAM Based Model for Policy Experiments." Presented at the International Symposium on the Social Accounting Matrix—Methods and Applications, Naples, Italy, June 17–19.

Pyatt, G., and J. Round. 1985. *Social Accounting Matrices: A Basis for Planning*. Washington: The World Bank.

Taylor, L. 1979. *Macro-Models for Developing Countries*. New York: McGraw-Hill.

13

Plan Austral and Other Heterodox Shocks—Phase II

Lance Taylor

Heterodox shocks are ancient history as far as economic policymakers in Argentina, Brazil, and Peru are concerned. The issue now at hand is macroeconomic management in a period of political disphoria and transition toward "normal" market relationships (albeit with substantial indexation). Problems that arise during such a "Phase II" adjustment are discussed in this paper, with special reference to Argentina. Historical precedents are briefly reviewed in section 13.1, and the relevant linkages among macro variables in section 13.2. A graphical presentation of the policy options appears in section 13.3, and they are illustrated numerically with a simple macro model in section 13.4. Conclusions are drawn in section 13.5.

13.1 History

Morals from the European hyperinflations *de riguer* when heterodox shocks are discussed; indeed, history has something practical to say about managing policy to make an innovation like a Rentenmark or an Austral take hold. As is well-known, there are two schools of thought about the German stabilization: the structuralist as practiced by the conservative Karl Helfferich and set out for scholars by Graham (1930), and the monetarist as advocated by the Marxist Rudolph Hilferding and chronicled in magisterial fashion by Bresciani-Turroni (1937). We follow the structuralist line here because it is more relevant to policy *after* a stabilizing move. Franco (1986) gives an eloquent structuralist reading of the history; he provides the institutional support for the model used here. Its algebra can be read from Taylor (1986).

Structuralists argue that although stable-value currencies like the Rentenmark and Austral partially de-index the economy as they anchor markup and public enterprise prices to an external standard by a fixed exchange rate, they do *not* obviate the underlying causes of inflation. Uncontrollable price increases stem fundamentally from conflicting claims to output. They tend to show up first in "flex-price" sectors like food products and services, but then they propagate through the rest of the system via indexation. The conflicts may be among national classes or between the nation and the rest of the world. We focus on the external contradiction here, as mirrored in the trade account. The greater the externally imposed excess of exports over imports, the more internal inflationary pressure there will be.

This diagnosis applied in Germany. In the structuralist view the inflationary impetus came from the large reparation obligations after World War I, which approached 10 percent of GDP. An exchange rate weak enough to generate such a trade surplus implied an extremely low real wage. A strong labor movement emerging from the ashes of 1918 resisted, and triggered inflation by bidding up money wages to drive the real exchange rate down. The Rentenmark cure of October 1923 did not take firm hold until the reparations began to be recycled under the Dawes Plan in August 1924.

Before Dawes, there were several mini-crises in which prices began to rise, the margin between the official and parallel rates for the dollar widened, and austerity was stepped up. Sufficiently unfavorable shocks to the trade balance, capital movements, or the fiscal deficit could have set off another inflation. The Dawes loan and the access to international capital markets it implied lifted the external constraint and permitted full stabilization. Similar endings occurred elsewhere in the 1920s: Silesian coal exports permitted stabilization in Poland, and adroit use of secondary capital markets did the same in Hungary. Fortune may not smile so favorably on Argentina and other Latin countries since there is no immediate source of extra dollars. The policy question becomes how to sustain stabilization while the economy remains externally constrained. Limited import capacity makes the prices of traded goods elastic to the level of activity; other macro variables have to adjust to make the saving, and trade gaps come into line.

13.2 Trade-offs

We opt for the usual structuralist view that imports are complementary to national goods: Intermediates are required to keep production going, foreign capital goods play an essential role in investment, and purchases of exotic consumer products are virtually nil. In Argentina the licensing scheme has bitten so hard that intermediates made up over 80 percent of the import total in 1984. Capacity to bring in imports follows from the major autonomous elements in the balance of payments—exports less interest payments plus capital inflows. The trade limit in Argentina is further complicated by the state's refusal to borrow from the banking system. There were net capital inflows of about U.S.$3.5 billion (Au$2.8 billion) in 1985, which simultaneously covered the public sector's borrowing requirement of Au$2.2 billion and staunched the loss of reserves. The second effect helped support the remonetization of the economy discussed below. However, had the dollars been available for extra imports instead of financial uses, price pressure from import shortages would have been less.

How does the national economy adjust to an import-imposed restriction on output, or in other words, how does aggregate demand meet a limited aggregate supply? Considering the main components of demand in Argentina, it is clear that capital formation has been cut *à outrance*—gross domestic investment amounted to only 11 percent of GDP in 1985. Public consumption had already stagnated in real terms by 1980. If exports are to be stimulated (see below), private consumption is left to bear the brunt of adjustment. Several policy-linked and/or endogenous macro variables can help bring total final demand toward equilibrium. One is tax policy, as the state intervenes to ensure market clearing. Others are rates of interest and inflation. We explore their effects in turn.

Regarding inflation, the key question is whether prices following the imposition of Plan Austral have settled into a pattern of persistent growth. So long as only isolated flex-prices—of beef or school uniforms—were going up, one could hope not. But with the wage and exchange rate increases of 1986 which fed into costs and a further round of higher markup prices late in the year, it is clear that a mild (by recent standards) but economywide price-cost spiral is underway. Given the Argentine nation's acute sensitivity to inflation, it is fair to assume along Wicksellian (or enlightened monetarist) lines that price and especially markup increases accelerate in response to an incipient excess of aggregate demand over import-limited supply. We have to explore how changes in the inflation rate feed back into demand.

On this issue the literature presents no dearth of possible effects. The main ones go as follows:

1. Faster price growth may stimulate capital formation directly or by reducing real interest costs if the nominal rate does *not* adjust instantly à la Irving Fisher to hold the real rate stable when inflation moves up or down. The slow adjustment hypothesis is reasonable so that a positive "Tobin effect" of inflation on investment is likely to appear.

2. There is a well-known negative relationship between effectiveness of tax collection and the inflation rate due to lags in the fiscal system, etc. The apparent austerity of the 1920s European stabilizations stemmed directly from an endogenous increase in tax revenues due to slower inflation. The tax lag can be called the "Olivera effect" after Olivera (1967); because of it slower inflation cuts demand by fattening the public purse.

3. Consumption demand may fall with faster price increases due to the inflation tax. Ever since classic monetarists like Wicksell and Robertson vanished from the scene, this tax has been analyzed only from the financial side, leaving out its real effects. The financial argument amounts to differentiation of the accounting balance for the consolidated banking system when the public sector has nowhere else to place its debt. An increase in bank credit to the state relative to the value of output must then be reflected in inflation or output growth (both terms proportional to the initial credit/output ratio). The output contribution is "seigniorage" while rising prices impose an "inflation tax" which acts by reducing the real value of national money held by the private sector. What these calculations ignore is the fact that rational folk will not only hold less money with inflation (the 1950s Chicago monetarists' beloved increase in velocity) but will also step up their saving to make good their real loss in wealth. Contrariwise, slower inflation will lead to both increased monetization of the economy and an increase in consumer demand. Both effects appeared smartly in wake of the Austral and Cruzado plans.

4. Another classical mechanism, "forced saving," may also be at work. Real wages are reduced by markup inflation, cutting workers' purchasing power at least in the short run. If their propensity to consume exceeds that of recipients of markup incomes, demand will fall. In a more complete description of the functional income distribution, the differential impact of inflation on all classes may either step up or cut back consumption, but simple wage versus nonwage income conflict probably applies in Argentina.

If inflation is reduced, effects 1 and 2 cut investment and the fiscal deficit—demand declines. Slower price increases ease the bite of the inflation tax and forced saving, leading to higher consumption. With the low investment and fiscal deficit levels now observed in Argentina, the consumption effects are likely to dominate. Although we consider both positive and negative effects of faster inflation on demand in what follows, the inverse linkages take center stage.

Turning to interest rates, we follow the usual approach in assuming that monetary expansion, either as a policy move or due to monetization of an increased public deficit, will drive them down. By increasing demand pressure on limited import capacity, fiscal expansion may also bid up prices, but its monetary impact will go through the interest rate and not the quantity theory channel.

Interest rate changes have four effects worth noting, three in the commodity market and one in the financial sphere:

1. A higher cost of funds will cut back on investment demand.

2. Higher domestic rates may stimulate capital inflow (or brake capital flight). If effectively intermediated internally, the incoming dollars permit import capacity and the level of output to rise, thereby easing inflationary pressures on the demand side.

3 With real rates at high levels, firms will be chronically starved of working capital. Under such circumstances credit tightness can drive prices up, as has long been recognized in Argentina. Peril to overall economic stability also is associated with high interest rates, as firms come closer to the edge of financial collapse.

4. In financial markets higher rates reduce demand for money and credit. Since faster inflation reduces money demand, there is a negative association between price increases and nominal rates in the short run. Over a longer period Fisherian arbitrage between inflation and interest rates will emerge but will not affect the direction of the results derived below.

In the following section we trace through the implications of these different adjustment mechanisms in diagrams; they are illustrated numerically in section 13.4. The shocks to the system that we consider include rises in net exports or net capital inflows (the latter due to revisions in lenders' attitudes or lower international interest rates) which permit slower inflation and faster output growth. Standard fiscal and monetary policy moves are also discussed. In the longer run both financial depth of the economy (measured by the ratio of fiscal liabilities to capital stock) and the real wage will evolve. We consider changes in these variables as well.

13.3 Thought-Experiments about Policy

For theoretical analysis we take the level of GDP as fixed by the trade constraint. Thereby the inflation and interest rates become the key internal adjustment variables, affecting aggregate demand and financial markets as discussed in the last section.

On the real side of the economy, a higher interest rate, say, will influence the inflation rate in several ways. It will reduce investment, so price in-

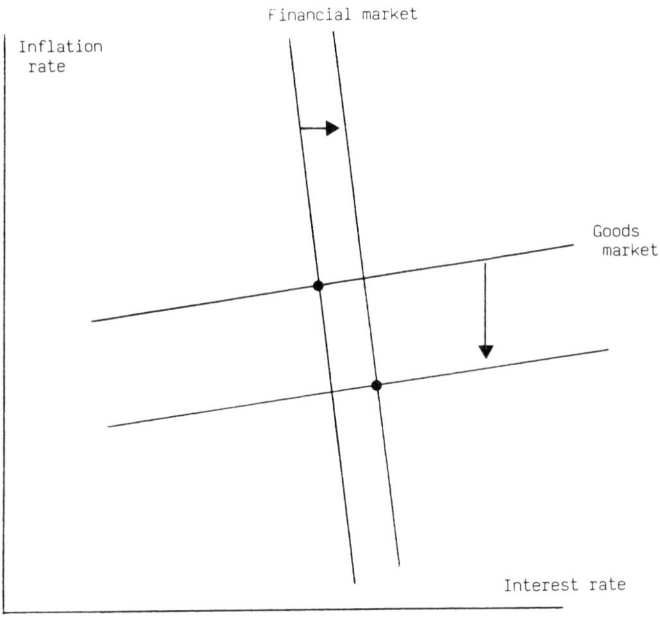

Figure 13.1
Impact of increased capital inflows or exports: inflation declines while increased economic activity causes the interest rate to rise

creases would have to decelerate to restore macro balance if the inflation tax dominates the demand responses discussed above. On the other hand, higher interest costs will drive up prices through working capital cost push. In practice, the latter effect may be more important, giving the positive "goods market" relationship between interest and inflation rates shown in figure 13.1. The slope is shallow since by structural theory inflation is mostly determined by cost pressures from increases in the nominal wage and exchange rates and a balance of offsetting interest rate effects is involved.

In financial markets we have already noted a negative impact of inflation on the interest rate. The schedule is likely to be steep (the interest rate is not strongly affected by changes in inflation in the short run) and even changing to a positive slope if Fisher effects come into play.

The shifted curves in figure 13.1 show what happens when additional foreign exchange enters the system, say, from external transfers to the public sector. In commodity markets supply rises from import capacity, letting inflation slow at a given rate of interest. In financial markets the increased activity will lead money demand and interest rates to rise for a

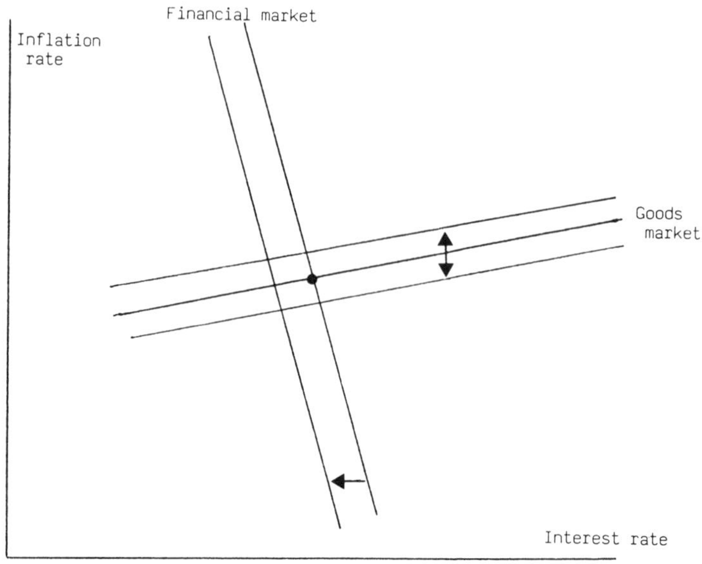

Figure 13.2
Impact of credit expansion: interest rate declines but change in inflation is ambiguous and presumably small

given rate of inflation. The net outcomes will be slower inflation and tighter credit, as the diagram shows.

In another exercise, suppose that public sector borrowing from the banking sector rises or the parallel exchange rate falls, slowing capital flight and reserve loss. Similarly the central bank could rediscount commercial and provincial bank paper (even more?) freely. In all cases credit conditions ease and the interest rate declines, shifting the financial market schedule leftward as in figure 13.2. Aggregate demand will rise and will have to be braked by higher markups if inflation tax and/or forced saving effects dominate household responses. However, there will also be less cost pressure from working capital. The goods market locus can shift either way, as shown. The final outcomes are a lowered interest rate and an ambiguous (but presumably not large) adjustment in inflation.

Finally, increased fiscal spending or lower taxes shift the goods schedule upward in the inflation tax/forced saving case. The outcome would be faster inflation *unless* the larger public deficit is monetized. Then lower interest costs could even make inflation decline via reduced cost pressures coupled with a leftward shift of the financial market curve. Similarly expansionary policy accompanied by additional access to foreign resources could allow output to rise without extreme inflationary pressure.

The principal moral from these exercises is that extra foreign resources may be essential to the stabilization effort—they will almost certainly permit inflation and (in connection with appropriate monetary policy) interest rates to decline. A second conclusion is that credit expansion is likely to reduce interest rates without unduly stimulating inflation—the real risk in such a move is a tendency toward capital flight. If it is not monetized, fiscal expansion is likely to bid up inflation; if it is monetized or (even better) financed from abroad, output gains rather than price increases will follow.

How do these results extend to the medium run? Here distributional conflicts become important—in particular, workers will want to maintain their real wage (especially in slow growth, zero-sum Argentina where real purchasing power has been stagnant for three decades). We consider one scenario in which financial depth (the ratio of fiscal debt to the current market value of the capital stock) and the real wage are state variables that evolve over time.

As we have already noted, a classic distributional model in Latin America is based on conflicting claims. With low real wages workers push for faster money wage increases; through markups the overall inflation rate will rise. Higher real wages are associated with slower price increases and thereby a more rapid increase in financial depth. The depth ratio's growth rate responds negatively to its own level (e.g., higher government debt leads to faster inflation and capital stock growth) so that real wages and financial depth trade off positively to hold the latter constant as in figure 13.3.

With regard to real wage growth, it declines with the wage itself (workers are less aggressive when their income is high) and also with price inflation. But inflation goes up with financial depth. Both state variables affect real wage growth negatively, and they trade off inversely to hold the growth rate to zero.

Now consider a more favorable external situation. As argued above, it would let the inflation rate decline. Real wage increases could be held to zero at a higher wage level, shifting the corresponding locus rightward in figure 13.3. Similarly fiscal debt could be higher, with the extent of the shift depending on tax collection lags which are destabilizing. (Greater fiscal depth increases the inflation rate, reducing tax collections, increasing the fiscal deficit, and making debt grow faster.) The final outcomes in a new steady with more ample foreign resources would be greater financial intermediation and (barring very strong Olivera effects which exaggerate the upward shift of the "constant depth" locus) a higher real wage. The benefits of easing the foreign resource constraint carry over to the medium run.

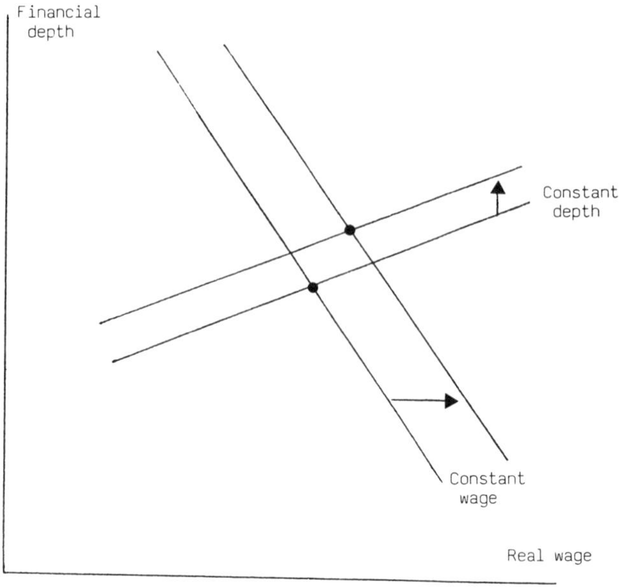

Figure 13.3
Impact of rise in foreign resources across steady states: both the domestic financial depth (the ratio of fiscal debt to the value of the capital stock) and the real wage rise

13.4 Policy Simulations

The quantitative significance of these results can be illustrated with a simple numerical model of the Argentine economy, based on a rough consolidation of the national income, balance of payments, and monetary accounts into a one-sector social accounting matrix (reproduced in an appendix) for 1985 as a base year. The model's salient features are as follows:

1. The price level is determined within each solution period (of one year) by a markup on input costs for imported and nationally produced intermediate goods, labor, and working capital. The markup rate is mildly responsive to capacity utilization (with an elasticity of 0.5). In the "exchange constrained" version of the model, it also has an elasticity of five (5.0) with respect to the ratio of outflow to inflow items in the current account. Increased output draws in imports and cuts exports (see below), driving up the markup rate. Higher prices raise the concurrent rate of inflation, cutting demand through the inflation tax. The implication is that demand pressure is reflected into higher prices as well as increased output. Foreign exchange inflows reduce markups and let production rise. This

specification replaces the extreme assumption of last section that output is strictly limited by imports and prices bear all the burden of adjustment to extra demand.

2. Over time, nominal wages increase at the rate of last period's consumer price index—the indexation period is one year. The nominal exchange rate is devalued slightly faster than last year's rate of inflation for the implicit deflator, leading to slow but steady real depreciation over time.

3. Consumer demand responds to income changes in the usual way (savings propensities are zero for wage income and higher for other flows) but is cut back by the inflation tax. Private investment responds negatively to the interest rate and positively to capacity utilization. Public investment is prespecified in nominal terms; the real level declines with higher prices. Government current purchases of goods are set in real terms, but wage payments (the major component of current spending) are set nominally. Exports respond to the exchange rate and taxes or subsidies (elasticity of 0.75), but decline as national output goes up (elasticity of 0.5). The latter response is based on a vent-for-surplus industrial exports in countries like Argentina and Brazil—when sales at home slacken, manufacturers search for markets abroad. Output in the model is determined by demand, subject to the foreign trade/markup linkage discussed above.

4. Besides holding down investment, interest rate increases drive up the price level through working capital cost push. Financing of working capital accounts for about 6 percent of variable cost in the base year.

5. In the trade account export behavior has already been described. Intermediate imports substitute for national goods with an elasticity of 0.3, and of course rise with the level of activity. Capital goods imports are proportional to private investment demand. Foreign consumer goods substitute with national products in a complete demand system (the linear expenditure system) but from a very low base. Factor service and transfer items are set exogenously in terms of Australs.

6. A money demand-supply balance suffices to describe financial markets, with the nominal interest rate as the equilibrating variable. Money demand is adjusted outside the model to be consistent with trend levels of inflation, but there is no linkage within the equations in the short run.

Table 13.1 summarizes the comparative statics of the model around its base projection for 1986, which involves growth and inflation (implicit deflator) rates of 4.3 and 65.7 percent, respectively. The real interest rate is about 14 percent per year, and the trade surplus is 3.9 percent of GDP.

Table 13.1
Comparative statics for the Argentine model

	Real GDP (factor cost)	GDP deflator	Real capital formation	Real consumption	Real current-account deficit	Real public deficit	Interest rate
Demand-driven version							
D.1 Base run	46.287	1.657	6.221	41.136	0.906	1.208	0.813
D.2 Government investment increase of 1.0 or 29.5 percent	47.837	1.651	6.935	42.357	0.963	1.444	0.767
D.3 Government investment increase with offsetting monetary policy	47.483	1.660	6.820	42.032	0.934	1.465	0.813
D.4 Devaluation of 20 percent	46.381	1.664	6.454	40.087	0.447	0.876	0.796
Version with markup elastic to trade deficit							
M.1 Base run	46.225	1.657	6.225	41.065	0.905	1.217	0.811
M.2 Government investment increase of 1.0 or 29.5 percent	47.107	1.665	6.945	41.476	0.943	1.539	0.749
M.3 Government investment increase with monetary policy offset	47.074	1.669	6.807	41.555	0.919	1.518	0.811
M.4 Devaluation of 20 percent	46.910	1.653	6.442	40.726	0.461	0.801	0.809
M.5 Run M.3 with foreign transfer to government of 0.2 percent	47.784	1.652	6.938	42.293	0.827	1.325	0.811

Note: All real magnitudes in billions of Australes of 1985. In runs D.2 and M.2 investment increase is in billions of Australes of 1986.

In the purely demand-driven version of the model, run D.2 shows what happens when public capital formation is increased by one billion Australs in prices of 1986 (or Au$604 million in prices of 1985). Real GDP rises by Au$1.55 billion, for a multiplier of 2.6. The higher public spending is assumed to be financed by borrowing from the banking system. The consequent monetary expansion drives down the interest rate by 4.6 percent at an annual rate. This stimulates private capital formation and reduces the annual inflation rate by about a percentage point (less working capital cost push). Run D.3 shows that happens when the interest rate is held constant by restrictive monetary policy. The output multiplier declines to 2.0, while inflation is slightly faster than in the base solution. Finally, run D.4 illustrates the effects of a 20 percent devaluation. Real exports increase by about Au$820 million (prices of 1985), or 13 percent. Inflation is faster, cutting real consumption by Au$1.05 billion. The interest rate drops marginally, as government borrowing in Austral terms rises. The final outcome is an increase of real GDP of less than Au$100 million, plus of course improvement in the current account.

The second set of runs shows what happens when the markup rate responds to the ratio of total imports to exports. (The 1986 solution differs slightly from the demand-driven version because of rounding errors in the model algorithm.) A fiscal expansion of Au$1 billion in 1986 prices which is monetized now drives up prices instead of reducing them (compare runs M.2 and D.2), and the output multiplier drops from 2.6 to 1.45. When the interest rate is held constant by monetary policy (run M.3), inflation is four percentage points faster and the real output gain is only Au$900 million. The economy is obviously constrained when foreign exchange shortages lead markups to rise along with increments in aggregate demand. Run M.5 illustrates the magnitudes. When the public investment increase of one billion is accompanied by Au$200 million in foreign transfers to the public sector and the interest rate is held constant, the increment in real GDP exceeds that in the purely demand-driven scenario (compare run D.3). Finally, devaluation is expansionary in the exchange-constrained specification (run M.4) but still forces real consumption to decline.

Table 13.2 shows how these results carry over to the medium run, in a set of projections without and with foreign transfers. The transfer is set equal to 5 percent of the trade surpluses in 1987–89 in the base projection, amounting to about U.S.$100 million per year. This modest inflow leads to significantly faster growth (3.9 as opposed to 3.5 percent at an annual rate over the solution period) and slower inflation. Distributional conflict is potentially reduced as real consumption grows more rapidly, and the functional distribution shifts away from profits as markups increase less.

Table 13.2
Effects of a transfer from abroad when the markup rate is elastic to the trade deficit in the model for Argentina (percent)

	Growth of GDP	Inflation, GDP deflator	Interest rate	Growth of real consumption	Growth of real investment	Growth of public investment	Markup rate
Solution without transfer							
1986	4.3	65.7	81.1	3.0	4.9	5.4	10.4
1987	3.2	61.9	61.5	0.7	15.3	18.6	11.6
1988	3.1	55.5	54.7	1.3	5.4	0.0	12.6
1989	4.2	50.0	55.0	2.1	5.4	3.7	13.7
Solution with transfer							
1986	4.3	65.7	81.1	3.0	4.9	5.4	10.4
1987	4.3	60.8	62.7	2.2	15.2	19.2	11.1
1988	3.0	54.8	56.5	1.1	5.5	0.2	12.1
1989	4.4	49.4	57.4	2.3	5.4	3.8	13.2

Note: The transfer in nominal Austral terms is set equal to 5 percent of the trade surplus from the initial solution for the period 1987–89.

13.5 Policy Conclusions

Returning from phase diagrams and simulations to Argentina, what conclusions can we draw for policy? The reason for going through the formal analysis is that it points to clearcut recommendations, as follow:

1. In line with the original heterodox shock paper by Lopes (1984), the results show that there is no strong justification for fiscal and monetary stringency in Phase II. Moderately expansionary monetary policy will reduce interest rates and support investment without overly accelerating inflation. (Indeed, inflation may decline if working capital costs are as important as assumed in the simulations.) Moderate fiscal expansion creates output increases with low multiplier values. If it were directed toward export promotion and/or import substitution, public investment could substantially reduce inflationary pressures by widening the foreign exchange bottleneck. Extreme austerity would raise the trade surplus by cutting output but would serve no other useful purpose. Given the political need to generate reasonable rates of output growth, a deliberately contractionary policy stance in 1987 would be folly.

2. Breaking the foreign exchange barrier must be a vital concern since demand pressure against fixed supply can stimulate price increases that could feed back into faster inflation as in the early 1980s. The model simulations are perhaps overly sanguine with regard to this possibility since they have a relatively long indexation period of one year built in. The main justification, if any, for monetary tightness is that high interest rates may slow or reverse capital flight. Certainly dear money will do very little to brake inflation, as historical experience in Argentina amply shows.

3. So long as a trade surplus is to be run, measures to bolster exports and import substitution are in order. Directed subsidies to nonagricultural sales abroad are likely to be more effective in producing foreign exchange than reducing agricultural export taxes, given the elasticities and likely development in world markets. Credit lines for exporters should be developed, and administrative clearance procedures streamlined. On the import side relaxing licensing requirements will be counterproductive, except for commodities cheap enough to reduce producers's costs dramatically. And again, public investment projects directed toward trade improvement make a great deal of sense.

4. Overt devaluation is likely to be unhelpful except as a means to hold the real exchange rate steady in the face of Phase II inflation. Devaluation drives up the Austral cost of raising public resources as the internal coun-

terpart to the foreign transfer, and in a more disaggregated model of the economy would have little impact on the volume of agricultural exports. Manufactured exports are more effectively promoted by directed policies than full-scale exchange revision, with its destabilizing inflationary and redistributional effects that appear in the simulations.

5. The public sector's pledge not to borrow from the banking system is counterproductive. If capital inflows continue, they should be used to bring in imports to permit output to rise and slow down inflation. Using foreign resources to finance the public deficit and build up reserves is consistent with remonetization of the economy and helps confidence, but serves no other useful ends. The dollars could just as well underwrite a modest import-led increment in growth. Sustained economic expansion at a 3 or 4 percent annual rate can defuse social tensions and make recurrence of a conflicting claims inflationary spiral substantially less likely to occur.

6. Finally, the instabilities in the present conjuncture all trace back to Argentina's need to run a secular trade surplus. If a bad trade situation turns worse, the debt obligations can always not be met. But before a crisis erupts, thought should be devoted to mechanisms for partial repayment or funding of obligations. Given its potential for self-sufficiency, Argentina is the natural country to take the lead in designing rational ways to deal with Third World debt. It may have to do so, with no Charles Dawes at hand to conjure the destabilizing external constraint away.

Appendix: Social Accounting Matrix for Argentina, 1985 (billions of Australes)

	Structure of costs	Uses of firms' income	Uses of household income	Uses of government income	Uses of foreign income (border prices)	Export tax	Competitive imports	Stock changes	Net private investment	Depreciation (private)	Public investment	Total investment	Totals
Product demands	30.0		38.438	1.080	8.194	−1.059	0.0	0.0	3.288	0.0	1.936	5.224	81.877
Wage bill	29.025			4.837									33.862
Working capital costs	4.0												4.0
Gross profits of firms	4.450												4.450
Profits of government enterprises	2.022												2.022
Value added at factor cost	39.497			4.837									44.334
Social security tax	1.958												1.958
Import tariffs	0.215		0.200										0.415
Indirect taxes	6.705												6.705
Export tax						1.059							1.059
Consumption excise			0.713										0.713
Direct taxes			0.835										0.835
Subsidies and transfers				4.079									4.079
Total taxes	8.878		1.748			1.059							11.685

Appendix (continued)

	Structure of costs	Uses of firms' income	Uses of household income	Uses of government income	Uses of foreign income (border prices)	Export tax	Competitive imports	Stock changes	Net private investment	Depreciation (private)	Public investment	Total investment	Totals
Imports (border prices)	3.052		0.516										4.731
Other foreign income		0.34		3.903					0.713			0.713	4.243
Depreciation	0.0												0.0
Income of firms	4.450												4.450
Wage income	29.025			8.916									37.941
Profit income	4.0	3.288											7.288
Total household income	33.025	3.288		8.916									45.229
Government income	10.9		1.748			1.059							13.707
Foreign income	3.502	0.34	0.516	3.903					0.713			0.713	8.974
Savings		0.822	4.527	−0.192	0.780								5.937
Totals	81.877	4.45	45.229	13.707	8.974	0.0	0.0	0.0	4.001	0.0	1.936	5.937	

Note

This paper originally appeared (in Spanish) in *El Trimestre Economico* 54 (Numero Especial, 1987): 155–175.

References

Bresciani-Turroni, C. 1937. *The Economics of Inflation: A Study of Currency Depreciation in Post-War Germany, 1914–23*. London: Allen & Unwin.

Franco, Gustavo H. B. 1986. *Aspects of the Economics of Hyperinflations: Theoretical Issues and Historical Studies of Four European Hyperinflations of the 1920's*. Unpublished Ph.D. dissertation. Cambridge: Harvard University, Department of Economics.

Graham, Frank D. 1930. *Exchange, Prices and Production in Hyper-inflation: Germany 1920–23*. Princeton: Princeton University Press.

Lopes, Francisco. 1984. "Inflacao Inercial, Hiperinflacao, e Disinflacao: Notas e Conjecturas." Rio de Janeiro: Pontificia Universidade Catolica, Departmento de Economia.

Olivera, Julio. 1967. "Money, Prices and Fiscal Lags: A Note on the Dynamics of Inflation." *Banco Nazionale del Lavoro Quarterly Review* 20: 258–267.

Taylor, Lance. 1986. "Stabilization and Growth in Developing Countries—A Structuralist Approach." Cambridge: Massachusetts Institute of Technology, Department of Economics.

Index